/
1-10

D1130639

THE
SOUTHERN SOUTH

THE
SOUTHERN SOUTH

BY

ALBERT BUSHNELL HART, Ph.D., LL.D., Litt.D.
PROFESSOR OF HISTORY, HARVARD UNIVERSITY

NEGRO UNIVERSITIES PRESS
NEW YORK

Originally published in 1910
by D. Appleton and Company

Reprinted 1969 by
Negro Universities Press
A DIVISION OF GREENWOOD PUBLISHING CORP.
NEW YORK

SBN 8371-1890-5

PRINTED IN UNITED STATES OF AMERICA

CONTENTS

CHAPTER   PAGE

INTRODUCTION 1
I.—MATERIALS 7
II.—THE SOUTHLAND 20
III.—THE POOR WHITE 30
IV.—IMMIGRATION 48
V.—SOUTHERN LEADERSHIP 59
VI.—SOUTHERN TEMPERAMENT 66
VII.—ATTITUDE TOWARD HISTORY 80
VIII.—NEGRO CHARACTER 91
IX.—NEGRO LIFE 106
X.—THE NEGRO AT WORK 120
XI.—IS THE NEGRO RISING? 132
XII.—RACE ASSOCIATION 149
XIII.—RACE SEPARATION 166
XIV.—CRIME AND ITS PENALTIES 181
XV.—LYNCHING 205
XVI.—ACTUAL WEALTH 218
XVII.—COMPARATIVE WEALTH 231
XVIII.—MAKING COTTON 250
XIX.—COTTON HANDS 261
XX.—PEONAGE 278
XXI.—WHITE EDUCATION 288
XXII.—NEGRO EDUCATION 308
XXIII.—OBJECTIONS TO EDUCATION 323
XXIV.—POSTULATES OF THE PROBLEM 338
XXV.—THE WRONG WAY OUT 347
XXVI.—MATERIAL AND POLITICAL REMEDIES . . . 367
XXVII.—MORAL REMEDIES 378
MAP AND TABLES 395
INDEX 419

THE SOUTHERN SOUTH

INTRODUCTION

THE keynote to which intelligent spirits respond most quickly in the United States is Americanism; no nation is more conscious of its own existence and its importance in the universe, more interested in the greatness, the strength, the pride, the influence, and the future of the common country. Nevertheless, any observer passing through all the parts of the United States would discover that the Union is made up not only of many states but of several sections—an East, a Middle West, a Far West, and a South. Of these four regions the three which adhere most strongly to each other and have least consciousness of rivalry among themselves are often classed together as " The North," and they are set in rivalry against " The South," because of a tradition of opposing interests, commercial and political, which culminated in the Civil War of 1861, and is still felt on both sides of the line.

That the South is now an integral and inseparable part of the Union is proved by a sense of a common blood, a common heritage, and a common purpose, which is as lively in the Southern as in the Northern part of the Union. The dominant English race stock is the same in both sections: in religion, in laws, in traditions, in expectation of the future, all sections of the United States are closer together than, for instance, the three compo-

1

nents of the kingdom of Great Britain and Ireland. Whatever the divergence between Southerners and Northerners at home, once outside the limits of their common country they are alike; the Frenchman may see more difference between a Bavarian and a Prussian than between a Georgian and a Vermonter.

It is not to the purpose of this book to describe those numerous common traits which belong to people in all sections of the United States, but to bring into relief some of the characteristics of the South which are not shared by the North. For it is certain that the physical and climatic conditions of the South are different from those of the North; and equally sure that as a community the South has certain temperamental peculiarities which affect its views of the world in general and also of its own problems. Slavery, which had little permanent effect on the society or institutions of those parts of the North in which it existed up to the Revolution, was for two centuries a large factor in Southern life, and has left many marks upon both white and negro races. The existence of a formerly servile race now ten millions strong still influences the whole development of the South.

Unlike the North, which ever since the Civil War has felt disposed to consider itself the characteristic United States, the South looks upon itself, and is looked upon by its neighbors, as a unit within a larger unit; as set apart by its traditions, its history, and its commercial interests. The ex-president of the Southern Confederacy a few years ago at a public meeting declared that he appeared " In a defense of our Southland." A Southland there is, in the sense of a body of states which, while now yielding to none in loyalty to the Union and in participation in its great career, adhere together with such a sense of peculiar life and standards as is not to be found in any group of Northern communities except perhaps New England.

The Northerner who addresses himself to these special conditions of the South must expect to be asked what claim he has to form or express a judgment upon his neighbors. The son of an Ohio abolitionist, accustomed from childhood to hear questions of slavery and of nationality discussed, I have for many years sought and accepted opportunities to learn something of these great problems at first hand. As a teacher I have come into contact with some of the brightest spirits of the South, and among former students count at least two of the foremost writers upon the subject—one a White and the other a Negro. For some years I have carried on an active correspondence with Southern people of every variety of sentiment. I have diligently read Southern newspapers and have been honored by their critical and sometimes unflattering attention. In the last twenty-five years I have made a dozen or more visits to various parts of the South ranging in length from a few days to four months, and therein have gained some personal acquaintance with the conditions of all the former slave-holding states except Missouri and Florida. In the winter of 1907–8 I took a journey of about a thousand miles through rural parts of the belt of states from Texas to North Carolina, with the special purpose of coming into closer personal touch with some phases of the problem upon which information was lacking.

There need be no illusions as to the extent of the knowledge thus acquired. These various journeys and points of contact with Southern people have shown how large is the Southern problem, and how hard it is to discover all the factors which make the problem difficult.

THE SOUTHERN SOUTH

Every year opens out some new unexplored field which must be taken into account if one is to hope for anything like a comprehensive view of the subject. How shall any Northerner coming into a slave-holding region set his impressions alongside the experience of men who have lived all their lives in that environment? What is seven months' residence by a visitor, a fly on the wheel, against seventy years' residence by men who are a part of the problem?

There are two sides to this question of the value of the observations of an outsider. Sometimes he is the only one who thinks investigation worth while; and too much caution in hazarding an opinion would put a stop to all criticism by anybody except the people criticised. The observer over the walls may see more than the dweller within. A Southerner coming up to make a study of the government in Massachusetts would probably discover queer things about the Street Department of Boston that escape the attention of those who breathe the city's dust; he might learn more about the conditions of mill towns like Fall River than the citizen of Boston has ever acquired; he might attend a town meeting in villages like Barnstable, into the like of which the Fall River man never so much as sets his foot; he may find out more about the county commissioners of Bristol County than was ever dreamed by the taxpayers of Barnstable; he may inform the dairyman on Cape Cod of the conditions of the tobacco farms on the Connecticut; and hear complaints from the factory hands of New Bedford which never reach their employers. It is just so in the South, where many people know intimately some one phase of the race problem, while few have thought out its details, or followed it from state to state. A professor in the University of Louisiana might tell more about the race and labor con-

4

ditions of his State than the writer shall ever learn; but perhaps he could not contribute to knowledge of the Sea Islands of South Carolina or the Texas truck farms or the mountains of North Carolina. The privilege of the outside visitor to the South is to range far afield, to compare conditions in various states, and to make generalizations, subject to the criticism of better qualified investigators who may go over the same area of printed book and open country, but which have a basis of personal acquaintance with the region.

If this book make any contribution toward the knowledge and appreciation of Southern conditions, it must be by observing throughout two principles. The first is that no statement of fact be made without a basis in printed material, written memoranda, or personal memory of the testimony of people believed to speak the truth. The second is that in the discussion there be no animus against the South as a section or a people. I have found many friends there. I believe that the points of view of the reflective Northerner and the reflective Southerner are not so far apart as both have supposed; as a Union soldier's son I feel a personal warmth of admiration for the heroism of the rival army, and for the South as a whole; and I recognize the material growth, the intellectual uplift, and the moral fervor of the Southern people. In one sense I am a citizen of the Southland. When a few years ago at a Phi Beta Kappa dinner in Cambridge, the president of the University of North Carolina said: "I love North Carolina, I ought to love that State, because it is my native country!" President Eliot replied, when his turn came: "President Winston says that North Carolina is his native country; gentlemen, it's *our* native country."

For this reason has been chosen as the title of this book,

THE SOUTHERN SOUTH

" The Southern South." Leaving out of account those
parts of the South, such as the peninsula of Florida, which
are really transplanted portions of the North; setting
aside also the manifold national characteristics shared by
both sections, I shall attempt to consider those conditions
and problems which are in a measure peculiar to the South.
The aim of the work is not to cavil but to describe, with
full realization that many of the things upon which comment is passed are criticised in the South, and have a
counterpart in the North.

Properly to acknowledge the information and impressions gained from friends, and sometimes from persons
not so friendly, would require mention of scores of names;
but I cannot forbear to recognize the candor and courtesy
which, with few exceptions, have met my inquiries even
from those who had little sympathy with what they presumed to be my views. The ground covered by the book
was traversed in somewhat different analysis and briefer
form in a course of lectures which I delivered before the
Lowell Institute in Boston during February and March,
1908. Parts of the subject have also been summarized in
a series of letters to the *Boston Transcript,* and an article
in the *North American Review,* published in July, 1908.
While a year's reflection and restatement in the light of
additional evidence have not changed the essential conclusions, I have found myself continually infused with a
stronger sense that the best will and effort of the best
elements in the South are hampered and limited by the
immense difficulties of those race relations which most
contribute to keep alive a Southern South.

CHAPTER I

MATERIALS

FOR an understanding of the Southern South the materials are abundant but little systematized. In addition to the sources of direct information there is a literature of the Southern question beginning as far back as Samuel Sewall's pamphlet " Joseph Sold by His Brethren," published in 1700. Down to the Civil War the greater part of this literature was a controversy over slavery, which has little application to present problems, except as showing the temper of the times and as furnishing evidence to test the validity of certain traditions of the slavery epoch. The publications which are most helpful have appeared since 1880, and by far the greater number since 1900. Besides the formal books there is a shower of pamphlets and fugitive pieces; and newspapers and periodicals have lately given much space to the discussion of these topics.

So multifarious is this literature that clues have become necessary, and there are three or four serviceable bibliographies, some on the negro problem and some on the Southern question as a whole. The earliest of these works is " Bibliography of the Negroes in America " (published in the " Reports " of the United States Commissioner of Education, 1894, vol. i). More searching, and embracing the whole field of the Negro's life in

America, are two bibliographies by W. E. Burghardt
DuBois, the first being "A Select Bibliography of the
American Negro" ("Atlanta University Publications,"
1901), and "A Select Bibliography of the Negro Ameri-
can" ("Atlanta University Publications," No. 10, 1905).
A. P. C. Griffin has also published through the library
of Congress "Select List of References on the Negro
Question" (2d ed., 1906) and "List of Discussions of the
Fourteenth and Fifteenth Amendments" (1906). One of
the most useful select bibliographies is that of Walter L.
Fleming in his "Reconstruction of the Seceded States,
1865–76" (1905). The author of this book, in his
volume on "Slavery and Abolition" ("The American
Nation," vol. xvi, 1908), has printed a bibliographical
chapter upon the general question of negro servitude in
America. The study of the Southern question would be
much lightened were there a systematic general bibliography, with a critical discussion of the various works that
may be listed.

A part of the problem is the spirit of those who write
formal books, and a group of works may be enumerated
which take an extreme anti-Negro view and seek to throw
upon the African race the responsibility for whatever is
wrong in the South. Dr. R. W. Shufeldt (late of the
United States army) has published "The Negro a Menace to American Civilization" (1907), of which the theme
is sufficiently set forth by the wearisome use of the term
"hybrid" for mulatto; he illustrates his book, supposed
to be a logical argument on the inferiority of the Negro,
with reproductions of photographs showing the torture
and death of a Negro in process of lynching by a white
mob; and he sums up his judgment of the negro race
in the phrase "The Negro in fact has no morals,

8

and it is therefore out of the question for him to be immoral."

The most misleading of all the Southern writers is Thomas Dixon, Jr., a man who is spending his life in the attempt to persuade his neighbors that the North is passionately hostile to the South; that the black is bent on dishonoring the white race; and that the ultimate remedy is extermination. In his three novels, "The Leopard's Spots" (1902), "The Clansman" (1905), and "The Traitor" (1907), he paints a lurid picture of Reconstruction, in which the high-toned Southern gentleman tells the white lady who wishes to endow a college for Negroes that he would like—"to box you up in a glass cage, such as are used for rattlesnakes, and ship you back to Boston." One of these novels, "The Clansman," has been dramatized, and its production, against the remonstrances of the respectable colored people in a Missouri town, led directly to a lynching. No reasonable being would hold the whole South responsible for such appeals to passion; but unfortunately many well-meaning people accept that responsibility. In Charlotte, N. C., the most refined and respectable white people went to see "The Clansman" played and showed every sign of approval, as appears to have been the case in Providence, R. I., in 1909. A recent writer, John C. Reed, in his "Brothers' War," brackets Thomas Dixon, Jr., with John C. Calhoun as exponents of Southern feeling and especially lauds Dixon as the "exalted glorification" of the Ku Klux.

The volume from Dixon's pen which has had most influence is "The Leopard's Spots," the accuracy of which is marked by such assertions as that Congress made a law which gave "to India and Egypt the mastery of the

cotton markets of the world"; and that it cost $200,-
000,000 to pay the United States troops in the South in
the year 1867. The book has been traversed with great
skill by a negro writer. When Dixon asks: "Can you
change the color of the Negro's skin, the kink of his hair,
the bulge of his lip or the beat of his heart with a spell-
ing-book or a machine?" Kelly Miller replies: "You
need not be so frantic about the superiority of your race.
Whatever superiority it may possess, inherent or acquired,
will take care of itself without such rabid support. . . .
Your loud protestations, backed up by such exclamatory
outbursts of passion, make upon the reflecting mind the
impression that you entertain a sneaking suspicion of their
validity."

Many Southern writers are disposed to put their problems into the form of novels, and there are half a dozen
other stories nearly all having for their stock in trade the
statutes of Reconstruction, the negro politician who wants
to marry a white woman, and the vengeance inflicted on
him by the Ku Klux. In the latest of these novels the
President of the United States is pictured as dying of a
broken heart because his daughter has married a man
who is discovered to be a Negro.

A book very widely read and quoted in the South is
Frederick L. Hoffman, "Race Traits and Tendencies"
("Am. Economic Association Publications," xi, Nos. 1, 2,
and 3, 1896). "Race Traits" is written by a man of
foreign extraction who therefore feels that he is outside
the currents of prejudice; it is well studied, scientifically
arranged, and rests chiefly on statistical summaries carefully compiled. The thesis of the book is that the Africans in America are a dying race, but many of the generalizations are based upon statistics of too narrow a range

10

to permit safe deductions, or upon the confessedly imperfect data of the Federal censuses.

Quite different in its tone is a book which is said to have been widely sold throughout the South, and which seems to be written for no other purpose but to arouse the hostility of the Whites against the Negroes. The title page reads: "*The Negro a Beast or In the Image of God The Reasoner of the Age, the Revelator of the Century! The Bible as it is! The Negro and his Relation to the Human Family! The Negro a beast, but created with articulate speech, and hands, that he may be of service to his master—the White man. The Negro not the Son of Ham, Neither can it be proven by the Bible, and the argument of the theologian who would claim such, melts to mist before the thunderous and convincing arguments of this masterful book.*" This savage work quotes with approval an alleged statement of a Northern man that inside the next thirty years the South will be obliged to "Re-enslave, kill or export the bulk of its Negro population." It insists that the Negro is an ape, notwithstanding the fact that he has not four hands; he has no soul; the mulatto has no soul; the expression "The human race" is a false term invented by Plato "in the atheistic school of evolution." The serpent in the garden of Eden was a Negro. Cain was also mixed up in the detestable business of miscegenation, for the Bible says, "Sin lieth at thy door, and unto thee shall be his desire, and thou shalt rule over him." The writer has taken pains to point out that "The mere fact that the inspired writer refers to it in the masculine gender is no evidence that it was not a female." The mulatto being "doomed by Divine edict to instant death . . . neither the mulatto nor his ultimate offspring can acquire

11

the right to live. This being true, it follows that these monstrosities have no rights social, financial, political or religious that man need respect." Wherever you find the word beast in the Bible it means the Negro!

If such passionate and rancorous books were all that sprang from the South, the problem would end in a race war; but as will be seen throughout this discussion, there are two camps of opinion and utterance among Southern white people. On one side the Kingdom of Heaven suffereth violence and the violent take it by force; on the other side there is a body of white writers who go deeper into the subject, who recognize the responsibility of the white race as the dominant element, and who preach and expect peace and uplift. Such a writer is A. H. Shannon in his " Racial Integrity and Other Features of the Negro Problem " (printed in Nashville and Dallas, 1907). In good temper and at much length he argues that the Negro owes to the white man a debt of gratitude for bringing his ancestors out of African barbarism, though the principal evils of the negro question are due to the inferior race.

A widely read book of the same type is Thomas Nelson Page's " The Negro: the Southerner's Problem " (1904). Mr. Page accepts as a fact the existence of various classes of Negroes self-respecting and worthy of the respect of others; and he believes, on the whole, that the colored race deserve commendation. " The Negro has not behaved unnaturally," he says; " he has, indeed, in the main behaved well." The main difficulty with Mr. Page's book is that it fails to go to the bottom of the causes which underlie the trouble; and that while admitting the fact that a considerable fraction of the negro race is improving, he sees no ultimate solution. He suggests but three alternatives: removal, which he admits to be impossible; amalgamation, which is equally unthinkable; and an absolute separation of social and apparently of economic life, which could be accomplished only by turning over definite regions for negro occupation. Starting out with undoubted good will to the black race, the writer ends with little hope of a distinct bettering of conditions.

Quite a different point of view is William Benjamin Smith's "The Color Line—A Brief in Behalf of the Unborn" (1905), which is based on the assertion that the Negro is no part of the human race and hence that amalgamation is a crime against nature. The general trend of Professor Smith's book is an argument, somewhat technical and not convincing, that the blackman is physically, mentally, and morally so different from the white man that he may be set outside the community. This was of course the argument for slavery, and if it be true, is still an argument for peonage or some other recognized position of dependency. From this deduction, however, Smith sheers off; he uses the inferiority of the Negro chiefly as an argument against the mixture of the races, which he believes to be a danger; and he makes an ingenious distinction between the present mixture in which the fathers were Whites and a possible future amalgamation in which the fathers might be Negroes.

The most suggestive recent study of the negro question is Edgar Gardner Murphy's "Problems of the Present South" (1904). Mr. Murphy is an Alabamian, very familiar with Southern conditions. While not optimistic —nobody in the South is optimistic on the race question —he recognizes the possibility of a much better race feeling than the present one. It is interesting to see that this man who, as champion of the movement against child labor in the South, has been so successful in relieving children of a terrible burden, feels sure that the worst thing that can be done for the community is to keep the Negro ignorant. He is perfectly willing to face the issue that those who show the qualities of manhood should have the reward of manhood, namely, the right to participate in politics; and the acknowledgment of that right he says does not imply race fusion. He gives up nothing of his Southern birthright, and courageously asserts the ability of his section to work out its problem for itself.

Genial in tone, full of the ripe thought of an accomplished writer is William Garrott Brown, "The Lower South" (1902), which is not a discussion of the race question so much as of the character and point of view of the planter before the Civil War and the Southern gentleman since that time, a plea for a sympathetic understanding of the real difficulties of the South and its sense of responsibility.

These five books are proof not only that there is wide divergence of views, but also that genuine Southern men, strongly loyal to their own section, can set an example of moderation of speech, breadth of view, and willingness to accept and to promote a settlement of the Southern question through the elevation of the people, white and black, who have ultimate power over that question.

In slavery days almost all the discussion of race questions came from the Whites, Southern or Northern. Now, there is a school of negro controversialists and observers, several of whom have had the highest advantages of education and of a personal acquaintance with the problems which they discuss, and thus possess some advantages over many white writers. About twenty years ago George W. Williams published his "History of the Negro Race in

14

America " (1883), which, though to a large degree a compilation, is a respectable and useful book. Another writer, William H. Thomas, in his "The American Negro" (1901), has made admissions with regard to the moral qualities of his fellow Negroes which have been widely taken up and quoted by anti-Negro writers. Charles W. Chesnutt, in several books of collected stories, of which "The Conjure Woman" (1899) is the liveliest, and in two novels, "The House Behind the Cedars" (1900) and the "Marrow of Tradition" (1901), has criticised the rigid separation of races. No man feels more keenly the race distinctions than one like Chesnutt, more Caucasian than African in his make-up. One of the best of their writers is Kelly Miller, who has contributed nearly fifty articles to various periodicals upon the race problems; and in humor, good temper, and appreciation of the real issues, shows himself often superior to the writers whom he criticises. The most systematic discussion of the race by one of themselves is William A. Sinclair's "The Aftermath of Slavery" (1905), which, though confused in arrangement and unscientific in form, is an excellent summary of the arguments in favor of the negro race and the Negroes' political privileges.

The most eminent man whom the African race in America has produced is Booker T. Washington, the well-known president of Tuskegee. In addition to his numerous addresses and his personal influence, he has contributed to the discussion several volumes, partly autobiographic and partly didactic. His "Up from Slavery" (1901) is a remarkable story of his own rise from the deepest obscurity to a place of great influence. In three other volumes, "Character Building" (1902), "Working with the Hands" (1904), and "The Negro in Business " (1907), he has widened his moral influence upon his race. " The Future of the American Negro " (1899) is the only volume in which Washington discusses the race problem as a whole; and his advice here, as in all his public utterances, is for the Negro to show himself so thrifty and so useful that the community cannot get on without him.

Paul L. Dunbar, the late negro poet, contented himself with his irresistible fun and his pathos without deep discussions of problems. The most distinguished literary man of the race is W. E. Burghardt DuBois, an A.B. and Ph.D. of Harvard, who studied several years in Germany, and as Professor of Sociology in Atlanta University has had an unusual opportunity to study his people. Besides many addresses and numerous articles, he has contributed to the discussion his " Souls of Black Folk " (1903), which, in a style that places him among the best writers of English to-day in America, passionately speaks the suffering of the highly endowed and highly educated mulatto who is shut out of the kingdom of kindred spirits only by a shadow of color. Witness such phrases as these: " To be a poor man is hard, but to be a poor race in a land of dollars is the very bottom of hardships "; or this, " The sincere and passionate belief that somewhere between men and cattle, God created a *tertium quid,* and called it a Negro,—a clownish, simple creature, at times even lovable within its limitation, but straitly fore ordained to walk within the Veil."

The three groups just sketched, the violent Southerners, moderate Southerners, and negro writers, each from its own point of view has aimed to study the complicated subject, to classify and generalize. Nearly all the writers are sources, in that they are conversant with the South and have a personal acquaintance with its problems; but their books are discussions rather than materials. What is now most needed for a solid understanding of the question is monographic first-hand studies of limited scope in selected areas. Unfortunately that material is still scanty. Professor DuBois has made a series of investigations as to the conditions of the Negro; first, his elaborate monograph, "The Philadelphia Negro" (published by the University of Pennsylvania, 1899), then a series of sociological studies in the "Atlanta University Publications," and several "Bulletins" published by the United States Department of Labor, notably "Census Bulletin No. 8: Negroes in the United States" (1904). He has thus made himself a leading authority upon the actual conditions, particularly of the negro farmer. At Atlanta University and also at Hampton, Va., are held annual conferences, the proceedings of which are published every year, including a large amount of first-hand material on present conditions. One Northern white man, Carl Kelsey, has addressed himself to this problem in his "The Negro Farmer" (1903), which is a careful study of the conditions of the Negroes in tidewater, Virginia.

One practical Southern cotton planter has devoted much time and attention to the scientific study of the conditions on his own plantation and elsewhere as a contribution toward a judgment of the race problem. This is Alfred H. Stone, of Greenville, Miss., who has published half a dozen monographs, several of which are gathered into a volume, under the title "Studies in the American Race Problem" (1908). He is now engaged, under the auspices of the Carnegie Institution, on a study of the whole question. He has visited several Southern states and the West Indies, and brings to his inquiries the point of view of an employer of Negroes who wishes them well and sees the interest of his country in the improvement of negro labor. Perhaps his judgment is somewhat affected by the special conditions of Mississippi and of his own neighborhood, in which the Negroes are very numerous and perhaps more than usually disturbing. The results of his latest investigations will appear under the title "Race Relations in America"; and may be expected to be the most thorough contribution to the subject made by any writer.

Among less formal publications are the negro periodicals, which are very numerous and include *Alexander's Magazine* and a few other well-written and well-edited summaries of things of special interest to the race. The whole question has become so interesting that several of the great magazines have taken it up. The *World's Work* devoted its number of June, 1907, almost wholly to the South; and the *American Magazine* published in 1907-8 a series of articles by Ray Stannard Baker on the subject. In 1904 the *Outlook* published a series of seven articles by Ernest H. Abbott based upon personal study. An interesting contribution is the so-called "Autobiography of a Southerner," by "Nicholas Worth," published in the *Atlantic Monthly* in 1906. Whoever Nicholas Worth may be, there can be no doubt as to his Southern birth, training, and understanding, nor of his excellent style, sense of humor, and power to make clear the growth of race feeling in the South since the Civil War.

All these and many other printed materials are at the service of the Northern as of the Southern investigator. Among their contradictory and controversial testimony may be discerned various cross currents of thought; and

18

their statements of fact and the results of their researches form a body of material which may be analyzed as a basis for new deductions. But nobody can rely wholly on printed copy for knowledge of such complicated questions. Books cannot be cross-examined nor compelled to fill up gaps in their statements. The investigator of the South must learn the region and the people so as to take in his own impressions at first hand. Printed materials are the woof; but the warp of the fabric is the geography of the South, the distribution of soil, the character of the crops, the habits of the people, their thrift and unthrift, their own ideas as to their difficulties.

Yet let no one deceive himself as to what may be learned, even by wide acquaintance or long residence. It is not so long ago that a Southern lady who had lived for ten years in the neighborhood of Boston was amazed to be told that such Massachusetts officers as Robert G. Shaw, during the Civil War, actually came from good families; she had always understood that people of position would not take commissions in the hireling Federal army. If such errors can be made as to the North, like misconceptions may arise as to the South. All that has ever been written about the Southern question must be read in the light of the environment, the habits of thought, and the daily life of the Southern people, white and black.

CHAPTER II

IN what do the Southern States differ as to extent and
climate from other parts of the United States? First
of all, what does the Southland include? Previous to
the Civil War, when people said " the South " they usually
meant the fifteen states in which slavery was established.
Since 1865 some inroads and additions to that group have
been made. Maryland is rather a middle state than a
Southern; West Virginia has been cut off from the South,
and is now essentially Western, as is Missouri; but the
new State of Oklahoma is a community imbued with a
distinct Southern spirit. For many reasons the Northern
tier of former slave-holding states differ from their Southern neighbors; and in this book less attention will be given
to Virginia, North Carolina, Kentucky, and Tennessee
than to their South-lying neighbors, because they are becoming to a considerable degree mineral and manufacturing communities, in which the negro problem is of
diminishing significance. The true Southland, the region
in which conditions are most disturbed and an adjustment
of races is most necessary, where cotton is most significant,
is the belt of seven states from South Carolina to Texas,
to which the term " Lower South " has often been applied.

Physically, the Southern States differ much both from
their Northeastern and their Northwestern neighbors.

20

THE SOUTHLAND

No broken country like New England reaches down to the coast; no rocky headlands flank deep natural harbors; there are, except in central Alabama and in Texas, no treeless prairies. Three of these states, South Carolina, Georgia, and Alabama, include mountain regions which, though interesting in themselves, are little related to the great problem of race relations and of race hostility. Physically, they protect the cotton belt from the North, and thus affect the climate; and they are fountains of water power as yet little developed. South of the mountains and thence westward through northern Mississippi, Louisiana, and Texas, is a hill region which is from every point of view one of the parts of the South most interesting and at the same time least known by Northerners. This is the traditional home of the Poor Whites; whose backwardness is in itself a problem; whose industry contributes much more than the world has been prone to allow to the wealth of the South; and whose progress is one of the most encouraging things in the present situation, for they furnish the major part of the Southern voters. The hills are still heavily wooded, as was the whole face of the country as far as central Texas, when it was first opened up by Europeans. The hill region is also the theater of most of the manufacturing in the South, and especially of the cotton mills.

Below the hills is a stretch of land, much of it alluvial, extending from lower North Carolina to central Texas, which is the most characteristic part of the South, because it is the approved area of cotton planting, the site of great plantations, and the home of the densest negro population. The central part of it is commonly called The Black Belt originally because of the color of the soil, more recently as a tribute to the color of the tillers of the

21

soil, for here may be found counties in which the Negroes are ten to one, and areas in which they are a hundred to one. It includes some prosperous cities, like Montgomery and Shreveport, and many thriving and increasing towns; but it is preëminently an agricultural region, in which is to be settled the momentous question whether the Negro is to stay on the land, and can progress as an agricultural laborer.

The seacoast, along the Atlantic and Gulf, is again different from the Black Belt. It abounds in islands, some of which, especially the Sea Islands of South Carolina and Georgia, present the most interesting negro conditions to be found in the South. In this strip lie also the Southern ports, of which the principal ones are Norfolk, Wilmington, Charleston, Savannah, Brunswick, Jacksonville, Pensacola, Mobile, New Orleans, and Galveston. With the exception of Atlanta, Montgomery, Birmingham, and Memphis, and the Texan cities, this list includes nearly all the populous cities of the Lower South. The ports are supported not from the productions of their neighborhood, but as out-ports from the interior. Three of them, Savannah, New Orleans, and Galveston, have a large European commerce; the others depend upon the coasting trade, the fruit industry, and the beginnings of the commerce to the Isthmus of Panama, which everybody in the South expects is to become enormous.

In one respect the Southland and the Northland were originally alike, namely, that they were both carpeted with a growth of heavy timber, the pine and its brethren in some localities, hard woods in others. Here a divergence has come about which has many effects on the South; by 1860, outside the mountains, there was little uncleared land in the North, while most of the hill region, and large parts of the Black Belt and coast, in the South were still untouched by the ax. In the last twenty-five years great inroads have been made on the Southern forests, and clearing is going on everywhere on a large scale. Nevertheless, a very considerable proportion of the Southern Whites and many Negroes still live in the woods, and have retained some of the habits of the frontier. Population is commonly sparse; pretentious names of villages on the map prove to mark hamlets of two or three houses; nearly all the country churches are simply set down at crossroads, as are the schoolhouses and mournful little cemeteries. The good effects of frontier life are there, genuine democracy, neighborhood feeling, hospitality, courage, and honesty; but along with them are seen the drawbacks of the frontier: ignorance, uncouthness, boisterousness, lawlessness, a lack of enterprise, and contempt for the experience of older communities.

One of the characteristics not only of the lower classes, but of all sections of the South, is the love of open-air life; the commonest thing on the roads in any part of the South is the man with a sporting gun, and a frequent sight is a pack of dogs escorting men on horseback who are going out to beat up deer. In some parts of the back country and in many parts of the Black Belt the roads are undrivable several months of the year, and people have to find their way on horseback. So common is the habit of horseback riding that a mountain girl to whom a Northern lady lent a book on etiquette returned it with the remark: " Hit seems a right smart sort of a book, but hit is so simple; why, hit tells you how to sit on a horse! " As will be seen in the next chapter, the frontier is ceasing to be, but many of its consequences will long be left impressed upon Southern character. Meanwhile the woods are turning into dollars, and a farming community is emerging not unlike that of the hill regions of western Pennsylvania or southern Ohio.

The physical respects in which the South most differs from the North are its climate and its products. The South enjoys an unusual combination of climatic conditions; it is a subtropical country in which can be raised cotton, rice, sugar, yams, and citrous fruits; it is abundantly watered with copious rainfall and consequent streams; at the same time, it is subject to occasional frosts which, however destructive of the hopes of orange growers, are supposed to be favorable to cotton. Not one of the Southern crops is a monopoly, even in the United States; they are raising cotton and oranges in California, rice in the Philippines, sugar in Porto Rico, and tobacco in Connecticut; but the South is better fitted for these staples than any other section of the Union, and in addition can raise every Northern crop, except maple sugar, including corn, oats, buckwheat, considerable quantities of wheat, barley, rye, and garden fruits. Every year trucking—that is, the raising of vegetables—grows more important in the South; and Texas still remains a great cattle state. There is, however, little dairying anywhere, and it cannot be too clearly kept in mind that the great agricultural staple, the dramatic center of Southern life, is "making cotton."

Though agriculture is the predominant interest in the South, it is coming forward rapidly in other pursuits, and is putting an end to differences which for near a century have marked off the two sections. Down to the Civil War the South hardly touched its subterranean wealth in coal and iron, and knew nothing of its petroleum or its stores of phosphate rock. Mining has now become a great industry, especially in Alabama, and the states north and

24

northwestward to Virginia. The manufacture of iron has kept pace, and indeed has stimulated the development of the mines; and Birmingham is one of the world's centers in the iron trade. Cotton mills also have sprung up; and, as will be shown later, think they are disputing the supremacy of New England. Though the Black Belt shares little in these industries, or in the city building which comes along with them, it has two local industries, namely, the ginning of cotton and the manufacture of cotton-seed oil, together with a large fertilizer industry.

The South is not without drawbacks such as all over the world are the penalty for the fruitfulness of semi-tropical regions. While, with the exception of the lower Mississippi, perhaps no day in the summer is as hot as some New York days, the heat in the Lower South is steady and unyielding; and though the Negroes and white laborers keep on with little interruption and sunstrokes are almost unknown, the heat affects the powers, at least of the Whites, to give their best service. Colleges and schools find it harder to keep up systematic study throughout the academic year than in similar Northern institutions.

The South is much more infested by poisonous snakes, ticks, fleas, and other like pests than the North, and though the climate is so favorable for an all-the-year-round outdoor life these creatures put some limitations on free movement. The low country also abounds in swamps, many of them miles in extent, which if drained might make the most fertile soil in the world; but, as they lie, are haunts of mosquitoes, and therefore of malaria. Deaths by malarial fever, which are almost unknown in the North, mount up to some hundreds in Southern cities, and in the lowlands, particularly of the Mississippi and the Sea Islands, every white new-comer must pay the penalty of fever before he can live comfortably. The people accept these drawbacks good-humoredly and often ignore them, but they make life different from that of most parts of the North.

On the other hand, the rivers of the South, flowing from the wide extended mountains with their abundant rainfall, make a series of abundant water powers. In the upper mountains there are a few waterfalls of a height from twenty to two hundred feet, but the great source of power is where the considerable streams reach the "fall line," below which they run unimpeded to the sea. Places like Spartanburg and Columbia in South Carolina, and Augusta and Columbus in Georgia, have large powers which are making them great manufacturing centers. No part of the United States east of the Rocky Mountains is so rich in undeveloped water powers as is the South.

This prosperity extends also to the smaller cities which are now springing up in profusion throughout the South. Even in the Black Belt there are centers of local trade; and forwarding points like Monroe in Louisiana, Greenville in Mississippi, and Americus in Georgia, are concentrators of accumulating wealth and also of new means of education and refinement. In this respect, as in many others, the South is going through the experience of the Northwestern states forty years ago; and although its urban population is not likely ever to be so large in proportion as in those states, a change is coming over the habits of thought and the means of livelihood of the whole Southern people.

In Southern cities large and small, new and old, the visitor is attracted by the excellent architectural taste of most of the public buildings, of many of the new hotels and modern business blocks, and of the stately colonnaded

private houses. Texas boasts a superb capitol at Austin,
one of the most notable buildings of the country, which
will perhaps be thought abnormal in some parts of the
North, since it was built without jobbery and brought with
it no train of criminal suits against the state officers who
supervised its erection. The less progressive state of Mississippi has a new marble capitol at Jackson, which is as
attractive as the beautiful statehouse at Providence. The
same sense of proportion and dignity is shown in many
smaller places, such as Opelika, Alabama, or Shreveport,
Louisiana, which contain beautiful churches and county
buildings appropriate and dignified.

The cities in many ways affect the white race, chiefly
for the better; they furnish the appliances of intellectual
growth, tolerable common schools, public high schools, public libraries, and a body of educated and thinking people.
In the cities are found most of the new business and professional class who are doing much to rejuvenate the
South. The interior cities much more than in former
times are centers for the planting areas in their neighborhood; and through the cities are promoted those relations
of place with place, of state with state, of section with
section, of nation with nation, which broaden human life.
Unfortunately in the cities, although their negro population is less in proportion than in the open country, the race
feeling is bitter; and some of the most serious race dis-
turbances during the last twenty years have been in large
places; although the presence of a police force ought to
keep such trouble in check.

Still the South remains a rural community. Leaving
out of account Louisville, Baltimore, and St. Louis, which,
although within the boundaries of slave-holding states,
were built up chiefly by middle-state or western state

trade, the ante-bellum South contained only three notable cities: Richmond, Charleston, and New Orleans. As late as 1880 out of eight million people in the lower South only half a million lived in cities of eight thousand inhabitants and upward. In 1900, though a third of the people of the whole United States lived in cities, the urban population of the states extending from South Carolina to Texas was only about a ninth. Since that time the cities have been going forward more rapidly; but the drift out of the open country is less marked than the similar movement in the Northern states, and the influence of foreign immigration is negligible.

Nevertheless the cities have become a distinct feature of the New South; and their healthy growth is one of the most hopeful tokens of prosperity. The largest is of course New Orleans, which has now passed the three hundred thousand mark and, in the estimation of its people, is on the way to surpass New York City. What else does it mean when the Southern port in one year ships more wheat than the Northern? But New Orleans is only the fourteenth in size of the American cities, and the Lower South has only one other, Atlanta, which goes into the list of the fifty largest cities of the Union.

Though these figures show conclusively that the South is not an urban region, they do not set forth the activity, the civic life, and the prospective growth of the Southern cities. Charleston is still the most attractive place of pilgrimage on the North American continent, beautiful in situation, romantic in association, abounding in people of mind, and much more active in a business way than the world supposes; Savannah is a seaport, with a few incidental manufactures, but one of the busiest places on the Atlantic coast; Mobile has become metropolitan in its

28

handsome buildings, and in a spirit of enterprise which the Yankees have not always been willing to admit to be a Southern trait. Atlanta is the clearing house of many financial enterprises, such as the great life insurance companies and trust companies, and has become a wholesale center. While three other interior cities of this region, Columbia, Montgomery, and Birmingham, are among the active and progressive places of the country. In Texas there is certain to be a large urban population, and Houston, San Antonio, and Dallas have not yet decided among themselves which is to be the Chicago of the South.

CHAPTER III

THE broad and beautiful Southland is peopled by about thirty million human beings (26,000,000 in 1900), who constitute the " South " as a community conscious of a life separate in many respects from that of the North. What is there in these thirty millions which sets them apart? First of all is the sharp division into two races—two thirds of the people Whites and one third Negroes, which in uncounted open and obscure ways makes the South unlike any other country in the world. In the second place account must be taken of the subdivision of the white people into social and economic classes—a division common in all lands, but peculiar in the South because of the relations of the strata to each other.

An analysis of the elements of white population may begin with the less prosperous and progressive portion commonly called the Poor Whites. As used in the South the term means lowlanders; and it is necessary to set off for separate treatment the mountaineers, who are, if not typical Southerners, at least unlike anything in the North. No other inhabitants of the United States are so near the eighteenth century as the people to whom an observer has given the name of " Our contemporary ancestors." For nowhere else in the United States is there a distinct mountain people. The New England mountaineers live

30

nowhere higher than 1,500 feet above the sea, and have no traits which mark them from their neighbors in the lower lands; in the Rocky Mountains the population is chiefly made up of miners; the Sierra Nevadas are little peopled; in the South alone, where some elevated valleys have been settled for two hundred years, is there an American mountain folk, with a local dialect and social system and character.

The mountains and their inhabitants are a numerous and significant part of the population in all the upper tier of the Southern States, including Oklahoma; and though they are much less numerous in the lower South, they furnish a large body of voters, and their slow progress is in itself a difficult problem. The Appalachian range, from Canada to Alabama, is made up of belts of parallel ridges; in a few places, such as Mount Washington in New Hampshire, and Mount Mitchell in North Carolina, they rise above 6,000 feet, but they include comparatively few elevations over 3,000 feet, and no lofty plateaus. Between the ridges and in pockets or coves of the mountains are lands that are easily cultivated, and in many places the mountains, when cleared, are fertile to their summits. The scenic culmination of the Appalachians is Blowing Rock in North Carolina, 3,500 feet above the sea, where the rifleman without stirring from one spot may drop his bullets into the Catawba flowing into the Atlantic, the New, which is a head water of the Ohio, and the Watauga, a branch of the Tennessee. Above this spot rises, 3,000 feet higher, the mass of Grandfather's Mountain; and below is an enchanting series of mountains, range after range, breaking off to the eastern foothills.

Within the Appalachians, south of Pennsylvania, dwell

about two and a half million people of whom but a few thousands are of African or European birth. These are true Americans, if there are any, for they are the descendants of people who were already in the country as much as a century and a half ago. In a Kentucky churchyard may be found such names as Lucinda Gentry, John Kindred, Simeon Skinner, and William Tudor. Side by side stand Scotch-Irish names, for many of that stock drifted southwestward from Pennsylvania into these mountains; and in the oldest burying ground, on the site of Daniel Boone's Watauga settlement, the first interment seems to have been that of a German. Just as in central Pennsylvania, and the Valley of Virginia, the English, Scotch-Irish, and Pennsylvania Dutch were intermingled. It is an error to suppose that these highlanders are descended from the riffraff of the colonial South; they have been crowded back into the unfavorable parts of the mountains because, as the population increased, there was a lack of good land; and the least vigorous and ambitious of them, though sons or grandsons of stalwart men, have been obliged to accept the worst opportunities.

The life of the Mountain Whites is not very unlike that of New England in the seventeenth century, New York in the eighteenth, and Minnesota in the nineteenth century. The people are self-sustaining in that they build their own houses, raise their own food, and make their own clothing. There have been instances where in the early morning a sheep was trotting about wearing a pelt which in the evening a mountaineer was wearing, it having been sheared, spun, woven, dyed, cut, made, and unfitted in that one day. Abraham Lincoln, as a boy in Indiana and a young man in Illinois, lived the same kind of life that these people are now going through; for here is the last refuge of the American frontier. These conditions seem not in themselves barbarous, for there are still thousands of Northern people who in childhood inhabited intelligent and well-to-do communities with good schools, in which most of the families still made their own soap and sugar, smoked their own hams, molded their own candles, and dyed their own cloth, where the great spinning-wheel still turned and the little wheel whirred.

The Mountain Whites, however, are more than primitive or even colonial, they are early English; at least among them are still sung and handed down from grandmother to child Elizabethan ballads. Lord Thomas still hies him to his mother to know

> Whether I shall marry fair Elender,
> Or bring the brown girl home.

Local bards also compose for themselves such stirring ditties as " Sourwood Mounting."

> Chickens a-crowin' in the sourwood mountain,
> Ho-de-ing-dang, diddle-lal-la-da.
> So many pretty girls I can't count 'em,
> Ho-de-ing-dang, diddle-lal-la-da.
>
> My true love lives up in the head of a holler,
> She won't come and I won't call 'er.
>
> My true love, she's a black-eyed daisy,
> If I don't get her, I'll go crazy.

The most unfavorable mountain conditions are fairly illustrated by eastern Kentucky, a veritable back country. Along the roads the traveler passes a number of one-

room houses, without glass windows, and is told many
tales of the irregular or no-family life of the people. Perhaps along a creek he chances on a traditional Mountain
White family, such as Porte Crayon drew fifty years ago,
when these people were first described as a curiosity. Below a dirty and ill-favored house, down under the bank
on the shingle near the river, sits a family of five people,
all ill-clothed and unclean; a blear-eyed old woman, a
younger woman with a mass of tangled red hair hanging
about her shoulders, indubitably suckling a baby; a little
girl with the same auburn evidence of Scotch ancestry;
a boy, and a younger child, all gathered about a fire made
among some bricks, surrounding a couple of iron sauce-
pans, in which is a dirty mixture looking like mud, but
probably warmed-up sorghum syrup, which, with a few
pieces of corn pone, makes their breakfast. A counter-
balance to the squalor is the plump and pretty girls that
appear all along the way, with the usual mountain head-
dress of the sunbonnet, perched at a killing angle. Such
people have their own peculiarities of speech like the
mountain woman's characterization of a forlorn country-
seat: "Warn't hit the nighest ter nowhar uv ary place
ever you's at?"

The miserable family described above are a fair type
of what a writer on the subject calls the "submerged
tenth among the mountaineers"; but they belong to the
lowest type, to which those who know them best give no
favorable character; they live in the remotest parts of the
mountains, in the rudest cabins, with the smallest provision of accumulated food. Most of them are illiterate and
more than correspondingly ignorant. Some of them had
Indian ancestors and a few bear evidences of negro blood.
The so-called "mountain-boomer," says an observer, "has

little self-respect and no self-reliance. . . . So long as his corn pile lasts the 'cracker' lives in contentment, feasting on a sort of hoe cake made of grated corn meal mixed with salt and water and baked before the hot coals, with addition of what game the forest furnishes him when he can get up the energy to go out and shoot or trap it. . . . The irregularities of their moral lives cause them no sense of shame. . . . But, notwithstanding these low moral conceptions, they are of an intense religious excitability. . . . They license and ordain their own preachers, who are no more intelligent than they are themselves, but who are distinguished by special ability in getting people 'shouting happy,' or in 'shaking the sinner over the smoking fires of hell until he gets religion.'" They are all users of tobacco—men, women, and children. They smoke and chew and "dip snuff." . . . Bathing is unknown among them. . . . When a garment is put on once it is there to stay until it falls to pieces. The washtub is practically as little known among them as the bathtub. . . .

The same authority has abundant praise for the better type of the mountaineer, who loves the open-air life, cares nothing for luxury, and "has raised the largest average families in America upon the most sterile of 'upright' and stony farms, farms the very sight of which would make an Indiana farmer sick with nervous prostration. He has sent his sons out to be leaders of men in all the industries and activities in every part of our country."

If there were no improvement in the mountaineer who remains on his land, the South would rue it; but in some parts of the mountains one may have such experiences as those of the writer in 1907 on a pedestrian journey across the mountains of North Carolina, among what has been supposed to be the most primitive and least hopeful people in the Southern mountains. He found beside a lonely creek near the little village of Sugar Grove the house of the son of a Swiss immigrant, the best one for many miles. It is also the Telephone Exchange in that remote region. The stranger is received hospitably, and sits down to a meal of a dozen good dishes, including the traditional five kinds of sauce. He is not required to sleep in the Telephone Exchange itself, which is the living room of the family occupied by the husband, wife, two babies, two older children squabbling in a trundle bed, and a space for two more, but receives a clean and comfortable room to himself. The host is justly proud that Sugar Grove has a good two-story school house put up by the labor of the people of the neighborhood, who tax themselves to increase the school term from the four months supported by the State fund to eight months. In that valley the people are as prosperous as in the average Maine village, and for much the same reason; it is lumber that has brought money and prosperity; for railroads were not built thither till the lumber was worth so much that the owners received considerable sums in cash, and the thrifty ones have saved it. A few nights later was tested the hospitality of a young couple newly married, who were running a little mill. They furnished a good room, a capital supper of eggs, bacon, good coffee, corn pone, and the equally delicious wheat pone, and arose in the dark so as to favor a five-o'clock departure; and they " allowed " that the entertainment was worth about twenty-five cents.

What has been done in Boone County, N. C., is likely to be done in most of the other mountains sooner or later; the coal and the timber draw the railroad, establish the village, make possible the school and start the community upward; but the mountaineers are slow to move, and the boarding schools, established partly by Northerners, are a godsend to the people. When in one such school mustering a hundred and fifty boys one hundred and thirty "guns" (that is, pistols) are turned over to the principal upon request, it is clear that the mountaineers need a new standard of personal relations. As you ride through parts of Kentucky, people point out to you where Bill Adams lay in wait to kill Sam Skinner last fall; or the house of the man who has killed two men and never got a scratch yet.

There is good in these mountain people, there is hope, there is potentiality of business man and college president. Take, for example, the poor mountain boy who, on a trip across the mountains with a fellow Kentuckian, seems to be reading something when he thinks he is not observed, and on closer inquiry reluctantly admits that it is a volume of poetry which some one had left at the house. "Hit's Robert Burns's poems; I like them because it seems to me they are written for people like us. Do you know who I like best in those poems? It is that 'Highland Mary.'"

The reason for hope in the future of the Mountain Whites is that they are going through a process which has been shared at one time or another by all the country east of the Rocky Mountains. The Southern mountaineers are the remnant of the many communities of frontiersmen who cleared the forests, fought the Indians, built the first homes, and lived in a primitive fashion. Much of the mountains is still in the colonial condition, but railroads, schools, and cities are powerful civilizing agents, and a people of so much native vigor may be expected in course of no long time to take their place alongside their brethren of the lowlands. The more prosperous South is too little interested in these people, and is doing little direct civilizing work among them, in many districts leaving that task to be performed by schools founded by Northerners. But there are some good state schools among them, as, for instance, that at Boonesboro', N. C.; and numerous small colleges mostly founded before the Civil War.

The Mountain Whites ought not to be confused with the Poor Whites of the lowlands. Although there are many similarities of origin and life, the main difference is that the mountaineers have almost no Negroes among them and are therefore nearly free from the difficulties of the race problem. In the lowlands as in the mountains, men whose fathers had settled on rich lands, as the country developed were unable to compete with their more alert and successful neighbors, who were always ready to outbid them for land or slaves; therefore they sold out and moved back into the poor lands in the lowlands, or into the belt of thin soil lying between the Piedmont and the low country. Hence the contemptuous names applied to them by the planting class—" Tar Heels " in North Carolina; " Sand Hillers " in South Carolina; " Crackers " in Georgia; " Clay Eaters " in Alabama; " Red Necks " in Arkansas; " Hill Billies " in Mississippi; and " Mean Whites," " White Trash," and " No 'Count " everywhere.

These so-called Poor Whites are to be found in every state in the South. They are the most numerous element in the Southern population. They are the people who are brought into the closest personal relations with the Negroes. A survey of their conditions and prospects is therefore essential for any clear understanding of the race question.

The present dominant position of the Poor Whites is different from that of their predecessors in slavery times.

THE POOR WHITE

Distant from the highways of trade, having no crop which they could exchange for store goods, satisfied with primitive conditions from which almost none of them emerged, the Poor Whites then simply vegetated. With them the negro question was not pressing, for they had little personal relation with the rich planters, even when they lived in their neighborhood; and the free Negroes who were crowded back like themselves on poor lands were too few and too feeble to arouse animosity. Mountain people have little prejudice against Negroes: but in the hills and lowlands, where the two races live side by side, where the free black was little poorer than his white neighbor, the slave on a notable plantation felt himself quite superior to the Poor Whites, who in turn furnished most of the overseer class, and had their own opportunities of teaching how much better any white man was than any nigger.

The isolation of these Poor Whites was one if the greatest misfortunes of ante-bellum times: it was not wholly caused by slavery, but was aggravated because the slave owner considered himself in a class apart from the man who had nothing but a poor little farm. " Joyce," said a Northern officer to a Poor White in Kentucky forty years ago, " what do you think this war is about? " " I reckon that you'uns has come down to take the niggers away from we'uns." " Joyce, did you ever own a nigger? " " No." " Any of your family ever own a nigger? " " No, sir." " Did you ever expect to own a nigger? " " I reckon not." " Which did the people that did own niggers like best, you or the nigger? " " Well, 'twas this away. If a planter came along and met a nigger, he'd say, ' Howdy, Pomp! How's the old massa, and how's the young massa, and how's the old missus, and how's the young missus? ' But if he met me he'd say, ' Hullo, Joyce, is that you? ' "

But Joyce and his kind went into the Confederate army of which they furnished most of the rank and file, and followed Marse Robert uncomplainingly to the bitter end; and they had a good sound, logical reason for fighting what was apparently the quarrel of their planter neighbor. A white man was always a white man, and as long as slavery endured, the poorest and most ignorant of the white race could always feel that he had something to look down upon, that he belonged to the lords of the soil. In the war he was blindly and unconsciously fighting for the caste of white men, and could not be brought to realize that slavery helped to keep him where he was, without education for his children, without opportunities for employment, without that ambition for white paint and green blinds which has done so much to raise the Northern settler. Though a voter, and a possible candidate for office, he was accustomed to accept the candidates set up by the slave-holding aristocracy. Stump speakers flattered him and Fourth-of-July orators explained to him the blessings of a republican government.

The Poor White, in his lowest days, had a right to feel that he was a political person of consequence, for did he not furnish three presidents of the United States? Jackson was born a Poor White, and had some of the objectionable and most of the attractive qualities of those people; Andrew Johnson came from the upper Valley of the Tennessee; Abraham Lincoln was a Poor White, the son of a shiftless Kentucky farmer. Materially the Poor Whites contributed little to the community, except by clearing the land, and they took care that that process should not go uncomfortably far.

Let a Southern writer describe his own ante-bellum neighbors: "These folk of unmixed English stock could not cook; but held fast to a primitive and violent religion, all believers expecting to go to heaven. What, therefore, did earthly poverty matter? They were determined not to pay more taxes. They were suspicious of all proposed changes; and to have a school or a good school, would be a violent change. They were 'the happiest and most fortunate people on the face of the globe.' Why should they not be content?.... holding fast to the notion that they are a part of a long-settled life; fixed in their ways; unthinking and standing still; ... unaware of their own discomfort; ignorant of the world about them and of what invention, ingenuity, industry, and prosperity have brought to their fellows, and too proud or too weak to care to learn these things."

What is the present condition of the Poor White? The greater number of white rural families own their farms, though there is a considerable class of renters; and they till them in the wasteful and haphazard fashion of the frontier. Their stock is poor and scanty, except that they love a good horse. Most of their food except sugar they raise on their own places, and up to a few years ago they were clad in homespun. There are still areas such as southern Arkansas and northern Florida in which the life of the Poor Whites has little changed in half a century.

Otherwise, if one now seeks to find this primitive and sordid life in the South, he will need to search a long time. After the Civil War the disbanded soldiers went back to their cabins, and for a time resumed their old habits, but at present they are undergoing a great and significant change. Though there are five or six millions of Poor Whites scattered through the South, especially in the remote hill country, for the most part away from the rich cotton lands and the great plantations, you may literally travel a thousand miles through the back country without finding a single county in which they do not show a distinct uplift. Take a specific example. On January 2, 1908, on a steamer making its way up the Mississippi River, was a family of typical Poor Whites, undersized, ill-fed, unshaven, anæmic, unprogressive, moving with their household gods, the only deck passengers among the Negroes in the engine room. On inquiring into the case, it came out that they could no longer afford to pay the rent on the tenant farm which they had occupied for several years. "How do you expect to get started on a new farm?" "Oh, we've got some stock. You see it right over there on the deck. Seven head of cows." "That isn't your wagon, I suppose, that good painted wagon?" "Oh, yes, that's our wagon, and them's our horses, three of 'em." "Is that pile of furniture and household goods yours too?" "Yes, that plunder's ours; we've got everything with us. You see I want to take my little boys where they can have some schooling." And this was the lazy, apathetic, and hopeless Poor White! He had more property than the average of small Southern farmers, and was moving just as the Iowa man moves to Nebraska, and the Nebraska man to Idaho, because full of that determination to give his children a better chance than he had himself, which is one of the main props of civilization.

Wherever the abject Poor White may be, a personal search shows that he is not in the hill country of Louisiana, Mississippi, or Alabama, nor in the enormous piney woods district of southern Alabama and Georgia. Visit Coosa County, Alabama, supposed to be as near the head waters of Bitter Creek as you can get, lay out a route which will carry you through by-roads, across farms, and into coves where even a drummer is a novelty. You will find many poor people living in cabins which could not be let to a city tenant if the sanitary inspectors knew it, some of them in one-room houses, with a puncheon floor, made of split logs; with log walls chinked with clay and moss, with a firestead of baked clay, and a cob chimney. Around that fire all the family cooking is carried on; the room is nearly filled up with bedsteads and chests or trunks, a few pictures, chiefly crude advertising posters, and not enough chairs to seat the family.

That is the way perhaps a fifth of the hill Whites live, but four fifths of them are in better conditions. The one-room cabins have given way to larger houses, a favorite, though by no means a type, being the double house with the "hall" or open passage from back to front; besides the two rooms there will probably be a lean-to, and perhaps additional rooms built on; and very likely a separate kitchen, used also as a dining room. Instead of the three to twelve little out-buildings scattered about, decent shelters begin to appear for the stock, and tight houses for tools and utensils.

Of the morals of these people it is difficult for a stranger to judge, but the intimate family life in the better cabins is in every way decorous. The pride of the family is the splendid patchwork bed quilt, with magnificent patterns, representing anything from the Field of the Cloth of Gold to the solar system. The children, who may be anywhere from two to fifteen in number, are civil, the spirit of the family hospitable; and though there are none of the books and newspapers which help to furnish both the sitting room and the brains of the Northern farmer's family, they are a hopeful people. Some embarrassing questions arise when there are nine people, old and young, sleeping in the same room, but even in the one-room

43

houses the people commonly have ways of disposing of themselves which are entirely decent. The poorest families live on "hog and hominy," a locution which does not exclude the invariable salaratus biscuit, corn pone, and real or alleged coffee and string beans.

It is hardly fair to compare these people, who are at best only ten or twenty years away from the frontier, with New Englanders or Middle States or far Western farmers. In the Southern climate people get on with smaller houses, fewer fireplaces and stoves, and more ventilation through the walls. There is little necessity for large farm buildings, and the country is too rough to use much farm machinery. Their outside wants are simple—coffee, sugar, or the excellent cane-syrup, clothing (inasmuch as they no longer make their own), wagons and utensils; these can all be bought with their cotton, and they raise their own corn and "meat" (pork). In comparison with the North a fair standard would be to set a dozen of the Coosa County houses alongside a mining village in Pennsylvania, and the advantage of cleanliness, decency, and thrift would show itself on the Southern side.

Those people are rising; though still alarmingly behind, both in education and in a sense of the need of education. Unusually well-to-do farmers may be found who boast that they are illiterate, and who will not send their children steadily to good schools in the neighborhood; but they are learning one of the first lessons of uplift, namely, that the preparation for later comfort is to save money. Saving means work, and perhaps the secret of the undoubted improvement of the Poor Whites is that there is work that they can do, plenty of it at good wages. That is a marvelous difference from slavery times, when there was nothing going on in their region except farm-

44

ing, and it was thought ignoble to work on anybody else's farm, for that was what niggers did. Nowadays some Whites are tenants or laborers on large plantations. Near Monroe, La., for instance, is a plantation carried on by Acadians brought up from lower Louisiana, with the hope that they will like it and save money enough to buy up the land in small parcels. There are plantations on which white tenants come into houses just vacated by negro tenants, on the same terms as the previous occupants; the women working in the fields, precisely as the Negroes do; there are plantations almost wholly manned by white tenants. But there are other more attractive employments, and it is so easy for the white man to buy land that there is no likelihood of the growth of a class of white agricultural laborers in the South.

The son of the Poor White farmer, or the farmer himself, if he finds it hard to make things go, can usually find employment in his own neighborhood, or at no great distance. Large forces of men are employed in clearing new land, a process which is going on in the hills, in the piney woods, and in the richest agricultural belt. Little sawmills are scattered widely, and the turpentine industry gives employment to thousands of people. Day wages have gone up till a dollar a day is easy to earn, and sometimes more; and the wages of farm laborers have risen from the old eight or ten dollars a month to fifteen dollars a month and upward. The great lumber camps give employment to thousands of people, both white and black, and are on the whole demoralizing, for liquor there flows freely; and though families are encouraged to come, the life is irregular, and sawmill towns may suddenly decay.

The great resource of the Poor White is work in the cotton mills, for which he furnishes almost the only available supply of the less highly skilled kinds of labor. Here the conditions are wholly different from those of half a century ago; he can find work every day for every healthy member of his family, and sometimes prefers adding up the wages of the women and children to making wages for himself. Whatever the drawbacks of the mill town, it has schools, the Sunday newspaper, and some contact with the outside world; and the man who really loves the farm may always return to it.

Even in slavery times the ambitious Poor White could get out of his environment, and furnished many of the business and political leaders of his time; and there was a class of white farmers working their own land. That class still exists, though no longer set off so sharply from the ordinary Poor Whites, inasmuch as the lower element is approaching the higher. As an instance, take a farmstead in Coosa County, Alabama, containing perhaps a hundred acres, and alongside the disused old house is a new and more comfortable one, flanked by a pump house; grouped near it are nine log outhouses, and one frame building intended for cotton seed. The front yard is beaten down flat, for it is very hard to make grass grow in the South near to houses; but it is neat and reasonably tidy; in the foreground stands an old syrup pan with red stone chimney, and near by is the rude horse-mill used for grinding the cane. Such a farm is a fair type of the average place, but still better conditions may be seen in new houses of four and even six rooms, with the front yard fenced in, and a gate, and a big barn for the storage of hay, just such as you might find in southern Iowa.

The evident uplift among the Poor Whites in their own strongholds is only a part of the story; for ever since the Revolution there has been a drift of these people into the more promising conditions of southern Ohio, Indiana, Illinois, and the far West. If from the number of born South Carolinians now living in other states be subtracted the natives of other states now living in South Carolina, the State will still have contributed 179,000 to other communities. Georgia has lost 219,000, and there are similar though smaller drifts out of Alabama and Mississippi; while Texas counts more than 600,000 people born in other states, principally the South. Former Poor Whites and descendants of Poor Whites can be found in every Northwestern and Pacific state, and constitute a valuable element of population. The truth is, as the evidence adduced in this chapter proves, that the term " Poor Whites " is a misnomer; that a class of poor and backward people which has existed for decades in many parts of the South is now disappearing. There are poor farmers in every part of the South; but poor farmers can be found in every northwestern state. The average of forehandedness and intelligent use of tools and machinery is less among the back country farmers in the South than in other parts of the Union; but there is such uplift and progress among them —particularly since the high price of cotton—that the Poor Whites are ceasing to be an element of the population that needs to be separately treated.

CHAPTER IV

IN every other section of the United States the element of the population descended from English colonists is flanked by, and in some places submerged by, a body of European immigrants; and every state is penetrated by great numbers of people from other states. Considering that the South has contributed to other sections of the Union about two and a half millions of people, the return current from the North has been comparatively small. " Why is it," asks the Louisville *Courier Journal*, " that so few of these home-seekers come South where the lands are cheaper and better, where the climate is more congenial, and where it is much easier to live and become independent from the soil? " Among the inhabitants of the Southern States were enumerated in 1900 only 400,000 people born in the North, of whom 250,000 originated in the Northeastern states from Maine to Pennsylvania, and 150,000 came from the Middle Western group extending from Ohio to Kansas; but this 400,000 people are so widely scattered that outside of Texas and Florida there are few groups of Northern people. Some farmers are said to be coming from the Northwestern states into tide-water Virginia; others to Baldwin County, in southern Alabama· others to northern Mississippi; and to Lake Charles, Louisiana; chiefly with a view to the trucking industry. Two

48

or three communities made up wholly of Northern people can be mentioned, such as Thorsby in Alabama and Fitzgerald in Georgia, which last is apparently the only flourishing experiment of the kind.

Of the 400,000 Northerners in the South the greater number are in the cities and manufacturing towns, as business men, bosses and skilled laborers in the mills, in professions and mechanical trades. As a rule they do not adhere to each other, and many of them seem to wish to hide their origin. Why is it that there is a flourishing Southern Club in New York, and smaller ones in other cities, yet no Northern club anywhere in the South? The Southern explanation is that the Northerner who settles in the South, within a .few weeks discovers that the convictions of a lifetime on all Southern questions are without foundation; and he takes on the color of the soil upon which he lives. If it be true that the Southern man and woman in the North continues to feel himself Southern to the end of his days, while the Northern man in the South tries to identify himself completely with the community in which he means to stay permanently, perhaps there is some explanation other than the impregnability of the Southern position.

The Southern emigrant to the North finds no door shut to him because he comes from elsewhere; his origin is interesting to the people he meets; and unless very violent in temper and abusive to the section of his adoption, he may criticise his home and set forth the superiority of the Southland without making enemies. The South, on the contrary, expects people who are to be elected to clubs and become full members of the community to agree with the majority; and on the negro question insists that all Whites stand together. While courteous to the occasional visitor, notwithstanding his presumed difference of view, the South is not hospitable to those who plume themselves upon being Northern; and as a community has shown decided hostility to the Northern teachers and organizers of negro schools, and even of schools for the Poor Whites. The Northerner who stands out on the question of the Negro's rights not only has seven evenings of hot discussion upon his hands every week, but finds himself put into the category of the " nigger lover," which includes not only the white teachers of Negroes, but a President of the United States.

Nevertheless, there is a strong Northern influence in the South, exercised partly through Southern men who have, either as students or as business men, become familiar with the North; partly through the Northern drummers; partly through Northern business and professional men, including many Northern teachers and college professors, who are scattered through the South, and who in general support the principle of the right of discussion and the privilege of differing from the majority, for which the best element in the South contests with vigor.

Small as is the number of Northerners in the South, the number of aliens is not much larger. In the whole United States there were in 1900, 10,500,000 foreign-born, of whom only 727,000 were in the whole South; while the lower South from North Carolina to Texas contained 303,-000, and the five states from South Carolina to Mississippi only 45,000. Of the 16,000,000 additional persons of foreign parentage in the Union the South had again 1,500,000. That is, with a third of the total population of the country, the South contains about one eleventh of the foreigners and children of foreigners. These general figures may be enforced by the statistics of particular

50

cities. Baltimore and Boston have each a population rising 600,000; but in 1900 there were 69,000 foreigners in Baltimore against 197,000 in the Northern city. New Orleans and Milwaukee are not far apart in total numbers, but Milwaukee had 90,000 foreigners to 30,000 in New Orleans. Atlanta, with a population of near 100,000, had only about 3,000 foreign-born people; Saint Paul with a similar population had 47,000.

This condition and its causes go very far back. When immigration began on a large scale about 1820 the Northern states were nearer to the old world, had better and more direct communication, and populous cities were already established; hence the foreign current set that way. No doubt the immigrant disliked to go to a region where labor with the hands was thought to be menial, but his real objection to the South was not so much slavery as the lack of opportunity for progressive white people. After the Civil War cleared the way and the South began to develop its resources there was a demand for just such people as the foreign immigrants to work in sawmills and shops; and in addition they were eagerly coveted as a source of field labor to compete with and perhaps supplant the Negro. All the Northern states have encouraged and some have fostered immigration; and the South has recently reached out in the same direction, though with caution. As Senator Williams, of Mississippi, puts it: "Nor, last, would I neglect foreigners of the right types. Resort would have to be had to them very largely because of the fact that our own country could not furnish immigrants in sufficient numbers."

During the last twenty years some systematic effort has been made to attract foreigners to the South; some of the Southern railroads, notably the Illinois Central, have attempted to stimulate immigration, in order to fill up the vacant lands and increase railroad business. Private agencies are at work in Northern cities, which try to direct immigrants southward. Immigration societies have been formed, and a great effort was made in 1907 to induce a current of immigration. A Southern State Immigration Commission was established under the chairmanship of the late Samuel Spencer, President of the Southern Railroad, and there are several similar local societies. Following an example originally set by some of the Northwestern states seventy years ago, several states appointed commissioners or bureaus of immigration, particularly North Carolina, South Carolina, Florida, and Louisiana. The most active of all these bodies is the State Immigration Bureau of Louisiana, which has busily distributed Italians and Bulgarians through the State. The Federal Government has taken a hand in steering foreigners southward, through a bureau in New York which puts before newly arrived immigrants the opportunities of the South. By this bureau and by liberal and even strained construction of the statutes the Federal authorities have aided in the effort to bring the South to the attention of the incomer and to facilitate his distribution.

In 1906 South Carolina took a part in the process by agreeing practically to act as the agent of the planters and mill owners of the state, who raised a fund of twenty thousand dollars which, to avoid the Federal statute against the coming in of immigrants under contract to find them work, was turned over to the State authorities. They thereupon made a contract with the North German Lloyd Steamship Company to import several immigrants whose passage was paid out of the fund. In consequence, in November, 1906, appeared in the harbor of Charleston the steamer *Wittekind,* having on board 450 steerage passengers, an arrival which was declared to be the first successful undertaking to promote foreign immigration from Europe to the South Atlantic section of the United States in half a century. These immigrants—137 Belgians, 140 Austrians, and 160 Galicians—were fêted by the Charleston people and triumphantly distributed throughout the State. Part of them were not mill hands at all; others had been misinformed as to the scale of wages and conditions; one of them thought it monstrous that he should have been a week in South Carolina without ever seeing a bottle of beer. They wrote home such accounts of their unhappiness that the steamship company declined to forward any more immigrants, and Mr. Gadsden was sent by the State as a special commissioner to Europe to investigate. He reported in 1907 that the people were writing home to say that they did not like their work or housing. He diagnosed the trouble as follows: " Our efforts have been almost entirely expended in inducing immigrants to come to the South, and we have thought little or nothing of how the immigrant is to be treated after he has come in our midst; . . . it seems to me that we have entirely overlooked our industrial conditions, namely, that the wage scale throughout the South is based on negro labor, which means cheap labor . . . our attitude throughout the South to the white laborer will have to be materially altered before we can expect to have the immigrant satisfied to remain as a laborer with us."

The only considerable groups of foreigners living together in the South are a small German colony in Charleston and a larger one in New Orleans, a body of Germans in central Texas (a settlement dating back to the Civil War), and a few thousand Italian laborers in the lower

Mississippi valley who have been brought there chiefly through private agencies in New Orleans and New York. Some Slavs have been introduced into the lower South where they are collectively known as " Bohunks "; and a few efforts have been made to bring in the Chinese.

For the slenderness of the immigrant movement there are two principal reasons: the first is that the South does not like immigrants, and the second is that the immigrants do not like the South. One constantly encounters a sharp hostility to foreigners of every kind. The Georgia Farmers' Union in 1907 unanimously voted against foreign immigration, because it would bring undesirable people who would compete with the Georgians for factory labor and would raise so much cotton that it would lower the price. A Texan lawyer in a Pullman car painted for the writer a gloomy picture of the unhappy condition of the North, which is obliged to accept " the scum of the earth " from foreign countries and is thereby overrun with Syrians, Russian Jews, and Sicilians, who are not capable of becoming American citizens and fill the slums of the cities; the South, in his judgment, was free from such difficulties. The *Manufacturers' Record* of Baltimore is fearful of " masses of elements living largely unto themselves, speaking foreign tongues and kept alien to the country through having no contact with its people and its institutions save only through their own leaders. Such an immigration, it is easily understood from experience in other parts of the country, might become a dangerous fester upon the body politic." A correspondent of the *Richmond Times Despatch* objects to immigrants because they will prevent the reëstablishment of the labor conditions which existed before the war, and will interfere with the plantation system; and he especially deprecates any effort " to try any of the races that have become inoculated with union notions, and who are so quick to overestimate their contributions to the success of the enterprises upon which they work and demand wages accordingly."

Another argument is that of competition. As a Southern writer puts it: "The temptation of cheap alien labor from abroad is obvious as one of the ways in which a home population may be dispossessed. When it ceases to fill the rank and file with its own sons . . . it ceases to be master or possessor of the country." From another source the Negro is warned that: "When the European who has been used to hard work begins to make a bale and a half of cotton to where the negro makes but half a bale, . . . then the farm labor will pass from the hands of the negro forever."

On this question of immigration, as on many other matters, there is a divergence between the responsible and the irresponsible Whites, or rather between the large property owners and people who look to the development of the whole section, and the small farmers and white laborers. The criticism of the foreigner comes chiefly from the people who hardly know him; from the town loafer or the small plantation manager who " hates the Dago worse than a nigger." Between such people and the few foreigners occasional " scraps " occur, and there have been instances of Italians or Bohunks who have been driven out by main force because their neighbors did not like them.

To be sure the foreigner in the North is not unacquainted with brickbats; but the real question is not whether the Southerner likes him, but whether he likes the South. He is under no such restraint as, for instance, in Buenos Ayres, where, if he is not satisfied, he must steam back six thousand miles to Europe; trains leave every part of the South every day bound for the North. Hence, as soon as the problem of getting the immigrant to the South is solved, the next point is how to keep him there. Of the immigrants brought over by the *Wittekind* in 1906, at the end of a year the larger part had left South Carolina. The authorities of the State were guiltless of holding out untrue inducements; but the immigrants did not expect to be charged their rail fares from Charleston to the place of labor; they found the wages less than they had supposed; sometimes less than they had received at home; they were obliged to deal with the company's store, instead of being paid in cash. Especially they complained that farm hands were not so " intimately received by their employers " as their cousins were in the Northwest. When the *Wittekind* was ready to sail from Bremen two hundred people who expected to join her refused to gó, because they had just heard of the race riot in Atlanta and thought the South could not be a pleasant place. Rumors of peonage, and a few actual cases, had also a deterring effect.

Nevertheless, there are a score or more of little agricultural communities in which a considerable part of the people are foreigners. Most of these people are Italians, that being an immigrating race accustomed to field labor in a warm climate, and traditionally inured to the peasant system. As these people bring little capital, most of them are assembled on some plantation which undertakes on the usual terms to advance them necessities until their crop can be made. It costs in central Louisiana about $60 per head to get Italians, and that is deducted out of their first year's earnings. In some cases the Italians come out as railroad and levee hands and afterward bring over their families. At Alexandria, La., in the neighborhood of

56

Shreveport, at Valdese, N. C., and elsewhere, are independent Italian villages.

The most successful plantation worked by Italian labor is undoubtedly Sunny Side, founded by the late Austin Corbin on very rich land in southeastern Arkansas. It dates back to 1898; the original plan was to subdivide the estate and sell it to the immigrants; and at one time there were perhaps fifteen hundred to two thousand Italians there, many of whom were not farmers and soon grew tired of the place. At one time they were reduced to less than forty families, but people have drifted back and new ones have come in, until in 1908 there were over one hundred and twenty families. They are sober, industrious, and profitable both to themselves and to the plantation owners, who have placed the same kind of labor on other plantations and would gladly extend the system if they could get the people.

Some other race elements are to be found in the South; a few Greeks have made their appearance; Bulgarians, Hungarians, and "Austrians" (probably Slavs) may be found in Louisiana; but the greater number of recent accessions are laborers or small business men, who play a very small part in the economic and social development of the region.

This whole question of the foreigner is in close relation to the negro problem. Even where the "Dagoes" are brought into close contact with the Negroes, they neither make nor meddle with them; but the main reason for interest in their coming is the scarcity and the ineffectiveness of negro labor. If the number of foreigners should largely increase, there is little doubt that they would join in the combination of the white race against the Negro. On the other hand they furnish a more regular field labor than the planter is otherwise able to employ, and when put alongside the Negro sometimes they stimulate him to unwonted effort, as witness the experience of an old cotton hand related to A. H. Stone: " I 'lowed to Marthy, when I heered dem Dagoes had done bought the jinin' tract, dat I was gwine ter show de white folks dat here was one nigger what wouldn' lay down in front er no man livin', when it come to makin' cotton. En I done it, too, plumb till pickin' time. It blowed me, too, sho's you bawn, blowed me mightily. But jis ez I thought I had um bested, what you reckon happened? I'z a natchel-bawn cotton picker, myself, and so is Marthy, and right dar is whar I 'lowed I had um. But 'tother night when me and de old 'oman 'uz drivin' back fum church, long erbout 12 o'clock, en er full moon, what you reckon I seen, boss? Fo' Gawd in Heaven, dat Dago en his wife en fo' chillum wuz pickin' cotton by de moonlight. I do' 'no how it looks to you, but I calls dat er underhanded trick myself!"

CHAPTER V

IMMIGRANTS either from the North or from abroad may be ignored as a formative part of the South; but the Poor Whites are only a part of the rank and file. There are many independent farmers, handicraftsmen, skilled laborers, and small laborers, all parts of a great democracy; and one of the causes of uplift is the coming of this democracy to a consciousness of its own power. Nevertheless, in the South as elsewhere in the world, the great affairs are carried on, the great decisions are made, by a comparatively small number of persons; and in no part of the Union has a select aristocracy such prestige and influence.

Before the war this leading element was very distinctly marked off, because it was nearly restricted to slaveholders and their connections by blood and marriage. Very few people, except in the mountain districts, ever held important state or national office who did not come from the slaveholding families, which never numbered more than three hundred thousand; and half of those families owned less than five Negroes and could hardly claim to belong to the ruling class. The slaveholding aristocracy included nearly all of the professional and commercial men, the ministers, the doctors, the college instructors, es-

59

pecially the lawyers, from whom the ranks of public service were to a great degree recruited.

These people were organized into a society of a kind unknown in the North since colonial times. In any one state the well-to-do people, perhaps two to five thousand in all, knew each other, recognized each other as belonging to a kind of gentry, intermarried, furnished nearly all the college and professional students, and were the dignitaries of their localities. In organization, if not in opportunities or in the amenities of life, they were very like the English county gentry of the period.

Those conditions are now much changed. In the first place, the old ruling families have almost all lost their wealth and their interstate position. Deference is still paid to them; a John Rutledge is always a John Rutledge welcomed anywhere in South Carolina, and a Claibourne carries the dignity of the family that furnished the first Governor of Mississippi; but it is a mournful fact that hardly a large plantation in the South is now owned by a descendant of the man who owned it in 1860. Some of the most ambitious of the scions of these ancient houses, whose communities no longer give them sufficient opportunities, have found their way to New York and other Northern cities, and are there founding new families. Many more are upbuilders of the Southern cities; some of them are again becoming landed proprietors. Still the element dominant in society, in business, and in administration, includes a large number of people who have come up from below or have come in from without since the Civil War.

Distinctly above the traditional Poor White, though often confused with him by outsiders, is the Southern white farmer. In ante-bellum days there was in every

Southern state, and particularly in the border states, a large body of independent men, working their own land without slaves, with the assistance of their sons—for white laborers for hire could not be had—and often prosperous. They were on good terms with the planters, had their share of the public honors, and probably furnished a considerable part of the Southern Whig vote. Their descendants still persist, often in debt, frequently unprogressive, but on the whole much resembling the farmer class in the neighboring Northern states. The destruction of slavery little disturbed the status of these men, and they are an important element in the progress of the South.

The old leaders have lost preëminence, partly because the South now requires additional kinds of leaders. In the modern Southern cities may be found classes of whole-sale jobbers, attorneys of great corporations, national bank officers, manufacturers, agents of life insurance and investment companies, engineers, and promoters, who were hardly known in the old South. In the social world these people still have to take their chance, for the foundation stones of society in every Southern state are the descendants of the leaders of the old régime, including many people whose former back-country farm with its half-dozen slaves has become magnified into a tradition of an old plantation. As a Southern writer says: "Legends had already begun to build themselves, as they will in a community that entrusts its history to oral transmission. For instance, the fortunes of many of our families before the war became enormous, in our talk and in our beliefs."

Notwithstanding this presumptive right of the old families to figure in modern society many are shut out by poverty and some by moral disintegration. Of course in the South as elsewhere the newcomers have more money and set a difficult standard of social expense; but, measured by New York criterions, there are few wealthy people in the South. Leaving out the Northern men who play at being Southern gentlemen it is doubtful whether there are thirty millionaires in the whole Lower South; and it must never be forgotten that nothing in the world is so democratic within its narrow bounds as Southern society. The social leaders recognize on equal terms other Southern high-class people, and also outsiders whom they reckon as high class. There is a sharp difference between the poor farmer and the well-to-do proprietor or the city magnate; but there is not necessarily a social distinction between the family which has an income of three thousand a year and the family which disposes of thirty thousand a year.

Furthermore, between all the members of the white race there is an easier relation than in the North; Pullman Car conductors are on easy and respectful terms with lady passengers who frequently use their line, the poorest White addresses the richest planter or most distinguished railroad man with an assured sense of belonging to the same class; society is distinctly more homogeneous than in the North. It is also more gracious. What is more delightful than the high-bred Southern man and woman, courteous, friendly, and interested in high things, bent on bringing to bear all the resources of intellectual training, religion, and social life for the welfare of the community? The high-class Southerner believes in education; he has a high sense of public duty; he stands by his friends like a rock; unfortunate is the Northerner who does not count among his choicest possessions the friendship of Southern men and women!

In business the South is developing a body of modern

go-ahead men who are alive to the needs of improvement in business methods, who adopt the latest machinery, seek to economize in processes, and have built up a stable and remarkably well-knit commercial system. The South before the war had many safe banks, and no state in the Union enjoyed a better banking law than Louisiana. All that capital was swept away by the Civil War, and for twenty years was not replaced, outside the cities; now little banks are springing up at small railroad stations, and in remote little county seats; and there is a concert and understanding between the country and city bankers which is of great assistance to the material growth of the South. The Southern business system calls for prudent and courageous men, and there is no lack of good material.

In politics, however, a new type of leaders has in the last twenty years sprung up as a result of the genius of Benjamin R. Tillman in discovering that there are more voters of the lower class than of the upper, and that he who can get the lower class to vote together may always be reëlected. As a matter of fact Tillman comes of a respectable middle-class family; but it is his part to show himself the coarsest and most vituperative of Poor Whites. Such men as ex-Governor Vardaman of Mississippi, and Senator Jeff Davis of Arkansas, are also evidences that the hold of the old type of political leader is weakened. Some people say that the present system of primary nominations is a sure way to bring mediocrity to the front.

On the other hand, the leaders of society and business and politics and intellectual pursuits fit together much more closely than in the North. In part this is the result of a social system in which people of various types imbibe each other's views; in greater part it is due to the influence of slavery, and the half century of contest over

63

slavery, in which the great property owners were also the heads of the state, the pillars of the church, and the formers of opinion.

The problem of the leader in the South is also the problem of the led; shall those who concentrate and shape public opinion, who carry on the corporations, write the newspapers, teach the university students, decide law cases, and preach the sermons, shall they also set forth a lofty spirit? Will the mass, the voters, the possessors of the physical force of the community, accept their decisions? In general, the tone of the leaders in the South is sane and wholesome; commercial influences are less strong on the press ·and on state and municipal governments than they are in the North. There is at least a greater sentimental and abstract respect for learning, a larger part of the community is in touch with and molded by the churches.

The lower Whites, though manifestly advancing, are still on the average far inferior to the similar class of white farmers of kindred English stock in the North; and also to many of the foreigners that have come in and settled the West. Education is going to help their children, but can do little for the grown people who are now the source of political power in the South; and there is a turbulence and uncontrolled passion, sometimes a ferocity, among the rural people which is to be matched in the North only in the slums.

In some ways the Northern visitor is struck by a crudeness of behavior among respectable Southern Whites such as he is accustomed in the North to experience in a much lower stratum of society. A large proportion of the Poor Whites in the South and many of the better class go armed and justify it because they expect to have

need of a weapon. Tobacco juice flows freely in hotel cor-
ridors, in railroad stations, and even in the vestibules of
ladies' cars; profanity is rife, and fierce talk and unbridled
denunciations, principally of black people. There is
doubtless just the same thing in Northern places, if you
look for it, but in the South it follows you. With all the
aristocratic feeling classes are more mixed together, and
it is a harder thing than in the North to sift your acquaintances. Still there is an upward movement in every
stratum of society; as Murphy puts it: "The real struggle of the South from the date of Lee's surrender—through
all the accidents of political and industrial revolution—
was simply a struggle toward the creation of democratic
conditions. The *real* thing, in the unfolding of the later
South, is the arrival of the common man." The North
has always had confidence in the average man; in the
South the upper and lower strata are in a more hopeful
way of mutual understanding than perhaps in the North.

CHAPTER VI

T HE South has not only its own division of special classes, its own methods of influence, it has also its own way of looking at the problems of the universe, and especially that department of the universe south of Mason and Dixon's line. To discover the temperament of the South is difficult, for upon the face of things the differences of the two sections are slight. Aside from little peculiarities of dialect, probably no more startling than Bostonese English is to the Southerner when he first hears it, the people whom one meets in Southern trains and hotels appear very like their Northern kinsfolk. The Memphis drummer in the smoker tells the same stories that you heard yesterday from his Chicago brother; the members of the Charleston Club talk about their ancestors just like the habitués of the Rittenhouse Club in Philadelphia; the President of the University of Virginia asks for money for the same reasons as the President of Western Reserve University; Northern and Southern men, meeting on mutual ground and avoiding the question of the Negro, which sometimes does not get into their conversation for half an hour together, find their habits of thought much the same: the usual legal reasoning, economic discussion, and religious controversy all appeal to the same kind of minds. Northerners read Lanier with the

66

same understanding with which Southerners read Long-fellow.

Nevertheless there is a subtle difference of temperament hard to catch and harder to characterize, which may perhaps be illustrated by the difference between the Northern "Hurrah" and the "Rebel yell"; between "Yankee Doodle" and "Dixie," each stirring, each lively, yet each upon its separate key. Upon many questions, and particularly upon all issues involving the relations of the white and negro races, the Southerner takes things differently from the Northerner. He looks upon himself from an emotional standpoint. Thomas Dixon, Jr., characterizes his own section as "The South, old-fashioned, medieval, provincial, worshipping the dead, and raising men rather than making money, family-loving, home-building, tradition-ridden. The South, cruel and cunning when fighting a treacherous foe, with brief, volcanic bursts of wrath and vengeance. The South, eloquent, bombastic, romantic, chivalrous, lustful, proud, kind and hospitable. The South, with her beautiful women and brave men."

This self-consciousness is doubtless in part a result of external conditions, such as the isolation of many parts of the South; but still more is due to an automatic sensitiveness to all phases of the race question. People in the South often speak of their "two peoples" and "two civilizations"; and at every turn, in every relation, a part of every discussion, is the fact that the population of the South is rigidly divided into two races marked off from each other by an impassable line of color. The North has race questions, but no race question: the foreign elements taken together are numerous enough, and their future is uncertain enough to cause anxiety; but they are as likely to act against each other as against the group of people of English stock; as likely to harmonize with native Anglo-Saxon people as to oppose them—they are not a combined race standing in a cohort, watchful, suspicious, and resentful. The North has twenty race problems; the South has but one, which for that very reason is twenty times as serious. In every field of Southern life, social, political, economic, intellectual, the presence of two races divides and weakens. The blacks and the Whites in the South are the two members of a pair of shears, so clumsily put together that they gnash against each other continually. Though one side be silver, and the other only bronze, neither can perform its function without the other, but there is a terrible strain upon the rivet which holds them together.

This state of tension is not due wholly to the Negroes, nor removable by improving them, as though the straightening only the bronze half of the shears you could make them cut truly. If no Negroes had ever come over from Africa, or if they were all to be expatriated to-morrow, there would still remain a Southern question of great import. One of the mistakes of the Abolition controversy was to suppose that the South was different from the North simply because it had slaves; and that the two sections would be wholly alike if only the white people felt differently toward the Negro. The Negro does not make all the trouble, cause all the concern, or attract all the attention of thoughtful men in the South. In every part of that section, from the most remote cove in the Tennessee mountains to the stateliest quarter of New Orleans, there is a Caucasian question, or rather a series of Caucasian questions, arising out of the peculiar make-up of the white community, though alongside it is always the shadow of the African.

Nobody can work out any of the Caucasian problems as

though they stood by themselves; what now draws together most closely the elements of the white race is a sense of a race issue. The white man cannot build new school-houses or improve his cotton seed or open a coal mine without remembering that there is a negro race and a negro problem. This consciousness of a double existence strikes every visitor and confronts every investigator. As Du Bois says, the stranger " realizes at last that silently, resistlessly, the world about flows by him in two great streams: they ripple on in the same sunshine, they approach and mingle their waters in seeming carelessness,— then they divide and flow wide apart." Henry W. Grady asserted that " The race problem casts the only shadow that rests on the South." Murphy says, " The problems of racial cleavage, like problems of labor and capital, or the problems of science and religion, yield to no precise formulæ; they are problems of life, persistent and irreducible."

Various as are the opinions in the South with regard to the race problem and the modes of its solution, society is infused with a feeling of uneasiness and responsibility. Sometimes the visitor seems to catch a feeling of pervading gloom; sometimes he hears the furious and cruel words of those who would end the problem by putting the Negro out of the question; sometimes he listens to the hopeful voice of those who expect a peaceful and a just solution; but all thinking men in the South agree that their section has a special, a peculiar, a difficult and almost insoluble problem in which the North has little or no share.

Here comes in the first of many difficulties in dealing with the Southern question, a diversity of voices such that it is hard to know which speaks for the South, or where the average sentiment is to be found. Public opinion on some moral and social questions is less easily concentrated than in the North; though the prohibitionists have recently made a very successful campaign through a general league, all efforts to focus public opinion on the negro question through general societies and public meetings have so far failed.

Agitation or even discussion of the race problem is not much aided by the press, though in some ways journalism is on a higher plane than in the North. Most cities, even small ones, have a newspaper which is edited with real literary skill, and which does not seem to be the servant of any commercial interest. There is a type of Southern paper of which the *Charleston News and Courier* is the best example, which has for its stock-in-trade, ultra and Bourbon sentiments. No paper in the South is more interesting than the *News and Courier,* but it represents an age that is past. The conservative, readable, and on the whole, high-toned Southern newspapers, do not in general seem to lead public sentiment, and the yellow journal has begun to compete with them. Still the paper which by its lurid statement of facts, large admixture of lies, and use of ferocious headlines, was one of the chief agents in bringing about the Atlanta riots of 1907 afterwards went into the hands of a receiver; and journals of that type have less influence than in the North.

A temperamental Southern characteristic is an impatience of dissent, a characteristic which has recently been summed up as follows by a foreigner who has lived twelve years in the South and is identified with it. " There are three phases of public sentiment that I must regard as weaknesses, . . . The public attitude of Southern temper is over-sensitive and too easily resents criticism . . . Then, I think the Southern people are too easily swayed by an apparent public sentiment, the broader and higher conscience of the people gives way too readily to a tin-pan clamor, the depth and real force of which they are not disposed to question. . . . Again, . . . the South as a section, does not seem fully to appreciate the importance of the inevitables in civilization—the fixed and unalterable laws of progress." Illustrations of this sensitiveness to criticism are abundant. For instance, the affectionate girl in the Southern school when a Yankee teacher gives her a low mark, bursts into tears, and wants to know why the teacher does not love her.

From slavery days down, there has been a disposition to look upon Northern writers and visitors with suspicion. Still inquirers are in all parts of the South received with courtesy by those whose character and interest in the things that make for the uplift of both the white and the black race furnish the most convincing argument that there is an enlightened public sentiment which will work out the Southern problem. In any case there is no public objection to criticism of Southerners by other Southerners; nothing, for instance, could be more explicit and mutually unfavorable than the opinions' exchanged between Hoke Smith and Clark Howells in 1907, when rival candidates for the governorship of Georgia. In politics one may say what he likes, subject to an occasional rebuke from the revolver's mouth.

It is not the same in the discussion of the race question. In half a dozen instances in the last few years, attempts have been made to drive out professors from Southern colleges and universities, on the ground that they were not sufficiently Southern. In one such case, that of Professor

Bassett, at Trinity College, North Carolina, who said in print that Booker Washington was the greatest man except Lee, born in the South in a hundred years, it stood by him manfully, and his retention was felt to be a triumph for free speech. Other boards of trustees have rallied in like manner, and there is a fine spirit of fearless truth among professors of colleges, ministers, lawyers, and public men. It is no small triumph for the cause of fair play that John Sharp Williams, of Mississippi, in 1907 came out in opposition to Governor Vardaman's violent abuse of the Negro, on that issue triumphed over him in the canvass for the United States Senate; and then in a public address committed himself to a friendly and hopeful policy toward the Negro.

In part, this frame of mind is due to a feeling neatly stated by a Southern banker: "The Southern people are not a bad kind, and a kind word goes a long way with them; they have odd peculiarities; they cannot argue, and as soon as you differ with them, you arouse temper, not on the Negro question especially, but on any." This diagnosis is confirmed by "Nicholas Worth": "Few men cared what opinion you held about any subject. . . . I could talk in private as I pleased with Colonel Stover himself about Jefferson Davis or about educating the negro. He was tolerant of all private opinions, privately expressed among men only. But the moment that an objectionable opinion was publicly expressed, or expressed to women or to negroes, that was another matter. Then it touched our sacred dead, our hearthstones, etc." This state of feeling has much affected politics in the South and is in part responsible for the phenomenon called the Solid South, under which, whatever be its causes, the South is deprived of influence either in nominating or supplying candidates for national office, because its vote may be relied upon in any case for one party and one only.

The dislike of the critic is specially strong when criticism comes from foreigners, and aggravated when it comes from Northerners. A recent Southern speaker says: "Now, as since the day the first flagship was legalized in its trade in Massachusetts, . . . the trouble in the race question is due to the persistent assertion on the part of northern friends and philanthropists that they understand the problem and can devise the means for its solution." That Northerners do not all lay claim to such understanding, or hold themselves responsible for race troubles, is admitted by a Southerner of much greater weight, Edgar Gardner Murphy, who has recently said: "Beneath the North's serious and rightful sense of obligation the South saw only an intolerant 'interference.' Beneath the South's natural suspicion and solicitude the North saw only an indiscriminating enmity to herself and to the negro."

To these characteristics another is added by "Nicholas Worth," in his discussion of the "oratorical habit of mind" of a generation ago—"Rousing speech was more to be desired than accuracy of statement. An exaggerated manner and a tendency to sweeping generalizations were the results. You can now trace this quality in the mind and in the speech of the great majority of Southern men, especially men in public life. We call it the undue development of their emotional nature. It is also the result of a lack of any exact training,—of a system that was mediæval." Another form of this habit of mind is the love of round numbers, a fondness for stating a thing in the largest terms; thus the clever but no-wise distinguished professor of Latin is "Probably the greatest classical scholar in the United States," the siege of Vicksburg was "the most terrific contest in the annals of warfare"; the material progress of the South is "the most marvelous thing in human history."

This difference of temperament between North and South is not confined to members of the white race. The mental processes of the Southern Negro differ not only from those of the Southern White, but to a considerable degree from those of the Northern Negro; and the African temperament has, in the course of centuries, in some ways reacted upon the minds of the associated white race. The real standards and aspirations of the Negroes are crudely defined and little known outside themselves, and if they were better understood they would still have scant influence upon the white point of view. The "Southern temperament," therefore means the temperament of the Southern Whites, of the people who control society, forum, and legislature. It is always more important to know what people think than what they do, and every phase of the race question in the South is affected by the habits of thought of thinking white people.

Both sections need to understand each other; and that good result is impeded by the belief of a large number of people in the South that the North as a section feels a personal hostility to the South; that in Reconstruction it sought to humiliate the Southern Whites, and to despoil them of their property; that it planted schools in the South with the express purpose of bringing about a social equality hateful to the Whites; that it arouses in the Negro a frame of mind which leads to the most hideous of crimes; and that Northern observers and critics of the South are little better than spies.

74

SOUTHERN TEMPERAMENT

The North is doubtless blamable for some past ill feeling and some ill judgment, but it cannot be charged now with prejudice against the South. It is not too much to say that the North as a section is weary of the negro question; that it is disappointed in the progress of the race both in the South and in the North; that it is overwhelmed with a variety of other questions, and less inclined than at any time during forty years to any active interference in Southern relations. An annual floodtide carries many Northern people into Florida and other pleasure resorts, where they see the surface of the negro question and accept without verification the conventional statements that they hear; the same tide on its ebb brings them North with a tone of discouragement and irritation toward the Negro, which much affects Northern public sentiment.

This apathy or disappointment is unfortunate, for from many points of view, the North has both an interest and a responsibility for what goes on in the South. First of all, from its considerable part in bringing about present conditions. Besides an original share in drawing slavery upon the colonies, the North by the emancipation of the slaves disturbed the preëxisting balance of race relations, such as it was. Then in Reconstruction the North attempted to bring about a new political system with the honest expectation that it would solve the race question. Surely it has a right to examine the results of its action, with a view either to justify its attitude, or to accept censure for it.

If either through want of patience or skill or by sheer force of adverse circumstance a dangerous condition has come about in the South for which the dominant white Southerners are not responsible, they are entitled to an understanding of their case and to sympathy, encouragement and aid in overcoming their troubles. No thinking person in the North desires anything but the peaceful removal of the evils which undeniably weigh upon the South. To that end the North might offer something out of its own experience, for it has expert knowledge of race troubles and of ways to solve them. The Indian question ever since the Civil War has been chiefly in the hands of Northern men; and if it has been a botchy piece of work, at least a way out has been found in the present land-in-severalty plan; and from the North in considerable part has proceeded the government of the Filipinos. The North carries almost alone a mass of foreigners who contribute difficulties which in diversity much exceed the negro problem, and which so far have been so handled that in few places is there a crisis, acute or threatening. The North has further its own experiences with Negroes, beginning in Colonial times; it now harbors a million of them; and it has in most places found a peaceful living basis for the two races, side by side.

Perhaps Southern people do not make sufficient allowance for the scientific love of inquiry of the North. It is a region where Vassar students of sociology visit the probation courts; where Yale men descend upon New York and investigate Tammany Hall; where race relations are thought a fit subject for intercollegiate debate and scientific monographs, on the same footing with the distribution of immigrants, or the career of discharged convicts. In Massachusetts, people are ready to attack any insoluble problem, from the proper authority of the Russian Douma to the reason why cooks give notice without previous notice. As a study of human nature, as an exercise in practical sociology, the Southern race problem has for the North much the same fascination as the preceding slavery question.

Doubtless the zeal for investigation, and the disposition to give unasked advice, would both be lessened if the Southern problem were already solved or on the road to solution by the people nearest to it. The Southern Whites have had control of every Southern state government since 1876 and some of them longer; they are dominant in legislature, court and plantation; yet they have not yet succeeded in putting an end to their own perplexities. Some of them still defiantly assert themselves against mankind; thus Professor Smith, of New Orleans, says apropos of the controversy over race relations: "The attitude of the South presents an element of the pathetic. The great world is apparently hopelessly against her. Three-fourths of the virtue, culture, and intelligence of the United States seems to view her with pitying scorn; the old mother, England, has no word of sympathy, but applauds the conduct that her daughter reprehends; the continent of Europe looks on with amused perplexity, as unable even to comprehend her position, so childish and absurd." Professor Smith's answer to his own question is: "The South cares nothing, in themselves, for the personal friendships or appreciations of high-placed dignitaries and men of light and leading." He does not speak for his section; for most intelligent Southern people, however extreme their views, desire to be understood; they want their position to seem humane and logical to their neighbors; they are sure that they are the only people who can be on the right road; but they do not feel that they are approaching a permanent adjustment of race relations.

How could such an adjustment be expected now? The negro question has existed ever since the first landing of negro slaves in 1619, became serious in some colonies before 1700, gave rise to many difficulties and complications during the Revolution, was reflected in the Constitutional Convention of 1787, later proved to be the rock of offense upon which the Union split, and has during the forty years since the Civil War been the most absorbing subject of discussion in the South. It hardly seems likely that it will be put to rest in our day and generation.

Yet some settlement is necessary for the peace and the prosperity of both races; and one of the means to that end is a frank, free and open discussion in all parts of the Union. Nothing was so prejudicial to slavery as the attempt to silence the Northern abolitionists; for a social system that was too fragile to be discussed was doomed to be broken. One of the most encouraging things at present is the willingness of the South to discuss its problems on its own ground, and to admit that there can be a variety of opinions; and to meet rather than to defy the criticisms of observers.

If the thinking people of the South were less willing to share the discussion with the North, it would still be a Northern concern; for the Southern race problem, like the labor unions of the manufacturing North, the distribution of lands in the far West, and the treatment of Mongolians on the Pacific Coast, is nobody's exclusive property. There must be freedom for the men of every section to discuss every such question; it is the opportunity for mutual helpfulness. For instance, how much might be contributed to an understanding of the decay of the New England hill towns by a Southern visitor who should visit them and then report upon them from his point of view. Violent, ignorant, and prejudiced discussion of any section of the Union by any other section is, of course, destructive of national harmony; but the days have gone by when it could be thought unfriendly, hostile, or condemnatory for Northern men to strive to make themselves familiar with the race questions of the South. "We are everyone members of another," and the whole body politic suffers from the disease of any member. The immigrant in the North is the concern of the Southerner for he is to become part of America. The status of the plantation hand in Alabama is likewise a Northern problem; as Murphy has recently said: "The Nation, including the South as well as the North, and the West as well as the South and the North, has to do with every issue in the South that touches any national right of the humblest of its citizens. Too long it has been assumed, both at the North and at the South, that the North is the Nation. The North is not the Nation. The Nation is the life, the thought, the conscience, the authority, of all the land."

CHAPTER VII

THE history of the United States is a rope of many strands, each of which was twisted into form before they were united into one cable. Each state marks the sites of its first landings, puts monuments on its battle-fields, commemorates its liberty days, and teaches its children to remember the great years of the past. The South has a full share of these memories, which are both local events and foundation stones of the nation's history. Jamestown, St. Mary's, Charleston, Fort Moultrie, York-town, Mobile, belong to us all, as much as Providence, Bunker Hill, Saratoga, and San Francisco.

The Southern mind likes to think of its episodes as contributions to the national history, and at the same time to claim as specifically Southern all that has taken place in the South since the foundation of the Federal Union. School histories are written and prescribed by legislatures to teach children a Southern point of view; the South of Washington and Jefferson, of Jackson and Calhoun, is looked upon as something apart from the nation. To some extent there is reason for this frame of mind; slavery, or rather the obstinate maintenance of slavery after it had disappeared in other civilized communities, put the South in a position of defiance of the world for near three quarters of a century; hence the

history of the South from 1789 to 1861 can be separated
from that of the Union as a whole in a manner impossible
for New England and the West.

This separate history needs, like other eras of human
history, to be envisaged in the light of things that actually
were. Such calm and unbiased approach to the study
of past times is difficult in the South because of the exaggeration of one of the fine traits of Southern character,
of its respect for the past, its veneration for ancestors.
In a world of progress a main influence is the conviction
that things need to be improved, that the children are
wiser than their fathers; but this spirit is out of accord
with the Southern feeling of loyalty to section, to state, to
kindred, and to ancestors. Charles Francis Adams spends
years in showing up the inconsistencies of the character of
his Puritan forbears; but to the Southern mind there
would be something shocking in a South Carolina or
Virginia writer who should set forth unfavorable views
of the courage of General Moultrie or the legal skill of
Patrick Henry.

For this reason, or for more occult reasons, there is a
disposition in the South to hold to local traditional views
of the history of the United States as a whole and of the
South in particular. For instance, most North Carolinians
seem addicted to the belief that Mecklenburg County drew
up certain drastic resolutions of Independence, May 20,
1775; and the man who is not convinced of it had better
live somewhere else than in North Carolina. In like
manner many Southerners suppose it to be an established
fact that the aristocracy in the South were descended from
English Cavaliers, and the leaders in New England from
the Puritans. Yet there is little evidence of permanent
Cavalier influence in any Southern colony. The most

81

recent historian of early Virginia, Bruce, says: "The principal figures in the history of Virginia in the seventeenth century were men of the stamp of Samuel Mathews, George Menefie, Robert Beverley, Adam Thoroughgood, Ralph Wormeley, William Fitzhugh, Edmund Scarborough, and William Byrd." Are these names more heraldic than those of John Winthrop and John Endicott and Thomas Dudley? Aside from the titled governors who did not remain in the colonies, Lord Fairfax possessed the only Virginia title, and he may be balanced by Sir William Phipps, the Yankee knight. George Washington's ancestors are known to have been respectable English squires, but where are the Cavalier forefathers of Patrick Henry and Thomas Jefferson, John C. Calhoun and Jefferson Davis? The bone and sinew of the Colonial South, as of the North, was made up of the English middle class, yeomen and shopkeepers; and in both sections the descendants of those men chiefly came to eminence.

Another of the unfortified beliefs which have wide currency in the South is that under slavery the South was a prosperous, happy, and glorious community. Robert Toombs, of Georgia, in a lecture delivered in Boston in 1856, said of the slave states: "In surveying the whole civilized world, the eye rests not on a single spot where all classes of society are so well content with their social system, or have greater reason to be so, than in the slaveholding States of this Union. . . . They may safely challenge the admiration of the civilized world." Later books of reminiscence carry you back to the delightful days when " the old black mahogany table, like a mirror, was covered with Madeira decanters standing in silver casters, and at each plate was a glass finger bowl with four pipestem glasses on their sides just touching the water "; when "woman's conquests were made by the charms and graces given them by nature rather than by art of women modistes and men milliners . . . and the men prided themselves, above all things, on being gentlemen. This gave tone to society."

This system was assumed to be especially happy for the slave; witness a recent Southern writer: "Hence, to the negro, the institution of slavery, so far from being prejudicial, was actually beneficial in its effects, in that, as a strictly paternal form of government, it furnished that combination of wise control and kind compulsion which is absolutely essential to his development and well-being." Minor, in his recent "The Real Lincoln," urges that "the children of slaveholders may be saved from being betrayed into the error of regarding with reprobation the conduct of their parents in holding slaves"; and justifies slavery on the ground that the slaves had "a more liberal supply of the necessaries of life than was ever granted to any other laboring class in any other place, or other age." Reed, in his "Brothers' War," holds that "Any and every evil of southern slavery to the negro was accidental. . . . Slavery, so far from being wrong morally, was righteousness, justice, and mercy to the slave." No wonder that "Nicholas Worth" exclaims: "What I discovered was that the people did not know their own history; that they had accepted certain oft-repeated expressions about it as facts; and that the practical denial of free discussion of certain subjects had deadened research and even curiosity to know the truth."

This theory that slavery was harmful, if harmful at all, only to the white race, has gone to the extent of insisting that slavery was educational; thus Thomas Nelson Page says that at the end of the War, among the able-bodied Negroes there was "scarcely an adult who was not a trained laborer or a skilled artisan. In the cotton section they knew how to raise and prepare cotton; in the sugar belt they knew how to grow and grind sugar; in the tobacco, corn, wheat, and hay belts they knew how to raise and prepare for market those crops. They were the shepherds, cattle-men, horse-trainers and raisers. The entire industrial work of the South was performed by them. . . . Nearly all the houses in the South were built by them. They manufactured most of the articles that were manufactured in the South." And Mrs. Avary, in her "Dixie After the War," thinks that "the typical Southern plantation was, in effect, a great social settlement for the uplift of Africans." These arguments are perhaps not intended to suggest that the present free laboring population would be better off if reduced to slavery; but they fix upon the present generation the unhappy task of justifying all the mistakes of previous generations.

The natural and wholly justifiable pride in the military spirit of the South during the Civil War extends over to the constitutional, or rather psychical, question of Secession. No issue in the world is deader than the question whether states have a right to secede, for the simple reason that the experience of forty years ago shows that in case any state or group of states hereafter may wish to secede, the other states will infallibly combine to resist by military force: no state or section can ever again assert that it has reason to suppose that secession is a peaceful and constitutional remedy, which should be accepted quietly by the sister states. To justify the doctrine of secession now would mean to pull out the bracing of the Union, no part of which is more determined to be a portion of one great and powerful American nation than the

Southern States. It can hardly be expected that the North, after sacrificing five hundred thousand lives and four billions of treasure, will, half a century later, come round to the point of view of the defeated section.

It is equally idle at this period of the world's history to deny to the Southern leaders in the Civil War sincerity and courage, or to withhold from the nation the credit of such lofty characters as Lee and Stonewall Jackson; but if they are to become world heroes alongside of Cromwell and Iredell, consistency demands that the corresponding Northern leaders shall likewise be accepted as sincere and courageous, and in addition as standing for those permanent national principles to which the children of their adversaries have now given allegiance. It is discouraging to discover such a book as Charles L. C. Minor's "The Real Lincoln; from the Testimony of his Contemporaries," which has gone to a second edition and the purpose of which is, by quoting the harsh and cruel things said of Lincoln in the North during his lifetime, to show that he was weak, bad, and demoralized. Far more modern the testimony of Grady in his New York speech of 1886, when he referred to him "who stands as the first typical American, the first who comprehended within himself all the strength and gentleness, all the majesty and grace of this republic—Abraham Lincoln. He was the sum of Puritan and Cavalier; for in his ardent nature were fused the virtues of both, and in the depths of his great soul the faults of both were lost. He was greater than Puritan, greater than Cavalier, in that he was American."

If the South looks on the Civil War through some favorable haze, it is chiefly in the direction of magnifying genuinely great men, and few of the Confederate soldiers retain any bitterness toward the other side. This is not the case with Reconstruction—toward which, for a variety of reasons, the South feels the bitterest resentment. Only a few months ago a flowery speaker in Baltimore, addressing an audience composed chiefly of Northern people, declared that "all the ignominy, shame, bloodshed, moral debasement that followed the crowning infamy of the Fifteenth Amendment must be laid at the door of the North alone. . . . The whole movement was thoroughly revolutionary—anarchy, chaos, ruin was the inevitable result." Thomas Dixon, Jr., rings all the changes and more on this theme. He makes Thaddeus Stevens, in the intervals that he can spare from his negro paramour, set out to confiscate the property of all the Southern Whites; and he supposes that the North sends down as its agents in the South "Army cooks, teamsters, fakirs, and broken-down preachers who had turned insurance agents." He charges that by the North the attempt was "deliberately made to blot out Anglo-Saxon society and substitute African barbarism."

The years from 1865 to 1871 were indeed sorrowful for the Southern States, and have planted seeds of hostility between North and South and also between the races in the South; but declamation and exaggeration add nothing to the real hardships of the process. Many Southerners still believe that their section was impoverished only by emancipation, which they say swept away two thousand million dollars' worth of property; they overlook that the South was politically and economically ruined by the losses of four years of a war which, besides the actual destruction in the track of armies, by its terrible drain took all the accumulated capital of the section. After the war the South still retained the land and the Negroes to work it. The community as a whole lost nothing except from the dislocation of industry. Inasmuch as the South has recovered its productive capacity, and there is not a man of any standing in the South who, from the point of view of the white man's interest, would go back to slavery if he could, it is time that the charges of spoliation by emancipation were withdrawn.

Both the duration and the intensity of the Reconstruction process have been overestimated. It was a period of general disorganization; the time of the Credit Mobilier scandals; the exact decade when the people of New York City were paying eighty million dollars for the privilege of being plundered by Boss Tweed. The Southern state governments had previously been economically administered, and the people keenly felt the degradation of corruption from which Northern States were also suffering; but the actual period of Reconstruction was much shorter than has usually been supposed. After the first attempts to reorganize the governments in 1865, they went back into the hands of the military, and the consensus of testimony is that the military government if harsh was honest. There they remained in all cases until 1868 and in Georgia until 1871. Within little more than a year after 1868 the Conservatives of Virginia regained control; in Alabama Reconstruction lasted only twenty-eight months; in the tidal wave of 1874 the carpetbag and scalawag power was broken in all the Southern States except South Carolina and Louisiana.

One year or five years of bad government was too much, but Southern lawlessness was not the monopoly of the Reconstruction governments. One of the greatest evils of the period was the Ku Klux Klan which Reed says " becomes dearer in memory every year." There was reason for recovering white supremacy in the South, even though the conditions of the Reconstruction government have been somewhat exaggerated; but the Ku Klux aroused a spirit of disorder, a defiance of the vested rights of white men as well as of Negroes, which has been a malign influence for forty years. The night-riders in Kentucky are almost a conscious imitation of the Ku Klux, and only a few months ago it was suggested that it be reorganized in Georgia to deal with negro crime. It is one thing to read of the gallant struggle of the Ku Klux to protect womanhood and to asert the nobility of the white race; it is quite another to be told, incidentally, that in a certain county of Mississippi the Ku Klux "put a hundred and nineteen niggers into the river." That is what some people call a massacre.

The attitude of some Southerners toward the Civil War and Reconstruction suggests the story of the Georgia captain who, after three years of honest fighting, reappeared on his farm and was welcomed home by his faithful Penelope. "The war is over," said he; "I have come home to stay forever." "Is that true, Jim? Have you licked the Yankees at last?" "Yes, I have licked them at last, but if they don't stay licked, I don't know but I may have to go up North and lick 'em again."

Is the North to be "licked again" indefinitely? The suffering, the sacrifice, and the heroism of the Civil War were as great on its side of Mason and Dixon's line as on the other side; and the historical perspective of that period of conflict covers some incidents which the North forgets with difficulty. For instance, the prison of Andersonville was hateful to the whole North. After forty years it is easier than at the time to understand the difficulties of an impoverished government guarding thousands of prisoners with a scanty force in a region lacking in food.

Nevertheless, it is a deep conviction of the survivors among the prisoners and in the minds of many thousand other persons that these inherent difficulties were aggravated by the incompetency and heartlessness of Captain Wirz, who by accepting command assumed the responsibility for the condition of things. By the best showing of his friends he was an incompetent man, who had the power of life and death over thousands of his fellow-men, and let many of them die for want of humanity and common sense. The only reason for remembering Wirz is that he was obnoxious to the Northern soldiers in a time of great excitement. Yet the South of Lee and Jackson and Sidney Johnston has erected a monument to that man who performed no service to the Confederacy except to be executed, who led in no heroic action, represents no chivalry, and who did not so much as capture a color or an army wagon. It is an example of what in other parts of the world is thought an emotional disinclination to look facts in the face.

As to the period since Reconstruction—that is, the last thirty years—the acute sensibility of the South no longer takes the form of accusing the North of an attempt to submerge the white race, but rather is turned toward enlarged news of Southern wealth and prestige, which will be examined later in this book. It has been the service of Southern writers, teachers, and public men to look facts more squarely in the face. Still, one finds now and then an old man of the old Benton spirit. About two years ago a Mississippi newspaper greeted a visitor who had previously expressed some opinions on the South, as " an object of distaste to all decent people of Mississippi. . . . This blue-abdomened miscreant . . . would have the world believe that the South has burnings, lynchings, and such horrors, with special trains, and the children of the public schools to witness. Are the people of Jackson going to hear this traducer of them; this man who prints broadcast over the country baseless slanders against the people who misguidedly invited him down here? Are they going to hear a man filled with venom who will take their good name." And a high-toned Southern gentleman, up to that time a personal friend of the Northerner, thought it necessary to print a card in a newspaper, setting forth the fact that he at least had no responsibility for the presence of the Yankee.

CHAPTER VIII

NEGRO CHARACTER

THE social organization of the Anglo-Saxons in the South, their relations with each other, their strife for leadership, takes little account of the other race, though it is diffused throughout the country; it is everywhere with the Whites, but not of them. Although to the Southern mind the community is made up entirely of white people, numerically almost one third of the inhabitants of the former slaveholding states are Negroes, and in the Lower South there are five million blacks against seven million Whites. The moral and material welfare of the South is intimately affected by their presence, and still more by their character. They are as much children of the soil as the Whites; they are everywhere distributed, except in the mountains; their labor is necessary for the prosperity of the section; they have a social organization of their own and many of the appliances of civilization; they own some land, travel, are everywhere in evidence, yet they are distrusted by nearly all the Whites, despised by more than half of them, and hated by a considerable and apparently increasing fraction.

Even the names habitually used by the Whites for their neighbors show contempt. "Nigger," though often used among the blacks, is felt by them to be depreciatory; "Darky" is jocular; "Negro" is condescending;

" Blacks " as a generic term is incorrect in view of the light color of a large fraction of the race. Afro-American, the invention of the Negroes, is pedantic. The Negroes themselves much prefer " Colored person," which is also a term used in directories.

Every Southern man and woman consciously or unconsciously makes generalizations as to the whole race from those comparatively few individuals with whom he is acquainted. Hence conventional and offhand statements, obviously based upon little direct knowledge of the Negro, abound in private conversation, in public addresses and in print. For example, a few months ago the mayor of Houston, himself the son of a Massachusetts man, who went down to Texas before the Civil War, was led by an accidental question to deliver an extempore indictment of the whole negro race under twelve heads then and there noted down as follows:

(1) The old Negroes in slavery times were a good lot, but Negroes nowadays are worthless.

(2) The Negro is the best laborer that the South ever had.

(3) Education destroys the value of the Negro, by making him unwilling to work.

(4) The South makes great sacrifices to educate the Negroes.

(5) The Negroes on the farms often do well; but those are the old slaves.

(6) The young Negroes will not work on the land but drift off, probably to the cities.

(7) The pure Negro is much superior in character to the Mulattoes, who are the most vicious part of the race.

(8) The mulatto is physically weak and he is rapidly dying out.

(9) Five sixths of all the Negroes in this city have some white blood.

(10) The educated Negroes fill the prisons.

(11) Booker T. Washington has good ideas.

(12) Negroes must be " kept in their place," otherwise there will be general rapine and destruction.

Some curious errors of perspective are discernible in this picture: the Negro is at the same time the best laborer and the worst laborer; the South continues to make great sacrifices to educate blacks who will not work and who fill the prisons; the mulatto is at the same time dying out and furnishing five sixths of the colored population of a large city. Such generalizations are the daily food of the South. Judge Norwood, of Georgia, on retiring from the bench of the city court of Savannah, where he had tried twelve thousand colored people, recently left on record his formal opinion that the Negro never works except from necessity or compulsion, has no initiative, is brutal to his family, recognizes no government except force, knows neither ambition, honor nor shame, possesses no morals; and the judge protests against " the insanity of putting millions of semi-savages under white men's laws for their government." The mayor of Winona, Miss., publicly announces that "The negro is a lazy, lying, lustful animal, which no conceivable amount of training can transform into a tolerable citizen." Senator Tillman, of South Carolina, on the floor of the Senate has said: " So the poor African has become a fiend, a wild beast, seeking whom he may devour, filling our penitentiaries and our jails." Governor Vardaman, of Mississippi, in his farewell message to the Legislature, in January, 1908, called the Negroes, who are in a majority in his state: " A race inherently unmoral, ignorant and superstitious, with a congenital tendency to crime, incapable unalterably of understanding the meaning of free government, devoid of those qualities of mind and body necessary to self-control, and being unable to control themselves."

One of the sources of confusion with regard to the Negro is that people speak of "the African Race" which they suppose to be pictured on the Egyptian monuments, to be briefly mentioned by Herodotus, and to be in the same condition now in Africa as it was when first described. As a matter of fact, there are several native races, varying in color from the intensely black and uncouth Guinea Negro of the West Coast to the olive-brown Arabs of the Sahara desert, and in civilization from the primitive dwarf tribes of Central Africa to the organized kingdoms of the Zulus and the thriving states of the Central lake region. Many arguments as to the negro character are based upon the supposed profound barbarism and cannibalism of all Africa. The truth is that the African tribes, with all their ferocity and immorality, had advanced farther in the path of civilization previous to their first contact with the Europeans than the North American Indians of the Atlantic and Mississippi regions; they had gone farther in the arts, had built up more numerous communities, and established a more complex society. The curse of Africa, from which the Indians were not free, was slavery and slave-hunting, which from time immemorial have led to ferocious wars and reckless destruction of life. On the side of religion, the African has built up a weird and emotional system, honeycombed with witchcraft and a belief in magic, stained with bloodshed and human sacrifice. Yet all explorers and residents in Africa find many attractive traits in the Negro; he loves a joke, makes a tolerable soldier, often shows faithful affection for his leaders, and under the supervision of white officials, seems capable of a peaceful and happy life.

That the character of the Negro should need to be a matter of absorbing interest to the Southern Whites and a study to Northern observers, is the fault of the Sixteenth Century European. The Negroes have for ages been in contact with white races on their northern and eastern borders; Ethiopian captives were brought to Rome, and the black slave is a favorite character in the " Arabian Nights." But that this race, situated on the other side of the globe, should affect the commerce and obstruct the political development of America, is one of the oddities of history. The Negroes, who have never made a conquest outside their own continent, who were first brought to Europe on the same footing as ostrich feathers and elephants, as objects of trade and as curiosities, have, through the greed and cruelty of our ancestors, planted a colony of ten million people in our land; and other groups, mounting up to several millions, in the West Indies and Brazil.

Many attempts are made to determine the ability of the Negro by what he has done in Africa and in Latin America. He has not lifted himself out of barbarism in his own continent, though he has founded large and prosperous states carried on solely by Africans; and Winston Spencer Churchill, from his recent visit to the heart of Africa, sees reason to predict that he will form permanent communities. The curses of Africa for centuries have been inhuman superstitions and devastating slave raids, dignified by the name of wars, for which the white and Arab slave dealers are partly responsible. Torture of captives, sack of towns, murder of infants, coffles of slaves marching to a market, are not so far away from the practice of European nations two or three centuries ago that we can brand them as evidence of irreclaimable barbarism. Pappenheim at Magdeburg and Lannes at the taking of Saragossa could match many of the worst crimes of the African impi on a raid, or of a white agent of the Congo Free State collecting his rubber tax. Protestant Germany and England left off the cruelest treatment of supposed witches only about two centuries ago. Cannibalism and the slave trade seem now on their last legs in Africa, and those white men who have lived longest in the heart of Africa seem to have the largest hope that the Dark Continent may be enlightened and a confidence in an African capacity for an existence much above the savage traditions.

These hopes are based in most cases on the expectation that white people will furnish the government and direct the industries. Whatever Africa may do for itself, the one notable effort to create an African state on an Anglo-Saxon model has been a failure. The Republic of Liberia was founded nearly a century ago, as a means of regenerating Africa by Christian civilization diffused from this spot on the coast into the interior; it was to be an outpost for tropical products and to furnish Africa an example of democratic state building. Liberia is the African state in which the United States is especially interested, for it was planted by American missionaries and agents of the Colonization Society; and has been an offshoot and almost a colony of this country. From the first it has been cursed by malaria, by the inroads and pressure of savages, and by a situation off the world's highways of commerce. To be sure its 15,000 civilized people have a public revenue of about $300,000, with a total import and export trade of about $1,000,000; but all efforts to induce a considerable number of Negroes from America to try their fortunes in Liberia have been failures. A colored magazine in Boston has had the humor and good-temper lately to reprint the following squib upon the opportunities in that country for the American Negro:

> Liberia's bridges, mills, and dams,
> Need many thousand Afro-Ams.
>
> Liberia's ewes, Liberia's lambs,
> Like black sheep, baa for Afro-Ams.
>
> Liberia's road, Liberia's trams,
> For steady jobs want Afro-Ams.
>
> The barber shops, like Uncle Sam's,
> Give hope to myriad Afro-Ams.
>
> There's bacon, hominy, yes, hams,
> For all industrious Afro-Ams.
>
> With faintest praise Liberia damns
> The slow-arriving Afro-Ams.
>
> Unless their woes at home are shams,
> Why don't they go, the Afro-Ams?

The inquiry of the final stanza is to the point, for though the American Colonization Society is still in existence, and within a few years has tried to send out a shipload of Negroes, Liberia attracts almost nobody and is a failure, either as a tropical home for the American Negro or as a center of Christianity and civilization for Africa.

How is it with the colonies and independent states of Americanized Africans in the West Indies, where there have been blacks for as much as four centuries? Of these communities Cuba, Porto Rico, Jamaica, Trinidad, the Windward and Leeward Islands were, or have been until recently, European colonies. Cuba's population is about half Negro; and they come nearer social and political equality with the Whites than anywhere else in the world; but there the dominant element is the pure Spanish or Spanish mestizo. In Jamaica since the emancipation of 1833 the races have had but one conflict, that of 1866, which was at the time thought to be due to the cruelty and panic of Governor Eyre. The blacks of Jamaica, to a large extent small proprietors, support themselves in the easy fashion of the tropics; but the 15,000 Whites who live among the 750,000 blacks seem less able than the like class in the Southern states to organize negro labor and make it profitable. The Negroes are taught to read and write, they have furnished thousands of acceptable laborers for the Panama Canal, and their death-rate is nearly down to the normal figures of the white people for their latitude. Their illiteracy, however, is about that of their brethren in the United States and nearly two thirds of all the children are illegitimate. Their government is practically still, as for two centuries and a half, out of their hands and in control of the English.

The Negroes in Hayti are popularly supposed to have deteriorated intellectually and morally. To be sure the alternating series of despotism and anarchy in that unhappy country are not very different from the course of things in the white community of Venezuela; and it would be a great mistake to suppose that the Haytian Negroes when they became independent a century ago had absorbed the civilization of their Spanish and French masters; most of them were still a fierce and intractable folk recently brought from Africa. Their experience, however, and

98

that of their neighbors in Santo Domingo, throws light upon the capacity of the African to build up a state, for both these lands are wholly governed by people of the African race. Neither has gained stability or improved in education or morals in half a century, though the Haytians are trying to set forth one of the arts of civilization by borrowing more money than they are willing to pay. The moral, or rather unmoral, conditions of this and other West Indian islands are a fair basis for argument as to the average character of the race.

The experience of the race in the Northern states leads rather to negative than to positive conclusions as to their intellectual and moral power. Time was when there were slaves on Beacon Hill; when Venus, "servant to Madam Wadsworth," was admitted to the First Church of Cambridge; and the Faculty of Harvard College warned the students not to consort with Titus, "servant of the late President Wadsworth." The colonial Negroes, who in no Northern colony were more numerous than six or seven per cent of the population, have left an offspring to which, since the Civil War, has been added a considerable immigration from the South. In 1900, 356,000 Africans born in the South were living in the North, and that proportion has since steadily increased. Nobody can pretend that this movement has improved the conditions of the Northern states, and the Negroes themselves encounter many hardships; they can vote, they get some small offices, and would get more if they could settle factional quarrels and unite behind single candidates; they have full and equal rights before the courts; they are commonly admitted to the public schools. On the other hand, separate negro schools have been provided in Indianapolis, in some places in New Jersey, and are likely to spread farther. Partly because many trades unions will not receive them, partly because they are thought to be less effective than Whites, partly from sheer race prejudice, they find many avenues of employment closed to them. Few people like them as neighbors, and though admitted to most Northern high schools and colleges they do not find that free intercourse of mind with mind which is not only one of the joys of living, but is a great upbuilder of character.

The situation of the Negroes in the North is frankly discouraging, both from their own point of view and that of the Northern White. Here if anywhere the race ought to show those qualities of determination and thrift and uprightness which its friends desire for it. Many of the Northern Negroes live on the same plane as the white people; many others do well, considering their lesser opportunities; and as a whole they earn their living; for where the men are lazy the women take care of them. But they are the objects of a steady prejudice; the reason for the school separation is that parents do not wish their children to be on such terms of acquaintance that they can learn all that the negro children know. Throughout the North there is a distrust of the negro voter, a belief that the Negroes furnish more than their share of the criminals.

To a large degree this is simply saying that the lowest part of the population is thought to be low; people dislike Negroes for the same reason that they object to many other persons, whether foreign or American born; the woeful difference is that any incompetent white individual may pull himself or push his children out of the slums and into association with the best, while color sets the Negro apart, no matter what his success in life; and the most respectable of them is treated as though responsible for the worst of his race. The door of opportunity is open in the North, but it does not open wide; the Northern colored man enters into what our ancestors called the half-way covenant; he, like his Southern brother, walks within the veil. Or is the bottom difficulty described by the immigrant from South Carolina to the North who said, " Yes, dere mought be more chances in New York than dere is in Charleston, but, please Gawd, 'pears like you ain't so likely to take dem chances."

The fundamental reason why race relations in the South are regulated by the white people, and are circumscribed by what they think best for themselves, is the universal white belief that the African is of an inferior race, so inferior that he cannot be trusted to take a part in the political life of the community, or even to manage his own affairs. That opinion is temperately stated by Thomas Nelson Page as follows: " After long, elaborate, and ample trial the Negro race has failed to discover the qualities which have inhered in every race of which history gives the record, which has advanced civilization, or has shown capacity to be itself greatly advanced." It is brutally stated by Governor Vardaman: " God Almighty created the Negro for a menial—he is essentially a servant. . . . When left to himself, he has universally gone back to the barbarism of his native jungles. While a few mixed breeds and freaks of the race may possess qualities which justify them to aspire above that station, the fact remains that the race is fit for that and nothing more."

The supposed inferiority of the negro race is not a foregone conclusion. First it rests on the tacit assumption that there is a " negro race " which can be distinguished from the white race, not only by color but also by aptitudes, moral standards and habits of mind. Some experts

101

in the South, who have studied the race as scientific men study the Indians of the Amazon, declare that they are unable to find any large body of traits which all Negroes possess; that they observe in no colored person characteristics which cannot be found in some Whites; and that they possess every variety of intellectual power and moral capacity. Then there is the question of the mulatto, who in his race mixture may be more white man than Negro. Is he to be included in the general indictment of inferiority? And, finally, what is to be argued from the men of power whom the negro race has displayed—a few in slavery days, and many in these later times?

The most extravagant statement of negro inferiority is that the worst white man is better than the best Negro because of the supernal quality of the white race. A Southern writer talks of "The endless creations of art and science and religion and law and literature and every other form of activity, the full-voiced choir of all the Muses, the majestic morality, the hundred-handed philosophy, the manifold wisdom of civilization—all of this infinite cloud of witnesses gather swarming upon us from the whole firmament of the past and proclaim with pentacostal tongue the glory and supremacy of Caucasian man." Judged by their achievements from the dawn of history to the present moment, the white race has indubitably achieved immensely more than the black race, but it has also achieved more than its own ancestors whom Taine thus characterizes: " Huge white bodies, . . . with fierce, blue eyes, . . . ravenous stomachs, . . . of a cold temperament, slow to love, home stayers, prone to brutal drunkenness: . . . Pirates at first: . . . seafaring, war, and pillage was their whole idea of a freeman's work. . . . Of all barbarians . . . the most cruelly ferocious."

NEGRO CHARACTER

After all, a race cannot be proved inferior by what it has not done; the United States as a war-making power has so far been inferior to the Germans and the Japanese, but its strength has not been tested. The real question is, does the Negro now, in the things that he is actually doing, show as much power as low and ignorant white people who have had no more than his opportunity? The Reconstruction governments, which are the stock in trade of those who decry the Negro, are little to the point, because they were to a considerable degree engineered by Whites, and because they lasted only from one to eight years. On the other hand, the great powers of a few select members of the race, and the excellent mentality and character of many others, are not proof that its average stamina is up to that of the white man; they must be tested by what they do.

The African in America has had little opportunity to work out a civilization of his own, and it certainly cannot be charged against him as a fault that he has accepted the white civilization which was at first forced upon him. As one of their own number says: "The Negro has advanced in exactly the same fashion as the white race has advanced, by taking advantage of all that has gone before. Other men have labored and we have entered into their labors." Yet, having accepted a heritage of literature, law and religion, from his white brother, the Negro cannot escape from the standard of the white man among whom he lives who have had like opportunities; and if he does not measure up to it it is impossible to avoid the conclusion that the race is inferior. Either the Negro is a white man with a black skin, who after a reasonable term of probation must now take the responsibilities of equal character (though not as yet of equal performance), or else it must be admitted that, though a man, he is a somewhat different kind of man from the White.

A favorite Southern phrase is: " The Negro is a child," and many considerable people accord him a child's privileges. The ignorant black certainly has a child's fondness for fun, freedom from care for the morrow, and incapacity to keep money in his pocket; but some planters will talk to you all day about the shrewdness with which he manages to get money out of the unsuspecting white man; and when it comes to serious crime, it is not every judge who makes allowance for childishness in the race. The theory that the negro mind ceases to develop after adolescence perhaps has something in it; but there are too many hard-headed and far-sighted persons, both full bloods and mulattoes, who have unusual minds, to permit the problem to be settled by the phrase, " The Negro is a child."

Genuine friends and well-wishers of the Negro feel intensely the irresponsibility of the race. A business man who all his life has been associated with them says: " He has all the good qualities of the lazy, thriftless person, he is amiable, generous and tractable. He has no activity in wrongdoing. He has the imitative gift in a remarkable degree, and always I love him for his faults, he is without craftiness, without greed. You will find no Rockefellers nor Carnegies among them. He is not a scoundrel from calculation. . . . He takes as his pattern the highest type of white man he is acquainted with. He has no sort of regard for what he thinks the poor white trash. . . . I don't know how best to help him, but I like him, like him and his careless devil-may-care ways. I like him because his whole soul is not absorbed in this craze for getting money. I like him because he does no evil by premeditation, because he sees no evil in everything he does, then goes and does it. I like him because some day in the distant past I was like him."

The main issue must be fairly faced by the friends as well as the enemies of the colored race. Measuring it by the white people of the South, or by the correspondingly low populations of Southern or Northern cities, the Negroes as a people appear to be considerably below the Whites in mental and moral status. There are a million or two exceptions, but they do not break the force of the eight or nine millions of average Negroes. A larger proportion of the mulattoes than of the pure bloods come up to the white race in ability; but if fifty thousand people in the negro quarter of New Orleans or on the central Alabama plantations be set apart and compared with a similar number of the least promising Whites in the same city or counties, fewer remarkable individuals and less average capacity would be found. Race measured by race, the Negro is inferior, and his past history in Africa and in America leads to the belief that he will remain inferior in race stamina and race achievement.

CHAPTER IX

THE negro problem in the South cannot be solved, nor is much light thrown upon it by the conditions of the race elsewhere. The immediate and pressing issue is the widespread belief that the great numbers of them in the South are an unsatisfactory element of the population. The total Negroes in the United States in 1900, the last available figures, was 8,834,000. They are, however, very unequally distributed throughout the Union; in twenty Northern states and territories there are only 50,000 altogether; in the states from Pennsylvania northward there are about 400,000; from Ohio westward about 500,000; while in the one state of Georgia there are over a million; 7,898,000 lived in the fifteen former slaveholding states; 7,187,000 in the eleven seceding states; and 5,055,000 in the seven states of the Lower South. At the rate of increase shown during the last forty years there will soon be 10,000,000 in the South alone. These figures have since 1900 been somewhat disturbed by the natural growth of population and by the interstate movement, so that the proportion of blacks in the North is doubtless now a little larger; but the fact remains that the habitat of the black is in the Southern States. Even there, great variations occur from state to state, and from place to place. In Briscoe County, Texas, there are 1,253 Whites and not a single Negro; in Beaufort County, S. C., there are 3,349 Whites and 32,137 Africans; on the island of St. Helena in this last county are 8,700 colored and 125 white people; and on Fenwick's Island there are something like 100 Negroes and not a white person.

As between country and city, the Negro is a rural man; the only Southern cities containing over 50,000 of them in the Lower South are New Orleans and perhaps Atlanta; in the former slaveholding states out of 8,000,000 Negroes only about 1,000,000 lived in cities of 8,000 people and upwards, which is less in proportion than the Whites. In a very black district like the Delta of the Mississippi they form a majority of the city population. In 72 of the Southern places having a population of 2,500 or more at least half the population is African; but their drift cityward is less marked than that of the white people, eighty-five per cent of all the Negroes live outside of cities and towns. The Negroes have no race tradition of city life in Africa, are no fonder than Whites of moving from country to city, and throw no unendurable strain on the city governments.

A favorite assertion is that the American Negroes are either dying out or nearing the point where the death-rate will exceed the birth-rate. Hoffmann, in his " Race Traits," has examined this question in a painstaking way, and proves conclusively that both North and South the death-rate of the black race is much higher than that of the Whites. In Philadelphia, for instance, the ratios are 30 to 1,000 against 20 to 1,000. Upon this point there are no trustworthy figures for the whole country; but an eighth of the Negroes live in the so-called " registration area," which includes most of the large cities; and in that area the death-rate in 1900 is computed at 30 to 1,000 for

Negroes and 17 to 1,000 for the Whites. This excess is largely due to the frightful mortality among negro children, which is almost double that among Whites in the same community. In Washington in 1900 one fifth of the white children under a year old died and almost one half of the colored children.

When Hoffmann attempts to show that the negro death-rate is accelerating, he is obliged to depend upon scanty figures from a few Southern cities. In Charleston, for instance, the records show in the forties (a period of yellow fever) a white death-rate of 16 and a colored death-rate of 20, against recent rates of 22 and 44 to the 1,000 respectively; but in New Orleans Mr. Hoffmann's own figures show a reduction of the colored death-rate from 52 in the fifties to 40 in the nineties. The only possible conclusion from these conflicting results is that the earlier mortality statistics on which he relies are few and unreliable.

Nevertheless, the present conditions of negro mortality are frightful. They appear to be due primarily to ignorance and neglect in the care of children, and secondly, to an increase of dangerous diseases. The frequent statement that consumption was almost unknown among Negroes in slavery times is abundantly disproved by Hoffmann; but the disease is undoubtedly gaining, for much the same reason that it ravages the Indians in Alaska, namely, that the people now live in close houses which become saturated with the virus of the disease. Syphilis is also fearfully prevalent, and the most alarming statements are made by physicians who have practice or hospital service among the Negroes; but the testimony as to the extent of the disease is conflicting, and there are other race elements in the United States which are depleted by venereal disease. The blacks also suffer from the use of liquor, though drunkards are little known among the cotton hands; but drugs, particularly cocaine and morphine, are widely used. In one country store a clerk has been known to make up a hundred and fifty packages of cocaine in a single night.

Notwithstanding the undoubtedly high death-rate, the birth-rate is so much greater that at every census the negro race is shown to be still growing; as Murphy says: "Whenever the Negro has looked down the lane of annihilation he has always had the good sense to go around the other way." The census of 1870 was so defective that it must be thrown out of account, but the negro population, which was about 4,400,000 in 1860, and 6,600,000 in 1880, had grown to 8,800,000 in 1900. It is true that the rate of increase is falling off both absolutely and in proportion to the white race. In the South Central group of states, which includes most of the Lower South, the population increased about forty-eight per cent from 1860 to 1880 and only thirty-nine per cent in the next double decade; while the white population has in both periods increased at about sixty per cent, with a rising ratio.

The urban Negro has a high death-rate, not only in the South but in Northern cities; in Boston and Indianapolis the birth-rate of the Negroes does not keep pace with the deaths, and they would disappear but for steady accessions from the South. The Southern blacks on the land are doing better and are growing steadily; neither statistics nor observations support the theory that the Negro is dying out in the South; and comparatively slight changes in resort to skilled physicians, in the spread of trained nurses, in infants' food, may check the child mortality. On the other hand, any increase in thrift and in saving habits will almost certainly affect the size of families and diminish the average birth-rate.

The very words "The Negro" suggest the misleading idea that there is within the Southern states a clearly defined negro race. In fact, physically, intellectually, and morally, it is as much subdivided as the white race. What is supposed to be the pure African type is the Guinea Negro, very black, very uncouth, and hard to civilize. What these people are is easy to find out, for a great part of the inhabitants of the Sea Islands of South Carolina and Georgia are of that race and speak what is called the Gullah dialect, which Joel Chandler Harris has preserved in his "Daddy Jack." Besides these children and grandchildren of imported Negroes there is near Mobile a small group of sturdy people perfectly well known to have been brought into the United States in 1858 in the yacht *Wanderer*. These may be part of a cargo from which Senator Tillman's family bought a gang, and he says of them: "These poor wretches, half starved as they have been, were the most miserable lot of human beings—the nearest to the missing link with the monkey I have ever put my eyes on."

The whole African problem is immeasurably complicated and contorted by the fact that of the Negroes in the United States not more than four fifths at the highest are pure blacks. The remainder are partially Caucasian in race, and occupy a midway position, often of unhappiness and sometimes of downright misery. As to the number of mulattoes, there is no trustworthy statistical statement; the census figures for 1890 reported that out of the total "negro" population eighteen per cent was mulatto in the northern group of Southern states, and about fifteen per cent in the Lower South; but these figures are confessedly defective and are probably vitiated by including some members of the lighter negro races as mulattoes.

Shannon, in his " Racial Integrity," while unhesitatingly accepting these very imperfect figures, attempts to supplement them by calculations made from an inspection of crowds; and it is his opinion that in the smaller cities, the towns and villages, about twenty-two per cent are mulattoes—" and that unless this amalgamation is effectually checked in some way, this ratio will continue to rise until practically the whole of the negro race will come to be of mixed blood." Shufeldt, in his " The Negro, A Menace," asserts that at least sixty per cent of the Negroes have some white blood, and is confident that the proportion is increasing. The census authorities of 1900 commit themselves only to the generalization that the mulattoes are most numerous in proportion to the number of Whites in any given community. As to the testimony of observers, there is every variety of appearance. You may see crowds of Negroes at a railway station in Georgia, of whom two thirds are purely mulatto; you may visit islands in South Carolina in which not one fortieth part have white blood.

The number of mulattoes is less important than their character and general relation to the negro problem. Most Southerners assert and doubtless believe that the mulatto is physically weak; but you see them working side by side with pure blacks, as roustabouts and plantation hands, and some planters tell you that one is as good as another in the field. People assert that mulattoes are more susceptible to disease, so that they are dying out; and some authorities say that there are no mulatto children after the third or fourth generation. There is no scientific ground for these assertions, and one of the highest medical authorities in the South is of the conviction that except for a somewhat greater liability to tuberculosis they are as healthy as the full bloods. Of course, the greater number of mulattoes in the United States are the children of mulattoes, and to what extent the proportion is kept up by further accessions from the white race is absolutely impossible to determine. Many statements on the whole subject come from people who hate the mulatto and like to think that he is a poor creature who is going to relieve the world of a disagreeable problem by leaving it.

From the same source comes the assertion that the mulatto is fundamentally vicious, frequently made by people who argue in the same breath that the so-called progress of the negro race means nothing, because it is all due to mulattoes. The mulattoes do include a much larger proportion of the educated than the pure bloods, and hence are more likely to furnish such criminals as forgers and embezzlers; but there seems no ground for the widespread belief that the mulattoes are more criminal than the pure blacks. That there is a special temptation more likely to come to some members of the mulatto section than to the pure black was suggested by a Southern gentleman when he said: "The black girls won't work and the yellow girls don't have to, they are looked after!" When asked to suggest who it was who looked after them, the conversation languished. The question of the character of the mulatto is a serious one, because most of the spokesmen and markedly successful people of the race are not pure bloods; and because of the unhappy position of thousands of men and women who have the aptitudes, the tastes, and the educations of white people; yet in the common estimation are bracketed with the rudest, most ignorant and lowest of a crude, ignorant and low race.

NEGRO LIFE

The status of the Negroes is in many ways altered by the steady though limited movement from South to North. The Negroes are subject to waves of excitement, and in 1879 a colored agitator created a furore for colonization by spreading abroad the news that in Liberia there was a "bread tree" and another tree which ran lard instead of sap, so that all you had to do was to cut from one and catch from the other. A systematic effort has been made to settle colored people in Indiana, in order to hold that State in the Republican column; and there are now probably nearly a hundred thousand there, a third of whom are settled in Indianapolis, where they furnish a race problem of growing seriousness. The Negroes in the city of Washington have increased eight times in forty years. They have repeatedly been brought into the North as strike breakers, often with the result of serious riots. In 1879 thousands of them left various parts of the South for Kansas, and in some cases the river boats refused to take them. As a result some Southern states passed statutes requiring heavy license fees (sometimes as much as $1,000 a year) from labor agents who should induce people to go to other states. Nevertheless, there are now over 50,000 in Kansas and over 100,000 in the neighboring new State of Oklahoma. At present there are in New York and Philadelphia nearly a hundred agents who draw Negroes northward, and they bring thousands of people every year, chiefly to enter domestic service. The movement is ill organized and does not by any means include the most thrifty, since passage money is often advanced by the agents.

The numbers of the Negroes are not in themselves alarming. In most Southern states they are fewer in proportion than the foreign element in many Northern states. The hostility to the Negro is not based on his numbers, but on his supposed inferiority of character. On this point there is a painful lack of accurate knowledge, because there is so little contact between the Whites and their negro neighbors. The white opinion of the blacks is founded with little knowledge of the home life of the other race. How many white people in the city of Atlanta, for instance, have actually been inside the house of a prosperous, educated Negro? How many have actually sat over the fire of a one-room negro cabin? The Southern Whites, with few exceptions, teach no Negroes, attend no negro church services, penetrate into no negro society, and they see the Negro near at hand chiefly as unsatisfactory domestic servants, as field hands of doubtful profit, as neglectful and terrified patients, as clients in criminal suits or neighborhood squabbles, as prisoners in the dock, as convicted criminals, as wretched objects for the vengeance of a mob.

An encouraging sign is the disposition of both white and colored investigators to study the Negro in his home. Professor DuBois has directed such researches both in Southern cities and in the open country; there are also two monographs upon the religious life of the Negro, one directed by Vanderbilt University and the other by Atlanta University; and Mr. Odum, of the University of Mississippi, has prepared a study upon the Negro in fifty towns in various states which, still in manuscript, is one of the most instructive inquiries ever made into negro life.

Naturally, such investigations are easier in the cities, and we know much more about the urban Negro, a sixth of the population, than of the rural black, who are five sixths. In the large cities there is an African population,

114

a considerable part of which is prosperous. Here are the best colored schools, the greatest demand for African labor, the largest opportunity for building up small businesses among the Negroes themselves. Here are to be found most of the rich or well-to-do Negroes; and there is a large contingent of steady men employed in all kinds of capacities, about whom there is little complaint. On the other hand, a broad fringe of the population lives in houses or rooms actually less spacious and less decent than the one-room cabin in the fields. This floating and unsteady part of the negro race finds a favorable habitat in the towns and small cities, where there is less opportunity for steady employment than in the large cities. From this class come the domestic servants, who will be considered in a later chapter.

The typical social life of the Negro is that of the field laborer, who lives in a poor and crude way. The most common residence is the one-room house, without a glass window, set in a barren and unfenced waste, with a few wretched outhouses, the worst cabins being on the land of the least progressive and humane planters. You may see on the land of a wealthy White one-room houses with chinks between the logs such that the rain drives into them, the tenant family crowded into the space between the fireplace and the unenticing beds, dirty clothing hanging about, hardly a chair to sit upon, outside the house not a paling or a building of any kind, and pigs rooting on the ground under the floor. On a tolerable Mississippi plantation with seventy-four families, seventeen had one-room cabins, and one of those families comprised eleven persons. Some Southerners have a theory that you can be sure that a cabin with a garden is occupied by a White; but that is a fallacy, for there are many negro gardens, although some planters prohibit them on the ground that they will become weed spots. In the cities the Negroes live for the most part in settlements by themselves, in which there are miserable tenements, usually owned by white people and no better than the one-room country house. Of course, thrifty colored people in country or city are able to build comfortable houses for themselves.

Inasmuch as both father and mother work either in the fields or in domestic service, there is little family life either in country or city. The food is poor and monotonous; it is chiefly salt pork, bacon, corn bread (usually pone), and some sort of molasses. Fresh meat is almost impossible to get outside of town, chickens are raised though not very plentiful, vegetables are few. For little children this diet is intolerable, and that is why so many of them die in infancy. Close observers declare that Negroes are brutal to their children, but one may be much among them without seeing any instances. They are also accused of deserting their old people; children often wander away and lose track of their parents, but you will find districts where the old are well looked after by their kindred. The most serious interference in family life is the field work of the women, and the breaking up of families by the desertion of the father; but somehow in all these family jars the children are seldom left without anyone to care for them.

Public amusements are almost wanting for the Negro. They are commonly not admitted to white theaters, concerts, and other similar performances. In the country there is nothing better than to crowd the plantation store of a Saturday night in a sort of club. Few of them read for pleasure, and there is little to relieve the monotony. Perhaps for that reason they are fond of going about the country, and you see them everywhere on horseback, or in little bull carts, or on foot. They will spend their last dollar for an excursion on the railroad, and at the turn of the year, January 1st, many of them may be seen moving. The circus is one of the greatest delights of the Negro; he will travel many miles for this pleasure. The field hand is thrown back on coarse enjoyments; hard drinking is frequent among both men and women, yet the habitual drunkard is rare; the country Negro is fond of dances, which often turn out unseemly and lead to affrays and murders.

For their social and jovial needs Negroes find some satisfaction in their church life. Their own statisticians claim 3,254,000 communicants worshiping in 27,000 church buildings, of which the greater part are in the country. Contrary to expectation forty years ago, the Negroes have been little attracted to the Catholic Church, which is so democratic in its worship, and possesses a ritual which might be expected to appeal to negro nature. Nearly half the church members are some sort of Baptists, and half of the rest adhere to the Methodist denominations. Some city churches have buildings costing twenty, thirty, and even fifty thousand dollars, and they are pertinacious about raising money for construction and other similar purposes.

These churches do not represent an advanced type of piety. Conversions are violent and lapses frequent, and the minister is not certain to lend the weight of his conduct to his words. There are many genuinely pious and hard-working ministers, but at least half of them in both city and country are distrusted by the Whites and discredited by their own people. Simply educating the minister does not solve the problem, for what the people want is somebody who will arouse them to a pleasurable excitement. That is, the present type of piety among the negro churches is about that which prevailed among the white people along the frontier fifty years ago, and which has not entirely died out in the backwoods and the mountains. A genuine colored service is extremely picturesque, the preacher working like a locomotive going up a heavy grade, while the hearers assist him with cries of, "Talk to um, preacher—Great God—Ha! Ha! You is right, brudder—Preaching now—Talk 'bout um—Holy Lord." Then the brethren are called upon to pray; in that musical intoning which is so appropriate for the African voice; then the minister lines out the hymns and the congregation bursts out into that combination of different minor keys which is the peculiar gift of the negro race.

Another negro enjoyment is the secret orders, which are almost as numerous as the churches and probably have as many male members. These societies are first of all burial and benefit orders with dues ranging from fifty cents a month upward, for which sick benefits of four dollars a week are paid and about forty dollars for burial. The societies build lodge houses not only in cities but in plantation regions; and the judgment of those who have most carefully examined them is that they are on the whole a good thing. They give training in public speaking and in common action; they furnish employment to managers and clerks; and their considerable funds are for the most part honestly managed. Some of them publish newspapers chiefly devoted to publishing the names of officers and members. In Mississippi there are thirty-four licensed orders with 8,000 members. They carry $30,000,000 of risks, and in a year paid $430,000 to policy holders. Naturally they have rather high-sounding names, such as "Grand Court of Calanthe," "Lone Star of Race Pride,"

"United Brethren of Friendship and Sisters of Mysterious Ten," "Sons and Daughters of I Will Arise." Some efforts are making to build up national societies such as the "Royal Trust Company" and "The Ethiopian Progressive Association of America," which, according to its own statement, is "incorporated with an authorized Capital Stock a hundred times larger than the next most heavily capitalized Negro corporation on Earth. It is designed to fraternize, build and cement the vital interests of Negroes throughout the world into one colossal Union." The order and the church are both social clubs and include a good part of the race both in city and country, and these organizations are the work of the last forty years, for in slavery times the negro churches were closely watched by the Whites, and secret societies would have been impossible.

CHAPTER X

NOBODY accepts church or fraternal orders as the measure of the Negro's place in the community, for the gospel which he hears most often is the gospel of work; and that comes less from the preacher than from the reformer; as DuBois says: " Plain it is to us that what the world seeks through desert and wild we have within our threshold—a stalwart laboring force, suited to the semi-tropics." The labor system and labor ideal of the South are very different from those of the North. First of all, there is the old tradition of slavery times that manual toil is ignoble; that it is menial to handle prime materials, and to buy and sell goods across the counter. But somebody must perform hard labor if the community is to go on; and there is an immense field for uneducated men. Besides the so-called " public works "—that is, turpentine, sawmills, building levees and railroads, and clearing land— there is the pulling and hauling and loading in the ports, the rough work of oil mills and furnaces and mines, and above all the raising of cotton, where the demand for labor is always greater than the supply.

Some of this labor is done by white gangs, and many of the blacks are engaged in other and higher pursuits; but the chief function of the Negro in the South is the rough labor which in the North was once chiefly performed by

Irishmen, later by Italians, and now in many places by Slavs. This vast industrial system is almost wholly officered by Whites, who are the owners, employers, and managers of nearly every piece of property in the South on which laborers are employed. They set, so far as they can, the terms of employment; but what they get in actual work is settled by the Negroes, notwithstanding a condition of dependence hard to realize in the North. It is firmly fixed in the average white employer's mind that the Negro exists in order to work for him, and that every attempt to raise the Negro must steer clear of any suspicion that it will lead him to abandon work for the white man. The slow drift of Negroes to the towns and cities cannot be prevented, nor some shifting from plantation to plantation; but the white man's ideal is that the Negro is to stay where he is, and hundreds of thousands of them are living within sight of the spot where they were born.

Therefore, whoever wishes to know the conditions of the typical Negro must look for them on the plantation, where he is almost the only laborer, and is at present prodigiously wanted. As a keen Southern observer says: "The protection of the Negro is the scarcity of labor"; for it is literally true that some plantations could profitably employ more than double the hands that they can get. Nevertheless it is an axiom in the South that "the nigger will not work." Thus General Stephen D. Lee gives currency to the declaration that "It is a fact known to those best acquainted with the negro race since the war, that more and more of them are becoming idle, and are not giving us as good work as they used to do." Another authority says: "Some few of the race are reliable—many hundreds are not. The farmer cannot get his land turned in the winter, because ninety hundredths of these laborers have not made up their minds as to what they want to do in the coming year. All would go to town if fuel was not high and house rent must be paid." An engineer in charge of large gangs in Galveston says he never would employ Negroes if he could help it, because they cannot be depended upon to rush work in an emergency. A planter met on a Mississippi steamer declares that wage hands at a dollar a day would not actually put in more than two thirds of the hours of labor; and would accomplish no more in two weeks than a cropper working on shares would do in two days. A Negro who employs large numbers of men says: "If a Negro can get what he wants without working he will do it."

Another standard accusation is that the Negro will not work steadily; that he never turns up on Monday, and will leave for frivolous reasons; that if he has been working for five dollars a week and you raise his wages to ten dollars he will simply work the three days necessary to earn the five dollars, having adjusted himself to that scale. In this charge there is a good deal of truth, but the difficulty is not confined to the African race. Northern employers are well acquainted with the hand who never works on Monday; and in the cotton mills of South Carolina, which are carried on solely by white labor, it is customary to have a " Reserve of Labor " of one fourth or one fifth in order to meet the case of the hands who wish to go fishing, or simply are not willing to work six days a week. Probably the remedy for the Negro is to increase his wants to the point where he cannot satisfy them by less than a whole week's work.

As to the general accusation that the Negro will not work, many white employers scout the suggestion. A brickmaker in St. Louis has for years employed them and likes them better than any other kind of labor. A Florida lumberman says: " I would not give one black man in the lumber camps of the South for three Italians, or three of any other foreigners. We can't get along without them, and for one, I don't want to try." And planter after planter will tell you that, however it may be with his neighbors, he has no trouble in keeping his people up to their work.

Another reason for skepticism is what one sees as one goes through the country. In the first place, enormous amounts of cotton are raised where there is nothing but negro labor. In the second place, even in winter, the season of the year when the Negro is least busy, there are plenty of evidences that he is at work and likely to keep at it. He may be seen at work on his own little farm, taking care of his stock, picking his cotton, fixing up or adding to his house, his fifteen-year-old girl plowing with one mule. A Negro's farm is generally more slovenly than a white man's, but the crops are raised. You see the hired hands on the great plantations, driving four-mule teams, working in the gins, coming for directions about breaking ground. The truth is that the Negro on the land is doing well, far better than might be expected from people who have so little outlook and hope of improvement, working more intelligently and doing better than the fellahin of Egypt, the ryots of India, the native Filipino, quite as well as the lowest end of the Mountain Whites and the remnants of the lowland Poor Whites. It is a race-slander, refutable by any honest investigator, that the American Negro as a race is unwilling to work.

It is another question how far they are competent to act as foremen or independent workers. An iron manufacturer in Alabama says he has found that the moment Negroes are promoted to anything requiring thinking power they fail disastrously, and ruin all the machinery put in their charge; as miners they handle tools with skill just as long as they are furnished the motive power, but they have little discretion or ambition. On the other hand, the writer has seen in the Richmond Locomotive Works white men working under negro gang bosses without friction; and in many parts of the South the building trades are almost wholly in the hands of blacks.

Why should the belief of the African's incapacity be so widely disseminated? First, because nineteen twentieths of the people who talk about the lazy Negro have no personal knowledge of the field hand at work. Their impression of the race is gained from the thriftless and irregular Negroes in the towns and cities. If we formed our notions of Northern farm industry from the gypsies, the dock loafers, the idle youths shooting craps behind a board fence, we should believe a generalization that Northern farmers are lazy. The shiftless population living on odd jobs and the earnings of the women as domestic servants, committing petty crimes and getting into rows with the white youths, cannot be more than one tenth of the Negroes, and the poorest tenth at that.

Domestic service is the most exasperating point of contact between the races. It has been reduced to a system of day labor, for not one in a hundred of the house servants spend the night in the place where they are employed. Great numbers of the women are the only wage earners in their family and leave their little children at home day after day so that they may care for the children of white families. Some mistresses scold and fume and threaten, some have the patience of angels; in both cases the service is irregular and wasteful. Nobody ever feels sure that a servant will come the next morning. Most of the well-to-do families in the South feed a second family out of the baskets taken home by the cook; and in thousands of instances the basket goes to some member of a third family favored by the cook. Hence the little song taken down from a Negro's lips by a friend in Mississippi:

> "I doan' has to wuk so ha'd,
> 'Cause I got a gal in de white folks' ya'd;
> And ebry ebnin' at half past eight
> I comes along to de gyarden gate;
> She gibs me buttah an' sugah an' lard—
> I doan' has to wuk so ha'd!"

Let one story out of a hundred illustrate this trouble. A newly married couple, both accustomed to handsome living, set up their own establishment in a Mississippi town, in a new house, well furnished and abounding in heirlooms of mahogany and china; the only available candidate for waitress is a haughty person who begins by objecting to monthly payments, and shortly announces to her mistress: "I ain't sure I want to stay here, but I will give you a week's trial." The patient and good-natured lady accepts the idea of a week's experience on both sides, but before that time expires the girl comes rushing up in a fury to announce that "I'm gwine ter leave just now, kase you don't give yo' help 'nough to eat." It develops that she has had exactly the same breakfast as the white family, except that the particular kind of bacon of which she is fond has run short. There is plenty of bacon of another brand, but that will not satisfy her; she will not stay "where people don't get 'nough to eat." She thereupon shakes the dust of the place off her feet and blacklists the family in the whole place, making it almost impossible for them to find another servant; and probably some other white mistress within a week takes up this hungry person as being the best that she can do.

Other people have more agreeable tales of good-tempered and humorous servants; and the negro question would be half solved if the people who undertake domestic service and accept wages would show reasonable interest, cleanliness, and honesty; and a million of the race might find steady employment at good wages in the South within the next six months, and another million in the North, if they would only do faithfully what they are capable of doing.

There is little hope of regeneration by that means; the difficulty is that capable Negroes do not like domestic service and seek to avoid it. The average Southerner sighs for the good old household slaves, and harks back to the colored mammy in the kitchen and stately butler in the drawing-room in slavery times, as evidence that the Negroes are going backward. He forgets that under slavery the highest honorable position open to a colored woman was to be the owned cook in a wealthy family; that Booker T. Washington and DuBois and Kelly Miller in those days would have been fortunate if raised to the lofty pinnacle of the trusted butler or general utility man on the plantation. The house servants in slavery times were chosen for their superior appearance and intelligence, and were likely to be mulattoes; the children and grandchildren of such people may now be owners of plantations, professional men, professors in colleges, negro bankers, and heads of institutions; while the domestic servant commonly now comes from the lowest Negroes, is descended from field hands, and chosen out of the most incompetent section of the present race. The problem of domestic service is chiefly one of the village and the city, in which only about a seventh of the Negroes live.

Even many Southerners have very hazy ideas about the subdivisions of plantation laborers; and do not distinguish between the renters and croppers, who are tenant farmers in their way, and the wage hands who are less ambitious and not so steady. There is complaint on many plantations that negro families do not finish their contracts, though the main outcry is against the day laborer; yet on many of the large plantations there is little complaint that even he does not work steadily, and little trouble in securing from him a fair day's work.

Another disturbance of the easy generalization that the Negro will not work is due to the variations from county to county and from place to place. Much more depends than the outside world realizes on the capacity of a plantation manager "to handle niggers"; and the testimony of a perfectly straightforward planter who tells you that he knows that the Negroes as a race run away from work because he has seen it, is no more true of the whole people than the assurance of his near neighbor that he knows the blacks are all industrious because they work steadily for him. Here we come back to the essential truth that it is unsafe to generalize about any race. There are thousands of good Negroes in the towns and thousands of lazy rascals on the plantations; but the great weight of testimony is that the colored man works tolerably well on the land.

Another of the statements, repeated so often that people believe them without proof, is that the Southern Negro has lost his skilled trades. Two Southern writers say: "Now, most of the bricklayers are white. The same is

127

true with respect to carpenter work. The trade of the machinist is practically in the hands of white men." "They have been losing ground as mechanics. Before the war, on every plantation there were first-class carpenters, blacksmiths, wheelwrights, etc. Half the houses in Virginia were built by Negro carpenters. Now where are they?" Nothing could better illustrate the fact that Southerners who reprehend the interference of the North in questions which it does not understand, are themselves myopic guides. If the negro trades have disappeared, how does it come about that in Montgomery, Ala., there are practically no other laborers of that type? that the bricklayers, carpenters, masons, blacksmiths, are all Negroes, and no white boys seem to be learning those trades. The census of 1890 showed in Alabama about 13,000 colored men who had some sort of skilled employment, many of them in trades which did not exist in slavery times, such as iron-working, steam fitting, and service on railroads. It is true that they are shut out of most of the callings in which there is authority over others; there are no negro motormen or trolley conductors, no negro engineers, though plenty of firemen; no negro conductors, though negro brakemen are not uncommon, and in Meridian, Miss., the trains are called in the white waiting room by a buxom negro woman.

In some Southern cities Whites, very often Northern men, have absorbed certain trades supposed to be the peculiar province of the Negro: barber shops with white barbers are found; the magnificent Piedmont Hotel in Atlanta has a corps of white servants; wherever the trades unions get into the South they are likely to work against the Negro; but in some cases he has unions of his own; or there are joint unions of Whites and Negroes. Considering the great opportunity for white men in callings where blacks are not admitted it does not seem likely that they will ever be excluded from skilled trades, though subject to more competition than in the past.

Another employment for which the African has in many ages and countries been found suited is military service. Even in slavery times military companies of free Negroes were not unknown, and some of them actually went to the front for the Confederacy in the first weeks of the Civil War. Then came the enlistment of nearly 200,000 in the blue uniform, and after the war some thousands of men remained in negro regiments. A brief attempt to educate colored officers in West Point and Annapolis was, for whatever reason, not a success; and the negro troops are almost wholly under the command of white officers. Since Reconstruction times negro militia companies have not been encouraged, and in some states have been wholly disbanded. The difficulty in Brownsville, Texas, in 1907, has tended to prevent negro enlistment in the army and navy. In the Spanish War and later in the Philippines negro regiments gave a good account of themselves. There are a few negro policemen in the cities, but in the South they are likely to disappear. The white man resents any assertion of authority over him by a Negro, and in general considers him unfit to exercise control over people of his own race.

Even in ante-bellum times there were occasional negro business and professional men, some of whom had the confidence of their white neighbors and made little fortunes. Since the Civil War these avenues have much widened. The 16,000 or 17,000 ministers are still to a large degree uneducated persons, as indeed is the case in many white churches. Negro physicians are numerous,

129

educated partly in Northern institutions, partly in medical colleges of their own, partly in schools officered by white professors, as, for instance, in Raleigh, N. C. Like the lawyers they cannot practice without the certificate of state officers not very friendly to them or easy to convince of their abilities; and the cream of the practice among colored people goes to the Whites. In business, negro merchants, manufacturers, builders, and bankers have become very numerous. Recently a Negro Bankers' Convention was held in the South. Most of the transactions of these men are carried on with their own people, though they often find customers and credit with Whites. So far, there are few or no large negro capitalists, but many promising groups of small capital have been brought together; and at the Expositions of Charleston and Jamestown they showed creditable exhibits of their own industries.

Two entirely new professions have opened up since the Civil War. The first is that of journalist, and there are many negro newspapers, none of which has any national circulation, or extended influence. The other is teaching, which has opened up a livelihood to thousands of young men and women. Some of the negro colleges are wholly manned by members of the race, many of them graduates of Northern institutions, who seem to make use of the same methods and appeal to the same aspirations as the faculties of white colleges.

Though often accused by his white neighbor of attempts to unite in hostile organizations, the Negroes show little disposition to rally around and support leaders of their own race. Booker T. Washington, the man of most influence among them, has encountered implacable opposition, and efforts have even been made by hostile members of his own race to break up his meetings in Boston. Inasmuch as the Negroes are excluded from politics in the South, it is hard for any man to get that reputation for bringing things about which is necessary in order to attract a strong following. As DuBois points out " If such men are to be effective they must have some power,—they must be backed by the best public opinion of these communities, and able to wield for their objects and aims such weapons as the experience of the world has taught are indispensable to human progress."

One of the strong influences is the conferences gathered in part at such institutions as Hampton and Tuskegee, and Atlanta University, in part called in other places. A considerable number of Negroes have the money and the inclination to attend these meetings, where they learn to know each other and to express their common wants.

CHAPTER XI

THAT the Negro is inferior to the Whites among whom he lives is a cause of apprehension to the whole land; that his labor is in steadiness and efficiency much below that of his intelligent white neighbors is a drawback to his section. Yet neither deficiencies of character nor of industry really settle his place in the community. A race may be as high as the Greeks and yet go to nothingness; a race may be as industrious as the Chinese, and have little to show for it. The essential question with regard to the Negro is simply: Is the race in America moving downward or upward? No matter if it be low, has it the capacity of rising?

To answer these questions requires some study both of present and past conditions. A very considerable number of Southern Whites are sure that physically and morally the Negro is both low and declining; and some go so far as to assert that every Negro is physically so different from the white man that he ought not to be considered a member of the human race. The argument was familiar in slavery times, and has been recently set forth by F. L. Hoffman in his " Race Traits of the American Negro "; from chest measurements, weight, lifting strength, and power of vision, he is convinced that " there are important differences in the bodily structure of the two races, dif-

132

ferences of far-reaching influence on the duration of life and the social and economic efficiency of the colored man." Professor Smith, of Louisiana, in his "The Color Line, A Brief for the Unborn," goes much farther in an argument intended to show that the brain capacity of the Negro, the coarseness of his features, the darkness of his color, the abnormal length of his arm, his thick cranium, woolly hair and early closing of the cranial sutures, prove that he may be left out of consideration as a member of a civilized community.

The tendency of scientific investigators during the last forty years has been to minimize the distinctions between races; and the argument that the Negro is to be politically and socially disregarded because of structural peculiarities, though the stock in trade of the proslavery writers two generations ago, now seems somewhat forced. To the Northern mind there is a kind of unreality in the whole argument of physical inferiority; it is like trying to prove by anatomy, physiology, and hygiene that the Hungarian laborer is always going to be an ignorant and degraded element in our population.

These technical arguments throw very little light upon the real African problem, which is not, what does the structure of the Negro indicate that he must be, but what is he really and what does he perform? If the Negro can work all day in the cotton field, save his wages, buy land, bring up his children, send them to school, pay his debts, and maintain a decent life, no cranial sutures or prognathism will prevent his being looked upon as a man; and the whole physical argument, much of which is intended to affect the public mind against amalgamation, cannot do away with the plain fact that the white and the black races are so near to each other that some hundreds of thousands of people come of white fathers and negro or mulatto mothers. The Negro is entitled to be measured, not by brain calipers, nor by two-meter rods, but by what he can do in the world.

What he can do in the world depends upon the inner man and not the outer; and here we approach one of the most serious problems connected with the race. Has the Negro character? Can he conceive a standard and adhere to it? Can he fix his mind on a distant good and for its sake give up present indulgences? Can he restrain the primal impulses of human nature?

That the Negroes as a race are impure and unregulated is the judgment of most white observers whether ill-wishers or fair-minded men. Thomas Nelson Page, for instance, declares that the immorality of the negro race has increased since slavery times. Thomas, himself a Negro, asserts that the sexual impulse " constitutes the main incitement to the degeneracy of the race, and is the chief hindrance to its social uplifting." Kelsey, a Northern observer, says: " Many matings are consummated without any regular marriage ceremony and with little reference to legal requirements." On this subject as on all others the most preposterous exaggerations are rife; a plantation manager will tell you that not two in a hundred couples on his plantation are married; a stock statement, a thousand times repeated, is that there is no such thing as a virtuous negro woman. Yet the truth is gruesome enough; there are plenty of plantations where barely half the families are married; bastard children are very numerous; and this condition applies not only in the cities and towns where people are put into new and trying environments, but everywhere among the Negroes upon the land. It is the most discouraging thing about

134

the race, because it saps the foundation of civilization. Nor is it an explanation to say that under slavery family ties were disregarded. The race has now had forty years of freedom and undisturbed religious training, such as it is. Still they ought to show decided improvement in morals if the race is capable of living on a high moral plane.

This is a gloomy and delicate subject, but cannot be allowed to pass without a few positive illustrations. When Kelsey suggested to a Negro that he might go back to the plantation and board in a negro family, he replied: "Niggers is queer folks, boss. 'Pears to me they don' know what they gwine do. Ef I go out and live in a man's house like as not I run away wid dat man's wife." A girl whose mistress was trying to put before her a higher standard of conduct said: "It's no use talking to us colored girls like we were white. A colored girl that keeps pure ain't liked socially. We just think she has had no chance." A negro boy twelve years old has been known to reel off two hundred different obscene rhymes and songs. Divorce is frequent, particularly the easy form which consists of the husband throwing his wife out of doors and bringing in another woman. The negro preachers are universally believed to be the worst of their kind, and very often are. If the things that are regularly told by white people and sometimes admitted by colored people are true, the majority of the Southern Negroes, rural and urban, are in a horribly low state both physically and morally.

The more credit to those members of the race who are pure and upright; who are showing that it is a libel to brand as hopelessly corrupt ten million people, including probably two million mulattoes; to say nothing of the numerous examples of chaste and self-respecting Negroes of both sexes in the Northern states. The most furious assailant of negro character will usually tell you of one or two Negroes that he knows to be perfectly straightforward; and the writer can bear personal testimony to the apparent wholesomeness of family life in negro homes that he has chanced to visit. Here, a young mother in her scrupulously clean log house hovering over her little children as affectionately as though she and they were white; there, gathered around the hearth of a new house with good furniture and pretty pictures, a family of seven children, neat, clean, attractive, respectful, intelligent, and apparently attached to father and mother. Again, a fine specimen of the thrifty colored man who boasts that he has lived forty-one years with one wife: " I got a good wife, she take keer of me." Where such homes are, all is not vile. It is a favorite Southern delusion that education and Christian teaching have no effect on the animal propensities of Negroes; there are thousands of examples to the contrary.

It would do no good to anybody to minimize the terrible truth that the Negroes as a race are in personal morality far below the Anglo-Saxons as a race, that the heaviest dead weight upon them is their own passions; but it would be equally futile to blink at the fact that the Whites do not set them in this respect a convincing example. Anglo-Saxons the world over are not unreasonably virtuous; and the divorce cases of Pittsburg might not be safe reading for impressionable people like the blacks. If the negro race is depraved it cannot but have a demoralizing effect on the white race, most of whom have colored nurses; and the male half of whom have all their life been exposed to a particularly facile temptation. Heaven has somehow shielded the white woman of the South from the noxious influences of a servile race; in slavery times and now there is not a fairer flower that blooms than the white Southern girl; although it is a delusion that she is never pursued by men of her own race. No visitor, no clean Southern man, knows the abysses in both races or can fix the proportion in which both need to rise if the Southland is to be redeemed from its most fearful danger. Great numbers of the Negroes are immoral, and great numbers of white men can testify to their immorality, for the building up of character is a long and weary process in both races.

So far as the future of the Negro is concerned, the real problem is whether he can suppress his bad traits and emphasize his higher nature, but that is a question with regard to all other races. The blacks are ignorant, not only of books, but of the world, of life, of the experience of the race. They are untrustworthy, but at the same time faithful; as one of their own number says: "They'll loaf before your face and work behind your back with good-natured honesty. They'll steal a watermelon, and hand you back your lost purse intact."

In any case, it may safely be affirmed that the Negro is not retrograding. On the Sea Islands, where it has been reported that the Negroes had sunk to savagery, where on one small island a white face had not been seen for ten years, there is undoubtedly a widespread belief in magic, or what a fluent colored preacher, in a discourse apparently intended for white ears, referred to as "Hindooism." On such subjects the Negroes are reticent; but no evidence of paganism is visible to long-time residents on the islands. When it comes to fortune-telling and charms, and a fetich that will insure you against having your mortgage foreclosed, about the same thing may be found among otherwise intelligent people in any Northern city. Degradation is frequent; and marital relations are loose on the islands, though no more so than on the plantations of Mississippi, or among the Negroes of the cities of Georgia. The population is in general healthier than on the mainland, though much exposed to severe malaria. Two or three of the African superstitions do survive; one is that you must always keep a door open during the day so that you may not shut the bad spirit in with you; but at night doors and shutters must be closed to keep the spirit out. Another superstition is the "Basket-name," which is the plague of the Northern teachers, who are a long time in learning that Louisa's basket name is "Chug," or that when you call Ezra, "Mantchey" will come. Churches of various denominations are kept up, and, together with the various lodges, furnish the principal social life of the people. To be sure they often have African dances at their religious services; but these are very like the Shaker dances, which can hardly be called pagan worship.

The error as to the progress of the Negro arises both from an unfounded notion of the virtues and the civilization of the Negroes under slavery, and an equally unfounded idea that the average conditions of the Negro to-day are hopeless. The Negro was busier in slavery times than now because there was always the whip in the background, but there is no reason to suppose that his average annual product was as great as that of the present freeman. Falsehood, thriftlessness, and immorality are the charges which were constantly brought against the slaves, both by outsiders and by their own masters. Judged by the standards which the white man most readily applies to himself—namely, the proportion of educated and progressive men and women, the average amount of property, the interest in the welfare of the race—there is no reason to doubt that the Negro is higher up than he was half a century ago.

How far does the desire for uplift extend, and how far is it effective? The negro population shows a distinct interest in the future of the race. The field hand who has the ambition to save and improve, to buy his own land, feels that he is benefiting not only himself, but giving an object lesson of the power of his race. Some of the leaders have personal ends to gain, but they all expect to gain them by showing a power to improve the conditions of their fellows. Yet even though the Negro may be working steadily, he may also be gaining nothing from generation to generation; if he gets better wages, he may be squandering them; a small part of the race might conceivably be going forward, while a large part was dropping back.

A piece of testimony on the highest phases of negro character which is too often forgotten in the South is that on the occasion when the race had the best opportunity to show black-heartedness it gave the world a noble example of patience, forbearance, and forgiveness. As that great Southerner, Grady, wrote: "History has no parallel to the faith kept by the negro in the South during the war. Often five hundred negroes to a single white man, and yet through these dusky throngs the women and children walked in safety, and the unprotected homes rested in peace. Unmarshalled, the black battalions moved patiently to the fields in the morning to feed the armies their idleness would have starved, and at night gathered anxiously at the big house to 'hear the news from marster,' though conscious that his victory made their chains enduring.

139

Everywhere humble and kindly. The body guard of the helpless. The rough companion of the little ones. The observant friend. The silent sentry in his lowly cabin. The shrewd counsellor. And when the dead came home, a mourner at the open grave. A thousand torches would have disbanded every Southern army, but not one was lighted." That achievement was a vast advance above the savagery of the native African; and why should the capacity for improvement stop there?

Keeping in mind the fact that with all his patience the slave in the best days of slavery was still a low and vicious type in whom his slavehood strengthened native propensities to lying, theft, and lust, it is undeniable that the greater part of the race has made great advances; even John Temple Graves, a harmful enemy of the Negro, admits that "The leaders of no race in history have ever shown greater wisdom, good temper and conservative discretion than distinguishes the two or three men who stand at the head of the negro race in America to-day." Under slavery no such success or influence was possible; there could be no negro orators, or reformers, or leaders in the South.

An invariable answer to the plea that the character of the negro leaders is a proof of the capacity for uplift is that they are substantially white men. At the same mo-ment the critics deny to those substantially white men the privileges of actual white men. But may not "substantially white men" have an uplifting influence such as indubitably white men had in earlier times? Most candid white observers, however hostile to the race, admit that somewhere from a tenth to a fourth of all the Negroes are doing well and moving upward; and this applies to the Negro on the land as well as in cities. In many

140

scattered areas in the South, groups of plantation Negroes have bought land and are saving money. Here are a few examples taken from the writer's notebook:

At Calhoun, Ala., may be found nearly a hundred Negroes who have bought or are buying their own farms, and have made $60,000 of savings to do it. A negro woman on one of those farms said of her new house: "We don't need no rider (overseer) now, dis house is our rider. It will send us into the field, it will make us work, and it will make us plan. We's got to plan. When Ise out in the pit I has to stop to look up at dis house, and den Ise so pleased I don't know how I am working." Near Nixburg, Ala., is another settlement started by a Negro, Rev. John Leonard, soon after the war, which is called thereabouts "Niggerdom," because the blacks have acquired the best tract of land in the region, have put up the best schoolhouse in the county, and as a neighbor said of them: "They have got to the place now where they're no more service to the Whites. They want to work for themselves." At Kowaliga, Ala., is the Benson settlement, where a Negro has bought his former master's plantation, largely extended it, has built a dam and mill, owns three thousand acres of land with many tenants, and is one of the few large planters of that section who combines cattle raising with cotton. He gave land and assistance to a good school with commodious buildings, carried on entirely by Negroes (including Tuskegee graduates); is building what is probably the best planter's house in the county, and has plenty of outside investments. At Mound Bayou, Miss., is another purely negro settlement, with a population of about two thousand, among whom not a single white man lives. Under the guidance of two brothers named Montgomery, they bought their land direct from the

141

railroad company, claim to own 130,000 acres, and have paid for considerable parts of it; maintain their own stores, carry on a little bank, and elect a negro municipal government. The results show as much capacity for managing their own affairs as the neighboring white towns.

There are two or three settlements of the same kind in the South, on a smaller scale, as at Goldsboro, Fla., and one in Alabama. Different in type, but a proof of prosperity, are the negro settlements on the Sea Islands; here is no personal leader like Leonard, or Benson, or Montgomery; but on several of the islands is a large group of colored landowners who have been there ever since the Civil War, and whose houses are much superior to the usual negro cabins. While not progressive, they hold on to their land with great tenacity, and are not running into debt.

These specific examples prove beyond question that Africans can advance. Every one of the settlements above mentioned is planted in an unpromising region, among Negroes presumably of a lower type than the average. Lowndes County, in which Calhoun is situated, is one of the most backward in the South; the Sea Islands have the densest negro population to be found anywhere. Similar instances, on a smaller scale may be found in every state and almost every county of the South. However backward the people, you are everywhere told that a few save money, buy land, and try to give their children better conditions. Nor is it the mulattoes only who show this disposition to get on in the world; the pure Negroes sometimes are the most industrious and sensible of their race.

Houses and lands are not the only measure of uplift;

and the numerous Negroes who, according to the impression of white men not likely to exaggerate, are really thrifty, might be unable to raise the average of their race; but it seems clear that the Negro is nowhere reverting to barbarism; that a considerable part of the race, certainly one fourth to one fifth, is doing about as well as the lowest million or two of the Southern Whites; though perhaps a fifth (of whom a great part are to be found in towns and cities) are distinctly doing ill; that the Negroes on the land, though on the average low, ignorant, and degraded, are working well, making cotton, and helping to enrich the South. For, as one of themselves puts it: " The native ambition and aspiration of men, even though they be black, backward, and ungraceful, must not lightly be dealt with." The real negro problem is the question of the character and the future of the laborer.

But deep in the breast of the Average Man
  The passions of ages are swirled,
And the loves and the hates of the Average Man
  Are old as the heart of the world—
For the thought of the Race, as we live and we die,
Is in keeping the Man and the Average high.

The only real measure of uplift is character, but character cannot be reduced to statistical tables. The accumulation of property, especially by a race nearly pauperized when it first acquired the right to hold property, can be traced and throws much light on the important question whether the Negroes are rising or falling. It is difficult to separate out the contribution which the Negro makes to the wealth of the South, and to estimate his own savings, because the only available census figures on this

143

subject deal with the three classes of owners, renters, and croppers of land; and do not, and probably cannot, make a separate account of negro wage hands on the plantations, and workmen and jobbers of every description. As nearly as can be judged, more than half the cotton comes off plantations tilled by negro laborers, or tenants; and for the rest, a notable portion is raised by independent negro farmers, chiefly on the hills—some on the lowlands. The wage hands and the town Negroes have, in general, little to show for their work at the end of the year. They receive or are credited with wages, live on them, and they are gone. Negroes are extravagant, tempted by peddlers and instalment-goods men, and fond of spending for candy, tobacco, and liquor. There are few savings banks in the South, and the failure of the Freedman's Bank in Reconstruction times was a terrible blow to the long process of building up habits of thrift. It seems to be the conviction of the best friends of the Negro in the South that the great majority of the day laborers have made little or no advance in habits of saving during the last forty years, although most of them have more to show in the way of clothing and furniture than their fathers had.

This is a great misfortune to the race, because, as Booker Washington never wearies of pointing out, now is the golden time for the Negro to acquire land. After the war, good farm land could be bought up at from $1 to $5 an acre; and to-day a family with $500 in cash, and saving habits, can, in most parts of the South, pick up an out-of-the-way corner of land, with a poor house on it, and begin the kind of struggle to support the family and pay for improvements which has been the practice of the Northwest. It is true that good land has now

144

become expensive; there are under-drained Delta lands which are held at $50 to $100 an acre, and although planters grumble at the trouble and loss of making cotton with shiftless hands, not one in a hundred wants to break up his plantation and sell it out to the Negroes. The successful communities of negro farmers who have acquired land during the last ten years have, with half a dozen exceptions, been organized by Northern capitalists, or philanthropists who have bought estates in order to sell them out. The reason for this reluctance of the planter is very simple: his business is to raise cotton on a large scale; if he sells out even at a good figure, he loses his occupation; and the South, as a community, has not yet seized the great principle that the prosperity of everybody is enhanced by an increase in the productive and purchasing power of the laborer.

No figures can be found for the city real estate holdings of Negroes, but in 1900 there were 188,000 so-called farms owned by Negroes, subject, of course, like white property, to mortgages for part of the purchase money, or for debts afterward incurred. In addition, 560,000 negro families were working plots of land, as croppers and renters, and received either a share or the whole of the crop that they made. These people altogether were working 23,000,000 acres, an average of about 30 acres to a family; and produced $256,000,000 worth of products. These 750,000 "farmers" represent something over 3,000,000 individuals, which figures to an annual output of $80 per head; and it is difficult to see how that value could possibly be produced if the Negroes were not there. The families of the day laborers count up to at least 3,000,000 more; and their product was probably somewhere near as large as that of the renters and croppers, although the share

145

of the planter is rather greater. It would seem reasonable to assert that $500,000,000 of the $1,200,000,000 of farm products in the South was raised by negro labor; and that by their work in the cities and towns they probably add another $200,000,000 to the annual product.

It is not, however, certain that the Negroes have accumulated in their own hands so much as the value of one year's output. A. H. Stone, a practical planter, says that, on his plantation, negro property was irregularly subdivided; his renters had property accumulated to an average of $400 a family, while the share hands did not average $50 a family. That is, the greater part of the negro property is owned by the smaller part of the population. That is not peculiar to Negroes; in New York City nearly the whole property is said to be owned by 20,000 people; and in Galveston most of the valuable real estate is said to be in the hands of, or controlled by, a score of individuals. In the cities and towns, many prosperous Negroes are rent payers, and own no real estate, but there may be 50,000 owners besides the 190,000 farm owners. In Kentucky half the Negroes who are working land independently own their farms. Even in Mississippi the owners and renters together are more than the share hands.

Since no Negro can successfully rent unless he owns mules and farm tools, and the renters are considerably more numerous than the owners, we may add 250,-000 more families on the land who have accumulated something. That makes 550,000 families, or between a third and a fourth of the Southern Negroes, who are getting ahead. If the 550,000 families averaged $900 each of land and personal property they would hold $500,000,-000; $900 is, however, a high figure, and it may be roughly

146

estimated that negro land owners and renters had accumulated in 1900 not more than $300,000,000 or $400,000,000 worth of property. The rest of the Southern Negroes are about 7,000,000 in number; at the low average of $15 a head of accumulations they would count up nearly $150,000,000 more. A fair estimate of negro wealth in the South, therefore, would be something above $500,000,000, and constantly rising.

This estimated proportion is confirmed by investigations into taxes paid by Negroes. In 1902 the 2,100,000 Negroes in the four states of Virginia, North Carolina, Georgia, and Arkansas were assessed for taxes on $54,000,000. At the same proportion throughout the South, their assessment would have been about $170,000,000, which by this time has probably increased to over $200,000,000; and $200,000,000 is a fortieth of the present total assessment. The sum is great, but the proportion to the wealth of the South is small. At best it can be said that the Negroes, who are a third of the population, own a fortieth of the property in the South; and that one fourth of the Negroes own four fifths of all the negro property. The taxes do not tell the whole story, and there are probably rich Northern cities in which the poorest third of the population does not directly pay more than a fortieth of the taxes. If a race is to be held up as worthless because it is not on the tax books, what will become of some of the most lively members of the Boston City Council and New York Board of Aldermen? Everybody knows that in every community the poorest people pay the largest proportionate taxes through their rent, and through the increased cost of living which is pushed down upon them by landlords and storekeepers. If the colored people were all to move out of their tenements and farms and to go on general strike and earn nothing with which to buy their supplies, the taxpayers of record would very quickly find out who paid a part of their taxes for them. Nevertheless, whatever excuses are made for him, it is undeniable that the Negro has no such spirit of acquisition, no such willingness to sacrifice present delight for future good, as the Northern immigrant, or even the Southern Poor White.

CHAPTER XII

IN the preceding chapters the effort has been made to analyze and describe the white race and the negro race, each as though it lived by itself, and could work out its own destiny without reference to the other. The white race is faced with the necessity of elevating its lower fourth; the negro race should be equally absorbed in advancing its lower three fourths. In both races there is progress and there is hope; if either one were living by itself it might be predicted that in a generation or two the problems would cease to be specially Southern and would come down to those which besiege all civilized communities. But neither race lives alone, neither can live alone. The commercial prosperity of the Whites largely depends on negro labor; high standards for the negro race depend on white aid and white example; neither race is free, neither race is independent. They are the positive and negative poles of a dynamo, and terrific is the spark that sometimes leaps from one to the other.

In one sense, the Southern Whites are the South, inasmuch as they have complete control of the state and local governments, of the military, of public education, of business on a large scale, and of society; but the Negroes are one third of the population, furnish much more than half the laborers for hire, have schools, property, and

149

aspirations; hence whatever term is used, " Southern Problem," " Race Problem," or " Negro Problem," it refers to the antagonism between those two races. How keen is the Southern consciousness of this peculiar condition may be learned from some of the Southern critics:

Thomas Nelson Page thus states it: " A race with an historic and a glorious past, in a high state of civilization, stands confronted by a race of their former slaves, invested with every civil and political right which they themselves possess, and supported by an outside public sentiment, which if not inimical to the dominant race is at least unsympathetic. The two races . . . are suspicious of each other; their interests are in some essential particulars conflicting, and in others may easily be made so; . . . the former dominant race is unalterably assertive of the imperative necessity that it shall govern the inferior race and not be governed by it." Less drastic is the statement of Judge William H. Thomas: " The white man and the negro together make up the citizenship of our Southern country, and any effort to deal with either ignoring the other will diminish the chances of ultimate success. That religion and sentiment, the fixed ideals and prejudices, if you please, of the South are *substantial facts* that cannot be ignored and must always be reckoned with." Murphy speaks of the " problem presented by the undeveloped forces of the stronger race. These must largely constitute the determining factor, even in the problem presented by the negro; for the negro question is not primarily a question of the negro among negroes, but a question of the negro surrounded by another and a stronger people."

To all these attempts to state the case the Northerner is tempted to reply that the South has no monopoly of race problems; that he too has prejudices and repulsions and race jealousies resembling those of the South; and that since he sees them melting away around him, those of his Southern brethren will also disappear of themselves. That is all true, yet much less than all the truth. In the South every white man is determined that there shall be two races forever. Nobody ever stated the Southern point of view on this subject better than the late Henry Grady: "This problem is to carry on within her body politic two separate races, equal in civil and political rights, and nearly equal in numbers. She must carry these races in peace; for discord means ruin. She must carry them separately; for assimilation means debasement. She must carry them in equal justice; for to this she is pledged in honor and in gratitude. She must carry them even unto the end; for in human probability she will never be quit of either."

"The South" in Grady's mouth really means the white South, for it is not in the purpose of any Southern man or woman of influence to permit the Negro to take part in deciding race issues. Furthermore, to the settlement of these difficult problems the South along with a genuine humanity, a desire to act in all things within justice and Christianity, brings habits of mind which have been discussed in an earlier chapter, and which make especially difficult moderate public statements on the race question. As in slavery times the simple assertion that there is a race question seems to some people an offensive attempt to bring ruin on the South: there is still something of the feeling candidly set forth by the old war-time Southern school geography: "The Yankees are an intelligent people upon all subjects except slavery. On that question they are mad."

Especially delicate and hazardous is any investigation of the most intimate race relation which in the nature of

151

things is better understood in the South than in the North. The sexual relation between Whites and Negroes is in such contradiction to much of the indictment against the negro race, and is so abhorrent even to that section of the white race that practices it, that there is no easy or pleasant way of alluding to it. Actual race mixture is proven by the presence in the South of two million mulattoes; it is no new thing, for it has been going on steadily ever since the African appeared in the United States, though there are people who insist that there was little or no amalgamation until Northern soldiers came down during the war and remained in garrison during Reconstruction. Every intelligent traveler in the ante-bellum period, every candid observer, is a witness to the contrary. Since the earliest settlements there have continuously been, and still exist, two different forms of illicit relations between the races— concubinage and general irregularity. Whence came the hundreds of thousands of mulattoes in slavery days? Of course the child of a mulatto will be normally light, and of the two million mulattoes now in the country, very likely three fourths are the children of mulattoes. But what are the other five hundred thousand? To that fateful question a reply can be made only on the testimony of Southern Whites now living down there, and not likely to paint the picture blacker than it is. Here are some striking instances of negro concubinage; and the judgment of competent men is that hundreds of like incidents could be collected:

CASE I.—A white business man in a small city of State A has lived twenty years with a mulatto woman. They have eight children, two of whom are successful business men, one of them a banker. The white man says that the woman has always been faithful to him, and though under the laws of the state he cannot marry her, he looks upon her as his wife and does what he can for the children.

CASE II.—A judge of State B has recently sentenced two different white men for cohabitation, though many Whites remonstrated and told him that there was no use in singling out for punishment a few cases among so many.

CASE III.—In State C a retiring judge suggests that cohabitation be made a hanging offense for the White, as the only way of stopping it.

CASE IV.—In State D one of the leading citizens of a town is known by all his friends to be living with a black mistress.

As to irregular relations, in one state a judge renowned for his uprightness proposes that a blacklist be kept and published containing the names of men known by their neighbors to visit negro women. A recent governor of Georgia says that "Bad white men are destroying the homes of Negroes and becoming the fathers of a mongrel people whom nobody will own." A newspaper editor says that he knows Negroes of property and character who want to move out of the South so as to get their daughters away from danger. There is no Southern city in which there are not negro places of the worst resort frequented by white men. Heads of negro schools report that the girls are constantly subject to solicitation by the clerks of stores where they go to buy goods. The presumption in the mind of an average respectable Southern man when he sees a light-colored child is that some white man in the neighborhood is responsible.

Whether the evil is decreasing is a question on which Southerners are divided. The number of white prostitutes has much increased since slavery days, when there were very few of them; and the general improvement of the community, the spread of religious and secular instruction, ought to have an effect. But the real difficulty is that, although it is thought disgraceful for a white man to live with a colored mistress, it does not seem to destroy his practice of a profession, or his career as a business man. There seems to be lack of efficient public sentiment.

If these statements of fact are true, and every one of them goes back to a responsible Southern source, there is something in the white race which in kind, if not in degree, corresponds to the negro immorality which is the most serious defect of his character. It is not an answer to say that the cities and even some of the open country in the North are honeycombed with sexual corruption. That is true, and some Southerner might do a service by revealing the real condition of a part of Northern society. Perhaps to live with a colored mistress to the end of one's life is, from a moral standpoint, less profligate than for a Pittsburg business man of wealth and responsibility to drive his good and faithful wife out of the house because she is almost as old as he is, and marry a pretty young actress. The mere ceremony of marriage no more obliterates the offense than would in the minds of the Southerner the marriage of the white man with his concubine; and everybody who associates with such a man thereby condones the offense.

The point is, however, not only that miscegenation in the South is evil, but that it is the most glaring contradiction of the supposed infallible principles of race separation and social inequality. There are two million deplorable reasons in the South for believing that there is no divinely implanted race instinct against miscegenation; that while a Southern author is writing that " the idea of

154

the race is far more sacred than that of the family. It is, in fact, *the most sacred thing* on earth," his neighbors, and possibly his acquaintances, by their acts are disproving the argument. The North is often accused of putting into the heads of Southern Negroes misleading and dangerous notions of social equality, but what influence can be so potent in that direction as the well-founded conviction of negro women that they are desired to be the nearest of companions to white men?

There is, of course, a universal prohibition in the South against marriage of the two races, and these statutes express the wish of the community; they put such practices to the ban; they make possible the rare cases of prosecution, which commonly break down for lack of testimony. Nevertheless the law does not persuade the negro women that there can be any great moral wrong in what so many of the white race practice. The active members of the negro race are in general too busy about other things to discuss the question of amalgamation which there is no prospect of legalizing; but it lies deep in the heart of the race that the prohibition of marriage is for the restraint of the Whites rather than of the Negroes; that it does not make colored families any safer; and that if there were no legal prohibition many of these irregular unions would become marriages.

One of the curious by-currents of this discussion is the preposterous conviction of many Southern writers that, inasmuch as these relations are between white men and negro women, there is no " pollution of the Anglo-Saxon blood;" thus Thomas Dixon, Jr., insists that the present racial mixture " has no social significance . . . the racial integrity remains intact. The right to choose one's mate is the foundation of racial life and civilization. The

South must guard with flaming sword every avenue of approach to this holy of holies."

On the other hand, and just as powerful, is the absolute determination of the Whites never to admit the mulattoes within their own circle. The usual legal phrase "person of color" includes commonly everybody who has as much as an eighth of negro blood, and in two states anyone who has a visible trace. But social usage goes far beyond this limit, and no person supposed to have the slightest admixture of negro blood would be admitted to any social function in any Southern city. In 1905 there was a dramatic trial in North Carolina brought about by the exclusion from a public school of six girls, descendants from one Jeffrey Graham, who lived a hundred years ago and was suspected of having negro blood. The Graham family alleged that they had a Portuguese ancestor, and brought into court a dark-skinned Portuguese to show how the mistake might have arisen; and eventually the court declared them members of the superior race.

The reason for the intense Southern feeling on race equality is to a large extent the belief that friendly intercourse with the Negro on anything but well-understood terms of the superior talking to the inferior is likely to lead to an amalgamation, which may involve a large part of the white race. The evils of the present system are manifest. The most reckless and low-minded Whites are preying on what ought to be one of the best parts of the negro race. Thousands of children come into the world with an ineffaceable mark of bastardy; the greater part of such children are absolutely neglected by their fathers; the decent negro men feel furious at the danger to their families or the frailness of their sisters. Both races have their own moral blemishes, and it is a double and treble

156

misfortune that there should be inter-racial mixtures on such degrading terms.

As for a remedy, nobody seems able to suggest anything that has so far worked. A recent writer soberly suggests that a way out is to make a pariah of the mulatto, including that part of the mulattoes who are born of mulatto or negro parents; they are to be shut from the schools, excluded from all missionary efforts, made a race apart; and that action he thinks would be a moral lesson to the full-blooded Africans! Another method is that of the anti-miscegenation league of Vicksburg, Miss., which aims to make public the names of offenders and to prosecute them. A better remedy would be the systematic application of the existing laws of the state, with at least as much zeal as is given to the enforcement of the Jim Crow laws. In the last resort there is no remedy except such an awakening of public sentiment as will drive out of the ranks of respectable men and women those who practice these vices. Such a sentiment exists in the churches, the philanthropic societies, and an army of straightforward sensible men and women. The evil is probably somewhat abating; but till it is far reduced how can anybody in the South argue that education and material improvement of the Negro are what most powerfully tends to social equality? Just so far as the negro man and the negro woman are, by a better station in life, by aroused self-respect and race pride, led to protect themselves, so far will this evil be diminished.

The subject cannot be left without taking ground upon the underlying issue. All the faults of the Southern men who are practical amalgamators add weight to the bottom contention of the South that a mixture of the races, now or in the future, would be calamitous. That belief rests upon the conviction that the negro race, on the average, is below the white race; that it can never be expected to contribute anything like its proportion of the strength of the community; and hence to fuse the races means slight or no elevation for the Negro, and a great decline for the white race. With that belief the writer coincides. The union of the two races means a decline in the rate of civilization; and the fact that so much of it is going on is not a reason for legalizing it, but for sternly suppressing it. If amalgamation is dangerous and would pull down the standard of that higher part of the community which must always be dominant, then such steps must be taken in all justice, in all humanity, with all effort to raise both races, as are necessary to prevent amalgamation.

While thus in one way fully recognized as a human being and of like blood with the Whites, upon the other side the Negro is set aside by a race prejudice which in many respects is fiercer and more unyielding than in the days of slavery. One of the few compensations for slavery was the not infrequent personal friendship between the master and the slave; they were sometimes nursed at the same tawny breast; and played together as children; Jonas Field, of Lady's Island, to this day remembers with pride how after the war, when he became free, his old master, whose body servant he had been, took him to his house, presented him to his daughters, and bade them always remember that Jonas Field had been one of the family, and was to be treated with the respect of a father. The influence of the white mistress on those few slaves who were near to her is one of the brightest things in slavery. She visited the negro cabins, counseled the mothers, cared for the sick, and by life and conversation tried to build up their character. It is almost the universal testimony that such relations are disappearing; rare is the white foot that steps within the Negro's cabin. John Sharp Williams, of Mississippi, says: "More and more every year the negro's life—moral, intellectual, and industrial—is isolated from the white man's life, and therefore from his influence. There was a kindlier and more confidential relationship . . . when I was a boy than between my children and the present generation of negroes."

It is a singular fact that the feeling of race antagonism has sprung up comparatively recently; to this day there are remnants of the old clan idea of the great plantations. Thousands of Negroes choose some White as a friend and sponsor, and in case of difficulty ask him for advice, for a voucher of character, or for money, and are seldom disappointed. The lower stratum of the Whites, which is thrown into close juxtaposition with Negroes, finds no difficulty in a kind of rude companionship, provided it is not too much noticed. The sentimental and sometimes artificial love for the old colored " mammy " is a disappearing bond between the races, for though the white children are cared for almost everywhere by negro girls, there seems little affection between the nurse and her charge.

Some Southern authorities assert that race hatred was fomented toward the end of Reconstruction. Says " Nicholas Worth ": " Men whose faithful servants were negroes, negroes who had shined their shoes in the morning and cooked their breakfasts and dressed their children and groomed their horses and driven them to their offices, negroes who were the faithful servants and constant attendants on their families,—such men spent the day de-

claring the imminent danger of negro 'equality' and
'domination,'" The same genial writer goes on to describe
the gloom at the supposed flood of African despotism; they
said: "Our liberties were in peril; our very blood would
be polluted; dark night would close over us,—us, degenerate sons of glorious sires,—if we did not rise in righteous
might and stem the barbaric flood." Though in all the
states the Negroes were swept out of political power by
1876, to this day they are popularly supposed to be plan-
ning some kind of domination over the Whites. This
made-up race issue is not yet extinct. Nobody knows the
inner spirit of a certain section of the South better than
Thomas E. Watson, of Georgia, who has recently said:
"The politicians keep the negro question alive in the South
to perpetuate their hold on public office. The negro question is the joy of their lives. It is their very existence.
They fatten on it. With one shout of 'nigger!' they can
run the native Democrats into their holes at any hour of
the day."

How does this feeling strike the Negro? Let an intelligent man, Johnson, in his "Light Ahead for the Negro,"
speak for himself. He complains that the newspapers use
inflammatory headlines and urge lynchings—"a wholesale assassination of Negro character"; that it is made a
social crime to employ Negroes as clerks in a white store;
that the cultured Southern people spread abroad the im-
putation that the Negro as a race is worthless; that the
news agents are prejudiced against the Negro and give
misleading accounts of difficulties with the Whites; that
people thought to be friendly are hounded out of their
positions; that there is a desire to expatriate the negroes
from the country of their fathers. Kelly Miller, a professor in Howard University, Washington, objects to using

physical dissimilarity as a mark of inferiority, and thinks "that the feeling against the negro is of the nature of inspirited animosity rather than natural antipathy"; and that "the dominant South is determined to foster artificial hatred between the races."

Race prejudice has always existed since the races have lived together; but, whether because taught to the boys of the Reconstruction epoch, or whether because the Negroes have made slower progress than was hoped, it is sharper now than in the whole history of the question. Is it founded on an innate race repulsion? Does the white man necessarily fear and dislike the Negro? The white child does not, nor the lowest stratum of Whites, who are nearest the Negro intellectually and morally. John Sharp Williams says: "If I were to call our race feeling anything etymologically, I would call it a 'post-judice' and not a 'pre-judice.' I notice that nobody has our race feeling or any race feeling indeed until after knowledge. It is a conviction born of experience."

Right here the champions of the Negro discern a joint in the armor; thus, DuBois: "Men call the shadow prejudice, and learnedly explain it as the natural defense of culture against barbarism, learning against ignorance, purity against crime, the 'higher' against the 'lower' races. To which the Negro cries Amen! and swears that to so much of this strange prejudice as is founded on just homage to civilization, culture, righteousness, and progress, he humbly bows down and meekly does obeisance." Is not this the crux of the whole matter? Is it prejudice against a low race, or a black race? To say that the white Southerner looks down upon and despises every black Southerner would not be fair, for there is still much personal liking between members of the two races, and the South is right in claiming that it has a warmer feeling for individual Negroes than Northern people. Said a Southern judge once: " If my old black mammy comes into the house, she hugs and kisses my little girl. But if she should sit down in the parlor, I should have to knock her down." That is, he liked the mammy, but the nigger must be taught to keep her place.

The phrase commonly used to describe this feeling is, " The danger of social equality." Here is one of the mysteries of the subject which the Northern mind cannot penetrate. Southern society, so proud, so exclusive, so efficient in protecting itself from the undesired, is in terror lest it should be found admitting the fearful curse of social equality; and there are plenty of Southern writers who insist that the Negro shall be deprived of the use of public conveniences, of education, of a livelihood, lest he, the weak, the despised, force social equality upon the white race. What is social equality if not a mutual feeling in a community that each member is welcome to the social intercourse of the other? How is the Negro to attain social equality so long as the white man refuses to invite him or to be invited with him? It sounds like a joke!

The point of view of the South was revealed in 1903 when President Roosevelt invited Booker Washington to his table. The South rang from end to end with invective and alarm; the governor of a Southern state publicly insulted the President and his family; a boy in Washington wrote a scurrilous denunciation on the school blackboard; the *Charleston News and Courier* rolled the incident under its tongue like a sweet morsel; a Georgia judge said: " The invitation is a blow aimed not only at the South, but at the whole white race, and should be resented, and the President should be regarded and treated on the same plane with negroes," and from that day to this the invitation has been received as an affront and an injury to the Whites in the South. We are told of the terrible consequences; how a black boy refused any longer to call the sixteen-year-old son of his employer " Mister "; how the Negro from that time on has felt himself a person of consequence. It does not appear that the President's example was followed by any Southern governor; or that any Negro invited himself to dinner with a white person. To the Northern mind the incident was simply a recognition, by the acknowledged leader of all Americans, of the acknowledged leader of black Americans. The Southern mind somehow cannot distinguish between sitting at the same table with a man and making him your children's guardian. The whole argument comes down to the level of the phrase used so constantly when the question of setting the slaves free was before the country: " Do you want your daughter to marry a nigger? "

What the phrase " social equality " really means is that if anything is done to raise the negro race it will demand to be raised all the way. But demand is a long way short of reality. Northerners have their social prejudices and preferences; yet they are not afraid that an Arab or a Syrian immigrant is going to burst their doors and compel them at the muzzle of the rifle to like him, invite him, make him their intimate; nobody can establish social equality by law or public sentiment. Everybody should sympathize with the desire of the South to keep unimpaired the standards of civilization; but the friendliest Northerner cannot understand why a Southern business man feels such a danger that he writes of social equality: "Right or wrong, the Southern people will never tolerate it, and will go through the horrors of another reconstruction before they will permit it to be. Before they will submit to it, they will kill every negro in the Southern states."

This ceaseless dwelling on a danger which no thoughtful man thinks impending leads to attacks of popular hysteria in the South. A few months ago in the town of Madison, Ga., it was reported: "Last night great excitement prevailed in Madison caused by the appearance on the electric-light poles in the city of a yellow flag about two feet long, with the word 'Surrender' printed in large letters in the center of it. Women became hysterical and thought it was the sign of a negro uprising. Extra police was installed and it was thought of calling out the military company. At the height of the excitement, it was learned that the signs had been posted as an advertisement by a firm here. Cases have been made against the members of the firm."

The real point with regard to social equality is not that the Negro is inferior, but that his inferiority must be made evident at every turn. You may ride beside a negro driver on the front seat of a carriage, because any passerby sees that he is doing your bidding; but you must not sit on the back seat with a Négro who might be a fellow-passenger; you may stop at a Negro's house, if there is absolutely no other place to stay, sit at his table, eat of his food, but he must stand while you sit; else, as one of the richest Negroes in the South said, "the neighbors would burn our house over our heads." The whole South is full of evidence, not so much that the Whites think the Negroes inferior, as that they think it necessary to fix upon him some public evidence of inferiority, lest mistakes be made. It was against such confusion of the character and the color that Governor Andrew protested when he said: " I have never despised a man because he was poor, or because he was ignorant, or because he was black."

CHAPTER XIII

STRONG and passionate dislike and apprehension such as is set forth in the last chapter is certain to show itself in custom and law set up by that portion of the community which has the power of legislation. The commonest measures of this kind are discriminations between Whites and Negroes, especially in the use of public conveniences. In some cases the white people shut out Negroes altogether. There are perhaps half a dozen towns in the South in which none but Negroes live; there are scores in which the Negroes are not allowed to settle or stay. Two counties in North Carolina (Mitchell and Watauga) undertake to exclude Negroes; and people who attempt to go through there with a black driver are confronted by such signs as "Nigger, keep out of this county!" If that is not sufficient, a native comes swinging across the fields and remarks: "I don't want to have any trouble, and I don't suppose it makes any difference to you, but if that nigger goes two miles farther, he'll be shot. We don't allow any niggers in this county." Such exclusions are not unknown in other states. In the town of Syracuse, Ohio, for generations no Negro has ever been allowed to stay overnight; and the founder of a little city in Oklahoma heard his buildings blown up at night because he had ventured to domicile colored servants there.

166

RACE SEPARATION

In the two Northern settlements of Fitzgerald, Ga., and Cullman, Ala., the attempt was made to keep Negroes out altogether.

In addition to these artificial separations, there is a redistribution of the population going on all the while. Few of the owners of good plantations any longer live on them, and the outlying Whites move into town, or into counties where Negroes are fewer. The places thus vacated are taken up through rent or purchase by colored people; so that we have the striking phenomenon that black counties are getting blacker and white counties whiter. Thus in Pulaski County, Ga., in thirty years the Negroes doubled and the Whites increased only about twenty per cent. The same thing is true inside the cities and towns; most of them have well-marked negro quarters, near or alongside which none but the lowest Whites like to live. In Richmond, on one of the main streets, it is tacitly understood that the Negroes take the north sidewalk and the Whites the south sidewalk. Probably no place is now quite so strict in the matter as Morristown, Tenn., was twenty-five years ago, when white women first came to teach the Negroes; they were literally thrown off the sidewalks into the gutter because that was the only place where "niggers or nigger-lovers" were allowed to walk.

The principle of race separation extends from civil into religious matters. Before the Civil War Negroes were often acceptable and honored members of white churches, and there are still some cases where old members continue this relation, but they could now hardly sit in the same pews. There are also difficulties in attempts to unite separate black and white churches into one general denomination. The Protestant Episcopal Church is much perplexed over a proposition for separate negro bishops,

167

inferior to the regular bishops. However, not a twentieth of the Negroes to-day are members of churches which are in organic relation to white churches; they have their own presbyteries, and conferences, and synods; set their own doctrines and moral standards, and (if the white man is right in thinking the race inferior) they will necessarily develop an inferior Christianity.

The discriminations so far mentioned have to do with unwritten practices; with customs which differ from community to community; there is another long series upon the statute books. In 1865, in the so-called Vagrant Laws, special provision was made for the relations of colored people; four states allowed colored children to be "apprenticed," which practically meant a mild slavery; in South Carolina "servants," as the Negroes were called in the statute, were forbidden to leave their master's place without consent; Mississippi forbade people to rent land to Negroes outside the towns; South Carolina established a special court for the trial of negro offenses; several states forbade blacks to practice any trade or business without a license. These laws, which competent Southerners now think to have been a serious mistake, seemed to Congress evidence of a purpose to restore a milder form of slavery, and they were swept away by the Reconstruction governments. Nevertheless, in all the Southern states, constitutions or statutes forbid the intermarriage of Whites and Negroes; and either during Reconstruction or since, all the Southern states have provided for separate public schools for Negroes; and several states prohibit the education of Whites and blacks in the same private school.

The most striking discrimination is the separate accommodations on railroads and steamboats, which has entirely grown up since the Civil War. In slavery times few

RACE SEPARATION

Negroes traveled except as the obvious servants of white people; but in 1865 legislation began for separate cars or compartments, and of the former slaveholding states, only two, Missouri and Delaware, are now without laws on that subject. The term "Jim Crow" commonly applied to these laws goes back to an old negro song and dance, and was first used in Massachusetts, where, in 1841, the races were thus separated. The Civil Rights Act of Congress of 1875 forbade such distinctions, but was held unconstitutional by the Supreme Court in 1883. Several state and federal cases have given opportunity for the courts to decide that if there is a division between the two races, the accommodations must be equal. Hence, most Southern trains have a separate Jim Crow car, with a smoking compartment. The Pullman Car Company, perhaps because its business is chiefly interstate, has hesitated to make distinctions, and commonly will sell a berth to anybody who will show a railroad ticket good on the appropriate train; but in some states there are now demands for separate colored Pullmans, or for colored compartments, or for excluding Negroes altogether. But nobody who knows the Pullman Car Company will for a moment expect that it will do anything because patrons desire it. The discrimination in many states extends to the stations. For instance, in the beautiful new Spanish Mission building at Mobile, there are separate waiting rooms, separate ticket windows, and two exits—one for Whites and one for colored people. In Greensboro, N. C., the waiting room, a large and lofty hall, is simply bisected by a brass railing.

Similar laws apply to steamboats, though here it is not so easy to shut off part of the passengers from the general facilities of the boat. Even in the Boston steamers running to Southern ports there are separate dining

169

rooms, toilet rooms and smoking rooms for colored passengers. Eight Southern states separate street-car passengers; sometimes they have a separate compartment for Negroes—more often, a little movable sign is shifted up and down the car to divide the races. Elsewhere, Whites sit at one end and Negroes at the other, and fill up till they meet. In most of these laws there is an exception, allowing colored nurses with white children and colored attendants of feeble or sick people to enter the white car; and it has been thought necessary to provide that railroad employees, white or black, may circulate through the train.

In restaurants and hotels the distinction is still sharper, for except those which are kept only for the accommodations of Negroes, there is no provision for tables for colored people in any form outside of the railroad eating houses. It is hence practically impossible for any colored person to get accommodation in a Southern hotel.

These discriminations on travel have never been desired by the railroad companies, inasmuch as they involve trouble and expense, and are a check on the Negro's love for riding on trains and boats, which is an important factor in the passenger receipts. It is everywhere disliked by the Negroes, both because they do not, in fact, have accommodations as good as those of the Whites, and because it is intended to be a mark of their inferiority. The low-class white man who, in 1902, acted as ticket agent, baggage man and division superintendent and conductor on the three-mile branch road connecting Tuskegee with the main line remarked affably: " Been to see the nigger school, I suppose? That's all right, Booker Washington's all right. Oh, yes, he's a good man, he often rides on this train. Not in this part of the car, you know, but over there in the Jim Crow. Oh, yes, I often set down and talk to Booker Washington. Not on the same seat of course. Jest near by."

Besides these shackles of custom or of law, the Negro is in general excluded in the South from every position which might be construed to give him authority over white people. The civil service of the federal government is on a different footing; ever since war times there have always been some negro federal officials, collectors of internal revenue, collectors of ports, postmasters, and the like; but there is a determined effort in the South to get rid of them. At Lake City, S. C., in 1898, part of the family of Baker, the negro postmaster, was massacred as a hint that his presence was not desired. The people of Indianola, Miss., in 1903, practically served notice on a colored postmistress that she could not be allowed to officiate any longer; whereupon President Roosevelt directed the closing of the Indianola office. When in 1902 Dr. Crum was appointed collector of Charleston, there was an uproar in South Carolina and throughout the South. That episode involved some painful and some comical things; for instance, a white lady who bears one of the most honored names in American history, and who sorely needed the employment, was practically compelled by public sentiment to resign a clerkship in the customhouse when Dr. Crum came in; and the people who protested against his appointment, on the ground that he was unfit, had previously helped to select him as a commissioner in the Charleston Exposition.

In all these controversies the issue was double; first, that the white people thought it an indignity to transact any public business with a Negro representing the United States; and second, that it would somehow bring about race equality to admit that a Negro was competent to hold any

171

important office. The President was furiously censured because he did not take into account the preferences of the Southern people, by which, of course, was meant the Southern white people; that in South Carolina there are more African citizens than Caucasian seemed to them quite beside the question.

For minor offices the lines are not so strictly drawn; there are a few colored policemen in Charleston, and perhaps other Southern cities; Negro towns like Mound Bayou, Miss., have their own set of officials; and there are some small county offices which a few Negroes are allowed to hold. Nearly two thousand are employed in some capacity in the federal departments at Washington; about two thousand more under the District government; and a thousand more elsewhere, mostly in the South. These are chiefly in the postal service; there are some negro letter carriers in all the Southern cities, and in Mobile there are no others. They get these appointments, and likewise places as railway mail clerks on competitive examination—an especially hard twist to the doctrine of race equality; for what is the world coming to if a nigger gets more marks on an examination than a white man? For the feeling that the Negro in authority is overbearing and presumptuous there is some ground, but the attitude of the South is substantially expressed in the common phrase, " This is a white man's government," and is closely allied with the bogy of African domination, which is trotted out from time to time to arouse the jaded energies of race prejudice.

One of the most unaccountable things in this whole controversy is the evident apprehension of a large section in the South that unless something immediate and positive is done, the Negro will get control of some of the Southern

states, notwithstanding such protests as the following:
"And even where they represent a majority,—where do
they rule? or where have they ruled for these twenty years?
The South, with all its millions of negroes, has to-day not
a single negro congressman, not a negro governor or
senator. A few obscure justices of the peace, a few negro
mayors in small villages of negro people, and—if we omit
the few federal appointees—we have written the total of
all the negro officials in our Southern States. Every
possibility of negro domination vanishes to a more shad-
owy and more distant point with every year." As will
be shown a little later, the Negro's vote is no longer a
factor in most of the Southern states, and he shows no
disposition to take over the responsibility for Southern
government. The cry of negro domination has been more
unfortunate for the Whites than for the blacks because
it has thrown the Southern states out of their adjustment
in national parties; in the state election of 1908 for Governor of Georgia, the issue was between Clark Howells,
who was much against the Negro, and the successful candidate, Hoke Smith, who is mighty against the Negro; but
neither Howells nor Smith brought out of the controversy
any reputation that dazzled the Democratic Convention
of 1908.

No party founded on negro votes or organized to protect negro rights any longer exists in the South. In
Alabama there are still "black-and-tan Republicans"—
that is, an organization of Negroes and Whites, and one
of the most rabid Negro haters in the South is a dignitary
in that organization and helped to choose delegates for
the Republican national convention of 1908. Throughout
the South there are also what are called the "Lilywhite Republicans"—that is, people who are trying to build up their

party by disclaiming any partnership with the Negro or special interest in his welfare. Neither of these factions makes head against the overpowering " White Man's party," which is also the Democratic party; hence every state in the Lower South can be depended upon to vote for any candidate propounded by the national Democratic convention; hence the section has little influence in the selection of a candidate, who yet would not have a ghost of a chance without their votes. The net result of the scare cry of negro domination is that the Whites are in some states dominated by the loudest and most violent section of their own race.

Behind this whole question of politics and of office holding stands the more serious question whether a race which, whatever its average character, contains at least two million intelligent and progressive individuals, shall be wholly shut out from public employment. It is on this question that President Roosevelt made his famous declaration: " I cannot consent to take the position that the door of hope—the door of opportunity—is to be shut upon any man, no matter how worthy, purely upon the grounds of race or color. . . . It is a good thing from every standpoint to let the colored man know that if he shows in marked degree the qualities of good citizenship—the qualities which in a white man we feel are entitled to reward—then he will not be cut off from all hope of similar reward."

The discrimination between the Negro and the White has nowhere been so bitterly contested as with regard to suffrage, inasmuch as the right of the Negro to vote on equal terms with the white man is distinctly set forth in the Fifteenth Amendment of the Federal Constitution, and as during Reconstruction the Negro had full suffrage in all the Southern states. Without going into the history

174

of the negro vote, it may be worth while to notice that at the time of the Revolution, Negroes who had the property qualification could vote in all the thirteen colonies except two; that they never lost that franchise in Massachusetts and some other Northern communities, and that as late as 1835 about a thousand of them had the ballot in North Carolina. Then in Reconstruction times the suffrage was given to all the Negroes in the country; a process of which one of the most bitter enemies of the race to-day says: " To give the negro the right of suffrage and place him on terms of absolute equality with the white man, was the capital crime of the ages against the white man's civilization." In reality the North bestowed the suffrage on the Negro because its own experience seemed to have proved that the ballot was an instrument of civilization—for all the foreign immigrants had grown up to it.

Southerners are never weary of describing the enormities of the governments based on negro suffrage; as a matter of fact, however, nobody North or South knows what would have been the result of negro suffrage, for in no state longer than eight years, and in some states only about three years, did they actually cast votes that determined the choice of state officers, or any considerable number of local officers. Their habit of voting for " the regular candidate," without regard to his fitness or character, was not peculiar to the race or to the section. Disfranchisement began with the Ku Klux in 1870, and in most states the larger part of the Negroes at once lost their ballots because driven away from the polls by violence or terror. The only community in which they were disfranchised by statute, together with the Whites, was the District of Columbia. Then came the era of fraud, the use of tissue ballots and falsified electoral returns, and confusing systems of ballot boxes; then, in 1890, began a process of disfranchising them by state constitutional amendments which provided qualifications especially difficult for Negroes to meet: for instance, special indulgence was given to men who served in the Confederate army, or whose fathers or grandfathers were entitled to vote before the war. This movement has already involved six states, and is likely to run through every former slaveholding state.

Even the comparatively small number of Negroes who can meet the requirements of tax, education, or property find trouble in registering, or in voting. In Mississippi, where there were nearly 200,000 colored voters, there are now 16,000; in Alabama about 5,000 are registered out of 100,000 men of voting age. Sometimes they are simply refused registration, like the highly educated Negro in Alabama, who was received by the official with the remark: " Nigger, get out of here; this ain't our day for registering niggers! " In Beaufort County, S. C., where, under the difficult provisions of the law, there are about seven hundred negro voters and about five hundred Whites, somehow the white election officials always return a majority for their friends; and in the presidential election of 1908 the hundred thousand negro men of voting age in South Carolina were credited with only twenty-five hundred votes for Theodore Roosevelt.

It has puzzled the leaders of the conventions to disfranchise the greater part of the Negroes without including " some of our own people," and yet without technically infringing upon the Fifteenth Amendment, which prohibits the withdrawal of the suffrage on account of race, color, or previous condition of servitude; but they have been successful. As a Senator from North Carolina put it: "The disfranchising amendment would disfranchise ignorant negroes and not disfranchise any white man. No white man in North Carolina has been disfranchised as a result of this amendment."

It is impossible not to feel a sympathy with the desire of the South to be free from an ignorant and illiterate electorate; there is not a Northern state in which, if the conditions were the same, the effort would not be made to restrict the suffrage; but that is a long way from the Southern principle of ousting the bad, low, and illiterate Negro, while leaving the illiterate, low, and bad White; and then, in the last resort, shutting out also the good, educated, and capable Negro. For there is not a state in the Lower South where the colored vote would be faithfully counted if it had a balance of power between two white parties; and Senator Tillman's great fear at present is that the blacks will make the effort to come up to these complicated requirements, and then must be disenfranchised again. Have the Southern people confidence in their own race superiority, when for their protection from negro domination and from the great evil of amalgamation they feel it necessary to take such precautions against the least dangerous, most enterprising, and best members of the negro race? Nevertheless, the practical disenfranchisement of the Negroes has brought about a political peace, and there is little to show that the Negroes resent their exclusion.

Whatever the divergences of feeling in the South on the negro question, it is safe to say that the Whites are a unit on the two premises that amalgamation must be resisted, and that the Negro must not have political power. All these feelings are buttressed against a passionate objection to race-mixture, which is all the stronger because so much of it is going on; it branches out into the withdrawal of the suffrage, not because the South is in any danger of negro political domination, but because most Whites think no member of an inferior race ought to vote; it includes many restrictions on personal relations which seem like precautions where there is no danger.

Upon these main issues Northerners may share some of the sentiments of the South, but none of the terrors. If the Negro is inferior, it does not need so many acts of the legislature to prove it; if amalgamation is going on, it is due to the white race, can be checked by the white race, and by no one else; if the Negro is unintelligent, he will never, under present conditions, get enough votes to affect elections; if he does acquire the necessary property and education, he thereby shows that he does not share in the inferiority of his race. The South thinks about the Negro too much, talks about him too much, abuses him too much. In the nature of things there is no reason why the superior and the inferior race may not live side by side indefinitely. Is the Negro powerful enough to force his standards and share his disabilities with the superior white man? Is it not as the Chinese sage says: "The superior man is correctly firm, and not firm merely . . . what the superior man seeks is in himself."

So far as can be judged, the average frame of mind in the South includes much injustice, and unwillingness to permit the negro race to develop up to the measure of its limitations. Here the experience of the North counts, for it has many elements of population which at present are inferior to the average. If there is a low Italian quarter in a city, or a Slav quarter, or a Negro quarter, the aim of the Northern community is to give those people the best chance that they can appropriate. Woe to the city which permits permanent centers of crime and degradation! By schools, by reformatory legislation, by philanthropic societies, by juvenile courts, by missions, by that great blessing, the care of neglected children, they try to bring up the standard. This is done for the welfare of the community, it is what business men call a dollars and cents proposition. If a man or child has three fourths of the average abilities, the North tries to bring him to the full use of his seventy-five per cent; if he stands at 150 on the scale of 100, it aims to give him the opportunity to use his superior qualities.

This is just the point of view of the Southern leaders who are fighting for justice and common sense toward the Negro: men like the late Chancellor Hill, of the University of Georgia, like President Alderman, of the University of Virginia, like Rev. Edgar Gardner Murphy, of Montgomery; their gospel is that, notwithstanding his limitations, the Negro is on the average capable of higher things than he is doing, and that the gifted members of the race can render still larger services to their own color and to the community. That is what Dr. S. C. Mitchell, of Richmond College, meant when he said: " Friend, go up higher! " a phrase which part of the Southern press has unwarrantably seized upon as a declaration of social equality.

Every friend of the South must hope that that enlightened view will permeate the community; but, as a matter of fact, a very considerable number of people of power in the South, legislators, professional men, journalists, ministers, governors, either take the ground that the Negro is so hopelessly low that it is a waste of effort to try to raise him; or that education and uplift will make him less useful to the White, and therefore he shall not have it; or that you cannot give to the black man a better chance without bringing danger upon the white man. Contrary to the experience of mankind, to present upward movement in what has been a very low white element in the South, and to the considerable progress made by the average Negro since slavery days, such people hold that intelligence and education do nothing for the actual improvement of the colored race. Since the Negro is low, they would keep him low; since they think him dangerous, they wish to leave him dangerous; their policy is to make the worst of a bad situation instead of trying to improve it.

No Northern mind can appreciate the point of view of some men who certainly have a considerable following in the South. Here, for instance, is Thomas Dixon, Jr., arguing with all his might that the Negro is barely human, but that if he is not checked he will become such an economic competitor of the white man that he will have to be massacred. He protests against Booker T. Washington's attempt to raise the Negro, because he thinks it will be successful. Part, at least, of the customary and statutory discriminations against the Negro which have already been described are simply an expression of this supposed necessity of keeping the Negro down, lest he should rise too far. All such terrors involve the humiliating admission that the Negro can rise, and that he will rise if he has the opportunity.

CHAPTER XIV

SITTING one night in the writing room of a country hotel in South Carolina, a young man opposite, with a face as smooth as a baby's and as pretty as a girl's, volunteered to tell where he had just been, a discreditable tale. It soon developed that his business was the sale of goods on instalments, chiefly to Negroes, and that in that little town of Florence he had no less than five hundred and ninety transactions then going on; that his profits were about fifty per cent on his sales; that nineteen twentieths of the transactions would be paid up; but that sometimes he had a little trouble in making collections.

"For instance, only yesterday," said he, "I went to a nigger woman's house where they had bought two skirt patterns. When I knocked at the door, a little girl came, and she says: 'Mammy ain't to home,' says she, but I walked right in, and there was a bigger girl, who says, 'Mamma has gone down street,' but I says, 'I know better than that, you —— nigger!' And I pushed right into the kitchen, and there she was behind the door, and I walked right up to her, and I says, 'Do you think I'll allow you to teach that innocent child to lie, you —— nigger? I'll show you,' says I; and I hit her a couple of good ones right in the face. She come back at me with

181

a kind of an undercut right under the jaw. I knew it wouldn't do any good to hit her on the head, but I landed a solid one in the middle of her nose; and I made those women go and get those skirts and give them up before I left the place."

Once entered on these agreeable reminiscences, he went on in language the tenor of which is fortified by a memorandum made at the time. "But that isn't a circumstance to what happened three weeks ago last Tuesday. There's a nigger in this town that bought a cravenette coat from us for thirteen dollars and a half. It costs us about nine dollars, but he only paid instalments of four and a half, and then, for about six months, he dodged me; but my brother and I saw him on the street, and I jumped out of the buggy before he could run away, and says I, 'I want you to pay for that coat.' He had it on. He says, 'I hain't got any money.' Says it sarcastic-like. Well, of course I wouldn't take any lip from a nigger like that, and I sailed right in. I hit him between the eyes, and he up with a shovel and lambasted me with the flat of it right between the shoulder-blades, but I could have got away with him all right if his wife hadn't have come up with a piece of board and caught me on the side; my brother jumped right out of the buggy, and he hit her square and knocked her down, and we had a regular mix-up. We got the coat, and when we came away, we left the man lying senseless on the ground." "But don't those people ever get out warrants against you?" "Warrants against me, I guess not! I lay in bed five days, and when I got up, my brother and I swore out warrants against the nigger and his wife. We brought them up in court and the judge fined them forty-seven dollars, and he says to me, 'All the fault I find with you is that you didn't kill the double adjective nigger. He's the worst nigger in town!' "

With all allowances for the lies visibly admixed in this unpleasant tale, it undoubtedly lifts the cover off a kind of thing that goes on every day between the superior and the inferior races. On the one side stand the negro customers, shiftless, extravagant, slinking away from their debts, yet doubtless afterward puffed with pride to be able to boast that they had a knock-down fight with a white man and were not shot; the other actor in this drama of race hatred could not even claim to be a Poor White; he was the son of a traveling man, had some education, was successful above the average, and until he began to talk about himself might for a few minutes have passed as a gentleman; yet to save a loss of less than five dollars, and to assert his superiority of race, he was perfectly willing to put himself on the level of the lowest Negro, and to engage in fisticuffs with a woman.

It is not to be supposed that this thoroughgoing blackguard is a spokesman for the whole South, or that every local court inflicts a heavy penalty upon black people for the crime of having been thrashed by a white man. The story simply illustrates a feeling toward the Negroes which is widespread and potent among a considerable class of Whites; and it bears witness also to a disposition to settle difficulties between members of the two races by the logic of hard fists. It is a lurid example of race antagonism.

No section of the Union has a monopoly of violence or injustice. Men as coarse and brutal as the man encountered in South Carolina could probably be found in every Northern city. Homicides are no novelty in any state in the Union, and it is as serious for a Northern crowd to put a man to death because somebody calls him " Scab " as

183

for an equally tigerish Southern mob to burn a Negro because he has killed a white man. The annals of strikes are almost as full of ferocity as the annals of lynching, and it would be hard to find anything worse than the murder, in 1907, of some watchmen in New York City who were thrown down a building by striking workmen, who were allowed by the police to leave the building, and were never brought to justice.

Nevertheless, there is in the North a strong impression that crime is on a different footing in the South; that assaults, affrays, and homicides are more frequent; that the South has a larger crime record than seems reconcilable with its numerous churches, its moral standards, and its fairly good state and city governments. Light may be thrown on the problem of race relations by inquiring whether the South is as much shocked by certain kinds of crime and violence as the North, whether a criminal is as likely to be tried and convicted, whether the superior race, by its practice in such matters, is setting before the inferior race a high standard of conduct.

Statistics indicate that in desperate crimes against the person, and especially in murder, the South far surpasses other civilized countries, and other parts of the United States. In London, with a population of 6,500,000, there were in a year 24 homicides; 4 of the criminals committed suicide, and the 20 others were brought to justice. In New York City, with about two thirds the population of London, there were 331 homicides with only 61 indictments and 46 convictions. In the state of South Carolina, with a population about one third that of New York City, there were 222 homicides in a year, and not a single execution of a white man.

Popular phrases and the press in the South habitually

put a gloss upon many of these crimes by calling them
" duels "; but a careful study of newspaper cuttings shows
that the old-fashioned affairs of honor with seconds and
exactly similar weapons, measured distance, and the word
to fire, have almost disappeared. Nearly all the affrays
in which the murdered man is conscious of his danger
are simply street fights, in which each man lodges in the
body of the other as many shots as he can before he himself sinks down wounded. It can hardly be considered
an affair of honor when Mr. John D. Twiggs, of Albany,
Ga., walks through the streets with a shotgun loaded with
buckshot, looking for Mr. J. B. Palmer, who has gone home
to arm himself.

Even this uneven kind of warfare is less frequent than
the outright assassination of one white man by another.
Where was Southern chivalry when Gonzales, the editor
of the *Columbia State,* was in 1902 killed in the open
street before he could draw his pistol, by Lieutenant-Gov-
ernor Tillman of South Carolina, about whom the editor
had been telling unpleasant truths? Where do you find
the high-toned Southern gentleman when a man walks up
to a total stranger, seizes him, and with the remark, " You
are the man who wanted to fight me last night," plunges
his knife into the victim's back. The newspapers are full
of the shooting of men through windows, of their disap-
pearance on lonely roads, of the terror that walketh by
night, and the pestilence that waiteth at noonday.

Then there are the numerous murders of friend by
friend, on all kinds of frivolous occasions; a man trespasses
on another man's land, goes to apologize, and is shot; another makes a joke which his friend does not appreciate,
and there is nothing for it but pistols. The feeling that
a man must assert his dignity at the end of a revolver

185

was revealed in New Orleans in 1908 when Inspector Whittaker, head of the police, with five of his men, walked into the office of the *New Orleans World,* which had criticised his enforcement of the liquor laws, struck the editor in the face and several times shot at him. After he had taken such pains to vindicate the majesty of the law, it seems a hardship that his superiors compelled the Inspector to resign. There is hardly a part of the civilized world where homicide is so common as in the South, and the crime is quite as frequent in the cities as in the back country. Pitched battles by white men with policemen and with sheriffs are not uncommon; and sometimes three or four bodies are picked up after such a fight.

In many ways this unhappy state of things is a survival of frontier practices which once were common in the Northwest as well as in the South, but which have nearly disappeared there as civilization has advanced; but in the South there is a special element of lawlessness through the Negroes. One of the few advantages of slavery was that every slaveholder was police officer and judge and jury on his own plantation; petty offenses were punished by the overseer without further ceremony, serious crimes were easily dealt with, and the escape of the criminal was nearly impossible.

Freedom, with its opportunity of moving about, with its greatly enlarged area of disputes among the blacks, and between Whites and Negroes, has combined with the influence of the press in popularizing crime, and perhaps with an innate African savagery, to make the black criminal a terrible scourge in the South. To begin with the less serious offenses, there is no doubt that the Negro has a very imperfect realization of property rights, partly because of the training of slavery. The vague feeling that

whatever belonged to the plantation was for the enjoyment
of those who lived on the plantation is deliciously expressed by Paul Dunbar:

Folks ain't got no right to censuah othah folks about dey
 habits;
Him dat giv' de squir'ls de bushtails made de bobtails fu'
 de rabbits.
Him dat built de gread big mountains hollered out de little
 valleys,
Him dat made de streets an' driveways wasn't 'shamed to
 make de alleys.

We is all constructed diff'ent, d' ain't no two of us de same;
We cain't he'p ouah likes an' dislikes, ef we'se bad we ain't
 to blame.
If we'se good, we needn't show off, 'case you bet it ain't
 ouah doin'
We gits into su'ttain channels dat we jes' cain't he'p pu'suin'.

But we all fits into places dat no othah ones could fill,
An' we does the things we has to, big er little, good er ill.
John cain't tek de place o' Henry, Su an' Sally ain't alike;
Bass ain't nuthin' like a suckah, chub ain't nuthin' like a
 pike.

When you come to think about it, how it's all planned out,
 it's splendid.
Nuthin's done er evah happens, 'dout hit's somefin' dat's
 intended;
Don't keer whut you does, you has to, an' hit sholy beats
 de dickens,—
Viney, go put on de kittle, I got one o' mastah's chickens.

Not so genial is the usual relation of Negro with Negro;
both in town and city there is an amount of crude and

savage violence of which the outside world knows little, and in which women freely engage. Jealousy is a frequent cause of fights and murders; and whisky is so potent an excitant that many competent observers assert that whisky and cocaine are at the bottom of almost all serious negro crimes. Practically every negro man carries a revolver and many of them bear knives or razors; hence, once engaged in a fracas, nobody knows what will happen. A woman describing a trouble in which a man shot her brother was chiefly aggrieved because " Two ladies jumped on me and one lady bit me." There is constant negro violence against the Whites, and they occasionally engage in pitched battles with white gangs.

Here, as in so many other respects, even well-informed people run to exaggeration. Thus President Winston, of the North Carolina Agricultural College, declares in public that the Negroes are the most criminal element in the population, and are more criminal in freedom than in slavery (both of which propositions are indisputable) ; that " the negro is increasing in criminality with fearful rapidity "; that " the negroes who can read and write are more criminal than the illiterate "; that they are nearly three times as criminal in the Northeast as in the South; that they are more criminal than the white class, and that " more than seven tenths of the negro criminals are under thirty years of age." This statement, like almost all the discussions of criminal statistics, ignores the important point that as communities improve, acts formerly not covered by the law become statutory crimes; and hence that the more civilized a state the more likely it is that criminals will be convicted, and the larger will be the apparent proportion of criminals. In Connecticut are enumerated 68 white juvenile delinquents to 100,000 people, in Georgia only four, but the Georgia boys are not seventeen times as good as their brothers in the Northern state. It further overlooks the fact that most criminals of all races are under thirty years of age, for crime is the accompaniment of youth with white men as with Negroes.

To say that the Negroes furnish more than their proportion of criminals is no more than to say that the lowest element in the population has the lowest and most criminal members. The excessive criminality of the Negroes, which is marked in all the states of the Union, is of course a mark of their average inferiority, and a measure of the difficulty of bringing them up to a high standard; and the proportion is often exaggerated. In South Carolina where the Negroes are three fifths of the population they furnish only four fifths of the convicts. As for the assertion that the educated Negroes are specially criminal, the statement is contradicted by the records of the large institutions of negro education, and by the experience of thousands of people. Education does not necessarily make virtue, but it is a safeguard. As a matter of fact, white Southerners in general know little of the lives or motives of thousands of the immense noncriminal class of Negroes, with whom they have no personal relations; but are wide awake to the iniquities of the educated men who fall into crime.

The experience of two centuries shows that the Negroes are not drawn to crimes requiring previous organization and preparation; no slave insurrection has ever been a success within the boundaries of the United States; and blacks are rarely found in gangs of bandits. The incendiarism of which there is now so much complaint is probably the expression of individual vengeance. The Negroes, according to the testimony of those nearest to them, are inveterate gamblers, and many affrays result from consequent quarrels, so that murders may be most frequent where there is the best employment and largest wages and greatest prosperity among the thrifty. Murder, manslaughter, and attempts to kill make up three quarters of the recorded crimes of the blacks in the Mississippi Delta. Murders of Negroes by Negroes are very common and many of the criminals escape altogether.

Negro crime is much fomented by the low drinking-shops in the city and in country, by the lack of home influence on growing boys and girls, by the brutalizing of young people who are sent to prison with hardened criminals, and in general, by close contact with the lowest element of the white race, which leads to crimes on both sides. It is a striking fact that where the Africans are most numerous there is the least complaint of crime. The so-called race riots are usually rows between a few bad Negroes and the officers of the law, or a group of aggrieved Whites. Fights with policemen and sheriffs are frequent, and desperate men not infrequently barricade themselves in houses, and sell their lives as dearly as they can. Quarrels over the settlement of accounts are not uncommon, and the Negro who feels himself cheated sometimes takes his revenge at the end of a gun. As weapons are ordinarily sold without the slightest check, to men of both races and of every age, there is never any lack of the means to kill.

Occasionally a cry is raised that proof has been found of the existence of " Before Day Clubs "—that is, of organizations of Negroes for purposes of violence. The thing is possible and difficult to disprove, but a sequence of crimes through such an organization seems alien to the Negro's habits, and is at least unlikely. The serious charges that the blacks habitually protect any negro criminal who comes to them will be considered farther on.

CRIME AND ITS PENALTIES

The negro crime about which Southern newspapers print most, Southern writers say most, and which more than anything else aggravates race hatred, is violence to white women. The crime is a dreadful one, made worse by the spreading abroad of details, but it has such a fateful relation to the whole Southern problem that something must here be said, less on the thing itself than on some of the common misunderstandings and misstatements which cluster about it.

Statistics are unfortunately too available, inasmuch as for twenty years the number of such crimes has been nearly balanced by the number of lynchings for that offense, which have been tabulated from year to year by the *Chicago Tribune,* and have been thoroughly analyzed by Professor Cutler in his recent book " Lynch Law." From 1882 to 1903 these statistics show an average of thirty-two lynchings per year for violence or attempted violence to white women, though of late they have been reduced to under twenty. This includes some cases of innocent men, probably balanced by assailants who escaped. These figures completely dispose of the allegation that the crime is very frequent. Contrary to common belief in the North, some such cases are tried before regular courts; and in Missouri the Governor in 1908 very properly refused to pardon a Negro under a sentence of death for that crime. Adding in these cases, and the half dozen which perhaps escaped the newspaper reporter, at the utmost there are not over fifty authenticated instances of this crime in the whole South in a twelvemonth. Among something like 3,000,000 adult negro males the ratio of the crime to those who might commit it is about 1 to 600,000; and out of 6,000,000 white women, not over fifty become victims, or 1 in 120,-000. For this degree of danger to white women ten million

191

human beings are supposed to be sodden with crime and actuated by malice, and the whole South from end to end is filled with terror.

The allegation frequently made that these crimes are committed by highly educated Negroes, graduates of Hampton and Tuskegee, is absolutely without foundation. Most of them are by men of the lowest type, some undoubtedly maniacs. Most of these occurrences take place where the Whites and Negroes are most closely brought into juxtaposition, sometimes where they are both working in the fields. Hence they are of rare occurrence where the Whites are fewest and the Negroes most numerous. In many places in the Black Belt, white people have no fear of leaving their families, because sure that their negro neighbors would give their lives, if necessary, for the protection of the white women. The Northern white teachers, who are accused of arousing in the Negro's mind the belief that he is the equal of the Whites, have never in a single instance been attacked; and in communities where the Negroes are literally fifty to one, have not the slightest fear of going about alone at any necessary hour of day or night.

These statements are not intended to minimize the dreadful effects of a crime which brings such wretchedness upon the innocent. The two worst enemies of the white woman in the South are " The Black Brute," whom the Southern press is never tired of describing in unrepeatable terms, and the white buzzard journalist who spreads her name and her dreadful story abroad to become the seed of another like crime. Where is the Southern chivalry and respect for white women when every such crime is sought out and flashed abroad, in all the details obtainable, and the victim is doomed to a second wrong in the lifelong feeling that she is known and branded throughout the land?

A general and well-grounded complaint is that any fugitive, no matter what his reason for flight, even though he is guilty of rape, is fed and sent on his way by his own people, a practice which goes back to slavery days when there were many strays whose only offense was a love of liberty. "The worst feature," says an observer, "is that other negroes help to conceal them and their crimes. They seem to have entered into a racial agreement that they must help each one of their race to escape the penalties of the white man's law by resorting to every artifice of untruthfulness and concealment." Judge Cann, of Georgia, charges that "as a race, negroes shelter, conceal and protect the criminals of their race; that they produce riots by attacking officers of the law while in the discharge of their duty; that they openly show sympathy with the negro criminal; that they conspire against the enforcement of law; that they have made first a hero, and then a martyr, of a legally convicted and executed murderer."

Like all such general statements, these allegations go too far. In the first place, it is not altogether a sentiment of race solidarity. Negroes have been known to give similar shelter to white vagabonds and criminals. In the second place, black criminals are frequently apprehended through blacks, and large numbers are brought into court, tried and convicted, entirely on negro testimony. Something has been done in the way of negro Law and Order Associations, which pledge themselves to give up criminals. Still, it is discomposing to know that when a search was making for a particularly odious fellow in Monroe, La., who had for a year or two made himself the nuisance of the neighborhood by looking into windows, his father

193

and brothers, who must have known his practices, unhesitatingly signed such a law-and-order pledge. The Brownsville incident of 1907 also, with the apparent determination of scores of men not to " split " on some ruffians and murderers among them, produced a painful feeling throughout the country. In few respects could the Negroes do so much good for themselves as by helping in the detection of the crime of their own people.

If Negroes are violent to Whites and among themselves, they follow an example daily and hourly set them by the members of the Superior Race. In the first place, the Negro listens habitually to rough and humiliating language. You get a new view of race relations when a planter in his store on Saturday night calls up for you one after another three specimen Negroes. " This man Chocolate," he says, " is a full-blooded nigger, the real thing." " Chocolate " says nothing, shrugs his shoulders, and looks as he feels, literally like the devil. The next is introduced as " One of your mixed ones—How did that come about, hey ! " and the mulatto, who has been the official whipper on the plantation, grins at the superior man's joke. The third is called up and presented as " The Preacher, very fond of the sisters." This is a fair sample of what constantly takes place wherever there is a rough, coarse white man among Negroes.

The office of the whipper is usually performed by the master himself, if he is one of those numerous employers who believe in that method. As one such put it: " I follow up a hand and tell him to do what he ought? If he won't, I just get off and whip him." " Suppose he summons you before a magistrate? " " I lick him again before the magistrate and send him home." Other planters have given up whipping and charge a fine against the Negro's account. Of course such fellows would rather be whipped than prosecuted, and think that the riders (that is, the overseers), if they once take it out of them in a thrashing, will harbor no further malice. In some states, as North Carolina, whipping is unusual; in others it is frequent.

Another race trouble is the driving out of blacks who make themselves disliked by the Whites. A Negro passes an examination for post office clerk, but is warned that if he tries to take the place he will be shot. A colored editor, whose paper is much less offensive than any of the white journals in his neighborhood in bad language and incitement to crime, is thought well treated because he leaves the state alive. A Negro who is too conspicuous, who builds a house thought to be above his station, who drives two horses in his buggy, may be warned to leave the place; and if he refuses to sacrifice his little property, may be shot. A black doctor may be warned out of the county because there are enough white doctors. The South is not the only community where people that are obnoxious are hustled out of town, and Southern Whites sometimes receive the same unofficial " ticket of leave "; but it makes bad blood when irresponsible people, often in no way superior in character to the Negroes whom they assail, uproot their neighbors.

Then comes the long list of homicides of Negroes by Whites. Ever since Ku Klux times there have been occasional instances of " whitecapping "—that is, of bodies of disguised men riding through the country, pulling people out of their houses and whipping them. Such practices are not confined to the South and are condoned sometimes in the North. Down on Buzzard's Bay in Massachusetts a few years ago a jury absolutely refused to convict the perpetrators of a similar outrage on a white man; while

195

in Alabama, in 1898, five Whites were sentenced for twenty years each for killing a Negro in that sort of way. Still convictions of white men for killing Negroes are very unusual. Since practically every adult negro man has a gun about him, the theory of the White is that if you get into a quarrel and the Negro makes any movement with his hands, you must shoot him forthwith. To this purport is the testimony of a Mississippi planter who reproved a hand for severely whipping his child; the black replied that it was his business and nobody should stop it; the white man said he would stop it; whereupon the Negro drew, but was met by a bullet in his forehead; and, explained the planter, " A steel bullet will go through a nigger's skull." Take another case: An assistant manager on an estate in the Delta of Mississippi tried to take a pistol away from a new hand and felt himself safe because the man had his hands in his pockets; but the Negro fired through the pocket, instantly killed the white man, and decamped. It afterwards was shown that he had previously killed another white man.

The responsibility is not always on the Negro's side. There are many disputes over labor contracts, in which the Negro justly believes that the white man has cheated him, and his attempt to audit is stopped by a quarrel in which the black is killed. Even boys under twelve years of age have been known to shoot Negroes over trivial disputes, and a young lady in Washington recently shot and killed a black boy who was stealing fruit. The Negroes complain of harsh treatment by the police. For instance, a good-looking, very black young man is glad to get out of Savannah and among the white people on the Sea Islands. " They like the colored people better; even if they do get drunk and are fierce, they treat them better. In Savannah

196

the other day I saw a man going back to his vessel, and a policeman asked him where he was going. He answered up rough like,—I wouldn't do that, I'd go down on my hands and knees to 'em rather than have any trouble with em,—and the policeman broke his club over his head, arrested him, and they sent him to the chain gang. I don't want to be arrested; I never have been arrested in my life." That the police are often in the wrong is shown by such instances as the recent acquittal of a Negro by direction of an Alabama judge; he had shot a policeman who was arresting him without reason, and the judge who heard the case justified him.

Perhaps, comparing city with city, the North is as disorderly as the South, but the rural South is a much more desperate region than the farming lands of the North, as is shown by the statistics of homicide and similar crimes. In Florida in 1899, with a population of 528,000, there were about 40 murders and 200 assaults with attempt to murder. In Alabama in 1895–96 there were about 350 homicides. In one twelvemonth some years ago there were 6 murders in Vermont, 96 in Massachusetts, 461 in Alabama, and over 1,000 in Texas. Judge Thomas, of Montgomery, has shown that the homicides in the United States per million of population are 129 against 10 per million in England; and when the sections are contrasted, New England has about 47 per million, against 223 per million in the South.

It is not easy to compare the criminal spirit in the North and the South by the records of the courts or the statistics of convictions; acts which are penitentiary offenses in one state may be misdemeanors, or no crime at all, in another. A very recent tabulation, made from statistics of 1905, shows in the Lower South 16,000 prisoners against 13,000 in a group of Northwestern states having the same total population; and in the whole South, 27,000 prisoners against 24,000 in a group aggregating the same number of people in the North and West. Of the Southern prisoners, about two thirds are Negroes, the proportion of criminals to the total numbers of the African race being decidedly less than in the North. The only safe generalization from those statistics is therefore that the Southern courts send more people to jail, white and black, than the Northern. Statistics throw little light on the question of relative crime.

A comparison is, however, possible between the ordinary course of justice in the South and in the North. The most notorious defect in the South is the conduct of murder trials, as shown by the evidence of Southern jurists. Says one, " Unreasoning and promiscuous danger stalks in any community where life is held cheap by even a few, and where the laws are enforced by privilege or race. In such a community there is no sufficient defense against a mob, or even a drunken fool." If one credited all the editorials in Southern newspapers, he would believe that " a man who kills a man in this community is in much less danger of legal punishment than one who steals a suit of clothes "; and experienced lawyers tell you that they never knew of a white man being convicted for homicide.

These statements are exaggerations, for the records of pardons show that a certain number of white men have reached the penitentiary for that offense and leave it by the side door. The reason for the failure of justice in numerous cases is, first of all, the technicalities of the courts, which are probably not very different in that particular from those of the North; and, secondly, the unwillingness of juries to convict. It must be accepted as an axiom that the average plain man in the South feels that if A kills B the presumption is that he has some good reason. Counsel for such cases habitually appeal to the emotions of the jury, and ask what they would have done under like circumstances. Even conviction may not be uncomfortable; take the case of a young White in Florida, who killed a policeman, was sentenced to eighteen months' imprisonment, was then hired out as a convict by his uncle at fifteen dollars a month, and paraded the streets at his pleasure.

A general impression in the North is that the Southern courts are very severe with colored men; and (if he has not already been lynched) it is true that they are likely to pass heavy sentence on a Negro who has killed a white man, and juries are often merciless; but there are many cases where blacks are lightly treated on the express ground that they have had less opportunity to know what is right and wrong. In Brookhaven, Miss., a very rough region, in a year three white men have been heavily sentenced for killing Negroes; while many cases could be cited where a Negro was acquitted or let off with a light penalty for a like offense.

When it comes to less serious crimes, the Negro enjoys a special protection whenever he can call in a respectable white man to vouch for him as in general straightforward; the Court is then likely to impose a light sentence. Even in serious cases a man is sometimes acquitted or lightly treated at the request of his master, so that he may return to work. That is what the planter meant who boasted: " I never sent a nigger to jail in my life; and I have taken more niggers out of jail than any planter in Alabama." That is, he never gave information against one of his own hands, but inflicted such small penalties

199

as he saw fit; and he would pay the fine for his men who came before the courts, or even secure their pardon, so as to get them on his plantation. That principle sometimes goes terribly deep. In the case of a Negro who whipped his child to death, the natural inquiry was, "What did they do with him?" To which the nonchalant answer was, "Oh, nothing, he was a good cotton hand."

The great majority of negro convicts are sentenced for petty crimes, stealing, vagrancy, and the like, and for rather short terms; but the name for this punishment, "the chain gang," points to a system practically unknown in the North. There are literal chain gangs, with real shackles and balls, working in the streets of cities, white and black together; and large bodies of convicts are worked in the open, stockaded, and perhaps literally chained at night. Right here comes in one of the worst features of the Southern convict system. The men on the chain gang are perhaps employed on city or county work, and if their terms expire too fast, the authorities will run out of labor; hence, the Negroes believe, perhaps rightly, that judges and juries are convinced of their guilt just in proportion to the falling off of the number of men in confinement; and that if necessary, innocent people will be arrested for that purpose. That is probably one reason why Negroes feel so little shame at having been in prison. "Did you know I was in the barracks last night?" is a remark that you may hear at any railroad station in Georgia.

The whole subject is complicated with vagrant laws. For instance, in Savannah Negroes not at work, or without reasonable excuse for idleness, shall be arrested; and in Alabama if arrested as a vagrant the burden of proof is on the black to show that he is at work. It is a mistake to suppose that colored tramps are common in the South; but irresponsible men, loitering about a city and sponging on the working Negroes, are frequent, and furnish many serious criminals.

On the whole, one would rather not be a negro convict in a Southern state, or even a white convict, for many state and county prisons are simply left-over examples of the worst side of slavery. A Northern expert in such matters in Atlanta a few years ago, in a public address, congratulated the people on the new jail which he had just visited. At least it looked like the most improved of modern jails, for it had large airy cells provided with running water, and the only defect in it was that it was intended for the state mules and was far better than any provision made there for human prisoners.

The first trouble with the Southern convict system is that it still retains the notion, from which other communities began to diverge nearly a century ago, that the prisoner is the slave of the state, existing only for the convenience and profit of those whom he serves. In the second place, it has been difficult to find indoor employment for the men, and most of them are worked out of doors, a life which with proper precautions is undoubtedly happier and healthier than that inside. In the third place, whipping is still an ordinary penalty, and very frequently applied. Furthermore, a number of states in the Lower South have been in the habit of letting out convicts, and that is still done in several states, as Florida, Alabama, and Georgia. They used to be rented to cotton growers, and a planter could get as few as two convicts or even one, over whom he had something approaching the power of life and death. This was a virtual chattel slavery, which long ago ought to have been disallowed by the Supreme Court of the United States, as contrary to the Thirteenth Amendment. If still retained on a state or county plantation, the convicts are in the power of wardens whose interest it is to drive the men unmercifully. Governor Vardaman in a public message in 1908 thought it necessary to say that " Some of the most atrocious and conscienceless crimes that have been perpetrated in this State are chargeable to the county contractor. I have known the poor convict driven to exhaustion or whipped to death to gratify the greed or anger of the conscienceless driver or contractor. The tears and blood of hundreds of these unfortunate people cry out for this reform."

The Governor suggests that white men suffer under this system, and there have been recent cases where vagrant Whites were sold on the auction block for a period of months. It might perhaps be argued that the South is always more stern in its judicial punishments than the North, inasmuch as five years on a convict farm in Mississippi is worse than being decently hanged in Massachusetts. The modern and humane methods of reform, of separating the youthful first-term man from the others, of specially treating juvenile crime, are little known in the South. When a twelve-year-old black boy is sent to the chain gang by a white judge, the community suffers. With regard to all those penal institutions one might share the feelings of the good Northern lady, when told that her grandson had been sentenced to the penitentiary for ten years: " What did they do that for? why, he won't be contented there three weeks! "

This sympathy with the criminal the governors of the Southern states appear to feel, as is shown by some astonishing statistics. When Governor Vardaman went out of office January 1, 1908, he pardoned 8 white men and 18 Negroes, most of them convicted of murder or manslaughter, and 11 of them life men. A Memphis paper has tabulated the state pardons for a period of twelve months, and if the results are accurate, they show 1 in Wisconsin, 22 in Massachusetts, 81 in Georgia, 168 in Alabama, and over 400 in Arkansas. Just how the Negroes get sufficient political influence to secure pardons is one of the serious questions in Southern jurisprudence. For these lavish pardons the Whites are wholly responsible, for from them spring all the governors and pardoning boards.

The same responsibility rests on the Whites for the inefficiency of criminal justice and for the mediæval prison system. The North might fairly plead that its efforts to reform its judicial and punitive system are resisted by the lower elements of society, which have such power through choosing prosecutors and judges and legislators, in framing laws and constitutions, that the better elements cannot have things their own way. Not so in the South, where the Superior Race has absolute control of the making of law and the administering of justice, and the treatment of prisoners. Every judge in the South, except a few little justices of the peace, is a white man. Negroes, although still eligible to jury service, are rarely impaneled, even for the trial of a Negro. Negro testimony is received with due caution; hardly any court will accept the testimony of one black against one white man. For failures in the administration of justice, for unwillingness to try men for homicide, for technicalities in procedure, for hesitancy of juries, the Superior Race is wholly responsible. The system is bad simply because the white people who are in control of the Southern state governments are willing that it should be bad. With all the machinery of legislation, and of the courts in its possession, the white race still resorts to forms of violence which sometimes strike an innocent man, and always brutalize the community, and lead to a contempt for the ordinary forms of justice. The place for the white people to begin a real repression of crime is by punishing their criminals without enslaving them.

CHAPTER XV

LYNCHING

THE defects in the administration of justice in the South are complicated by a recognized system of punishment of criminals and supposed criminals by other persons than officers of the law—a system to which the term Lynch Law is often applied. In part it is an effort to supplement the law of the commonwealths; in part it is a protest against the law's delay; in greater part a defiance of law and authority and impartial justice.

In its mildest form this system of irresponsible jurisprudence takes the form of notices to leave the country, followed by whipping or other violence less than murderous, if the warning be disregarded. Such a method owes all its force to the belief that it proceeds from an organized and therefore a powerful race of people. Next in seriousness come the race riots of which there were many examples during the Reconstruction era; and occasionally they burst into serious race conflicts, of which half a dozen have occurred in the last decade. The responsibility rests in greater measure on that race which has the habit of calculated and concerted action: reckless Negroes can always make trouble by shooting at the Whites; but the laws, the officers of justice, the militia, the courts, are in the hands of the white people. Since they are always able to protect themselves by their better organization, their command of the police, and the conviction in the minds of both races that the white man will always come out victorious, most troubles that start with the Negroes could easily be dealt with, but for a panic terror of negro risings which harks back to slavery times. It is very easy to stampede Southern communities by such rumors. When, in 1908, six armed Negroes were arrested in Muskogee, Okla., telegrams went all over the country to the effect that a race war was on, and two companies of militia were ordered out; but apparently there was not a glimmer of real trouble. Negroes have repeatedly been driven out of small places. For instance, in August, 1907, in Onancock, on the eastern shore of Virginia, there was a dispute over a bill for a dollar and a quarter which ended with the banishment of a number of Negroes. In the year 1898 there was a similar riot in Wilmington, N. C., and several thousand Negroes were either ejected or left afterwards in terror. The trouble here began in excitement over the elections.

By far the most serious of these occurrences was the so-called race riot at Atlanta, September 22, 1906, caused primarily by that intense hostility to the Negroes which is to be found among town youths; and secondarily by some aggravated crimes on the part of Negroes, and the equally aggravated crime of a newspaper, the *Atlanta Evening News,* which, by exaggerating the truth and adding lies, inflamed the public mind; on the night before the riot it called upon the people of Atlanta to join a league of men who " will endeavor to prevent the crimes, if possible, but failing, will aid in punishing the criminals."

The whole affair has been examined by several competent observers, but the essential facts may be taken from the report of a committee of business men of Atlanta, who went into the matter at the time, and who declared that of the persons killed, " There was not a single vagrant. They were earning wages in useful work; . . . they were supporting themselves and their families. . . . Of the wounded, ten are white and sixty colored. Of the dead, two are white and ten are colored." This was not a riot, but a massacre, for which the Superior Race is responsible; and from every point of view it was damaging to the whole South. It kept back foreign emigrants, it deeply discouraged the best of the Negroes in Atlanta and elsewhere; it gave rein to the passions of the mob. Considering that nobody was killed from among the mob, it seems like a ferocious practical joke that scores of Negroes were arrested and charged with murder, while not a single one of the hundreds of real murderers has ever received the slightest punishment. Who can wonder at the grief and anguish of DuBois's "Litany of Atlanta!" Every large place is liable to disturbance; Northern cities have had race riots, and are likely to have more. The recent assaults on and murders of Negroes in Springfield, Ohio, and Springfield, Ill., are not different in spirit from those in the South; and though there were plenty of indictments, the leader of the latter mob was acquitted on his trial—a result which was reflected in the famous Cairo mob of 1909.

What progress can be made in breaking up the savage and criminal instincts of the Negro when he sees the same instincts in the Superior Race, which is in a position to do him harm? If the Negroes for any cause should in any Southern city, where they are in the majority, take possession of the streets and hunt white people to death as was done in Atlanta, it would bring on a race war which would devastate the whole South; and the lower race would be severely punished for aspiring to the same fashions in gunshots as its superiors. As a commercial traveler said on the general subject of race relations: "You do not understand how the young fellows in the South feel; when any trouble comes, they want to kill the nigger, whether he has done anything or not."

The third and most frequent form of race violence is lynching, a practice obscured by a mass of conventional and improbable statements. The subject has been set in its proper light in an impartial and scientific study by Professor Cutler entitled "Lynch Law," based on a compilation of statistics which come down to 1903. He sweeps away three fourths of the usual statements on the subject, first of all disproving the allegation that lynching is a comparatively recent practice brought about by negro crimes since the Civil War. The term Lynch Law has been traced back to Colonel Charles Lynch, of Virginia, who, in Revolutionary times, presided at rude assemblies which whipped Tories until they were willing to shout "Hurrah for Liberty!" Till about 1830 lynching never meant killing; it was applied only to whippings or to tarring and feathering. In the frontier conditions of the South and West, the habit grew up of killing desperadoes by mob law, as, for instance, the celebrated clearing out of five gamblers at Vicksburg, Miss., in 1835. This process was also applied to some murderers, both Whites and Negroes.

Professor Cutler also disposes of the assertion that the most serious offense for which lynching is applied was unknown previous to emancipation. In 1823, a Negro in Maryland was badly beaten, though not killed, for a supposed attack upon a white woman. In 1827 one was burned at the stake in Alabama for killing a white man. From that time on, lynching of blacks continued in every Southern state—commonly for murder, in a few cases for insurrection, in at least nine ascertained cases previous to the Civil War for violence to white women. It is evident, therefore, that the extremest crime had been sometimes committed, and the extremest punishment exacted by mob violence before the slaves were set free.

The lynching of Negroes was kept up after the war, and carried into a system by the Ku Klux Klan and later White Caps, though usually applied by them for political reasons. About 1880 lynching of Negroes began to increase, nominally because of more frequent rapes of white women; and to this day one often hears it said: "Lynchings never occur except for the one crime." In the twenty-two years from 1882 to 1903, Cutler has recorded 3,337 cases of lynchings, an average of 150 a year, rising to the number of 235 in 1892. In 1903 there were 125 persons lynched and 125 executed legally. Of these lynchings, 1,997 took place in the Southern states, 363 in the Western states, 105 in the Eastern states, and not a single one in New England. Of the 3,337 lynchings, 1,169 were of Whites (109 for rape) and 2,168 were Negroes, thus completely disposing of the notion that this practice either began because of negro crime, or was continued as a safeguard against it. Of the blacks lynched, 783 were charged with murder; 707 with violence to women; 104 with arson; 101 with theft; and from that on down to such serious crimes as writing a letter, slapping a child, making an insolent reply, giving evidence or refusing to give evidence. A Negro was lynched in 1908 for killing a constable's horse.

The common notion that rape of white women, the most serious crime committed by Negroes, is on the increase, is also exploded by these statistics, which show that the proportion, which has been as high as one half of all lynchings, has come down to about one fourth. It may be said, therefore, without fear of contradiction that lynching did not originate in offenses by Negroes, is not justified by any increase of crime, and is applied to a multitude of offenses, some of them simply trivial.

Successful attempts have been made to lynch Negroes in Northern states, and in 1903 one was burned at the stake, in Wilmington, Del., which, however, is a former slave state, and the last to adhere to the whipping-post. Lynching has also much diminished in the West, so that it is becoming more and more a Southern crime. In 1903, 75 of the 84 lynchings were in the South, in 1907 the total lynchings had come down to 63, of which 42 were in the four states of Louisiana, Mississippi, Alabama, and Georgia, and only 2 in the North. The proportion of causes of lynchings remained about the same: murder, 18; violence to women, 12; attempted violence, 11; miscellaneous causes, 22.

The methods of the lynchers are very simple. In 1906 a white man, accused of murdering his brother, on whose case the jury had disagreed, was dragged out of jail and shot. In a great many cases the supposed criminal is hunted down by what is called a " posse "—really a self-appointed body of furious neighbors; and very seldom is there the semblance of investigation. If the offender is lodged in jail, that sanctuary of the law is often invaded. In August, 1906, a mob of three thousand men, incited by a person who afterwards proved to be a released convict, broke open the jail at Salisbury, N. C., in despite of addresses by the mayor and United States senator, took out and killed three supposed negro criminals. Occasionally, when a criminal has been tried, convicted, and is awaiting execution, he is taken out and lynched, for the excitement of seeing the man die, and perhaps from fear that he will be pardoned.

Naturally, in this quick method, mistakes sometimes occur. At Brookhaven, Miss., on January 2, 1908, a Negro was lynched for killing a white man; a few days later they caught the actual murderer, but consoled themselves with the belief that inasmuch as the first Negro was wounded when captured, the presumption was that he must have killed some other white man. A few days later, at Dothan, Ala., a Negro was taken out, hanged, and two hundred shots fired at him, but was found the next morning alive and unwounded, and was allowed to escape. In a recent case at Atlanta a Negro positively identified by the victim of a most serious crime was allowed to go to trial, and was acquitted, because the court believed him innocent, and the woman subsequently identified another man.

How does it come about that these mobs, composed invariably of white men and none others, cannot be put down by the white authorities? The first reason is that there are no rural police in the South to make prompt arrests and protect prisoners; the sheriffs upon whom the custody of such persons depends are chosen by popular election, and usually have no backbone; one of them who had actually lodged his prisoners in jail said that he hated to do it, and didn't know how he could meet his neighbors. Jailors commonly give up their keys after a little protest; there are few cases where a determined sheriff, armed and ready to do his duty, could not quell a mob; but what can be expected of a sheriff who turns over a prisoner to the mob in order that they may "investigate" his crime? Occasionally a sheriff shows some pluck, and in December, 1906, President Roosevelt singled out for federal appointment a sheriff who had lost his reëlection because he had opposed a mob. Governors are sometimes very weak-kneed; a few years ago the governor of North Carolina delivered up to a mob a colored boy who had had such confidence in the Superior Race as to come to the executive mansion and ask for protection. At Annapolis, in 1908, neither the sheriff, jailor, nor municipal authorities made any effort to prevent the taking out of a prisoner; in Chattanooga, Sheriff Shipp, who permitted a Negro to be taken out of his hands and lynched, though the sheriff had been served by telegram with an order from a justice of the Supreme Court directing him to protect the criminal, was reëlected by a large majority; and apparently did not lose popularity when a year later he was sentenced to ninety days' confinement for contempt of court.

In all the Southern states the last state resort for keeping the peace is the militia, and there have recently been two scandalous instances where these volunteer soldiers have permitted themselves to be overrun by a mob, giving up their guns without an effort to fire a shot. In one of these cases it was recorded that " No effort was made to hurt any of the soldiers however, as it was plain to the crowd that they had gained their point." At Brookhaven, Miss., in 1908, the officer commanding the militia excused himself because the sheriff had not asked him to order his men to fire. These brave soldiers, these high-toned Southern gentlemen, these military heroes, called out for the special purpose of protecting a prisoner, would not draw a trigger!

The militia of course are not cowards, they are simply sympathizers with the mob; and throughout the South, in the press, and from the lips of many otherwise high-minded people, lynching is freely justified. Witness a cor-

212

oner's jury in Charlotte, N. C.: "We, the . . . jury to inquire into the cause of the death of Tom Jones, find that he came to his death by gunshot wounds, inflicted by parties unknown to the jury, obviously by an outraged public acting in defense of their homes, wives, daughters, and children. In view of the enormity of the crime committed by said Tom Jones, . . . we think they would have been recreant to their duty as good citizens had they acted otherwise." The rector of St. Luke's Church, Jacksonville, says: "I write as an upholder of law and order; as one who deprecates and denounces mob law; but I write as one who holds that law is but the will of the majority in a democracy, and that will is that every time a negro criminally assaults, or attempts to assault, a white woman, he shall be dealt with by mob law, which is law after all. Only I would say, let that mob be certain, 'beyond a reasonable doubt,' that they have the right man." Listen to the *Atlanta Georgian:* "Some good citizens will say they are shocked, and deplore these evil conditions, and the demoralization they are going to produce, and all that, but they really ain't shocked, although they think they are, and under proper provocation they would be lynchers themselves." Even the late D. H. Chamberlain, once Reconstruction governor of South Carolina, says: "Practically I come very near to saying that I do not blame the South for resorting to lynching for this crime," and Benjamin R. Tillman, Senator of the United States, has publicly declared: "I will lead a mob to lynch a man at any time who has attacked a woman, whether he be white or black," and that it would probably be necessary "to send some more niggers to hell."

The standard published reason for this acquiescence in lynching is that the usual course of law is inadequate;

people point to the legal delays and the technicalities of the courts, courts organized by white men, held by white judges, influenced by white counsel, before a white jury. They claim that lynching is a rude sort of primitive justice, " an ultimate sanction " which is simply a speedier form of law, though mobs are notoriously easily confused as to persons and circumstances. They consider lynching necessary in order to prevent the taking of testimony in open court in cases of rape, a necessity which any legislature could obviate. They plead that lynching is the only penalty which will keep the Negro in bounds, although there are such strings of lynchings as show conclusively that the publicity given to sickening details makes lynching simply a breeder of crime. In the little town of Brookhaven, Miss., there were two lynchings in the first eight weeks of 1908. The Southern defenders of lynching set forth the solemnity of this form of execution, closing their eyes to the fearful barbarities which have accompanied many cases and are likely to occur any day.

The most cogent reason for the practice of lynching is that it gives an opportunity for the exercise of a deep-seated race hostility. Most of the murders and other crimes which lead to lynchings happen where Whites and Negroes are living close together. A lynching is an opportunity for the most furious and brutal passions of which humanity is capable, under cover of a moral duty, and without the slightest danger of a later accountability. Spectators go to a lynching, as perhaps they went to the witch trial in Salem, or a treason case under Lord Jeffreys, to get a shuddering sensation. Kindred of the injured ones are invited to come to the front with hot irons and gimlets; special trains have repeatedly been furnished, on

214

request to the railroads, in order to carry parties of lynchers; in several instances the burning at the stake of Negroes has been advertised by telegraph, and special trains have been put on to bring spectators. After the *auto da fé* is over, white people scramble in the ashes for bits of bone. Within a few months a black woman was burned at the stake by a mob, though everybody knew she had committed absolutely no offense except to accompany her husband when he ran away after committing a murder. These are not incidents of every lynching, they are not condoned by those Southerners who disapprove of lynching; but when you have turned a tiger loose and given him a taste of blood, you are not entitled to say that you have no responsibility for innocent people whom he may devour.

The whole fabric of defense of lynching, which in some cases and for some crimes is justified by the large majority of educated white men and women in the South, may be exploded into fragments by a single test. If lynching under any circumstances is for the good of the community, why not legalize it? Why does not some state come out of the ranks of modern civilized communities in which public courts replace private vengeance and torture has ceased to be a part of judicial process, and enact that in every town the adult men shall constitute a tribunal which—on the suggestion that somebody has committed a crime—shall apprehend the suspect, and, with the hastiest examination of the facts, shall forthwith condemn him to be hanged, shot, or burned, and shall constitute themselves executioners, after due notice to the railroads to bring school children in special trains to witness the proceedings, and with the right to distribute the bones and ashes to their friends as souvenirs? Then the whole proceeding may be inscribed on the public records, so that later generations may see the care that has been taken to prevent lawlessness.

It would be unjust to leave this subject as though Southern people spent their lives in breathing out threatenings and slaughter. With all the conversation about homicide, all the columns of lurid dispatches about lynchings, in which again white people pen the dispatches and white editors vivify them, the everyday atmosphere seems peaceful enough; the traveler, the ordinary business and professional man, feels no sense of insecurity. Still one wonders just what was in the mind of the Alabamian who, after driving a Yankee a hundred miles through a wild part of his state, prepared to return by another way, but remarked: " I wouldn't be afraid to drive right back over the same road that we came." The chance that a respectable man in the South, who attends to his own business, will be shot, is very much greater than in any other civilized country; but powerful influences are at work to bring about better things. There are some indications that the Negroes will be compelled to give up carrying weapons, and then, perhaps, some of the Whites can also be disarmed. Sensible people deplore the insecurity of life. As for race violence, nobody who knows the South can doubt that the feeling of hatred and hostility to the Negro as a Negro, perhaps to the white man as a white man, is sharper than ever before; but that is the feeling of those members of both races who have no responsibility, of the idle town loafer, of the assistant plantation manager who could make more money if his hands would work better. On the other side stand the upbuilders of the commonwealth, the educators, the professional classes, the plantation owners, the capitalists, most of whom wish the Negro well, oppose violence and injustice, and are willing to coöperate with the best element of the Negroes in freeing the South from its two worst enemies—the black brute, and the white amateur executioner.

CHAPTER XVI

I N every discussion of Southern affairs an important
thing to reckon with is a fixed belief that the South
is the most prosperous part of the country, which fits
in with the conviction that it has long surpassed all other
parts of the world in civilization, in military ardor, and
in the power to rise out of the sufferings of a conquered
people. This belief is hard to reconcile with the grim fact
that the South under slavery was the poorest section of the
country. Visitors just before the outbreak of the Civil
War, such as Olmsted, and Russell, the correspondent of
the *London Times*, were struck by the poverty of the South,
which had few cities, short and poor railroads, scanty
manufacturing establishments, and in general small accumulations of the buildings and especially of the stocks of
goods which are the readiest evidences of wealth. Some
rich families there were with capital not only to buy slaves,
but to build railroads and cities; and when the Civil War
broke out there was in service a quantity of independent
banking capital. A delusion of great wealth was created
by the listing as taxable property of slaves to the amount
of at least two thousand millions. Although the legal right
to appropriate the proceeds of the labor of the Negroes
was transferable, it could go only to some of the 300,000
slaveholding families; and no bill of sale or tax list could

make wealth out of this control of capacity to produce in the future; or if it was wealth, then the North with its larger laboring population of far larger productivity was entitled to add five or six thousand millions to its estimate of wealth. The South was made richer and not poorer by unloosing the bonds of the negro laborer.

All the world knows that from 1865 to 1880 the South was comparatively a poor community, not because of the loss of slaves, but from the exhaustion of capital by the Civil War, and the disturbance of productive labor. The opportunity for a fair comparative test did not come till the region settled down again; and then the output in proportion to the working population remained decidedly small when compared with European countries, and still smaller when compared with the Northern states.

During the last quarter century, however, the South has experienced the greatest prosperity that it has ever known. Its progress since 1883 has been such that an editorial in a Southern newspaper says: "Leaving her mines and her mills out of the question, the great South is rich in the products of her fields alone—richer than all the empires of history. She is self-contained, and what is more, she is self-possessed, and she has set her face resolutely against the things which will hurt her." Since that statement was printed the material conditions of the South have improved, population has steadily increased; and the resources of the section have more than kept pace with it, manufactures have wonderfully developed, industry has been diversified, railroads and trolley lines are extended by Southern capital; the production of coal has been enormously increased; the utilization of the abundant water powers for electrical purposes is beginning; most of the older cities have been enlarged; and new centers of population have sprung up. The traveler by the main highways from Washington through Atlanta to New Orleans, or from Cincinnati through Chattanooga and Memphis to Galveston, sees a section abounding in prosperity.

What are the sources of this wealth? First of all comes the soil; beginning with the black lands in western Georgia and running through the lower Mississippi valley to the black lands of Texas, lies one of the richest bodies of land in the world, comparable with the plains of Eastern China. It is a soil incredibly rich and, once cleared of trees, easy of cultivation; blessed with a large rainfall and abundance of streams. This belt, in which the greater part of the Southern cotton is raised, is the foundation of the prosperity of the South, which for that reason is likely to continue permanently a farming community.

These rich soils are not to be had for the asking, and fully improved lands, especially the few plantations that are undrained, bring prices up to $100 an acre or more, but uncleared land is still very cheap, and away from the Black Belt may be had at low prices, especially in the piney woods regions, which when fertilized are productive and profitable.

Among the most valuable Southern lands are those under culture for fruits and " truck." This is one of the few methods of intensive agriculture practiced in the South. Success in such farming depends on climate, accessibility to market, and skill. A belt of land in Eastern Texas which has good railroad communication with the North, has suddenly become one of the most prosperous parts of the South because its season is several weeks earlier than that of most of its competitors. Truck farming bids fair to change the conditions of the Sea

Islands, of the Carolinas and of Georgia, since they are in easy and swift communication with the great Northern markets.

Scattered everywhere throughout the South are enormous areas of swamp land, partly in the deltas of the rivers, and partly caught between the hills. Under various acts of Congress 8,000,000 acres of so-called "swamp lands" were given to the states including much rich bottom land. The South is now making a demand upon the Federal Government to assume toward those lands a responsibility akin to that for the irrigated tracts in the Far West, and it seems likely that either a Federal or State system will undertake the reclamation of large tracts. The legislature of Florida, for instance, has authorized the levy of a drainage tax for the drainage of the everglades, where millions of acres could be made available. At present all the Federal projects under way, though they involve 2,-000,000 acres and $70,000,000 of expenditure, are in the Far West and on the Pacific Slope.

The fundamental fact that the South is mainly agricultural is brought out by the statistics of occupations in 1900. The greater part of the population of both white and black races is on the soil. By the census of 1900, in sixteen states counted Southern, thirty-eight per cent of the population were bread-winners. Out of the total population of 23,000,000 there were 8,100,000 persons engaged in gainful occupations, of whom 814,000 were in large cities and the remaining 7,300,000 in small cities and the country. The rapid growth of towns and small cities is due to the prosperity of the open country; and hence the large city is less important and less likely to absorb the rural population than is the case in the North.

Except the Pacific Northwest no part of the Union is

so rich in timber as the South. Until about ten years ago, enormous areas of timber land were so far from railroads that nobody could think of lumbering them; now that the hills of Louisiana, Mississippi, Alabama, Georgia, and the Carolinas are penetrated with main lines, now that branches are pushed out and that logging trams stretch still farther, few spots lie more than fifteen miles from rails. Before sawmills arrive, men can earn fair day wages at cutting railway ties and hauling them as much as fifteen miles, so that the poor land-owners have one unfailing cash resource. Up to the financial depression of 1907, lumbering of every kind was very prosperous; new mills were under construction and a large amount of labor found employment. In 1908 many concerns were shut down, and planters were rejoiced because Negroes were coming back to them for employment. The check to lumbering is only temporary. The South still furnishes more than one third of the total product of the country; and Louisiana comes next to the state of Washington in the amount of annual cut. But, as a native puts it, " Timber is a'gittin' gone "; and in ten years most of the Southern states will approach the condition of Michigan and Wisconsin in the decline of that industry. Nevertheless, one may still ride or drive for days through splendid pine forests that have hardly seen an ax. In most places when the timber is cut, farming comes in, and that is the cause of the extraordinary prosperity of the " piney woods " belt, through southern Georgia and Alabama; where the farmer of a few years ago was making a scanty living, he is now able to sell his timber, to clear the land, and to begin cotton raising on a profitable scale.

The South is conscious of the wastage of its timber resources, for the cut is now advancing far up on the highest slopes of the mountain ranges; hence the Southern members of Congress have joined with New Englanders in supporting a bill for an Appalachian Forest Reserve, which would set apart considerable areas at intervals from Mount Washington in New Hampshire to Mount Mitchell in North Carolina, to be administered by the federal government in about the same fashion as the similar reserves in the Rocky Mountains and the Sierra Nevada and Cascade Ranges. This movement is greatly strengthened by the manufacturers, who believe that the water powers require a conservation of the upper forests.

Growing trees are available not only for lumber and railroad ties, but for turpentine, and any two of these processes, or even all three, may be going on at the same time. On a tract of pine land, no matter where, usually the first process is to box the trees for turpentine, and the men in the business sometimes buy the land outright, but oftener simply pay a royalty. For this privilege the old-fashioned price was a cent a tree, which would be about $40 or $50 for a 160-acre tract; but lately farmers have received as much as a thousand dollars for the turpentine on their farms. The box or cut in the trunk can be enlarged upward every year for five years; then if the tree is left untouched for six or seven years it may be back-boxed on the other side and will yield again for five or six years; so that it takes about twenty years to exhaust the turpentine from a given area. The flow from the incision, collected in a hollow cut out of the wood, or by a better modern method of spigots and cups, not unlike that used for maple trees, is periodically collected and carried to the still, where the turpentine is distilled over, and the heavier residue makes the commercial resin. At the prices of the last few years this "naval stores" industry has been profitable and millions of trees are still being tapped.

In mining, the South has no such position as in timber. The coal product is respectable and growing—in 1906 nearly 40 million tons, which was a ninth of the national product. Iron ore is also plentiful; and lead and zinc are abundant in Missouri. Of the output of more than a hundred millions of precious metals, not half a million can be traced to the South—and there are no valuable copper mines.

" Varsification, that's what we want," was the dictum of the sage of a country store in the South; and diversification the South has certainly attained. The annual money value of manufactured products has now become considerably greater than of the agricultural products, though of course the crops are the raw materials to many manufactures. In 1880 the manufactured products of the South were under 500 million dollars, or one eleventh of the total of the United States; in 1900 they had risen to 1,500 millions, or about one ninth of the total; and in 1905 they were 2,200 millions—a seventh of the total.

The most striking advance in manufactures has been in iron, the production of pig rising from 1,600,000 tons in 1888 to 3,100,000 in 1906, a seventh of the national total; a prosperity due in part to the close proximity of excellent ore and coal. But the production in other parts of the Union has increased even more rapidly, so that the proportion of iron made in the South is smaller than at any time in twenty years. One difficulty of the manufacture is that it requires besides the crude labor of the Negroes a large amount of skilled labor, which cannot be furnished by the Poor Whites or the Mountain Whites.

Another large manufacture is that of tobacco which is

224

grown in quantities in many of the Southern states, particularly in North Carolina and Kentucky, the great centers of the tobacco industry being Richmond, Durham (North Carolina), and Louisville. The tobacco factories are one of the few forms of manufacture in which Negroes are employed for anything except crude raw labor.

In distilled spirits the South produces nearly a third of the whole annual output—the greater part in Kentucky; the Lower South does not provide for the slaking of its own thirst; and of the milder alcoholic drinks consumed in the whole country, the South furnishes only about a tenth.

This success in manufactures is due in part to cheap power, for both fuel and water power are abundant and easily available; and since the South requires little fuel for domestic purposes, it has the larger store for its factories and railroads. The South has also become a large producer of petroleum, phosphates, and sulphur, and in its bays and adjacent coasts has the material for a valuable fishing industry.

For carrying on these various lines of business, the South is indebted in part to Northern and foreign capital; but very large enterprises are supported entirely by the accumulations of Southern capitalists; and the savings of the region are turned backward through a good banking system into renewed investments. The South before the Civil War was probably better supplied with small banks lending to farmers than in any other part of the Union, and in the last ten years a similar system has been again worked out. There are nearly 1,500 national banks in the South, of which two thirds have been founded since 1900; and in addition, there are numerous joint stock and private banks. That the business is sound is shown by the fact that practically all the Southern banks weathered the crisis of

1907, which was more severe there than in the North. In a very remote rural parish of Louisiana, in a small and seedy county seat, is a little bank opened in November, 1907, which, within two months, had accumulated $65,000 of deposits, and was still enlarging. Through these widely distributed banks capital is supplied to small industries and to opportunities of profit which would otherwise be neglected.

One needs actually to pass over the face of the South in order to realize how much progress has been made in transportation facilities. That section has always been alive to the necessity of getting its crops to market, and Charleston has for a century been at work on communications with the interior; and the Pedee Canal, the first commercial canal in the United States, was constructed in 1795 to bring the crops to that port. The navigable reaches of the Southern rivers up to the "fall line" were early utilized for light-draught steamers, of which some still survive. Turnpike roads were also built into the interior of the state; and the railroad from Charleston to Hamburg—140 miles— completed in the thirties, was the longest continuous line of railroad then in existence. Down to the Civil War Charleston had an ambitious scheme for a direct line across the mountains to Cincinnati. The effort to keep transportation up to the times for various reasons was not successful; settlements were sparse, exports other than cotton scanty, distances great, free capital limited.

In the last ten years the South has seen a wonderful advance in railroad transportation. States like Louisiana and Georgia are fairly gridironed with railroads, and new ones building all the time; indeed, in the "Delta" of Mississippi a railroad can live on local business if it has a belt of its own twelve miles wide.

Nevertheless, the present railroad system in the South, comprising about 80,000 miles, has been mostly built since 1880. This system includes several lines from the Middle West to the seaboard, so that Baltimore, the James River ports, New Orleans, and Galveston are enriched by commerce passing through their ports to regions outside the Southern states. Nevertheless, as will be seen in the next chapter, this means that the great distributing centers in the Union are outside the limits of the South.

The progress of the country is measured also by the great improvement in accommodation for travelers. The testimony is general that down to about 1885 there were, outside half a dozen cities, no really good hotels to be found in the South; now you may travel from end to end of the region and find clean, comfortable, and modern accommodations in almost every stopping place. The demands of the drummers are in part responsible for this gratifying state of things.

The country roads do not share in the advance. Nominally the South has over 600,000 miles of public highway, but little of it has even been improved. Some of the old pikes have gone to ruin, others are still kept up by tolls; but in many regions which have been well settled and thriving for a century and a half there is a dearth of bridges, and in bad weather the roads are almost impassable. So far, the difficulty is not much relieved by trolley lines. The cities are well supplied and some of them have a superior system; but few parts of the South have such a string of populous places as will justify interurban lines, exceptions being the Richmond-Norfolk and Dallas-Fort Worth systems. The trolley lines have been much developed by a Northern syndicate which, under the name of Stone & Webster, has made a business of buying or building and operating electric plants, many of them with elaborate water power; and the current is distributed for power, light, and transportation. Stone & Webster's lines can be found all over the Union, as in Minneapolis and in the state of Washington, as well as in the South. The capital of the trolley roads in 1906 was 3,765 millions, or a fifth of the total trolley investment in the United States.

At the best points of contact between rail and water transportation great port enterprises are springing up. Galveston is the only port along the whole coast of Texas with easily obtainable deep water, and the Government has spent great sums in improving it, while the city has made the most gallant effort to rebuild and fortify itself against the invasion of the sea which a few years ago almost destroyed it. New Orleans feels itself the natural port of the lower Mississippi valley, and the Eads system of jetties keeps the mouth of the river open, though there is not water enough to float the great steamers that come into the large Atlantic ports, and the wharf charges are heavy; the actual commerce of New Orleans—exports and imports together—was in 1907 $28,000,000 less than that of Galveston. Inasmuch as New Orleans is a hundred miles from the open sea, an effort has been made to provide capital to build a gulf port about fifty miles to the eastward, but so far little progress has been made. The city of New Orleans has shown unusual enterprise in building a public belt line railroad ten miles long, intended to connect with all the roads entering the city; and the city thus steps alongside Cincinnati as the owner of a veritable municipal steam railroad. Between these ports there is unceasing rivalry, and the depth of water on the bar outside Galveston, or at the mouth of the Mississippi, is as interesting to the Southern business man as the bulletin of a football game is to a Northerner. Texas will prove to you by science, logic, and prophecy that no deep-draught vessel can get into New Orleans, or pay the awful port charges after it arrives; the Louisianian is confident that the next typhoon will silt up those Texan lagoon harbors which have no great river behind to scour them out.

Mobile, which is a place with increasing foreign commerce, can never hope to lead deep water to its present wharves, but about twenty-two miles below the city is an opportunity to bring large ships nearly inshore, and that is likely to be the future port of Mobile. Pensacola is the special favorite of the Louisville & Nashville Railroad, but seems to have no advantages which will bring it ahead of its neighbor Mobile. Of the lower Atlantic ports, Fernandina, Brunswick, Savannah, Charleston, and Wilmington are all limited in the depth of water, and several of them require difficult river navigation. The deep-water ports of Baltimore on the Chesapeake, and Norfolk, Portsmouth, and Newport News on the lower James, are on the extreme borders of the South and depend for their prosperity chiefly on Western commerce.

The transportation business of the South, as in other parts of the Union, has drifted into the hands of a comparatively few large corporations. The Southern Railroad, the Atlantic Coast Line, the Seaboard Air Line, and the Louisville & Nashville include nearly all the railroads between Virginia and Mississippi. The Baltimore & Ohio, Chesapeake & Ohio, Norfolk & Western, and the new Virginia Railroad connect the tide water of Virginia and North Carolina with the West. The Louisville & Nashville, Illinois Central, the Missouri Pacific and Queen and Crescent roads stretch southward from the Middle Western states to the Gulf. In Texas three or four railway systems compete for the business between the upper trans-Mississippi country and the Gulf, and there is a bewildering complex of branch lines. The net result is that the South outside the mountains is gridironed with railways. The areas more than ten miles from a railroad line in the South are now comparatively small. For this reason may be expected a more rapid development of the resources and wealth of that section in the next ten years than in the last decade.

CHAPTER XVII

WEALTH the South possesses—large wealth, growing wealth, greater wealth than that section has ever before approached. So agreeable is this state of things that Southern writers are inclined not only to set forth their prosperity but to claim that theirs is the most prosperous part of the whole country and is soon to become the richest. As Edmonds puts it in his " Facts about the South ": " Against the poverty, the inexperience, the discredit and doubt at home and abroad of ourselves and our section of 1880, the South, thrilled with energy and hope, stands to-day recognized by the world as that section which of all others in this country or elsewhere has the greatest potentialities for the creation of wealth and the profitable employment of its people." The Southern statements of the poverty of the South from 1865 to 1880 are more easily verified. The tracks of armies outside Virginia and parts of Tennessee were narrow; but at the end of the war the South had exhausted all its movable capital; the banks were broken; the state and Confederate bonds worthless; the railroads ruined; the cities disconsolate. And the labor system was, for a time, much disturbed, though never disrupted. As Henry Watterson, of Kentucky, puts it: " The South! The South! It is no problem at all. The whole story of the South may be summed up in a sentence:

231

She was rich, she lost her riches; she was poor and in bondage; she was set free, and she had to go to work; she went to work, and she is richer than ever before. You see it was a ground-hog case. The soil was here, the climate was here, but along with them was a curse, the curse of slavery."

The immense increase of wealth and productivity since 1880 is equally unquestionable. When it comes to the claim that it is the most prosperous part of the world, it cannot be accepted offhand. The fact that the South is well off does not prove that it is better off than its neighbors; the wealth and prosperity of the South are always limited by the character of its labor. Calculation of profits, adding of bank balances, cutting of coupons, have to some degree drawn men's minds away from the race question; but on the other hand the demand for labor and the losses of dividends or of opportunities to make money because the labor is inefficient are ever renewed causes of exasperation. At all times the South is subject to reverses like those of other regions. The crisis of 1907 hit that section hard by cutting down the demand for timber, minerals, iron, and other staples, and was one of the factors in a decline in cotton which touched the pocket nerve of the South; and the railroads felt the loss of business. Still, most Southern enterprises weathered the storm, and in 1909 the tide of prosperity is mounting again.

If it be true that the South is the most prosperous part of the world, a disagreeable responsibility falls upon somebody for having less than the best schools, libraries, buildings, roads, and other appliances of civilization; if it be not true, there must be some defect in the social or industrial system which out of such splendid materials produces less than a fair proportion of the world's wealth. To be sure a section or a state might lag behind in production and yet forge ahead in education, in the harmony of social classes, in respect for law, in good order. Switzerland is not a rich country, but it is an advanced country. The claims of superior productiveness can with difficulty be tested. The relative status of the two sections in intellectual and governmental ways has been examined in earlier chapters and the South cannot claim supremacy there. A similar comparison shall now be made as to the relative production and accumulation of the two sections.

A criterion of wealth much relied upon by Southern writers is the movement of commerce. We are told that two fifths of the inward and outward movement of foreign trade passes through Southern ports. The truth is that in 1907 that figure was $883,000,000 as against $2,432,000,-000 in all Northern Atlantic, Lake and Pacific ports. The bulk of this Southern business, however, is in exports—$742,000,000—a third of the total. Not a tenth of all the imports came into Southern ports, and three fourths of that through the three ports of Baltimore, Galveston, and New Orleans, from all which a part goes into non-Southern states. The explanation is that through the Southern ports pour the staples, but that the return cargoes, especially of manufactures, go to Northern ports, even though part of it is later distributed to the South. A second correction is due to the fact that about $536,000,000 of the exports goes through the five ports of Baltimore, Newport News, Norfolk and Portsmouth, New Orleans, and Galveston, all of which are entrepots for immense trade originating beyond the limits of the South. For instance, New Orleans and Galveston together shipped 24 million bushels of the 147 millions of wheat exports—practically not a Southern crop. Even in such an unreckoned increment of income as the federal pension lists, the South is less forward than the North, which drew 113 millions a year against 25 millions in the whole South and 11 millions in the seceded states—most of that to colored soldiers.

The relative wealth of the two sections is best measured not by foreign trade but by internal production and by public income and expenditure, calculated on a per-capita basis. Of course conditions vary greatly from state to state; in Alabama there is steady farm work most of the year, while in North Dakota the winter is a time of comparative leisure; California uses agricultural machinery, South Carolina depends chiefly on hand tools; Wyoming is so young that it has had little time to accumulate capital, Tennessee has large accumulations. It would be unfair to compare Arkansas with Connecticut, or Illinois with Florida, on a strictly per-capita basis. The only way to equalize conditions for a fair comparison is to take groups of states and set them against other groups of equivalent population and of similar interests, so that local errors may neutralize each other.

As a basis for such a comparison of resources, three sets of tables have been made up. The first sets apart the group of eleven seceding states with 17,000,000 people (West Virginia not included) as being typically Southern; and places against them a group of agricultural states extending from Indiana to Oklahoma, also containing 17,000,000 people. The second tables include the whole South—viz., the fifteen former slaveholding states (excluding West Virginia), together with the District of Columbia, including a population of about 28,000,000 people; to which is opposed the Middle West and Pacific states from Indiana to the Coast, together with Vermont and New Hampshire, which are added to make up a full 28,-

000,000. To such comparisons the objection has been made that it averages the confessedly inferior rural negro population with the picked immigrants from the East and abroad in the Northwest. The objection is a concession of the lower average productive capacity of the South; but in order to compare the white elements of the two sections by themselves, a third set of tables compares the whole South containing 17,900,000 whites and 8,000,000 blacks against a group of Northern agricultural states with a population of 18,000,000 whites and 234,000 blacks.

The materials for such comparisons are various. Every traveler has his impressions of the relative prosperity of South and North based on what he sees of stations, public and private buildings, cities and stocks of goods, and on the appearance of farms and work-people throughout the country. For precise indications, the population of the states is estimated year by year in the *Bulletins* of the Census Bureau; estimates of accumulated wealth are made every few years by the Department of Commerce; returns of annual crops by the Department of Agriculture; banking statistics by the Treasury Department. The annual *Statistical Abstract* prints summaries of manufactures and other industry, and on these topics the Census Bureau issues valuable bulletins. For tax valuations there is no general official publication, but the *World Almanac* collects every year from state auditors a statement of assessments. Most of these sources must be accepted as simply a series of liberal estimates, but the factors of error are likely to be much the same in the Northern and the Southern communities, and at least they furnish the basis for a comparison in round numbers. The tax assessments are significant, because they are revised from year to year, and the methods of assessment are not very different in the various parts of the country and are likely to err by giving too low a value or omitting property, so that comparisons from tax returns are relatively more favorable to the poorer than to the richer communities.

I. The Eleven Seceding States.

Tabulation based upon the principles stated above will be found in the Appendix to this volume; and a study of those tables reveals some interesting comparisons between the eleven communities which formed the Southern Confederacy and nineteen Western communities, the two groups each having in 1900 about nineteen million inhabitants. The assessed taxable valuation of the Southern group in 1904 was 4,200 millions; in the Northern group it was 9,700 millions, or more than double. Four years later the valuations were 5,200 millions as against 13,800 millions. Since tax assessments are subject to many variations, perhaps a fairer measure of sectional wealth is banking transactions. The bank deposits of the National groups of the Southern group were, in 1906, 700 millions, in the Northern group, 2,400 millions. Bank clearings in the same year were respectively 4 billions and 8½ billions.

All the eleven seceding states together in 1906 valued their real estate at 2,900 millions, their personal at 1,800 millions, total 4,700 millions. A corresponding Northern group (in which the richest state is Indiana), counts its real estate worth 7,700 millions, its personalty, 2,700 millions, a total of 10,400 millions. That is, the Northern land and buildings are counted nearly thrice as valuable, and personalty about a half more valuable, though every-

236

body knows that there is a vast deal of untaxed personalty in the North.

The miles of railroad in the Southern group were 55,000; in the Western, 94,000; the total value of agricultural products in the South was estimated at 1,060 millions, in the North at 1,945 millions. Even the cotton crop of the eleven states, worth 550 millions, was overbalanced by the Northern corn crop which brought 595 millions. The manufactures in the South for 1905 were 1,267 millions; in the Northwest 2,932 millions. The Southern group expended for schools 26 millions, the corresponding Northern states expended 91 millions. The value of Southern school property was 43 millions, of the Northern group it was 216 millions; the average annual expenditure per pupil in daily attendance in the South was $9.75; in the North about $28.45. For public benevolent institutions the South expended in 1903 net $3,000,000, the North $7,000,000; the Southern group had 1,070,000 illiterate Whites, of whom 76,000 were foreign born; the Northern group had 207,000 besides 389,000 illiterate foreigners. In the indices of accumulated property the comparison is about the same; the Southern deposits in all banks were, in 1906, 701 million dollars, the Northern 2,439 millions. In manufactures the Northern group, with a capital of 2,240 million dollars and 903,000 hands, produced 2,932 millions; against Southern capital of 1,140 millions, employing 659,000 persons and producing 1,267 millions.

The comparison of valuations brings out one unexpected result, namely, that several of the Southern states have actually less taxable property now than they had fifty years ago. This does not mean that they are poorer because they have lost their slaves. Leaving slaves out of account, in 1860 South Carolina had a valuation of $326,000,000; in 1906 of $250,000,000; in Mississippi the valuation of real estate in 1860 was $158,000,000; in 1906, with a population more than twice as great, it was $131,000,000; in the rich state of Georgia the valuation in 1860, deducting slaves, was $432,000,000 against $578,000,000 in 1906. The Southern people feel justly proud of the fact that the valuations of the eleven former members of the Confederacy between 1902 and 1906 increased by 962 millions, from a total of 3,799 millions to 4,761 millions, that their annual manufactures increased by 450 millions; from 819 millions in 1900 to 1,267 millions in 1905.

This increase in industry is so striking that the Southern states suppose they are unique in that respect; but the corresponding Northern group of equal population in the same periods gained 4,000 millions in valuations and 705 millions in annual manufactures. These figures may be checked off in various ways. Take, for instance, the annual value of crops; the South is very certain that with its cotton, its corn and other crops together it is far in advance of the North. In the Southern states which were in secession (excepting Texas) the value of farms and stock in 1900 was 2,100 millions, the value in an equivalent Northwestern group was 7,800 millions. The total farm product in the Lower South was 1,360 millions, in the Northern group of equal population 2,390 millions. If Texas be compared with a group of Pacific states, of equivalent population, the Texan farms are worth 960 millions, the Far Western 1,400 millions.

The Lower South has been saving money of late years and is proud of its growing bank deposits, from 168 millions in 1896 to 701 millions in 1906, an increase of 450 per cent; but the equivalent Northern population has in-

creased from 716 millions to 2,439 millions. The Lower
South in 1905 had 917 national banks with deposits of 308
millions and assets of 568 millions; the similar Northern
states had deposits of 834 millions and assets of 1,418
millions. Let us see whether the South makes up this
disparity by its state banks. In 1906 the Lower South,
including Texas, had deposits of 700 millions in all banks;
and total bank clearings of about 3,920 millions; the
equivalent Northern group had deposits of over 2,400 millions, with total clearings of about 8,500 millions. Measured, therefore, by accumulated savings, by bank capital,
by clearings, the South is poorer than the least wealthy
section of the North. If we were to take the rich Eastern
and Northwestern states, with their immense population,
enormous manufactures (New York City contains over
twenty thousand factories), and vast transportation lines,
the fact that the South is far behind the North in things
both material and intellectual would stand out even more
clearly.

II. The Whole South

It might fairly be said that it is unreasonable to compare the former seceding states which have gone through
the disruption of their labor by Civil War with new Western communities in which there has been no destruction of
capital. Accordingly the second set of tables compares the
whole South—fifteen states and the District of Columbia
—with a Northwestern and Pacific Coast group of equivalent population. Since a part of the contention of Southern writers is that the South was richer than the North
before the Civil War and is only returning to her rightful
place of supremacy, it is worth while to examine the supposed wealth of the South in 1860. The assessed valua-

tion of the Lower South was then 4,330 millions, which a Southern statistician attempts to show was 750 millions more than the combined wealth of New England and the Middle states; out of this sum, 3,100 millions was for personal property, including about 1,200 millions for slaves; but either the slaves should be left out or a capitalized value of Northern laborers should be added on a slave-market basis.

Passing by the figures of 1870, which are discredited by all statisticians, in 1880 the total property valued for taxes in the Lower South was 1,880 millions, in the whole South was 3,420 millions; while in similar blocks of North-western population they were respectively 2,712 millions and 4,640 millions. This is a splendid record for a people who had given their all in a civil war and who had to build up nearly every dollar of their personal property from the bottom. The land, of course, was always there, but was worth much less per acre in 1880 than similar good land in 1860.

How far has this rate of progress been continued since 1880 as shown by the inexorable method of comparing groups of Southern states with groups of Northwestern states of equal population? The tax valuation shows about the same proportion, so far as can be ascertained, to real values in one section as in the other. The local differences of mode of assessment when averaged would probably not disturb the result by more then ten per cent. The whole South (16 communities) as compared with a Northern group of the same number of people in 1907 showed 8.5 billions of assessed property against 13.7 billions in the North. It may therefore be set down as proven that the taxable wealth of the lower agricultural South is less than half that of similar agricultural communities in the North;

so that while mining and manufacturing states like Maryland, Kentucky, and Missouri have about the same wealth as similar Northern communities, the South as a whole has not one half the wealth. Take the former slaveholding states all together, including such a rich commonwealth as Missouri, and the farm value in the whole region in 1900, with 28 millions of people, was under 5,000 millions; while 28 million people in the West and Northwest owned farms to the amount of about 11,000 millions, or more than double. The total Southern crops in 1899, the last year in which the totals are obtainable, were worth 1,360 millions, the Northern crops counted up to 2,390 millions. The value of the Southern corn crop in 1905 was 416 million dollars; the equivalent population in the Northwest raised 601 million dollars' worth of corn. The whole South raises about 32 million dollars' worth of oats; the North raises 201 millions. The Southern potato crop is worth 19 millions; the Northern, 76 millions. Southern hay counts up to 66 millions and Northern to 258 millions. Even in tobacco, the North furnishes 7 million dollars' worth against 35 million dollars in the South. Cotton is the one crop that is exclusively Southern, and the crop of 1905, the year that we are considering, including the seed, was worth 632 million dollars. The Southern group had 127,000 teachers, school property of 84 millions, and total school revenue of 45 millions, against competing Northern figures of 199,000, of 293 millions, and of 120 millions. It is difficult in these figures to find justification for the notion that the South as an agricultural region is richer than the North, or is likely ever to rival it.

The actual figures for the present conditions of the South are sufficiently attractive. During the four years

THE SOUTHERN SOUTH

1904–1907 the big crops and high price of cotton gave to
the South such prosperity as it had never known before,
the total output being nearly fifty million bales, which sold,
in cash, for about 2,700 million dollars. This happy result
was reflected in every city and every county of the rural
South, for old debts were paid, new houses built, land
doubled or even trebled in value, and a spirit of hopfulness
pervaded the whole population. A buoyancy is reflected
in the press, and particularly in the *Manufacturers' Record* of Baltimore, the leading Southern trade paper. " The
South," says the *Record*, " is now throughout the world
recognized as the predestined center of the earth, based on
greater natural advantages that can be found anywhere
else on the globe." Or as another Southern paper put it
some years ago : " In 1860 the Richest Part of the Country
—In 1870 the Poorest—In 1880 Signs of Improvement—
In 1889 regaining the position of 1860."

Nobody can be more pleased with Southern prosperity
than New Englanders, who have long since found out that
the richer other sections of the country become, the more
business Northerners have with those sections; if there are
directions in which the South is making more rapid progress than the North, it should be candidly acknowledged.
Nobody can visit thriving cities like Richmond, Atlanta,
Birmingham, Memphis, New Orleans, and the galaxy of
future centers of population in Texas, without hearty
pleasure in the increasing evidences of civilization, but it
is very unevenly distributed. Off the main lines of transportation the towns are still ill-built and unprogressive,
and the greater part of the area of the South is no farther
along than states like Illinois and Minnesota were in the
late sixties.

It is, however, a ticklish thing to make these comparisons, because many Southerners, and particularly Southern newspapers, consider it an attack upon the South to intimate that it is still much improvable. As the *Macon Telegraph* said a few months ago: " After all what does it matter that a Harvard professor should consider us lazy and not even excuse us on the ground that we are victims of the hookworm? We still have the right to go on expanding the figures relating to our remarkable industrial upbuilding, until we have driven New England out of the business of cotton manufacturing."

The best measure of comparative wealth would be a statistical statement of accumulations. On this subject there are many wild guesses. The *Manufacturers' Record* in January, 1907, makes claims for the South which deserve especial examination: " England's wealth, according to the London *Express,* is increasing at the rate of $7,000,-000 a week. That is less than one seventh of the rate of the increase of wealth in the South. The increase in the true value of Southern wealth in the past twelve months was $2,690,000,000, or about $7,300,000 for every day in the year, including Sundays and holidays. Not only is the speed of increase in the South so much greater than that in England, but the South possesses resources, agricultural and mineral, that make certain in the future even a much greater rate of increase than England."

Except poor old poverty-stricken New England, all the world will welcome this prodigious accretion of wealth. Think how many opera tickets you might buy for two and a half billions of dollars! The only attempt at exact figures of our national wealth is the estimate of the *Statistical Abstract,* published about every four years, and not based on any exact figures. Such as it is, it is relied upon by the Southern writers; and it sets forth that in the four years from 1900 to 1904 the total national wealth increased by less than 20 billions, an average of 5 billions a year; it is hardly likely that a third of the population, which in other respects is below the Northwest, was contributing more than half this annual gain. The only ground for the assertion seems to be an alleged increase in the Southern tax valuation from 7 billions in 1906 to 8 billions in 1907; assuming that the average proportion of valuation to actual value is forty per cent, you have your two billions and a half.

The first comment on this statement, which is selected as typical of the broad claims which float through the Southern press, is that the figures furnished the *World Almanac* for 1908 by the state authorities show that the Southern valuations in 1906 were 7,813 millions, and in 1907, 8,474 millions; so that the increase of assessments is 650 millions instead of 1,000 millions. In the second place, the estimated true value by the *Statistical Abstract* in 1904 was about 20 billions for the whole South; and on a basis of comparison of the valuations of 1904 and 1907, the increase in the whole three years would be at best only two and a half billions. In the next place, two and a half billions a year means that every man, woman, and child, black and white, is on the average laying up a hundred dollars, which is an amazing rate of saving.

Having thus proven that the material progress of the South is exaggerated, the next logical step is to show that perhaps it has foundation, inasmuch as the equivalent 28,-000,000 people in the Northwest in 1905 are gaining wealth still more rapidly, having increased their estimated "true value" from 44 billions in 1904 to at least 50 billions in 1907. The South, which supposes itself to be getting rich faster than any other part of the globe, has in the last few years actually added less to its wealth than a similar Northwest agricultural region. In the year 1906–7, while the South added 650 millions to its tax duplicate, the North added 850 millions. If, as may be the case, the 650 millions of valuation meant 1,700 millions of new wealth, the Northwest was adding at least 2,300 millions.

In all this array of figures there is no criticism of the South, no denial that it is more prosperous than it has ever been before; no desire to minimize its splendid achievements which are helping on the solution of the race problem; but it is essential that the Southern people should measure themselves squarely with their neighbors. The single state of New York, with less than a fifth the population of the South, has as much property as the whole South (leaving out Missouri), and adds every year to its wealth as much as is added by the whole South (leaving out Texas). The South is really at about the same place where the Northwest was thirty years ago; it is developing its latent resources; building its cities; perfecting its communications; starting new industries; and in much less than thirty years it will come to the point that the Northwest has now reached; but that section is still driving ahead more rapidly, and thirty years hence may be proportionately richer than it is to-day. If the South is saving four millions a day, the Northwest is saving five millions; and the Middle and New England states, the other third of the country, are saving eight or ten millions a day. If the South is to range up alongside the Northwest, to say nothing of the Northeast, it must increase its production still faster, and the only way to accomplish that purpose is by improving the average industry, thrift, and output of its people.

III. Comparative Efficiency of White Populations North and South

Some Southern statisticians, while admitting these indubitable figures, contend that the South is improving at a much more rapid rate, and hence must in no long time overtake the North; but it must be remembered that in most of these fields of comparison the North not only shows from two to two and a half times the output, but that its annual or decennial increase is absolutely larger than in the South; that is, that the annual amount which the South must add to its present output, in order to catch up with the North, is larger than it was a year ago, or at any previous time. A conventional explanation of this state of things is that the Negroes constitute a large part of the Southern working force, and are much below the average of Americans in their productive output; but when comparisons are made between similar aggregations of white population, results are not very different. If the whole South (including the District of Columbia) be compared, not with a block of about 28,000,000 Northern people, but with a block of about 18,000,-000 white people corresponding to the 17,900,000 Whites in the South (both figures for 1900), the results are still startling; although the South has all the advantage of the labor and production of 8,000,000 Negroes besides the Whites. The debts of the Southern communities in 1902 were 374 million dollars; of the Northern, 301 millions. The total taxes raised in 1902 were: South, 116 millions; North, 202 millions. The estimated Southern wealth in 1900 was 16.7 billions; in 1904, 19.8 billions, an increase of 3.1 billions; in the North the corresponding figures are 25.8 billions and 31.4 billions, an increase of 5.6 billions. The Southern assessed valuation of 1907 was 8.5 billions, of the Northern group 10.7 billions.

What makes these differences? It certainly is not because the South is deficient in natural resources, in fertility, in climate, in access to the world's markets, in the enterprise of its business men. What is the reason for this discrepancy between the resources and the output of the South? Some of the Southern observers insist that the North is made rich through its manufactures. In order to eliminate that condition the comparisons in this chapter are all with Western and Northwestern states (Vermont being included simply to equalize the numbers); some of these states, as the Dakotas and Oregon, are very similar in their conditions to the purely agricultural and timber states of the South; in other states, such as Indiana and Wisconsin, there are large manufactures, which, however, are no more significant in proportion than those of Maryland and Missouri. The Northwestern states have more manufactures than the Southern, but they have more of everything, which indicates industry and prosperity. The obvious reason is that laborers in the South, both white and colored, are inferior in average productive power to Northern laborers; and the obvious remedy is to use every effort to bring up the intelligence, and the value to the community of every element of the population.

While the proof sheets of the foregoing chapter are passing through their revision there appears in *Collier's Weekly* for January 22, 1910, an article by Clark Howell of the *Atlanta Constitution* who makes, in italics, the statement that "*the trend of Southern development is incomparably in advance of that of any other section of the continent."* The opportunity to apply the cold bath of statistics to such torrid statements can still be taken, by adding to the tables in the Appendix some figures for 1907 and 1908, and even 1909, together with some generalizations based on figures not included in the tables. For example, the figures for public school education in 1907 show for the ten seceding states 78,000 teachers against 153,000 in the corresponding Northern group; school property to the value of 19 millions as against 41 millions; annual revenue of 24 millions as against 90 millions. The rich state of Texas, with 18,000 teachers, is balanced by the Pacific group with 28,000; its school property of 15 millions by 64 millions; its annual expenditure of 7 millions by 25 millions. Even the richer border state group of five communities, and an average daily attendance of a million school children, has school property of 48 millions against 86 millions in the corresponding Northwestern states; and the school revenue of 21 millions must be placed against the revenue in the corresponding group of 38 millions.

The assessed valuations of the states, as reported to the *World Almanac* for 1910, are as follows: the whole South in 1909 was assessed on 10,051 millions—a gain of 2,200 millions in three years; in the equal Northwestern group it was 19,884 millions—a gain in three years of 7,000 millions (out of which perhaps 2,500 millions should be deducted, on account of a bookkeeping increase in the assessments in Kansas and Colorado). The cotton crop of 1908 sold for 675 millions and the corn crop of the North for 886 millions. The railroads in the South in 1908 totaled 71,790 miles and in the Northwestern group 123,332 miles. The South " has just harvested a billion-dollar cotton crop " says Clark Howell, and he predicts twenty-cent cotton. The actual crop for 1909 was probably less than 11 million bales, and at the average price for the season of about 14 cents, it sold for something like 770 million dollars. The corn and wheat crops of the whole North (not the equivalent group) sold in the same year for 2,091 million dollars.

No good can result to anybody either from belittling or exaggerating the productivity of the South. That section is progressing, and the more it progresses the less become its difficulties of race and labor problems, the greater its connection with neighboring states, the larger the advantage to the whole nation. Still, on any basis of comparison with the least wealthy states and sections of the North—whether it be made between the total population of equivalent groups or between the white populations only, leaving out of account the productivity of the Negroes, the South is below the national standard of wealth and progress; it grows constantly in accumulations and in productivity, but its yearly additions are less than those of the Northwestern states, and much less than those of the Northeastern states.

CHAPTER XVIII

MAKING COTTON

THE South holds a call upon the world's gold to the extent of $450,000,000 to $500,000,000 for the cotton which it will this year furnish to Europe. . . . This money, whether paid in actual gold or in other ways, will so strengthen the financial situation, not only of the South, but of New York and the country at large, as to make the South the saving power in American financial interests. No other crop on earth is of such far-reaching importance to any other great country as cotton is to the United States."

This extract from the *Manufacturers' Record* is a somewhat grandiloquent statement of the conviction of the South that it possesses a magnificent cotton monopoly which no other part of the world can ever rival; that with proper foresight and with courage, the South may corner the world's market in the staple, and fix a price which will insure prosperity. In a country full of natural resources of many kinds, with a soil on which corn may be grown almost as good as in Indiana, where cattle can be raised and dairies may be established, the chief aim and object of life is to " make cotton." The talk of small farmers is cotton; every country merchant of any standing is a cotton buyer; and most of the large wholesale houses and banks are interested in cotton.

In all the large cities and some of the small ones are

cotton exchanges at which are posted on immense black-boards the day's data for " Receipts at Ports," " Overland to Mills and Canada," " Current Stock," " Southern Mill Takings," " Total in Sight to Date," " World's Possible Supply," and so on. The federal Census Bureau publishes from time to time estimates of the acreage and condition of cotton, which so affect the markets that great efforts have sometimes been made to bribe the officials to reveal the figures before they are published. The Census Office issues periodical reports showing the number of bales of cotton ginned throughout the South.

This is the more remarkable because cotton is not the principal product of the South, nor even the major crop of the rural sections; but the size and public handling of the crop carry away men's imagination. Timber, turpentine, mining, and iron making, taken together, produce a larger annual value than cotton. The total value of all other crops in 1907 was $758,000,000, which was about $90,000,000 more than the value of the cotton crop. The corn alone was over $485,000,000, or over two thirds the value of the cotton. Hay ($92,000,000), wheat, tobacco, oats, and potatoes make up $272,000,000 more. Though the Lower South grew only 9,000,000 bushels of wheat, rice, cultivated on rather a small scale in South Carolina, is a crop of growing importance in Louisiana and Texas. The South raises no sugar beets, little flaxseed, and not a twentieth of the wool; but the sugar and molasses are worth nearly $20,000,000. Trucking or the raising of vegetables, chiefly for the Northern market, is said to employ 700,000 freight cars in the season. The South has also about 15,000,000 cattle, 6,000,000 sheep, and 15,000,000 pigs, all of which are independent of cotton except that to some degree cotton seed is the food for stock.

THE SOUTHERN SOUTH

When all has been said, however, the typical Southern industry is cotton, upon the raising of which certainly nearly half of the population is concentrated, and it constitutes about a fourth of the whole annual product of the South. The field of the cotton industry extends from the foot of the mountains to the Atlantic and Gulf Coasts; and the Southern social problem is to a very large degree the problem of cotton raising under a system by which one race includes practically all the masters, and the other furnishes almost all the laborers for hire.

The history of cotton is in itself romantic. In 1790, about 4,000 bales were raised; in 1800, 150,000; in 1820, 600,000; in 1840, over 2,000,000. In 1860 there was a tremendous crop of nearly 5,000,000 bales, a figure not reached again until 1879. In 1904 the crop was 13,700,-000 bales—an amount not equaled since. The price of cotton has of late ruled much lower than in the first half of the century, when it sometimes ran up as high as 30 cents a pound. The 1860 crop brought about 11 cents. In 1898 the average price was about 6 cents, and some cotton sold as low as 3 cents, but the enormous crop of 1904 brought about 12 cents, and it has ruled higher since. In 1908 the slackening of the world's demand caused the price to drop, but it has risen again to the highest point for thirty years.

The significance of the cotton crop is to be calculated not by the Liverpool market, but by its remarkable effect on the life of the South. One reason for its importance is that it can be grown on a great variety of land. Most of the best American long staple, the Sea Island, comes from a limited area off the coast of South Carolina and Georgia, in which a seed trust has been formed by the local planters to prevent anybody outside their narrow

252

limits from raising that grade; for if the seed is renewed every few years, the fiber can be profitably raised on land now covered by the piney woods. Another variety of the long staple, the Floradora, is raised inland. The river bottoms and deltas of the numerous streams flowing into the Gulf of Mexico are a rich field for cotton, especially along the Mississippi river; but the Black Belt of the interior of Georgia and Alabama is almost equally productive; and the piney woods district and considerable parts of the uplands may be brought under cotton cultivation.

Northerners do not understand the significance of the fertilizer in cotton culture. George Washington was one of the few planters of his time who urged his people to restore the vitality of their land as fast as they took it out; but rare was the planter up to the Civil War who raised cattle, and the imported guano from the rocky islets of the Gulf and Pacific was little used. Then in the seventies discoveries were made of phosphate rocks in the estuaries of the Carolina rivers; and later, inland deposits in Tennessee. From these, with some admixture of imported materials, are made commercial fertilizers which have become indispensable to a large number of the cotton farmers, so that they are now spending 20 millions a year on that alone, every dollar of which is expected to add at least a dollar and a half to the value of the crop.

The word "plantation" has come to have a special meaning in Northern ears. It brings to the mind the great colonnaded mansion house with trim whitewashed negro quarters grouped about it, the pickaninnies running to open the gate for the four-in-hand bringing the happy guests, while back in the cotton field the overseer rides to and fro cracking his blacksnake whip. That kind of plantation is not altogether a myth. For instance, at Hermitage, just outside of Savannah, you see a brick mansion of a few large rooms, built a hundred years ago, surrounded by attractive sunken gardens, and one of the most superb groves of live oaks in the South; and near it are the original little brick slave cabins of one room and a chimney.

That kind of elaborate place was rare; in most cases the ante-bellum planter's house was a modest building, and nowadays very few large planters live regularly on the plantation. If the place is profitable enough, the family lives in the nearest town or city; if it is unprofitable, sooner or later the banks get it and the family goes down; even where the old house is preserved, it is likely to be turned over to the manager, or becomes a nest for the colored people. Inasmuch as cotton raising is an industrial enterprise, plantations are apt to change hands, or the owners may put in new managers; so that the ante-bellum feeling of personal relation between the owner and the field hand plays little part in modern cotton making.

The modern plantation can more easily be described than analyzed; the term is elastic; a young man will tell you that he has " bought a plantation " which upon inquiry comes down to a little place of less than a hundred acres with two houses. The distinction between a " farm " and a " plantation " seems to be that the latter term is applied to a place on which there is a body of laborers (almost universally Negroes) managed, with very few exceptions, by white men and devoted principally to one crop.

Individual plantation holdings vary in size from the thirty thousand acres of Bell, the central Alabama planter, down to fifty acres. Many large owners have scattered plantations, sometimes as many as twenty or thirty, each carried on by itself; or two or three adjacent groups under one manager. You are informed that the X brothers "own thirty-three plantations," which probably means thirty-three different large farms, ranging from two hundred to two thousand acres each. Three to five thousand acres of land under cultivation is as large a body of land as seems advantageous to handle together.

A fair example of the large plantation in the best cotton lands is the estate managed by Mr. Dayton near Jonesville, La., on the Tensas and Little rivers. It is an expanse of that incredibly rich land, of which there are millions of acres in this enormous delta, land which has in many places produced fifty to seventy-five successive crops of cotton without an ounce of fertilizer. Between the rivers, which are fenced off by levees, lie the fields, originally all wooded, but in these old plantations even the roots have disappeared from the open fields, although wherever the plantation is enlarged the woods have to be cleared, and the gaunt and fire-scarred dead trunks mark the progress of cultivation.

The negro houses stand in the middle of the field; for on modern plantations it is very rare to gather the hands in quarters near the great house; their cabins are distributed all over the estate. On the main road is a manager's house, distinctly better than any of the negro cabins. Near by a white family is moving in where a black family has moved out, for this plantation (though the thing is uncommon) has a few white hands working alongside the Negroes. In this free open, in the breadth of the fields and the width of the turbid streams, alongside the endless procession of scenic forests in the background, one forgets the long hot days of toil, the scanty living, the ignorance and debasement. It may all be as sordid as the mines or the iron works, but it is in pure air. These thousands

of broad acres with their mealy brown soil bearing the
"cotton-weed" (the common name for the stalk after the
cotton is picked) are a type of the lowland South from
Texas to North Carolina.

A plantation of somewhat different type is "Sunny
Side" in Arkansas, nearly opposite the city of Greenville,
Miss. "Sunny Side" is supposed by some people to be
extravagantly conducted because there are three or four
good managers' houses on the estate, and because there is
twenty-three miles of light railway track. Considering
that the plantation runs eight and a half miles along the
river, and that all its products and supplies would otherwise need to be hauled, there is a reason for the railroad,
whose one little locomotive fetches and carries like a well-
trained dog; and it is a special privilege of all the people
employed on the estate and of visitors to ride back and
forth as their occasions require. "Sunny Side," with an
adjacent estate under the same management, comprises
about 12,000 acres, of which 4,700 acres, including broad
hay lands and extensive corn fields, are under cultivation,
and the remainder is in timber; considerable areas have
been cleared in recent years. The annual cotton crop is
about 2,500 bales. As on most plantations, the houses of the
hands are distributed so that nobody has far to go to his
work. Twenty to thirty acres is commonly assigned to
a family; more to a large family, and the lands rented at
from $6 to $8 an acre, according to quality, with the usual
plantation privileges of firewood, a house, and pasture for
draft animals.

Here comes in one of the most important complications
in cotton culture. Northern wheat is usually grown by
farmers tilling moderate-sized farms, either as owners or
as money renters; a third or more of the cotton is raised

in the same way by farmers or small planters who till for themselves or employ a few families of hands; and like the wheat farmers they look on the land as a tool. On the large plantations, where perhaps as many as a thousand people are busied on the crop, the manager looks upon the laborer simply as an element of production; you must have seed, rain, and the niggers in order to get a crop. Even the most kind-hearted and conscientious plantation owner cannot avoid this feeling that the laborers are, like the live-stock, a part of the implements; he houses them, and if humane and far-sighted, he houses them better than the mules; he "furnishes them"—that is, he agrees to feed them and allow them necessities while the crop is making. All this is practically the factory system, with the unfavorable addition that the average plantation hand comes near the category of unskilled labor. A Negro brought up on one plantation can do just as well in a plantation ten or a thousand miles away; and there is no subdivision of labor except for the few necessary mechanics. That is, cotton planting on a large plantation is an industrial enterprise requiring considerable capital, trained managers, and a large plant of buildings, tools, animals and Negroes.

A characteristic of cotton culture is that it requires attention and keeps the hands busy during the greater part of the year. The first process is to break the ground, which begins as early as January 1st, then about March or April the seed is dropped in long rows, and during the seeding season the rural schools are likely to stop so as to give the children the opportunity to help. In the seed there is great room for improvement; as yet the Southern agricultural colleges seem to have made less impression on the cotton grower than their brethren in the Northwestern states have made on the corn and wheat farming, for some large and otherwise intelligent planters make very little effort to select their seed.

When the cotton is once up, it needs the most patient care, for it must be weeded and thinned and watched, and is gone over time after time. The "riders" or assistant managers are in the saddle all day long, and a prudent manager casts his eye on every plot of cultivated ground on his plantation every day; for it is easy to "get into the grass," and all but the best of the hands need to be kept moving.

Then comes the picking of the cotton, which lasts from August into February. It is a planter's maxim that no negro family can pick the cotton that it can raise, and extra help has to be found. Here is one of the large items of expense in raising cotton, for the fields have to be gone over two, three, and sometimes four times, inasmuch as the cotton does not all mature at the same time, and if it did, no machine has ever been invented which is practical for picking cotton. It is hand work to the end of the year. There is a plantation saying that it takes thirteen months to make a cotton crop, and it is true that plowing for the next crop begins on some parts of the plantation before the last of the two or three pickings is completed on other parts. When picked, the cotton goes into little storehouses or into the cabins, until enough accumulates to keep the gin busy.

Everybody in the great cotton districts talks about "A bale to the acre" as a reasonable yield, but one of the richest counties of Mississippi averages only half a bale, and the whole South averages about a third of a bale. What is a bale? The "seed cotton," so called, as it comes from the field, has the brown seeds in the midst of the

258

fiber, and the first process is to gin it—that is to take out the seed, and at the same time to make it into the standard package for handling. This requires machinery, originally invented by that ingenious Yankee schoolmaster, Eli Whitney. There are about 38,000 of these ginneries, some having one poor little old gin, others five or six of the latest machines side by side, with air suction and other labor-saving devices. It is an interesting sight to see the fluffy stuff wafted up into the gin with its row of saw-teeth, and then blown to the press, where a plunger comes down time after time until the man who runs it judges that about five hundred pounds have accumulated; then another plunger comes up from below; the rectangular mass thus formed is enveloped in rough sacking and fastened with iron cotton ties. The completed bale is then turned out, weighed, numbered, stamped, and recorded; and becomes one of the thirteen million units of the year's crop; but the number identifies it, and any particular bale of cotton may be traced back to the plantation from which it came and even to the negro family that raised it. Sea Island cotton has a much woodier plant, and the seed cotton contains less lint and more numerous although smaller seeds; hence it requires special picking, a special gin, cannot be so compressed, and must be much more carefully bagged. Sea Island cotton at 23 cents a pound is thought to be no more profitable than the short staple at less than half the price.

About 1897 a great effort was made to substitute a round bale, weighing about half as much as the standard bale, and in 1902 the output reached nearly a million. It is still a question whether that package is not an improvement, but the machinery was more expensive, complaints were made that the round bale was harder to stow for export; the railroad companies refused to give any advantage in freight rates; and the compressor companies, who are closely linked in with the railroads, were opposed to it altogether; and the round bale has almost disappeared from the South. Only two per cent of the cotton is thus baled.

One of the things remarked by Duke Bernhard of Saxe Weimar, when he visited the South in 1824, was that the people seemed unaware that there was any value in cotton seed. Some planters put it on the field as a fertilizer, where it has some value; others threw it away. During the last twenty years, however, the cotton seed has become a great factor in the production. About one third the weight of the seed cotton is seed, and its value is over one tenth that of the baled cotton. In the high cotton year of 1906 the cotton seed was thought to be worth nearly ninety millions. Immense quantities go to the oil mills which are scattered through the South. Besides the clear oil they produce oil cake which is used as a food for animals or a fertilizer. The seed practically adds something more than a cent a pound to the value of the product.

CHAPTER XIX

SO far cotton cultivation has been considered as though it were a crop which came of itself, like the rubber of the Brazilian forests, but during a whole century the cultivation of cotton has had a direct influence on the labor system and the whole social organization of the South. Such close relations sometimes exist in other commodities; for instance, the election of President McKinley, in 1896, seems to have been determined by a sudden rise in the price of wheat; but cotton is socially and politically important every year, because upon it the greater part of the negro labor is employed, and to it a large portion of the white management and capital is devoted.

Furthermore, the conditions of the old slavery times are more nearly reproduced in the cotton field than anywhere else in the South. The old idea that the normal function of the African race is field labor is still vital; and the crude and unskilled mass of Negroes still find employment in which they succeed tolerably well. As in slavery times, the cotton hands are more fixed in their locality than in other pursuits; they are less ambitious to move about, and find their way more close hedged in if they try to go elsewhere. The relation of the white man as task-master to the Negro as a deferential class is still distinctly maintained; while the system of advances

261

to laborers resembles the old methods of feeding the hands.

The Negro is not the sole cotton maker; fully one third of the cotton in the South is never touched by a black hand, being raised by small white farmers both in the lowlands and in the hill regions, who produce one, two, or more bales a year and depend upon that crop to pay their store bills. Something like one sixth of the crop is raised by independent negro land owners or renters working for themselves; this leaves nearly or quite one half the crop to negro labor under the superintendence of white owners or managers.

Even where the Negro is employed on wages, he looks on himself as part of the concern and expects due consideration in return for what Stone calls the "proprietary interest he feels in the plantation at large, his sense of being part and parcel of a large plantation. Then, too, there is his never-failing assurance of ability to pay his account, no matter how large, by his labor, when it is not too wet or too cold, his respect, and his implicit and generally cheerful obedience."

Inasmuch as more than half the Negroes are raising cotton, and most of the others are working on farms, it is important to know what kind of laborers they make. It is the opinion of their greatest leader, Booker Washington, that the best place for the Negro is in the rural South, and that he is not fitted for the strife of the great cities South or North. Is he perfectly fitted for any service? Is it true, as one of the employers of Negroes alleges, that "their actions have no logical or reasonable basis, that they are notional and whimsical, and that they are controlled far more by their fancies than by their common sense?"

COTTON HANDS

In cotton culture there is little to elevate a man. One of the numerous errors flying about is that the slave in the cotton fields was a skilled laborer, and that there is intellectual training in planting, weeding, and picking. The owner or renter must of course accustom his mind to consider the important questions of the times of plowing and seeding, and he must submit to the anxiety which besets the farmer all over the world; but cotton culture is a monotonous thing, the handling of the few tools is at best a matter of dexterity, and the only man who gets an intellectual training out of it is the manager. When cotton is high, a plantation is a more or less speculative investment, and many people who save money put it into land and hire a manager. Cotton broking and banking firms sometimes carry on plantations of their own. City bankers and heavy men get plantations on mortgage, or by purchase; and banks sometimes own too much of this kind of property.

Of course many planters run their own plantations; but on all large estates, and many small ones, there is a manager who is virtually the old overseer over again. Commonly he is a good specimen of the lower class of the white population; in a very few cases he is a Negro. Successful managers command a salary as high as $3,000 a year or more, and have some opportunity to plant on their own account; business sense such a man must have, but above all he must be able to "handle niggers," an art in which, by common consent, most Northern owners of cotton land are wanting. On a large plantation there will also be one or more assistant managers, commonly called "riders"; a bookkeeper, who may be an important functionary; a plantation doctor, sometimes on contract, sometimes taking patients as they come and charging their bills on the books of the plantation. On one plantation employing a hundred and thirty Italian families there is even a plantation priest.

The manager subdivides the estate into plots, or "plows"—you hear the expression "he has a fifteen-plow farm"—of from ten to thirty-five acres, according to the number of working hands in the squad that takes it. A "one-mule farm" is about thirty acres. He settles what crop shall be grown; some insist that part of the acreage be planted in corn, others raise all the corn for the estate on land worked by day hands. The secret of success is unceasing watchfulness of all the details, and especially of the labor of the hands.

Outside of the administrative force and their families there are commonly no white people on a cotton plantation. The occasional white hands make the same kind of contracts, live in the same houses, and accept the same conditions as the Negroes; but their number is small and they are likely to drift out either into cotton mills or into sawmill and timber work. The foreign agricultural laborers, as has been shown in the chapter on immigration, are few in number. The Germans, the so-called Austrians, the few Bulgarians, Greeks, Syrians, and Italians, all taken together, are probably less than 10,000, and there seems little reason to suppose that their number will soon increase. The main source of plantation labor has always been the Negroes who furnish about two million workers on other people's land, and with their families make up more than half of all the Negroes in the United States.

With their families—for the unit on the plantation is not a hand, but a family, or where three or four unmarried men or unmarried women work together, a gang. This practice, combined with the child labor in cotton mills, accounts for the large number of persons under fifteen years old—more than half the boys in some states—who are employed in gainful occupations. This is one of the most striking divergences from any kind of Northern farming where plenty of farmers' wives ride the mowing machine, and farmers' sisters pick fruit, and farmers' children drop potatoes, where foreign women often work in garden patches, but where people do not habitually employ women and children at heavy field labor.

The best Negroes, unless they own land of their own, seek the form of contract most advantageous to themselves, paying either a money rent of two dollars to eight dollars an acre, or an equivalent cotton rent. It is generally believed that the renters are the people most likely to save money and buy property for themselves. In Dunleith, Mississippi, a crew of seven people came in with a hundred dollars' worth of property, and three years later went away with more than a thousand dollars' worth of accumulated stock, tools and personal property. A renter must have animals of his own, and is obliged to feed them and to keep up his tools. Some planters find that renters leave them just as they are doing well, and that the land is skinned by them. In general, however, a Negro who has the necessary mules can always find a chance to rent land.

The share hand or cropper is next in point of thrift; the planter furnishes him house, wood, seed, animals, and implements; and at the end of the year the value of the crop is divided between owner and tenant, either half and half or "three fifths and four fifths," which means that the Negro gets three fifths of the cotton and four fifths of the corn.

A third class is the wage hands, who in general have not the ability to rent land on any terms; they receive a house and fuel, and wages, from fifteen dollars a month up to a dollar a day. Where steady wage hands can be found, this is considered the best arrangement for the planter.

Renters and croppers may be supplemented by extra work, paid for by them, or charged to them. If they get into a tight place with their cotton, the manager sends wage hands to their aid, and at picking time all available help of all ages is scraped together and sent out according to the needs of the plantation. Of course, a renter or a " cropper " may allow members of his family to work for others, if he cannot keep them busy. On some plantations tenants pay on an average nearly a hundred dollars a year for this extra help.

During the five years from 1903 to 1907 there was a phenomenal demand for cotton hands, and planters were eager to get anybody that looked like work; hence the Negro had the agreeable sensation of seeing people compete for him. Of course, if, at the " change of the year " (January 1st), the Negro moves to one planter, he moves away from another, and the man thus left behind has gloomy view of the fickleness and instability of the negro race. One of the best managed plantations in the Delta of Mississippi, supposed to be very profitable, has seen such a shift that at the end of five years hardly one of the original hands was on the place. Other planters in that region equally successful in making money say that they have little or no trouble with negro families moving, and there seems no good reason to believe that they are more restless than any other laborers. It is, of course, highly discouraging for a planter who has made every effort by improved houses, just treatment and clear accounts, to satisfy his people, to see them slipping away to neighbors who are notoriously hard, unjust, and shifty. While he remains on a plantation, the Negro feels, says a planter, " the certainty, in his own mind, that he himself is necessary to its success."

It is this dissatisfaction with the negro laborer which has led to the efforts, described above, to bring in foreigners, efforts which have been so far quite unsuccessful, first, because the number of people that could be induced to come is too small to affect the South, and secondly, because few of them mean to remain as permanent day laborers. Since the South seems better fitted than any other part of the earth for the cultivation of cotton, since at any price above six cents a pound there is some profit in the business, and at the prices prevailing during the last five years a large profit, it seems certain that the Negro will be steadily desired as a cotton hand; and the question comes down to that suggested by Nicholas Worth: " There ought to be a thousand schools, it seemed to me, that should have the aim of Hampton. Else how could the negroes—even a small percentage of them—ever be touched by any training at all? And if they were not to be trained in a way that would make the cotton fields cleaner and more productive, how should our upbuilding go on? For it must never be forgotten that the very basis of civilization here is always to be found in cotton."

If the master sometimes is dissatisfied with the laborer, the Negro in his turn has his own complaints, which Booker Washington has summed up as follows: " Poor dwelling-houses, loss of earnings each year because of unscrupulous employers, high-priced provisions, poor schoolhouses, short school terms, poor school-teachers, bad treatment generally, lynchings and whitecapping, fear of the practice of peonage, a general lack of police protection, and want of encouragement." In this list several of the items refer to the plantation system of accounts, which cannot be understood without some explanation of the advance system.

In slavery times plantation owners got into the habit of spending their crop before it was grown, and that is still the practice of by far the greater number of cotton planters and farmers, large and small. In flush times agents of large cotton brokers and wholesale establishments literally press check books into the hands of planters and invite them to use credit or cash to their hearts' content. There is some justification in the system as applied to cotton culture, which over large areas is the only sale crop; and under which (for the same system runs down to the very bottom) the planters themselves are in the habit of making advances to their tenants and hands. The white and negro land owner commonly make arrangements " to be furnished " by the nearest country storekeeper; or by a store or bank, or white friend in the nearest city. On the plantation, the planter himself commonly furnishes his own hands, and has a store or " commissary " for that purpose. Neither banker nor planter expects to lose money; both are subject to heavy deductions by the failure of planters and the departure of hands, and hence they recoup themselves from those who will pay. The effect is, of course, that when the cotton is sold and accounted for, the planter and his hand alike may not have any surplus to show, and begin the new year in debt. And the same round may be gone over again year by year during a lifetime.

The system is enforced by lien loans, through which the crop is the security for the loan, and in addition it is customary for the small farmer to mortgage mules, tools, and whatever else he may have. As Stone explains: " The factor's method of self-protection is to take a deed of

268

trust on the live stock and prospective crop, and is the same whether the applicant be a two-mule Negro renter, or the white owner of a thousand acres of land, wanting ten thousand dollars of advances. . . . There is, however, this difference: the white man gets his advances in cash, available at stated intervals, while the Negro gets the most of his in the shape of supplies." Many people believe that the whole crop lien system is an incentive to debt, that if it were abolished people would have to depend upon their character and credit; and hence a determined effort was made in South Carolina in 1908 to repeal the lien law outright.

The obvious defects of this system, the tendency to extravagance, the not knowing where you stand, the prevention of saving habits, are aggravated for the Negro because the white man keeps the books. The Negro is accustomed to be charged prices which in many cases are a half higher than the cash price of the same article in the nearby stores; he knows that there will be an interest charge at the rate of from ten per cent to forty per cent on his running account, and he suspects (sometimes with reason) that the bookkeeping is careless or fraudulent. Some planters make a practice of ending the settlement of every account with a row, and the consequent frame of mind of the Negro is illustrated by a stock story. A Negro has been trading with a local merchant and goes to a new store because they offer twelve pounds of sugar for a dollar instead of ten. On his way back he passes the old place, where they ask him in, weigh up his sugar, and show him that he has actually only nine pounds instead of twelve. "Yes, boss, dat's so, but after all, perhaps he didn't get the best of it; while he was weighing out that sugar, I slips dis yere pair of shoes into my basket."

The story precisely illustrates the futility of cheating the Negro; for whenever he thinks his accounts are juggled, he will see to it that his labor is no more conscientious than the bookkeeper's. Many of the really long-headed planters see that the less the relations of employer and hand are matters of favor, and the more they become affairs of business, the easier it will be to get on with their hands. Many of them have a fixed basis for advances, not more than about fifteen dollars a month for a family, and that in provisions only; others keep no book accounts for such advances, but issue coupon books of say fifteen dollars every month. A few pay their wage hands and give out the advances in cash, allowing people to buy where they will. A very few decline to have anything to do with advances in any form; but inasmuch as the Negroes must eat, in such cases the hands usually get somebody else to furnish them. Some planters close up their accounts at the end of the year, compelling the Negroes to turn in whatever they have in property to close out their accounts, and then start in afresh.

All these are only palliatives; the net effect of the system of advances to hands is to accentuate the industrial character of the cotton plantation. A big plantation in central Alabama or the Delta of Mississippi cannot be compared with any Northern farms, nor even with the great ranches of California; it is very like a coal mine back in a cove of the mountains of Pennsylvania; the same forlorn houses, the same company store, the same system of store orders and charges; only the coal mine sells its product from day to day and pays any differences in cash at the end of the month, while the cotton hand must wait till his particular bale is sold at the end of the season, before he can draw his profit. The Negro is therefore less likely than the miner to lay up money, and is even more at the mercy of the company's bookkeeper.

Here is an actual annual account of a plantation family in the Delta of Mississippi, two adults and one child, poor workers:

	Debit		Credit
Doctor	$24.45	Cotton....	$498.57
Mule	33.00	Cotton seed	91.00
Clothing	53.40		
Rations................	60.00		
Feed	11.25		$589.57
Rent	130.50		
Extra labor	179.45		
Seed	11.90		
Ginning...............	43.50		
Cash down	53.50	Debit.	$11.38
	600.95		$600.95

These people got their living and sixty-six dollars in cash and credit during the year; but the charge for extra labor shows that they were shiftless and did not work out their own crop. On the same plantation an industrious family of three adults and one child earned in a year $974, of which $450 was net cash.

An examination of various plantation accounts reveals the fact that the actual earnings of the negro hands, if industrious, are considerably greater than the average for the Pennsylvania miners, but of course the whole family works in the fields. The renters could do still better if they had money enough to carry them through the year; on a prosperous plantation in Arkansas, only about one fortieth of all the negro gangs kept off the books of the company and drew their earnings in cash at the end of the year, while two thirds of the Italians employed on the same plantation had no store accounts. In fact there is some complaint that the Italians club together and buy their provisions at wholesale.

The advance system is complicated by a system of " Christmas Money." You hear planters bitterly cursing the Negroes who have demanded $25, $50, or $100 to spend at Christmas time, as though the money were not charged against the Negro to be deducted at the end of the year; and as though it were not so advanced in order to induce the Negro to make a contract with them. Many planters refuse to give Christmas money and yet fill up their plantation houses. It is all part of a vicious system; the wage hands have to be paid somehow, though often not completely paid up till the end of the year; the share hands and renters are carried by the planter because they always have been carried; and because bad planters can take advantage of this opportunity to squeeze their hands. The difficulty is one known in other lands; in Ceylon, for instance, the laborers on tea and rubber estates draw advances, carry debts which have to be assumed by a new employer, trade at a " caddy," which is the same thing as a commissary, and complain of the accounts.

The system is just as vicious for the small land owners both negro and white. Most Southern states under their crop lien law allow the growing crop to be mortgaged for cash or advances, and hence any farmer has credit for supplies or loans up to the probable value of the crop when marketed. That value is variable, the advances are clogged with interest and overcharges, and the whole system is a heavy draft on the country. There are money sharks in the Southern country as well as in the Northern cities, and many scandalous transactions. One man in Alabama has

2,500 Negroes on his books for loans, in some cases for a loan of $5 with interest charges of $1.50 a month. Cases have been known where a Negro brought to a plantation his mules and stock, worked a season, and at the end saw all his crop of cotton taken, and his property swept up, including the mules, which are exempt by law. Many back plantations take the seed for the ginning—that is, they exact more than twice what the service is worth. A Negro has been known to borrow say $200; when it was not paid, the white lender seized on all his possessions, and without going through any legal formality gave him credit for $100, leaving the balance of the debt hanging over his head. A peddler has been known to insist on leaving a clock at the house of a poor colored woman who protested that she did not want a clock, could not afford a clock and would not take a clock. The man drove off, returned some months later, demanded payment for the clock which was just where he left it, never having been started, and when the money was not forthcoming proceeded to take away the woman's chickens—her poor little livelihood. She ran to a white neighbor, who came back with her and turned the scoundrel out. There is first and last much of this advantage taken of the ignorance and poverty of the Negro; a certain type of planter declares that he can make more money out of an ignorant black than out of an educated one. As one of the white friends of the colored race in the South says, the Negroes must receive at least sufficient education to enable them to protect themselves against such exaction.

Considering the immense importance of cotton to the South, it is amazing how wasteful is its culture and its distribution. Experts say that a great part of the cost of fertilizers could be saved by cultivating the cow pea.

About six per cent of the value of the fiber—a trifle of forty million dollars—is seriously injured by ginning. Comparatively few farmers or planters select their seed, though several of the Southern agricultural colleges have set up cotton schools, and the president of the Mississippi Agricultural and Mechanical College has actually begun to hold farmers' institutes for the negro farmers. The cotton bale is probably the most careless package used for a valuable product. It sometimes literally drops to pieces before it reaches the consumer; and of course the grower, in the long run, loses by the poor quality or the poor packing of his product. The grading of cotton requires that a large quantity be brought together in one place, and the small grower gets little advantage out of improvement in his staple.

What the South most needs in cotton is the improvement of the labor. As President Hardy, of the Mississippi Agricultural College, says: " So many of our negroes are directing their own work that their efficiency must be preserved and increased or great injury will result to our whole economic system. The prosperity of our section as a whole is affected by the productive capacity of every individual in our midst. The negro's inefficiency is a great financial drain on the South, and I believe this farmers' institute work for the negro is the beginning of a permanent policy that will be very far-reaching in its results. There is no doubt that this is one of the ways of increasing the cotton production of the country that has heretofore received very little attention."

It remains to consider the relation of the race question to cotton manufacture. Long before the Civil War it was seen that the Southern staple was being sent to foreign countries and to the North to be manufactured, and that the South was buying back its own material in cotton goods; therefore some cotton mills were constructed in the South. The labor in these mills seems to have been entirely white, but their product, which was of the coarser qualities, was never large enough to control the market. About 1880 came a new era of cotton manufacture, aided first by the extension of the railway system, second by the development of water power, and third by the discovery that the poor whites make a tolerable mill population. Hence grew up a chain of flourishing factory towns, most of them on or near the "fall line," so as to take advantage of the water powers, and there has been a steady growth of Southern manufactures. In 1887 the Southern mills worked up only 400,000 bales, which was one fifth of the staple used for manufactures in the United States. Twenty years later they were making up 2,400,000 bales, which was one half the consumption. The state of South Carolina alone in 1905 produced manufactures to the amount of $79,000,000.

The first thing to notice in this manufacture is that the mill hands are still exclusively white. Several efforts have been made in Columbia, Charleston, and elsewhere to carry on cotton mills with negro labor, and a few negro capitalists have built mills in which they expected to employ people of their own race; but every one of these experiments seems to have been a failure, partly because of the ignorance of the average Negro who could be drawn into the industry, and partly because of his irregularity. The Poor Whites do not make by any means the best mill help, and their output of yards per hand is considerably less than that in the Northern states. The supply of white labor also shows signs of depletion, though Mountain Whites are being brought down; it is still a question whether they will settle in the new places, or whether after they have saved money they will return to their mountains. Hence the frantic efforts to bring in mill hands from outside the South. Northern hands will not accept a lower wage scale and do not like the social conditions. It is plain that the Southern cotton manufacture is entirely dependent upon the supply of native white labor.

Notwithstanding the great growth of cotton manufacture in the South, the fine qualities are still made elsewhere; and the capital employed, the total wages paid, and the value of output are much greater in the North. The value of the product in South Carolina rose between 1890 and 1905 from $10,000,000 to $50,000,000, but in the same period the value in Massachusetts rose from $100,000,000 to $130,000,000. The output of cotton goods in Columbia, $5,000,000 is less than half the output of Nashua, New Hampshire. The New England states still furnish nearly one half the output of cotton manufactures, measured by value. The Northern states as a whole pay $65,000,000 a year for wages against $27,000,000 in the South; and their product is $270,000,000 against $268,-000,000 in the South. It is evident, therefore, that the scepter for cotton manufacture has not yet passed into the hands of the South.

The discussion of the economic forces and tendencies of the South in the last three chapters may now be briefly recapitulated. The South is a prosperous and advancing region on the highway to wealth, but advancing rather more slowly than other agricultural sections of the country, and in material wealth far behind the West and farther behind the Middle states and New England. It will be several decades before the South can possibly have as much accumulation as that now in possession of the region which most resembles it in the United States, the Middle West and Far West. Of its sources of wealth, the timber is temporary, mining and iron making limited in area. The chief employment must always be agriculture, and particularly cotton. Cotton culture on a large scale, as now carried on, is an industrial enterprise in which the laborer is likely to be exploited. The advance system is a curse to the South, inciting to extravagance and leading to dreams of wealth not yet created; it is especially bad for the Negro, who is at his best as a renter, or still more as the owner of land. Economically the progress of the negro laborer is very slow, but he is absolutely necessary to the welfare of the South, for no substitute can be discerned.

CHAPTER XX

FROM the earlier chapters on the Negroes and on the Cotton Hands it is plain that the Southern agricultural laborer is unsatisfactory to his employer, and not happy in himself; that the two races, though allied, are yet in disharmony. Of recent years a new or rather a renewed cause of race hostility has been found, because the great demand for labor, chiefly in the cotton fields, gives rise to the startling abuse of a system of forced labor, commonly called peonage, which at the mildest is the practice of thrashing a hand who misbehaves on the plantation, and in its farthest extent is virtually slavery. For this system the white race is solely acountable, inasmuch as it is the work of white men, sometimes under the protection of laws made by white legislatures, and always because of an insufficient public sentiment among white people.

When the slaves were set free, the federal government was careful to protect them against a relapse into bondage. The Thirteenth Amendment, which went into effect in 1865, absolutely prohibited " slavery or involuntary servitude except as a punishment for crime whereof the party shall have been duly convicted." In addition, in 1867, an act of Congress formally prohibited " the system known as peonage." A further statue of 1874 declared it a crime " to kidnap or carry away any other person with intent to hold him in involuntary servitude." The word "peonage" comes from the Mexican system of serfdom, the principle of which is, that if an employee owes his master he must continue to serve him until that debt is paid, the only escape being that if another employer is willing to come forward and assume the debt the employee is allowed to transfer his obligation to the new master. In practice, the system amounts to vassalage, inasmuch as the debt is usually allowed to reach a figure which there is no hope of paying off.

The term "involuntary servitude" is clear enough, and it is a curious fact that when the Philippine Islands were annexed there was a system of slavery in the Sulu Archipelago which was actually recognized by a treaty made by General Bates; but the federal government dropped the treaty, and there is no doubt that the United States courts would uphold any Sulu bondman who sought his liberty under the Thirteenth Amendment.

In 1865 some of the Southern states passed vagrant laws under which Negroes were obliged to make a labor contract for a year, and could be compelled to carry out that contract; and the belief in the North that these statutes were virtually intended to reënslave the freedmen was one of the mainsprings of the Fourteenth Amendment and the other Reconstruction legislation.

Inasmuch as the raising of cotton requires almost continuous labor, it is customary to make voluntary contracts with both renters and wage hands running for a year, commonly from the first of January; and breach of contract is a special grief and loss to the planter, inasmuch as if a Negro throws up a crop it is often impossible to find anybody else to finish it. Hence has grown up almost unconsciously a practice which closely resembles the Mexican peonage. It is unwritten law among some planters that nobody must give employment for the remainder of the year to a hand who is known to have left his crop on another plantation; and still further, that no contract should be made at the beginning of the year with a family which, after accounting for the previous crop, is still in debt to a neighbor, except that the new employer may pay the old debt and charge it as an advance against the hand. There is nowhere any legal sanction of this widespread practice, but the result is that thousands of Negroes are practically fastened to their plantation because nobody else in the neighborhood will give them employment; and far too many planters therefore make it a point to keep their hands in debt.

This system grew up slowly and attracted little attention till it began to be applied to Whites. During the last ten years the South has been opening up sawmills and lumber camps, often far back in the wilderness. In order to get men either from the South or the North, it was necessary to prepay their fare, which was subsequently taken out of their wages. Hence the proprietors of those camps felt that they had a claim on the men's service, and in some cases kept them shut up in stockades. For instance, in 1906, a Hungarian named Trudics went down to Lockhart, Texas, receiving $18.00 for railroad fare, on an agreement to work for $1.50 a day. He did not like the work and thought he had been deceived as to the terms; whereupon he used a freedman's privilege of bolting. He was trailed with bloodhounds by one Gallagher, caught, brutally whipped by the boss, and driven back, as he said, "like a steer at the point of a revolver."

Similar cases have been reported from various parts of the South, involving both native Americans and foreigners;

the latter have sometimes had the special advantage of aid from the diplomatic representatives of their country. Inasmuch as some of the state courts were unwilling to take action, cases were brought before the federal courts under the Peonage Act of 1867. Thus, though the personal abuse of Trudics by Gallagher was a state offense which seems to have escaped punishment, the violent laying of hands on him and restraint of his liberty was made a case before a federal court; and Gallagher was sent to prison for three months. It is plain that if foreigners and white Northerners can be practically enslaved, the same thing may happen to white Southerners; this and other like convictions have had a good effect. Quite beyond the injustice of the practice, it has been a damage to the South because it checks a possible current of immigration.

In 1908 an attempt was made to show a case of peonage of Italians on the Sunny Side plantation, Arkansas. It proved that one of the hands had grown dissatisfied and started to Greenville to take a train for the wide world, leaving unpaid a debt of about a hundred dollars at the commissary. One of his employers followed him to the station and told him that if he attempted to leave he would arrest him for breach of contract; whereupon the man returned to the plantation. This was certainly not peonage, and the grand jury consequently refused to indict; but it was an attempt to enforce specific performance of a labor contract. Peonage of Whites seems to have about come to an end; it was not stopped, however, by public opinion in the South, and it still goes on through the holding in bondage of hundreds, perhaps thousands, of Negroes, either in unabashed defiance of law or through the means of cruelly harsh and unjust laws, aided by bad judges.

In the first place, many planters assume that a Negro

who is on the debit side on their books has no right to leave the plantation, even for a few days, and as one of them expressed it to me: "If he goes away, I just go and get him." A case recently occurred in Monroe, La., where some colored men were brought from Texas by one Cole on the assurance that they were to be employed in Arkansas. Instead they were switched off and set to work in Louisiana. One of them departed and made his way to Texas, but his master followed him, seized him, brought him back in defiance of all law, and set him at work again. The master was tried for peonage in Texas, but was not convicted.

One of the worst criminal cases of this kind is that of John W. Pace, of Dade City, Ala., who not only shut in his own people, but would seize any black that chanced along that way and compel him to work for him a few days. Judge Thomas G. Jones, who in 1901 was put on the federal bench in that state, made it his business to follow up Pace; when a jury declined to convict him, the judge rated them soundly; another case was made out and Pace thought it prudent to plead guilty, and was sentenced to fifty-five years in the penitentiary. The Supreme Court of the United States affirmed the constitutionality of the peonage law and Pace threw up his hands; then, on the request of the judge, the President pardoned him. These and some like convictions have shaken the system of confining men because the employer thinks that otherwise they will go away.

Nevertheless, under cover of iniquitous state laws, peonage of Negroes goes on steadily, first by a most unjust enforcement of various special state statutes which require agricultural labor contracts to be made in writing, and to run for a year. The illiterate Negro often does not know what he is signing, and if he did know might see no means of helping himself. It is difficult to contrive a legal penalty for a Negro who simply leaves his contract and goes off; he might be arrested and held for debt, since almost all such hands owe their employer for supplies or money; but all the Southern states have constitutional provisions against imprisonment for debt. The difficulty is ingeniously avoided by most of the states in the Lower South, which make it a punishable offense to draw advances on " false pretenses "; thereby a hand who attempts to leave while in debt to his master can be arrested as a petty criminal. But how is it provable that the Negro might not intend to return and carry out his contract? In Alabama the legislature, with intent to avoid the federal peonage law, has provided that the acceptance of an advance and the subsequent nonperformance of the contract shall be proof presumptive of fraudulent intent *at the time of making the contract*. Now the employer can follow his absconding hand by a process thus described by a planter. You arrest him on the criminal charge of false pretenses, which is equivalent to a charge of stealing the money; you get him convicted; he is fined, and in lieu of money to pay the fine he goes to jail; then you pay the fine and costs and the judge assigns him to you to work out the fine, and you have him back on your plantation, backed up by the authority of the state.

Let a few actual illustrations, all based on Southern testimony, show what is done under such a system. A woman borrows six dollars of a neighboring planter, who afterwards makes a demand for the money. As it is not paid, he sets up without further ceremony the pretense that she is obliged to work for him, refuses to receive back the money which her present employer furnishes her, and attempts to compel her to labor. In South Carolina a man starts to leave his employer, asserting that he has paid up his debt; the employer denies it; the man is brought into court and fined thirty dollars, and in lieu of the money goes back to the same servitude, this time hopeless. A Negro in Alabama makes a contract January 1st and takes $5.00 earnest money, and works until May; the master refuses to give him a house. He works two months more, and then leaves, is arrested for breach of contract, and the courts hold that the acceptance of that five dollars proves that he did not mean to carry out his contract, although he has worked seven months. A woman makes a labor contract; and before it expires marries a man whom she had never met at the time of making her contract; held, that her marriage proves that she did not mean to carry out the contract when she made it, and she is therefore guilty of false pretenses.

Even without a contract a Negro may be legally obliged to labor for a white man under vagrancy laws, by which Negroes who are not visibly supporting themselves may be convicted for that crime, and then sent to the County Farm, or hired out to somebody who will pay their fine. Once in the hands of a master, they are helpless. For instance, one Glenny Helms, who was apparently guilty of no offense, was in 1907 arrested, fined and sold to one Turner, who in this case thought it prudent to plead guilty of peonage. The son of this Turner was the agent in the most frightful case of peonage as yet recorded. A woman was accused of a misdemeanor; it is doubtful whether she had committed any; but at any rate she was fined fifteen dollars; Turner paid the fine; she was assigned to him and he set her to the severe labor of clearing land. And then what happened? What was a hustling master to do with a woman who would not pile brush as fast as the men brought it, but to whip her, and if she still did not reform, to whip her again, and when she still would not do the work, to string her up by the wrists for two hours, and when she still " shirked," God Almighty at last came to the rescue; she was dead! When they tried to prosecute the man for murder in the state courts, the sheriff of the county (who was in the gang) came to the other slaves who had seen this, as they were summoned to the grand jury, and told them that if they gave any damaging testimony " we will put you in the river." Such things happen occasionally in all civilized lands. As dreadful a crime was committed in Paterson, New Jersey, not many years ago; but there are two differences between the Bosschieter and the Turner cases. Those Jersey murderers were all convicted; that man Turner walks the earth, unmolested, not even lynched. The public sentiment of New Jersey was clear that an offense against the humblest foreigner was an offense against the Commonwealth; but the blood of that poor black woman cries in vain to the courts of Alabama; and the thousands of people down there who feel furious about such matters are so far helpless.

The states by their statutes of false pretenses are partners in those iniquities, but the federal government has done its best in prosecutions. Between fifty and a hundred indictments have been brought. Federal Judge Boyd, of North Carolina, said of his district: " There has been evidence here of cruelty so excessive as to put to shame the veriest barbarian that ever lived." Federal Judge Brawley, of South Carolina, has held void an act of that State making breach of labor contract a misdemeanor. Convictions have been obtained in half a dozen states, and it is altogether likely that the Supreme Court of the United

States will confirm this good work by holding invalid all state statutes which attempt to enforce a debt by sending a man to prison, or still more by selling his services to a master.

Here, as in so many other phases of this question, the troublous thing is not that there should be cruelty and oppression or servitude. Gangs of Italians under a padrone in the North are sometimes little better than bondmen. Masters of almshouses and reform schools will sometimes be brutal unless their institutions are frequently and carefully inspected. The real difficulty is that the superior race permits its laws and courts to be used for the benefit of cruel and oppressive men; that public sentiment did not prevent the peonage trials by making the cases impossible; that a federal judge in Alabama should be assailed by members of the bar and members of Congress because he stopped these practices. Peonage is an offense which cannot be committed by Negroes; it requires the capital, the prestige, and the commercial influence of white men.

The federal government has instituted investigations of these practices, and Assistant Attorney General Russell has urged the passing of such federal statutes as shall distinctly reach these cases of detention; and also the amendment of the state laws so as to take away the authority to transfer the services of anyone from the state to an individual. This last is a reform of which there is especial need. Most of the cases of peonage arise out of the practice of selling the specific services of a convict to an individual; and it carries with it practically the right to compel such a person to work by physical force. What is to be done with a bondman who refuses to touch a hoe, except to whip him, and to keep on whipping him till he yields? The guards and wardens of prisons in the South use the lash freely, but they are subject at least to nominal inspection and control. To transfer the distasteful privilege to a contractor or farmer is to restore the worst incidents of slavery.

Sympathy must be felt for the planters and employers who make their plans, offer good wages, give regular employment, and see their profits reduced or eliminated because they cannot get steady labor. Much of the peonage is simply a desperate attempt to make men earn their living. The trouble is that nobody is wise enough to invent a method of compelling specific performance of a labor contract which shall not carry with it the principle of bondage. Men enlisted in the army and navy may be tracked, arrested, and punished if they break their contracts —but they cannot be lashed into shouldering a gun or cooking a meal. Sailors are, by the peculiar conditions of isolation at sea, subject to being put in irons for refusing to obey an order—but the cat has disappeared from the legal arguments to do their duty. It is the concomitant of freedom that the private laborer shall not be compelled to work by force; there is no way by which the South can cancel that triumph of civilization, the exercise of free will. When will people learn the good old Puritan lesson that the power to do well involves the power to refuse well doing? That you cannot offer the incitement of free labor without including the possibility of the laborer preferring to be idle?

CHAPTER XXI

WHITE EDUCATION

THE most progressive nations have now definitely come to the conclusion that there is no mode of increasing industrial and commercial efficiency so effective as universal education sufficiently prolonged to effect permanent improvement in the observing and reasoning powers of the children." So said that primate of American education, President Eliot, in an address at Tuskegee, Ala. Though speaking before an audience chiefly composed of colored people, he was laying down a general principle, for he goes on to say that in the Southern states " for both whites and blacks the school time is too short; a large proportion of the children leave school at too early an age; well-trained teachers are lacking; and the range and variety of accessible instruction are too small. Hence a large proportion of both the white race and the black race in the South are in urgent need of better facilities for education."

This is one point of view; at the other extremity stand such men as a Southern editor who has recently written, " As an educational influence the investment of $100,000 in a cotton mill is worth ten times the $100,000 given a Southern college." What does the South as a whole think on this question of education? What are its needs? What has it so far done? What is it prepared to do? How does education affect the race question?

288

WHITE EDUCATION

Throughout the South there has been and still persists an excellent tradition of reading and of education among the classes which may be presumed to afford such advantages for their children. Classical allusions and quotations from Scripture and Shakespeare are still recognized by all well-educated men. Some of the few fine old plantation houses contain elegantly appointed libraries, stopping short, however, at the year 1836, or whenever the owner died. The city of Charleston has better bookstores than the city of Albany. Probably more people in North Carolina can comment on Shakespeare than in Maine; and the man who can read Horace without a pony and quote Greek without looking at the book is a public character. Besides this admiration for an old-fashioned learning that is now passing, the South feels a genuine and lively interest in what goes on in the world. The present generation of fairly well-to-do people travel more, see more, read more that is written in their own time, think more than did their fathers and grandfathers. They feel a genuine interest in education, put intelligent thought on methods, show respect for the colleges, are willing to spend money on schools.

Like England in the Eighteenth Century the South abounded in readers of good literature, while the land was full of ignorance. Though in early Virginia suggestions were made for free common schools, and Thomas Jefferson strenuously advocated them, though in the forties and fifties several Southern states had elaborate paper systems of schools, outside the large cities there were no graded schools open to all white children such as were familiar in the North after 1840. Even New Orleans waited for good school buildings till the fortunate bequest of McDonogh; as for free rural schools, not a single Southern

289

state had organized and set in operation a system before the Civil War. From the first the sparse settlement of the South, the presence of the Negro, and the lack of that commercial connection with the rest of the world which so arouses the human mind, made it difficult and perhaps impossible to found a system of general popular education in that region.

For the higher education of the dominant class much more was done. Beginning with William and Mary in 1692—the first colonial college except Harvard—many colleges were established. The first state university was North Carolina, founded in 1790; the first American university of the German type was the University of Virginia, which began operations in 1825; the first institution to introduce coeducation was Blount College, which, about 1800, conferred the degree of A.B. upon a woman. But for various reasons there never were money enough, students enough, and trained educators enough to man the Southern colleges that were founded; and secondary schools to feed the colleges were lacking. The girls had a few boarding schools, some of which were called colleges by courtesy, but their education was superficial. Many students who could afford it found their way to Northern colleges, and that is why John C. Calhoun, the apostle of slavery, was a Yale graduate, and Barnwell Rhett, the protagonist of secession, was a graduate of Harvard.

After the Civil War came a dismal period, when some of the old universities were closed for want of means and of professors who could take the oath of allegiance. The training of the children of the best families at that period has been thus described by one who experienced it: " The schools that I attended—may God forgive the young women who one after another taught the children of the sparsely settled neighborhood—were farces and frauds. There was no public school. . . . We lived in sort of a secluded training place for Southern gentlemen. . . . We never saw a newspaper. . . . The professor of mathematics —so a rumor ran—was a freethinker. He was said to have read Darwin and become an evolutionist. But the report was not generally believed; for, it was argued, even if he had read Darwin, a man of his great intellect would instantly see the fallacy of that doctrine and discard it."

One of the few benefits conferred by the Reconstruction governments was a system of general public schools nominally open to every child in city or country; but just as the education of Negroes and Poor Whites was beginning, the schools were separated for the two races, and the Negroes were cut off from Southern white teachers. To start the new system there was no tradition of public school training and management, little sense of public duty in laying sufficient taxes, and the South was very poor. Hence it was about 1885 before the South put into operation a general educational system, supported by public taxation. The most recent statistics available (for 1906) show over 6,000,000 common school pupils in the South, besides 380,000 pupils in private schools, 118,000 pupils in public high schools, and 34,000 more in private secondary schools; 38,000 students in public and private universities, colleges and schools of technology. Every Southern state has now worked out some system of both rural and urban public schools, and several of them have a sizable State school fund which is distributed among the districts. The ordinary type of rural school is practically the district school of the North over again. City schools are graded in the usual fashion. Most states have a State Superintendent of Education, and the more progressive communities like Louisiana are introducing county superintendents with power to compel good schools. Surely with so many people and so much money, all must be happy in the South. It is an educational army, with common school infantry, secondary school cavalry, and in the institutions of higher learning the heavy artillery and the big guns. Yet it is an army in which every division, brigade, and regiment is divided into two camps, in which spear clashes on shield, for hardly anything in the South so brings out into relief the race question as the problem of education, and especially of negro education.

The Reconstruction governments made no provision for public high schools, but the growth of towns and cities in the South and the need of preparatory schools for the colleges, and the public sense of the value of secondary education, have compelled the founding of a great number of such schools, both for girls and boys. Normal schools have also developed till there are 45 with over 10,000 students. The colleges are also flourishing; and of professional schools the South has more than 160, with above 12,000 students.

A rough measure of the need of education is the statistics of illiteracy, which in the reports of the United States Commissioner of Education is defined as the status of a person over ten years of age who is able neither to read nor to write. Such illiterates in Germany are about one per cent of the population; in England about six per cent; in the whole of the United States about ten per cent. The various states of the Union show great variations: in Nebraska in 1900 it was two per cent; and the lowest Southern state, Missouri, with six per cent, showed a greater proportion of illiterates than any of 27 Northern

292

states; while the 12 highest communities on the list, from Arkansas with twenty per cent to Louisiana with thirty-eight per cent, are all Southern but two. Of 58,000,000 persons sufficiently old to be capable of both reading and writing in some language in the United States in 1900, 6,000,000 were illiterate, of whom about 4,000,000 lived in the South; of the 21 most illiterate states and territories, 15 are Southern, the worst being Alabama, South Carolina, and Louisiana, in all of which more than a third of the population was illiterate. This alarming state of things is not due wholly to the negro race; out of 5,700,000 blacks at least ten years of age, 2,700,000, or forty-eight per cent, were illiterate; out of 13,000,000 Whites, 1,400,000, or eleven per cent, were illiterates. The white illiterates, with all the advantages of their superior race, were half as numerous as the Negroes! Out of 1,900,000 white children of school age, 200,000, or ten and a half per cent, could not read or write; out of 1,000,000 colored children of the same age, 300,000 were illiterate, which is twenty-five per cent.

For both races this proportion of illiterates is steadily diminishing; and that is the effect of the schools and of nothing else. Never again will the South see a generation like the present, in which many adults have had no opportunity, or have neglected the opportunity of going to school when children. These figures accord with the experience of other states; for instance, New Hampshire in 1890 was as illiterate as Missouri was in 1900; and in both states illiteracy is steadily decreasing. As for the Southern Poor Whites, it is true, as Murphy says, that they have a potentiality of education. " I find no hopelessness in it, because it is the illiteracy, not of the degenerate, but simply of the unstarted. Our unlettered white people are native

293

American in stock, virile in faculty and capacity, free in spirit, unbroken, uncorrupted, fitted to learn."

The gross figures of illiteracy are misleading, because the old people who cannot now be taught to read and write reduce the general average against the children who are learning the arts of intelligence. The percentage of colored illiterates in the whole of the United States in 1900 was forty-four per cent as against seventy per cent in 1880; in Louisiana the percentage runs up to sixty-one per cent; but the Negroes between ten years old and twenty-five show only about thirty per cent of illiteracy, and that proportion is steadily decreasing. In 1900 the illiterate children from ten to fourteen years of age were in Mississippi only twenty-two per cent. With reasonably good schools and proper laws for compulsory attendance illiteracy may be expected to sink to about the figures of other civilized nations.

This raises at once the question of the actual efficiency of the schools in the South, their comparison with other parts of the country, their probable effect upon the future of the region. The ability to write one's name and to read a few words is only the beginning of education; the real educational question in the South is, What are the schools doing beyond the rudiments of the three R's? Some light is thrown on that question by comparing the school statistics of the Lower South with those of a block of similar Western and Northwestern agricultural communities from Indiana to Utah: 20,700,000 Southerners have 7,000,000 children of school age (five years to eighteen), of whom 4,400,000 are enrolled and the average daily attendance is 2,700,000; 20,700,000 Northerners with 6,000,000 children (a million less than the equivalent South) enroll 4,500,000 and have a daily attendance of 3,200,000. The

Southern group has 92,000 teachers; the Northern, 158,-000. The value of Southern school property is $42,000,-000; of Northern, $217,000,000, or over four times as much. The Southern school revenue is $26,000,000; the Northern, $92,000,000. The average expenditure per pupil attending in the South is under $10.00; in the North nearly $30.00. The South spent about 16 cents on each hundred dollars of valuation; the North spent about 20 cents.

When the whole South together, including such rich states as Maryland and Missouri, is compared with an equivalent population group in the North, the figures are more favorable to that section: 28,000,000 Southerners furnished an average daily attendance of 3,700,000 children; the same number in the North furnished 4,200,000. The South has 127,000 teachers; the North, 200,000. The total value of Southern school property is $84,000,000; of Northern, $294,000,000. A comparison of per-capita expenditure in the year 1900 showed an average school tax in the United States of $2.84 per head; but not a single state south of Washington raised above $2.10. Alabama raised only 50 cents, and even the rich state of Texas only about $1.50, as against $4.80 in North Dakota. Tennessee spent $1,800,000 a year in public education; Wisconsin, with an equivalent population, spent $5,500,000; South Carolina, with a population nine tenths that of California, spent one eighth as much. The state of Mississippi spent $6.17 per pupil annually; the state of Vermont spent $22.85.

Inasmuch as the Negroes contribute several million school children and not very much in taxes, it will be instructive to compare the 12,000,000 Whites of the Lower South with 12,000,000 Northwestern Whites, in those forms of education which are referable chiefly to the

Whites. The Lower South, on this basis, furnished in 1906 68,600 pupils in public secondary schools against 172,600 in the equivalent North; the secondary school plants in the South cost $23,000,000; in the North $52,-000,000. The college students in the South were 27,800; in the North, 27,200. The Southern college income was $6,000,000; the Northern, $7,500,000. Here, again, the comparison of the whole South with 18 million Whites against 18 equivalent millions in the Northwest is somewhat more favorable. The secondary plant costs $40,-000,000 against $77,000,000 in the North. The normal schools of the South have an income of $1,400,000, those of the North $2,400,000. The Southern college students are 38,-000 against 42,000; and the college income, $9,000,000 against $12,600,000.

The inevitable inference from these figures is that the South still needs to bring up its equipment and its expenditure if it is to educate as efficiently as its neighbors; and this presumption is strengthened by observation of schools of various grades. The Southern city schools are good, especially in the former border states; St. Louis, Baltimore, and Louisville come close up to Cleveland, Indianapolis, and St. Paul in the outward evidences of educational progress. Statistical comparison of a group of Southern cities with a group of Northern cities of the same aggregate population shows that in externals they are not far apart; the Northern schools have more schoolrooms, more teachers and more plant, but the annual expenditures are about as large in the Southern as in the Northern group.

The rural white schools are a different matter. It is, to be sure, nearly thirty years since old Bill Williams explained why there was no school in the Clover Bottom district in the Kentucky mountains: " They couldn't have no school because there wasn't nary door or winder in the school-house. I've got that door and winder, and I paid a dollar for 'em; but I've been keeping 'em, you see, because there was trouble about the title. Jim Harris gin us that land, and we 'lowed 'twas all right, because it belonged to his gran'ther and he was the favorite grandson; but when the old man died it 'peared like he had willed it to somebody else; and I wouldn't put no door nor winder into no school-house where there ain't no title, and there hain't been no school there sence. You want to know when all that trouble happened 'bout the title? I reckon it was fifteen or twenty year ago." There are still just such schools or rather such no schools in many parts of the South.

Even in prosperous regions, buildings, apparatus, and teacher may be alike, dirty and repellent. Take, for instance, Mt. Moriah school in Coosa County, Alabama. The building is twenty-five feet square, inclosing a single room with two windows and two doorways, one of them blocked up. In the middle is an iron stove, around which on a winter's day are parked four benches in a hollow square, upon which, or studying in the corner, huddle and wriggle twenty-three pupils, ranging from seven up to twenty-one years of age. They are reading physiology aloud, in the midst of the gaunt room, with very little in the way of blackboards or materials. An example of the better district schoolhouse is in a populous region near the mill town of Talassee; a new building with eleven windows, well ceiled throughout, with a clean gravel space in front, good desks and plenty of blackboard.

The curse of many of the rural schools is their easy money, for all the Southern states have a system of state school funds, the income of which is subdivided among the districts, and is in some of them about enough to keep up school three or four months on the usual scale of payment to teachers. When the school fund is exhausted, great numbers of districts close their schoolhouses, and the result is that the average number of school days in a year is far below that of Northern schools. In Massachusetts, Connecticut, and Rhode Island the public schools are in session about 190 days; in Georgia, 118; in Arkansas, 87. These are averages; and since the city schools commonly run seven or eight months, there must be many districts in which there are not over fifty or sixty days' school. One of the great educational reforms now going on in the South is to secure from the local governments appropriations to continue the schools after the state fund runs out. When the South is sufficiently aroused to the blessing of education, it will find that it has money enough for its needs.

Another defect is in the schoolhouses. The Southern towns and cities are coming to follow the example of the West and North in putting up imposing school buildings, though there is no such need for elaborate heating apparatus and ventilation as in the North, and they are in general simpler. The country schoolhouse is in many cases a big, dirty hut, often built of logs, wretchedly furnished, and devoid of the commonest appliances of civilization. There seems to be a feeling throughout the South that schoolhouses cannot be built wholly out of taxation, but the people on the ground must contribute at least a part of the cost. You may find neat and tidy rural schoolhouses, actually painted, but they are far from typical.

Another difficulty is the teachers. The monthly salaries for white teachers in several of the Southern states are high. A Coosa County farmer complains that a teacher in his district is getting $3.50 a day for twenty days in the month, which was more than any farmer in the district could earn. But of course her $70.00 a month would only run while school was in session, which might be five months. In Louisiana rural teachers receive higher salaries than in any other state in the Union, and no commonwealth is making such determined effort to improve its rural schools. In the remoteness of Catahoola Parish may be seen a system of wagonettes to bring children to central graded schools, a reform which goes very slowly in New England.

A further reason for the backwardness of the Southern rural schools is that they are in the hands of county superintendents, whose place until recently has too often been political. Now there is a body of trained superintendents who are giving people object lessons in what can be done even with poor buildings by well-trained teachers. The South is also bending its energies on normal schools, and the result is a growing body of teachers with professional spirit, who expect to make the schools their life work. The state superintendents are also improving in their professional power. The worst Southern rural schools are not too much behind those that Horace Mann found in Massachusetts when he began his work in 1837; the wages of the rural teachers are probably not so low as those in Maine; and the next decade will see a vast improvement in the rural schools throughout the South.

So with the secondary schools, where the number of pupils has astonishingly increased. In 1898 there were in the South 1,107 schools and 72,000 pupils; in 1906 there were 1,685 schools (Texas alone has 321), 5,100 teachers, and 118,000 pupils. A great change has come about in the education of girls. Nearly half the teachers and nearly two thirds of the pupils (70,000) in these schools are women, and that means that in connection with the normal schools, in which there are over 7,000 women students, the South is now training a body of teachers who are going to make a great change in the education of the next generation. The growth of secondary schools means further that the South is putting an end to a reproach of many years' standing—namely, that it could not adequately prepare pupils for college.

It was a severe lesson when the trustees of the Carnegie retiring allowance fund in 1906 laid down its principle that no grant would be made to professors in any college which did not come up to the following standard: " An institution to be ranked as a college must have at least six professors giving their entire time to college and university work, a course of four full years in liberal arts and sciences, and should require for admission not less than the usual four years of academic or high school preparation, or its equivalent, in addition to the preacademic or grammar school studies." To the surprise of the Lower South, it was discovered that only one institution,. Tulane University, had insisted on the condition of four years academic or high school preparation. Several other organizations are waking the South up to the need of improvements, such as the Association of Colleges and Preparatory Schools of the Southern states, with nineteen colleges as members; a commission of the Southern Methodist Church; the General Education Board of New York, with its fund of $43,000,-000; and the Southern Education Board.

In the South as in the North, there are two types of institutions of higher learning, the endowed (in most cases denominational) and the public. The number of Southern colleges is considerable; 166 out of 493 in the United States—which is not far from the proportion of the population; but only 8 of these institutions have upward of 500 undergraduate students, as against 42 in the rest of the Union; and the total number of undergraduate students in universities, colleges, and technological schools, 25,300, is about a fifth of the total of 122,000 in the United States, while the normal proportion would be a third. The property of the Southern colleges (.$99,000,000) is about a fifth of the total college property; the income of $7,-300,000 is about a sixth of the whole, the benefactions in 1906 ($2,400,000) about a seventh. That is, in number, wealth, and students, Southern institutions of higher learning represent about the same reduced proportion to the North as in the case of public wealth and public expenditures; that means that an average million of people in the South enjoy less than half the educational advantages possessed by an average million in the Northwest.

This rather favorable proportion does not obtain in women's education; of the fifteen colleges for women, recognized by the Bureau of Education as of full collegiate rank, only 4 are in the South; they include less than an eighth of the women students, and their property is less than a tenth. The 95 Southern institutions classified as " Colleges for women, Division B " are practically boarding schools of secondary grade, and are balanced by the greater number of Northern girls in high schools; 345,000 against 70,000 Southern high school girls; the 17,000 in private high schools and academies are overbalanced by 35,000 in the North. One of the great needs of the South at present is high-class colleges for girls, which shall turn out a well-grounded and well-trained body of women, interested in public affairs, and shall be a nursery of high school and college teachers.

The Southern denominational colleges are open practically to men only. The normal schools receive both sexes, and 4,000 women are registered in the Southern universities, colleges, and technological schools which are open to both sexes, as against 10,000 men. As the Southern states grow richer, they are giving more attention and more money to their public institutions, but so far few of their advanced institutions take rank alongside the great Northwestern universities. The University of North Carolina has 682 students and an excellent tradition; the University of Texas counts 1,100 men and 400 women, and is in many ways the most flourishing of the Southern institutions. The University of Virginia, though it has an annual grant from the legislature, is practically an endowed institution with 700 students; the University of Georgia has 408 students, though it at one time put forth the whimsical claim that it had the largest attendance in the United States, surpassing Harvard and Columbia, a result made up by adding in day scholars in affiliated schools below the high school grade. The state university funds, including the federal grants, are usually dispersed among two, or even three or four small institutions.

There is a vigorous intellectual movement in the South. The recent graduates, who at one time had a preference for college appointments in their own colleges, are now giving way to a throng of eager young scholars who have enjoyed graduate study in American or foreign universities and hold higher degrees. Wherever you fall in with a body of those men, you are impressed with their good training and their broad outlook. Politics are yearly less forceful in such institutions; and probably never again will there be such an episode as happened in a border state university about ten years ago. A new president discovered after a time that the janitor of the college buildings was not disposed to take instructions from him, whereupon he appealed to the board of trustees to put the man definitely under his control. The trustees held their meeting, at the end of which the janitor appeared with a bundle of blue envelopes, the first of which he offered to the president with the confidential remark, " You're fired ! " The others were addressed to the professors, every one of whom was summarily removed. Having thus gone back to first principles, the trustees elected a new president and a new faculty, including some of the old teachers; strange to say, that university has since become one of the most promising in its section. In all institutions of this kind and in the literary faculties of many colleges is a sprinkling of Northern professors, for the Southern colleges, like the Northern, are more tolerant than they were half a century ago. Most of the young men now receiving appointments in colleges and scientific institutions have studied in other Southern colleges, in the North or in Europe; and in all the learned associations they take their places as well-equipped and productive men.

Professional education has also made great strides in the South. Many of the most promising young men are sent to Northern law and medical schools, not only because of their supposed educational advantages, but because it is thought well for a young man to have a double horizon; but the greater number find instruction in nearby professional schools either established by practitioners or attached to some university. For the medical students the hospitals which are springing up everywhere furnish clinical material. Theological education is less systematized; the older and more settled denominations have good schools, but too many preachers in the back country have no other training than a natural " gift of the gab." In the agricultural and mechanical colleges, and the engineering departments of the endowed public universities, the South is educating her future engineers and scientific men.

The educative effects of travel and intercourse with other people are making themselves felt. In ante-bellum times few Southerners traveled widely, except the comparatively small number of the richer young men who found their way to Northern colleges, or abroad. Until ten years ago it was difficult to hold Southern conventions and gatherings of intellectual men of kindred aims because people could not afford to travel. Now there is more circulation, more knowledge of the world, more willingness to see in what respects the South lags behind, a greater spirit of coöperation between Southern states, and with some people of other sections. The norms of common schools, secondary schools, and higher institutions are now laid down on about the same principles as in the North, and it remains to develop them, to make paper systems actual, to get more of the school children registered, more of the registered children in attendance, more months of school for those who attend, better teachers for the longer sessions, new buildings to accommodate the larger numbers, more students to fill the little colleges and to enlarge the universities. White education in the South is in a progressive and hopeful condition.

In the means of education outside of schools and colleges the South is still much behind the richer North, and still more behind foreign countries. Museums and picture galleries are few, aside from private collections in Baltimore, Washington, Richmond, and New Orleans. The fine old paintings that one sees in clubs and public buildings come from an earlier age, for there are few Southern artists. Nevertheless, the architectural standard is quite as high as in the North, and the tradition of wide spaces and colonnades persists. In its public buildings the South is in general superior to the North; even in remote county seats one may find buildings old and new of classic proportions, dignified and stately.

The South has been poor in collections of books, but all the larger Universities have fair libraries, and the cities have public libraries, and the numerous gifts of Carnegie have stimulated this form of public education. Several Southern cities, as, for example, Galveston, have endowed institutions for lecture courses on the general plan of the Lowell courses in Boston.

The South has never been highly productive in literature, and too much of the Southern writing bears evidence of a purpose of speaking for the South or in a Southern fashion. A considerable part of the books written by Southerners are about the South in one way or another; there is a sense of sectional obligation. This is the less necessary for a region from which have sprung Poe, one of the world's acknowledged literary delights, and Lanier. There is a school of Southern writers, of whom the late Joel Chandler Harris is a type, who have found broader themes of life about them and have given to the world the delightful flavor of a passing and romantic epoch. The principal literary work of the South is now in its newspapers.

Another intellectual force is found in the Southern historical societies, of which there is one in almost every state. They have shown a lively interest in saving the records of the early history of the South and in preserving its memorials from destruction. There are also two or three literary periodicals of distinct literary merit, in which one finds an expression of the newest and most modern South.

In every direction, then, the white people of the South

are alert. The schools are fair and improving, the community is awake to the need of educating all the children, even in the remote country; and though the taxes for education are still very light, there is a disposition to increase them. In Texas, for example, where there is a state tax, the people have by constitutional amendment authorized all school districts to double that amount by local taxation. If the Whites were the only people to be educated, and if education were the panacea, if it brought assurance of good government, the Southern question would in due time take care of itself.

The most hopeful sign of intellectual progress is the association of those most interested for the promotion of their common ends; such is the Coöperative Education Association of Virginia which holds annual meetings and general conferences for education. These meetings are means of attracting public attention to the problems and of suggesting the solution.

For many years education of the Whites in the South has been aided from the North, first, through considerable gifts for the education of the Mountain Whites, and second, through more sparing aid to colleges for Whites in the lowlands. Recently, however, the attention of wealthy Northern givers has been turned to the importance of uplifting the whole white Southern community, and after several annual visits to the South under the patronage of Mr. Robert C. Ogden, of New York, a Southern Education Board was formed, the purpose of which is to rouse people to the need of improving their education; following it is the General Education Board, which makes small gifts to educational institutions usually on the stipulation that they shall raise a conditional amount varying from an equal sum to a sum three times as great. This is the more necessary as there are only two or three institutions in the South that have anything like an adequate endowment. Tulane University in New Orleans has a property of several millions, and the University of Virginia has recently raised a new million outright, but the South has no large body of people with superfluous funds and its giving turns habitually rather in the direction of church construction and foreign mission work than to educational institutions. Of $1,400,000 given to the University of Virginia during thirty years, $900,000 came from Northerners and $270,000 more from foreigners living in the South.

Of late, voices have been raised for some kind of Federal aid to Southern education on the plea that where there is the greatest intellectual destitution there is the most need for money. The appeal is contrary to the usual instincts of the South in matters of federal and state relations, and is strongly opposed by part of the Southern press, particularly the *Manufacturers' Record,* which has waged a campaign against even the private gifts made through the General Education Board.

CHAPTER XXII

NEGRO EDUCATION

HOWEVER cheering the interest in general public and higher education throughout the South, the Whites get most of the benefit; the lower third of the people, the most ignorant, the poorest, the least ambitious, those whose debasement is the greatest menace to the community, are less in the public eye; and the efforts to educate them arouse antagonism of various kinds. All calculations as to numbers of pupils, school expenditures, and public opinion as to education are subject to restatement when the Negroes are taken into account. Even in states like Maryland and Kentucky, where they are not a fourth of the population, they disturb the whole educational system, and in the Lower South, where they are in many places overwhelming in numbers, the problem of their education becomes alarming.

Most people suppose that negro education began during the Civil War, but it is as old as colonization; free Negroes were always allowed some privileges in this respect, and thousands of slaves were taught to read by kind-hearted mistresses and children of the family; the opinion of one who has carefully explored this field of inquiry is that of the adult slaves, about one in ten could read and write. Nevertheless, this practice was contrary to the principles and the laws of the South, as is proved by the dramatic prosecution of Mrs. Margaret Douglass, of Norfolk, in 1853, for the crime of holding a school for free negro children, in ignorance of the fact that it was forbidden as "against the peace and dignity of the Commonwealth of Virginia." In due time this person, who had admitted unhallowed light into little dark souls, was duly sentenced to thirty days' imprisonment, a penalty (as the judge explained) intended to be "as a terror to those who acknowledge no rule of action but their own evil will and pleasure."

Both the teachings and the prosecutions establish a general belief that Negroes could easily learn to read and write; and when during the Civil War refugees flocked into the Union camps at Beaufort and Hilton Head, charitably disposed people in the North sent down teachers; and, the federal government coöperating, schools were started among those Sea Island people, then rough, uncouth, and not far beyond the savage state, though now a quiet, well-ordered, and industrious folk. From that time till the giving up of the Freedman's Bureau in 1869, the federal government expended some money and took some responsibility for negro education. It was a pathetic sight to see old gray-headed people crowding into the schools alongside the children, with the inarticulate feeling that reading and writing would carry them upward. The Northern missionary societies kept up these elementary schools, and then began to found schools and colleges for the training of the most gifted members of the race. Out of their funds, and with the aid of the freedmen, they put up schoolhouses, they collected money to establish institutions like Fisk University in Nashville, Leland and Straight Universities in New Orleans, and Atlanta University. Such colleges were on the same pattern as other colleges for Whites both North and South, adopting the then almost universal curriculum of Greek, Latin, and mathematics, along with smatterings of other subjects; they included preparatory schools, which, as in some white colleges both North and South, included the larger number of the recorded students.

Now came the founding of rural schools, for both Negroes and Whites; all the Reconstruction constitutions provided for free public schools; and since that time there has been public organized education for the colored people, such as it is, in every state, in every city, and in most of the rural counties having a considerable black population. The reaction against Reconstruction for some time bore against these schools and they have come along slowly. When, about 1885, the South entered upon a new career of education, the negro schools came more into people's minds; but they have not advanced in proportion to the white schools, and they have encountered a lively hostility directed particularly against the higher forms of education.

The present status of the negro common schools may be summarized from the report of the Commissioner of Education for 1906. Taking the whole South together, there were, in that year, over 2,900,000 colored children five to eighteen years old, of whom 1,600,000, or little more than half, were enrolled in school, while of the white children of school age nearly three fourths were enrolled. Out of 1,-600,000 enrolled, the average attendance was 990,000, or about a third of the children of school age, while of the whites it was 3,000,000, or nearly half the children of school age. For the 1,600,000 enrolled negro children, there were 28,000 teachers, or 1 to 57; for the 4,500,000 white children over 100,000 teachers, 1 to 45. The annual expenditures for the 6,200,000 children enrolled (white and black) were $46,000,000, but to the negro children (about a third of the whole, and least likely to be educated otherwise) was assigned about a seventh of this sum. To state the same thing in another form, in nearly all the Southern states at least twice as much was spent per pupil on Whites as on Negroes.

A part of this disparity is due simply to the fact that the superior race produces the larger number of children capable of secondary and higher training and has more money to carry its children along, to pay their expenses and tuition where necessary, in order to give them a start in life. That consideration does not account either for the very low enrollment or low attendance of negro children. The truth is that the majority of white people, who have the sole power of laying taxes and of appropriating money for education, think that the Negroes ought not to have school advantages equal to those of white children, or advancing beyond a common school education.

The mere statistics of negro schools and attendance after all carry with them little information. What kind of pupils are they? What kind of school buildings are provided for them? What is the character of their teachers? Naturally, among both races, many are at work after twelve or fourteen years, but the percentages of enrollment and attendance are so much less than those of the white people that apparently colored children are less likely than white to be sent to school and to be kept there when started. Though every Northern state without exception has some kind of compulsory education, not a single Southern state, except Kentucky and Missouri, has enacted it.

Some personal knowledge of Southern schools, both in cities and the country, suggests several reasons why the attendance is small. Visit this negro wayside school in the

311

heart of the piney woods near Albany, Ga. The building is a wretched structure with six glass windows, some of them broken; the sky visible between the weatherboards. There is one desk in the room, the teacher's, made of rough planks; the floor is rough and uneven. Of the forty-four children enrolled, none of whom come more than about three miles, thirty-two are present on a pleasant day; six of them appear to be mulattoes. They wear shoes and stockings and are quiet and well-behaved but sit in the midst of dirt on dirty benches. The teacher is a pleasant woman, wife of a well-to-do colored man in the neighboring town, but apparently untrained. She teaches five months at $35 a month. Last year there was no school at all in this district.

Enter another school at Oak Grove, Ala. The house is a single room, twenty-five feet square; larger than is needed, like many of the schoolhouses, because it may serve also for church services. There is not a sash in any one of the seven windows, each having a hinged shutter. The teacher has a table, and for the pupils are provided several rude benches with or without backs; the room is furnished with a blackboard and is reasonably clean; the teacher, a young man eager and civil, a graduate of a neighboring school carried on by the Negroes for themselves, holds five months' school. Take another school near Albany, Ga., in a tolerably good schoolhouse built by the Negroes themselves with some white assistance, for the county commissioners will do no more than offer $100 to a district that will spend about $300 more on a building. The room overcrowded, four or five at a desk; twice as many girls as boys; a good teacher who has had some normal training; a book for each group of three in the reading class; the lesson about a brutal Yankee officer who

312

compels a little Southern girl to tell where the Confederate officer is hiding. The children read well and with expression.

These are probably fairly typical of the rural negro schools throughout the South, and better than some. As a matter of fact, thousands of negro children have no opportunity to go to school, because the commissioners simply refuse to provide school in their district; perhaps because the number of children is thought too few; perhaps merely because they do not wish to spend the money. In a town with perhaps 2,000 Negroes there is sometimes only one negro teacher.

Here comes in the effect of the separate school system which prevails in every Southern state, in the District of Columbia, in Indianapolis, and in parts of New Jersey. The system was inaugurated just as soon as the Whites obtained control of the Reconstruction government after the Civil War, and it goes all the way through: seperate buildings, separate teachers, separate influences, separate accounts. The reasons for it are: first, the belief of white parents that negro children, even the little ones, have a bad influence on the white children; second, the conviction that mixed schools would break down the rigorous separation of races necessary to prevent eventual amalgamation; third, the blacks are niggers. In cities and towns it adds little to the expense to keep up separate buildings and corps of teachers, but in rural districts, where the number of children is small, the expense of double schools may be a serious matter.

One reason why the schools are poor is that the pupils are irregular, and one reason why they are irregular is that the schools are poor. The wretched facilities of the rural schools, both white and negro, tend to drive chil-

313

dren out; and the incompetent teachers do not make parents or children fonder of school. For the white schools a supply of reasonably intelligent young men and women is now coming forward. As to the Negroes, with few exceptions, every teacher is a Negro, though appointed by and supervised by some white authority; it is doubtful whether half the negro teachers have themselves gone through a decent common school education. Many of them are ignorant and uneducated. The superintendent of the town schools at Valdosta, Ga., says: "There are to-day outside of the cities, not more than one half dozen teachers in each county in the state, upon an average, who can honestly make a license to teach. The custom in most counties is to license so many as we are compelled to have to fill the schools from among those who make the most creditable show upon examination. School commissioners do not pretend to grade their papers strictly. If they did three-fourths of the negro schools would be immediately closed."

Conditions are not much better in the towns, where many negro teachers earn only $150 to $200 a year; but in the cities the negro teachers are more carefully selected, for they can be drawn from the local negro high schools or the normal schools. But the colored people are said to scheme and maneuver to get this teacher out and that one in. They have been known to petition against a capable and unblemished teacher on the ground that she was the daughter of a white man, and it was immoral for her to be teaching black children.

If the negro common schools are inferior to the white, this is still more marked in their secondary public schools, such as they are. No principle is more deeply ingrained in the American people than that it is worth while to spend

314

the necessary money to educate up to about the eighteenth year all the young people who show an aptitude, and whose parents can get on without their labor. The Southern states accept this principle, but for such education the Negroes have few opportunities. Out of 151,000 Southern young people in public and private high schools, 6,500 high school pupils and 2,600 in the private schools are Negroes. That is, a third of the population counts a seventeenth of the secondary pupils. Most of the so-called negro colleges are made up of secondary and normal pupils who get a training very like that of the Northern academies, and some favored cities have public high schools for the Negroes. This is the case in Baltimore, and was the case in New Orleans until about 1903, when the high schools were discontinued, on the ground that the Negro could not profit by so much education, although the lower branches of the high schools were still taught in the upper rooms of the negro grammar schools.

It must not be forgotten that there are more than a hundred institutions for training the colored people, which draw nothing from the public funds. These schools, in part supported by the colored people themselves, in part by Northern gifts, which during the last forty years have amounted to between thirty and fifty million dollars, are usually better than the public schools, and have more opportunities for those lessons of cleanliness and uprightness which the Negro needs quite as much as book learning. Those schools are a thorn in the side of the South—so much so that for years it was hardly possible to get any Southern man to act as trustee; they are supposed to teach the negro youth a desire for social equality; they are thought to draw the Negroes off from cordial relations with the Southern Whites; above all, they include the higher institutions which are credited with spoiling the race with too much Greek and Latin. To a considerable degree the schools of this type are mulatto schools, probably because the people of mixed blood are more intelligent and prosperous, and more interested in their children's future; but many of them are planted in the darkest part of the Black Belt—such as the Penn School in the Sea Islands. Wherever they exist, they appeal to the ambition and the conscience of the Negro, and help to civilize the race; they are not only schools but social settlements. Alongside the earlier schools and colleges planted by Northerners in the regular academic type, during the last thirty years have arisen first Hampton, then Tuskegee, and then many like schools, built up on the principle of industrial training, which will be described in the next chapter.

The Northern schools for the education of the Negroes have brought about one of the unpleasant features of the Southern question in the boycotting of the Northern teachers, both men and women, who have come down to teach them. This practice is a tradition from Reconstruction times when it was supposed that the Northern teachers were training colored youth to assert themselves against Whites. They expected only to furnish examples and incitements to the Southern people themselves; hence a feeling of bewilderment and grief, because from the very beginning the white teachers in these institutions have been under a social ban the relentlessness of which it is hard for a Northerner to believe. An educated and cultivated white family has lived in a Southern city, superior intellectually and morally to most of the community about it; yet no friendly foot ever crossed its threshold. The beautiful daughter, easily first in the girls' high school, never exchanged a word with her classmates outside the school, except when called upon, as she regularly was, to help out her less gifted fellows, as an unpaid and unthanked tutor—because her father was spending his life in trying to uplift the Negro. The attitude of the South toward most of those schools is one of absolute hostility. Even an institution so favorably regarded in the South as Hampton Institute has been prohibited by the Legislature of Virginia (which makes it a small money grant) from selling the products of its industrial department.

The negro colleges in the South are far from prosperous; planted in the day of small things with limited endowments, frequented by people who have little money to pay for tuition, they have been supported from year to year by Northern gifts which are not sufficient to keep them up to modern demands. Though some of them have tolerable buildings, few have adequate libraries, laboratories, or staff of specialist instructors. The state institutions of this grade open to blacks are nearly all rather low in standards, and offer little inducement for academic training; they are either normal or industrial in type. The better off of the Negroes send their sons to Northern white colleges where they may receive the best instruction but have little contact with their fellow students. So far from the number of negro college graduates being too great, it is entirely too small for the immediate needs of the race. They must have educated teachers and trained professional men; the negro schools will never flourish without competent teachers and supervisors of the negro race. In many respects the colleges are the weakest part of negro education. One school in which numbers have had good training, Berea College, Kentucky, has now been abandoned under an act of the state legislature forbidding the teaching of Whites and Negroes together, but an industrial school of high grade will be provided exclusively for the colored race.

As DuBois says: " If, while the healing of this vast sore is progressing, the races are to live for many years side by side, united in economic effort, obeying a common government, sensitive to mutual thought and feeling, yet subtly and silently separate in many matters of deeper human intimacy,—if this unusual and dangerous development is to progress amid peace and order, mutual respect and growing intelligence, it will call for social surgery at once the delicatest and nicest in modern history. It will demand broad-minded, upright men, both white and black, and in its final accomplishment American civilization will triumph." DuBois calculates that in the twenty-five years from 1875 to 1900 there were only 1,200 or 1,300 negro graduates from all the colleges open to them North and South, an average of about fifty a year out of a race numbering during that period, on the average, six millions. Out of this amount about half have become teachers or heads of institutions, and most of the rest are professional men.

Many of the academic and normal training schools of various grades are situated in the midst of large colored populations, and take upon themselves a work similar to that of the college settlements in Northern cities. Such is the flourishing school at Calhoun, Ala., which is in the midst of one of the densest and most ignorant Negro populations in the South, and besides training the children sent to it, it has supervised the work of breaking up the land, which is sold to negro farmers in small tracts, thereby giving an object lesson of the comfort and satisfaction in owning one's own land. Most such schools aim to be centers of moral influence upon the community about them.

Here, again, they encounter the hostility of their neighbors on the ground that they are putting notions into the heads of the Negroes, and are destroying the labor system of the community. On the other hand, many of the Whites take a warm interest in these schools, although not a single one has ever received any considerable gift of money from Southern white people. The testimony is general that they are well taught, preserve good order, and inculcate decency of person and life.

Probably the most effective argument in favor of negro education is the success of Hampton and Tuskegee, two endowed schools, practically kept up by Northern benefactors, which are the great exemplifiers of industrial education. They are successful, both in providing for large numbers of students—about 3,000 altogether—and in producing an effect upon the whole South. The number of graduates is but a few score a year, and many of them go into professions for which they were not directly prepared in these schools. But great numbers of men and women who have spent only a year or two in these institutions carry out into the community the great lesson of self-help; and hundreds of schools and thousands of individuals are moved by the example of these two famous schools and similar institutions scattered throughout the South. They preach a gospel of work; they hold up a standard of practicality; they are so successful as to draw upon themselves the anathemas of men like Thomas Dixon, Jr., who says: " Mr. Washington . . . is training them *all* to be masters of men, to be independent. . . . If there is one thing a Southern white man cannot endure it is an educated Negro."

The question is imperative. With all the efforts at education, notwithstanding the great reduction in the percentage of illiteracy, the number of negro adult men and women in the South who are unable to read and write is actually greater than at any time since by emancipation they were brought within the possibilities of education. The actual task grows greater every day, and if the resources of the South are more than correspondingly increased, it is still a question how much of them will be devoted to this pressing need. Education will not do everything; it will not make chaste, honest, and respectable men and women out of wretched children left principally to their own instincts. Education is at best a palliative, but the situation is too serious to dispense even with palliatives.

Perhaps the first necessity is to improve the character and the training of the negro teachers. Both in the rural and the city schools appointments are in many cases made by white school board men who have little knowledge and sometimes no interest in the fitness of their appointees. The colleges and industrial schools all have this problem in mind. State normal schools for Negroes in many of the Southern states try to meet this necessity, but a great many of the country teachers, some of them in the experience of the writer, are plainly unsuited for the task. Some of them are themselves ignorant, few have the background of character and intellectual interest which would enable them to transmit a moral uplift.

One of the most serious difficulties of negro education is the attendance, or rather nonattendance. Within a few weeks after the beginning of school, pupils begin to drop out; often perhaps because the teacher cannot make the work interesting. One of their own number says: " Many of our children do not attend school because our teachers are incompetent; because many of the parents simply dislike their teachers; because some parents prefer Baptist teachers; because many children have their own way about all they do; because many children do not like a strict teacher; because some parents contend for a fine brick building for the school; because, as a whole, many parents are too ignorant and prejudiced and contentious to do anything, yet we have enrolled about 150 pupils this session in spite of the devil."

Some of the schools are overcrowded. There have been cases where 6 teachers were assigned for 1,800 children, of whom 570 enrolled, yet the average earnings of the six teachers would not be more than $100 a year. Against these instances must be placed a great number of intelligent, faithful teachers who make up for some deficiencies of knowledge by their genuine interest in their work.

For negro education as for white, but perhaps with more reason, it is urged that the federal government ought to come in with its powerful aid. The argument somewhat resembles that of the blind Chinese beggar who was sent to the hospital where he recovered his sight, and then insisted that, having lost his livelihood, he must be made porter to the hospital. Aside from any claim of right, it is true that the problem of elevating the Negroes concerns the whole nation, and is a part of the long process of which emancipation was the beginning. Federal aid for colored schools, however, can never be brought about without the consent of the Southern states, and they are not likely to ask for or to receive educational funds intended solely for the Negroes; while Northern members of Congress are not likely to vote for taxing their constituents who already pay two or three times as much per capita for education as the South, in order to make up the deficiencies of the other section. It is impossible to discover any way in which federal aid can be given to the Negroes without reviving sectional animosity; and it is a fair question whether such gifts could be so hedged about that they would not lead to a corresponding diminution in the amount spent by the Southern states. The Government grants to state agricultural colleges and experiment stations inure almost wholly to the advantage of the Whites; if a part of that money could be devoted to the education of the Negro, it might be helpful.

Several educational trusts created years ago for the benefit of the Negroes have now ceased their work. The Peabody fund of about three million dollars was much depleted by the repudiation of the Mississippi and Florida bonds, and has now been entirely distributed. For some years it was devoted to building up primary teaching on condition that the localities benefited should themselves spend larger sums. Then it went into normal schools. In 1882 the Slater fund of one million dollars was given solely for the education of Negroes. The General Education Board in its allocations to Southern institutions has liberally remembered several of the negro institutions as well as the white.

CHAPTER XXIII

OBJECTIONS TO EDUCATION

IN the two previous chapters white and negro education have been described as parts of the social and governmental system of the South; there, as in the North, the tacit presumption is that education is desirable, that it is essential for moral and material progress, that both the parents and the community must make great sacrifices to secure it. White education hardly needs defense in the South; most of the people wish to see the opportunities of life open to promising young people, believe in the spread of ideas, and look on education as the foundation of the republic.

Does the principle, as in the North, apply to all the elements of population? Is the education of the Negro as clearly necessary as that of the White? Should the same method apply to the training of the two races? On the contrary, there is in most Southern white minds hesitation as to the degree of education suitable for the blacks; and a widespread disbelief in any but rudimentary training, and that to be directed toward industrial rather than intellectual ends.

The first objection to negro education is that the race is incapable of any but elementary education and that all beyond is wasted effort. Has the Negro as a race an inferior intellectual quality, a disability to respond to opportunities?

With all the effort to educate the race, and with due regard to the fact that the proportion who can read and write is rapidly rising, the Negroes are alarmingly ignorant, the most illiterate group in the whole United States; and therefore they need special attention. In addition, they are subjected to the smallest degree of home training, and enjoy the smallest touch with those concentrated forces of public opinion which force the community upward. Some of the Negroes seek intellectual life at home, for occasionally you see a family grouped about the fire with the father reading a book to them; but hardly any of the rural people and probably few of the townsmen own a shelf of books and magazines and newspapers. Their journalism is in general rather crude. A class of patent inside newspapers is carried on by the heads of one or the other negro order; and they contain good advice, news of the order, advertisements of patent hair dressings which "make harsh, stubborn, kinky, curly hair soft, pliant and glossy"; and descriptions of the experiments of surgeons in making black skin white by the use of X-rays. Some of these papers are well edited, and all of them have discovered the great secret of modern journalism, which is to put as many proper names as possible into the paper.

One difficulty with the negro newspaper is that it cannot fill up entirely with colored news; and on general questions and the progress of the world the regular white newspapers, with their greater resources, are certain to be more readable. Still, few Negroes outside the cities read either weekly or daily papers regularly; and one of the necessities for raising the race is to cultivate the newspaper habit. To be sure, there is a type of highly successful white journalism that does not edify the white race. Yet even a bad newspaper cannot help telling people what is going on in the world. In spite of its freight of crime, such a paper carries people out of themselves, makes them feel a greater interest for mankind, brings in a throng of new impressions and experiences, helps to educate them.

Outside of newspapers the Negroes have access to the written works of members of their own race, which are at the same time a proof of literary capacity and a means of teaching the people. Of course it is always urged that such men as Booker Washington, the educator and uplifter; Dunbar, the pathetic humorist; Chesnutt, author of stories of Southern life that rival Joel Chandler Harris and Thomas Nelson Page; DuBois, who in literary power is one of the most notable Americans of this generation; Kelly Miller, the keen satirist; and Sinclair, the defender of his people—prove nothing as to the genius of the races because they are mulattoes; but they and their associates are listed among the Negroes, included in the censure on negro colleges, and furnish the most powerful argument for the education of at least a part of the race. Few men of genius among the Negroes are pure blacks; but it is not true that the lighter the color the more genius they possess. So far as the effects of a prolonged and thorough education are concerned, those men from any point of view prove that the mulattoes, who are perhaps a fifth of the whole, are entitled to a thorough education. Has not Du-Bois the right to say:

" I sit with Shakespeare and he winces not. Across the color line I move arm in arm with Balzac and Dumas, where smiling men and welcoming women glide in gilded halls. From out the caves of evening that swing between the strong-limbed earth and the tracery of the stars, I summon Aristotle and Aurelius and what soul I will, and they come all graciously with no scorn nor condescension. So, wed with Truth, I dwell above the Veil. Is this the life you grudge us, O knightly America? Is this the life you long to change into the dull red hideousness of Georgia? Are you so afraid lest peering from this high Pisgah, between Philistine and Amalekite, we sight the Promised Land?"

On the other hand, the history of the last thirty-five years proves conclusively that the great mass of negro children can assimilate the ordinary education of the common schools. Mr. Glenn, recently Superintendent of Education in Georgia, declares that "the negro is . . . teachable and susceptible to the same kind of mental improvement characteristic to any other race," and Thomas Nelson Page admits that the "Negro may individually attain a fair, and in uncommon instances a considerable degree, of mental development." About three fourths of the young people have already learned to read.

Many people intimately acquainted with the race assert that, although about as quick and receptive as white children up to twelve or fourteen years of age, the negro children advance no further; that their minds thenceforward show an arrested development. Certainly anyone who visits their schools, city or rural, public or private, is struck with the slowness of the average child of all ages to take in new impressions, and with the intellectual helplessness of many of the older children. Whether this is due to the backwardness of the race, or to the uncouthness of home life, or to the want of other kinds of stimulus outside of school, is hard to determine. That there is any general arrested development is contradicted by thousands of capable youths, mulatto and full blood.

The very slowness of the black children is a reason for giving them the best educational chance that they can take. That is why the Southern Education Association which met in 1907 passed a unanimous resolution that: "We endorse the accepted policy of the States of the South in providing educational facilities for the youth of the negro race, believing that whatever the ultimate solution of this grievous problem may be, education must be an important factor in that solution."

Another point of view is represented by the statement of Thomas Nelson Page that the great majority of the Southern Whites "unite further in the opinion that education such as they receive in the public schools, so far from appearing to uplift them, appears to be without any appreciable beneficial effect upon their morals or their standing as citizens." Governor Vardaman, of Mississippi, as late as 1908 recommended the legislature to strike out all appropriations for negro schools on the ground that "Money spent to-day for the maintenance of the public school for negroes is robbery of the white man and a waste upon the negro. It does him no good, but it does him harm. You take it from the toiling white men and women; you rob the white child of the advantages it would afford him, and you spend it upon the negro in an effort to make of the negro that which God Almighty never intended should be made, and which man cannot accomplish." He asserts that the most serious negro crime is due to "The manifestation of the negro's aspiration for social equality, encouraged largely by the character of free education in vogue, which the State is levying tribute upon the white people to maintain."

In Cordova, S. C., in 1907, a business man who had visited a colored school and spoken encouragingly to the pupils, felt compelled by public sentiment to print an apology and a promise never to do anything so dreadful again. This criticism comes not simply from demagogues like Vardaman or weaklings like the Cordovan; intelligent planters will tell you that they are opposed to negro education because it makes criminals; and think their accusation proven by instances of forgeries by Negroes, which of course they could not have committed had they been unable to write. A superintendent of schools in a Southern city holds that even grammar school education unsteadies the boys so that they leave home and drift away; though he candidly acknowledges that it keeps the girls out of trouble and provides a respectable calling as teachers to many negro women.

Side by side with this feeling of disappointment or hostility, as the case may be, is the conviction of most Southern people that enormous sacrifices have been made for the negro schools. Thomas Dixon, Jr., with his accustomed exactness and candor, wrote a few years ago: " We have spent about $800,000,000 on Negro education since the War." These figures show a poverty of imagination: it would be just as easy to write " eight thousand millions " as " eight hundred." The estimate of the Bureau of Education is that in the thirty-five years since 1870 about $155,000,000 has been spent to support common schools for the negro race, which is about a fifth of the amount spent on the white common schools in the same period, and not a hundredth of the supposed present wealth of the South; in addition, heavy expenditures are made out of the public treasury for secondary and higher education in which the Negro has a slender share.

Another more specious complaint with regard to Negro education is that it is an unreasonable burden on the Whites to make them pay for negro education, and repeated attempts have been made to lay it down as a principle that

328

the Negroes shall have for their schools only what they pay in taxes. Thus Governor Hoke Smith, of Georgia, says: " Is it not folly to tax the people of Georgia for the purpose of conducting a plan of education for the Negro which fails to recognize the difference between the Negro and the white man? Negro education should have reference to the Negro's future work, and especially in the rural districts it is practicable to make that education really the training for farm labor. If it is given this direction it will not be necessary to tax the white man's property for the purpose. A distribution of the school fund according to the taxes paid by each race would meet the requirements."

In at least two states this idea has been to some extent carried out. In Kentucky the state school fund is apportioned among the school children without regard to race, but for local purposes the Negroes appear to be thrown on their own payments. And in Maryland, under various statutes from 1865 to 1888, all the taxes collected from Negroes were devoted to negro schools, the state adding a lump sum per annum.

This point of view involves a notion of the purpose of education and the reasons for public schools so different from that which animates the North that it is hard to deal with the question impartially. Massachusetts makes the largest expenditure per capita of its population in the whole Union, almost the largest expenditure per pupil, and certainly the largest aggregate expenditure, except the more populous states of New York, Pennsylvania, Illinois, and Ohio; Massachusetts spends on schools two fifths as much every year as all the fifteen former slaveholding states put together. In that state people think that school taxes are not money spent but money saved: that they get back every cent of their $17,000,000 a year, several times over, in the increased efficiency of the people, in the diminution of crime, in the addition to the happiness of life. Schooling is insurance, schooling is the savings bank that can't break, schooling is that sane kind of poor relief which prevents poverty. The last thing which any Massachusetts community thinks of reducing is school expenditure!

Furthermore, no principle is so ingrained in the Northern mind as that since education is for the public benefit, every taxpayer must contribute in proportion to his property. The rich corporations in New York or Pittsburg, childless old couples, bachelor owners of great tracts of real estate, wealthy bondholders educating their children in private schools, never dream of disputing the school tax on the ground that they, as individuals, make no demands on the school fund.

Still less would it enter the mind of any Northern community to divide itself into social classes, each of which should maintain its own schools. Such a proposition would go near to bring about a revolution. First of all, the non-taxpayer is a taxpayer; it is the *pons asinorum* of finance that the poor are more heavily taxed in proportion to their means than any other class of the community, through indirect taxes and the enhanced rents of the real estate which they occupy. As a matter of fact, all the taxes eventually paid by the Negroes in the South probably amount only to a third or a half of the three millions or so spent upon their schools. What of that? Are the Southern states the only communities in the country in which a comparatively small part of the population pays most of the taxes; it is altogether probable that in Boston or New York the payers of nine tenths of the taxes do not furnish one tenth of the school children. Who educates the Irish, German, Italian, Jewish, Greek, and Syrian children of those cities? The well-to-do part of the community, and it does it uncomplainingly, with its eyes open, gladly. The South likewise is educating the Negroes principally for the advantage of the white race, for the efficiency of the whole region in which the Whites have the greatest stake, and from which they derive the greater benefit, material and moral.

One of the most obstinate Southern conventional beliefs, widely held, constantly asserted, and diametrically contrary to the facts, is that the Negroes have been spoiled by classical education which has totally unfitted them for ordinary life. Thus even Murphy holds that " We have been giving the Negro an educational system which is but ill adapted even to ourselves. It has been too academic, too much unrelated to practical life, for the children of the Caucasian." The intelligent man on the cars will tell you that the negro college graduates with their Greek and Latin are spoiling the whole race. Never was there such an advertisement of the vigor of college education; since the official statistics show that the actual number of Negroes studying Greek and Latin in 1906, both in the secondary and higher schools (except the public schools), was 1,077 men and 641 women, a total of 1,718 persons. With some possible additions from those in high schools, and higher institutions, the total number of colored people who are now taking any kind of collegiate training is not above 3,000, of whom only 180 took degrees in 1906; there are also 4,500 normal students, of whom 1,270 graduated. Of professional students there were in all (1906) about 1,-900 Negroes, a third of whom were in theology and another third in medicine. Of negro colleges and technical schools and private academies, 127 are enumerated, rang-

ing all the way from the Arkadelphia Baptist Academy
with 50 students, up to Tuskegee Normal and Industrial Institute with 1,621 students; but in all such colleges
those ranked as taking a college course are comparatively
few.

These figures throw light on the further conventional
·belief that it is the Northern endowed colleges that have
made the trouble in the colored race, through efforts to
teach the colored youth that they were the equals of the
Whites. By far the greater number of Negroes who are
really getting training above the secondary grade in the
South are in the state-sustained institutions—many of
them, of course, still of low grade; and full credit should
be given to the South for developing this type of negro
education, of which the North knows little. State Agricultural, Normal or Industrial colleges are to be found
in every former slaveholding state, except Arkansas and
Tennessee, and together include more than 5,000 students.

The attacks, chiefly from Southern Whites, upon negro
college education have of late been transformed into a controversy as to the relative importance of academic and
industrial training. The schools of the Tuskegee type furnished manual work to their students apparently not in
the first instance because it was thought to be educative,
but because they had to earn part of their living. This is
apparently the main source of the bitter hostility of Dixon
to the work of Tuskegee. The form his criticism takes
is that Booker Washington, instead of teaching the Negro
to be a good workman, is training him to take independent
responsibility; that if he is a good workman he will compete with the Whites, and if he is a good leader he will aim
to make the Negroes a force in the community. This line

of objection to education of the black is really based upon
the belief that they are a race capable of education, that
the Negro is not a clod, but may be improved by the systematic efforts of superior men; he has in him the potentiality of vital force.

Meanwhile throughout the country has been running a
current in favor of a more practical education than that
furnished by the ordinary schools, and the result has been
the Technical, Manual Training, and Commercial schools
scattered throughout the Northern states. The controversy
is not at all confined to questions of negro education. The
Southern white people have been well inclined toward the
new type of education for Negroes, although on the whole
much preferring the academic type for their own children.

A hot discussion has raged as to which of the two systems is most necessary to the Negro. The champions of
the academic side dwell upon the right of the Negro to the
same type of education as the white man. In many white
minds lies a lurking feeling that academic negro training
leads to discontent with present conditions; and that industrial training is more likely to bring about contentment
with the things that are. In fact, both types are most necessary. The fifty millions poured into the South by Northern generosity would have been worth while if they had
done no more than maintain a Hampton which could train
a Booker Washington. His ideas of thrift, attention to
business, building decent houses, putting money into banks,
are ideals specially needed by the negro race; but they also
need the DuBois ideal of a share in the world's accumulated
learning; of the development of their minds; of preparation
to educate their fellows. That a supply must be kept up
of people acquainted with the humanities, having some
knowledge of literature, able to express themselves cogently,

competent to train the succeeding generations, is as true for the negro race as for any other; if it is a low race it has the greater need for high training for its best members.

The two difficulties with manual training for either Whites or Negroes are, first, that it may be simply practice in handicrafts, without intimate knowledge of tools or processes, possessing no more educative value than the apprenticeship of a carpenter or a blacksmith. The other danger is that the manual part will be dilettante; and anyone who has ever visited any large industrial school for Whites realizes how hard it is to keep students busy with things that actually tell. The weekly hours available for shop work where there are large classes are too few to induce skill. Hence manual training may be simply a means of keeping young men and women in elevating associations for a series of years, without much positive education. The success of Hampton and Tuskegee and like institutions is due to a judicious mixture of book learning and hand learning, backed up by the personality of the founders, General Armstrong in Virginia and Booker Washington in Alabama, and of their successors and aids.

Against both industrial and academic training many people in the South feel a strong prejudice, because they believe that both tend to produce leaders who may dangerously organize the fellows of their race. A favorite form of slander has been to charge that the graduates of colleges furnish the criminals, and practically the worst criminals, of the negro race. Never was there a more senseless or a more persistent delusion. The total number of male graduates of all the Southern colleges during the last forty years is not above two thousand, besides perhaps five hundred graduates of Northern colleges who have found their way into the South. Many of those institutions have kept track of their graduates and are able to assert that the cases of serious crime among them are remarkably few, no more in proportion probably than among the graduates of Southern and Northern colleges for Whites. The moral effect of the colleges among Negroes is in the same direction as among Whites; the students include the more determined of the race or the children of the more determined. The negro college students are still only about one in one thousand of the children and young people of the race. The total number of living graduates of negro colleges or other institutions of college grade are not one in two thousand of the Negroes in the South.

It is true that even that number find it hard to establish themselves in professions or callings which can reward them for the sacrifices and efforts of their education. The negro doctors and lawyers have almost no white practice and not the best of negro practice, but there is an opening for thousands of Negroes in the development of the education of their people. The thousandth of the race in secondary schools and the two thousandth or more in colleges are enough to prove that a large number of individuals in the race are capable of and ought to have the advantages of higher training.

The denial to the Negroes of public secondary education at the expense of the state practically means that most of them will not have it at all. It is denied on the ground that it unfits boys and girls for life—exactly the argument which has been unsuccessfully brought against schools of that grade in the Northern states. It is denied on the ground that beyond twelve years of age most of the Negroes are stationary and cannot profit by a secondary education, a conclusion which does not seem justified by the experience of the few high schools and the numerous private and benevolent schools. Still more serious, the denial of secondary education means that the Negroes are deprived of the most obvious means of training for teachers of their own race.

In the last analysis most of the objections to negro education come down to the assertion that it puts the race above the calling whereunto God hath appointed it. The argument goes back to the unconscious presumption that the Negro was created to work the white man's field, and that even a little knowledge makes him ambitious to do something else.

One thing is certain: that no community can afford to neglect the academic side of education. The schools are to many people the only and the final appeal to the higher side of life, the only touch with the world's stock of great thoughts. The accusation is brought against the best Northern city schools that they are not practical, because they deal too much with literature and history and science. The negro child, like the white child, needs to have its mind aroused to the large things in the world; needs the education of thinking, as well as of learning; as DuBois puts it: "To seek to make the blacksmith a scholar is almost as silly as the more modern scheme of making the scholar a blacksmith; almost, but not quite."

On the side of the Negro there are other complaints. One is that his education has not had a fair trial; that the dominant South which lays and expends the taxes has not dealt with the Negro on an equal footing with white children; that the per capita expenditure on the black children in school is probably not more than a third that for white children; that the negro schools have often been exploited by white politicians who have put in their own favorites

336

as teachers; that even where the best intentions prevail, the schools are manned by incompetent teachers; nowhere do the rural colored people enjoy an education to the degree and with the kind of teachers and appliances common in the country districts of the North; the race can hardly be spoiled by education, for it has never had it, not for a single year. Only about a third of the negro children are at school on a given school day. Few of their rural schools hold more than five months, many not more than three, some not at all; and in from sixty to one hundred days in the year, irregularly placed, with teachers on the average not competent for the exceedingly elementary work that they do, the wonder is that children ever go a second day or acquire the rudiments of learning; yet many of them learn to read fluently, to write a good hand, and to do simple arithmetical problems. A race must have some intellectual quickness to pick up anything out of such a poor system. The arguments in favor of negro education have so far been convincing to every Southern community, since negro common schools are maintained and considerable amounts are spent for secondary and higher education.

The arguments against negro education destroy each other; they assume both that the Negro is too little and too much affected by the education that he receives. On one side we are told that he is incapable of anything more than the rudiments; on the other side, that education is a potent force making the Negro dangerous to the world. The incompetent can never be made dangerous by training into competence. Education cannot change the race weaknesses of the Negro; but it can give a better chance to the best endowed.

CHAPTER XXIV

THAT the South confronts a complexus of problems difficult and almost insoluble is clear to all onlookers, Northern or Southern, candid or prejudiced. So far this book has undertaken to deal rather with conditions than with remedies, to state questions without trying to answer them, to separate so far as may be the real aspirations and progress of the Southern people of both races from conventional beliefs and shop-worn statements which overlie the actualities.

Such an analysis of the physical and human elements of Southern life prepares the way for a discussion of a different nature. Shall the thriftless part of the Southern community remain at its present low average standard of productivity? Are the lower Whites and the still lower Negroes moving upward, however slowly? Can the two races come to an understanding which will mean peace in our time? Are there positive remedies for a state of things admittedly alarming? Any attempt to answer these questions means some repetition or restatement of things already treated at greater length. A first step may well be to summarize the whole Southern problem as it presents itself to the writer's mind.

(1) The South as a whole, on any basis of material advancement, is below the average of other parts of the Union

338

and of several foreign countries; it is poor where it ought to be rich; it needs economic regeneration.

(2) Measured by intellectual standards also the white South is below the other sections of the Union; the high standing of its leaders does not bring up the average of the more numerous elements. Any radical improvement, therefore, must include the uplift of the lower stratum of Whites.

(3) The South is divided between two races, one of which is distinctly inferior to the other, not only in what it now does, but in the potentialities of the future.

(4) The lower race is so far behind, and so likely to lag indefinitely, that it is necessary for the welfare of the community that the two be kept separate; and this stern edict applies not only to the pure African race, but also to the two millions of mixed bloods, many of whom in aptitude and habits of thought are practically white men.

(5) Both these races are improving, the Whites in great numbers and rapidly; fewer of the Negroes proportionally, and more slowly.

(6) The criminality of both races, and especially the violent criminality of the Negroes, brings into the controversy an element of personal rage and fear.

(7) Partly by superior abilities, partly by an inherited tradition, partly for the defense of the community, the white race dominates in every department of social, industrial, and political life; it owns most of the property; makes the laws for the black man; furnishes for him the machinery of government and of justice; and inexorably excludes him from both the social and political advantages of the community.

(8) This race division interferes with the American principle of equality—that is, the equal right of every man,

339

woman, and child to do the best thing that his abilities and training allow, the inferior doing the best in his stratum, the superior the better best of his class.

(9) The two races do not live together harmoniously. The Whites fear some kind of negro domination—the Negroes resent the complete control by the Whites; actual collisions are rare, but there is a latent race hostility.

(10) The white people, though they assume sole responsibility for whatever adjustment is made, know little of the private life of the best Negroes, and exercise small direct influence on the lower race. Hence the ordinary agencies of uplift—the church, the school, and contact with superior minds—are not brought into operation.

(11) The main reason for this want of touch with the Negroes is an apprehension that any common understanding will assist a social equality which might lead to miscegenation.

The Southern problem, therefore, to state it in a sentence, is how twenty million Whites and ten million Negroes in the Southern states shall make up a community in which one race shall hold most of the property, and all the government, and the other race shall remain content and industrious; in which one gets most of the good things of life and the other does most of the disagreeable work; in which the superior members of the inferior race shall accept all its disadvantages; in which one race shall always be at the top and the other forever at the bottom; yet in which there shall be peace and good will.

To these conditions, discouraging, hard, implacable to innocent people, out of accord with the usual American principles, any effective remedy must nevertheless adjust itself. Practically all Southern people agree that the question is alarming, but they are at odds among themselves as

340

to the remedy; and they may be roughly divided into the intolerant, the discouraged, and the moderate.

(I) Examples of passionate violence are plenty, and Professor J. W. Garner, a Southerner, suggests some reasons for their abundance: " Next to the difficulties arising mainly from the changed industrial conditions in the South and their resulting effect upon the character of the black race, the most serious obstacle in the way of maintaining harmonious relations between the two races is the persistent, ill-timed, and often intemperate agitation of the race question by a certain class of politicians lately sprung up in the South, whose chief stock in trade is the race issue. Their method consists in working upon the sympathies of a certain class of whites by appealing to their passions and prejudices, by dwelling upon the brutality and savagery of the negro, by conjuring up imaginary dangers of negro supremacy, by exaggerating real dangers and in every conceivable way exalting the negro problem, as a political issue, to a position out of all proportion to its real importance."

The truth of this statement may be illustrated from the published conclusions of some writers and speakers who are representative of the most radical type of Southern feeling. For instance, Hoke Smith, Governor of Georgia in 1908, has declared that " the development made by the Negro in the South came through the institution of slavery, from the control of an inferior race by a superior race. I believe that control was absolutely necessary for the development which the Negro made. The continuation of control is, in a measure, necessary to retain for the great mass of Negroes the progress made by them while in slavery."

(II) Hoke Smith is far from representing the general

341

or the average view in the South. Some of the best spirits there who feel the responsibility of their race are at their wit's end over the whole question and see no way out of the difficulty. Thus a lawyer of Birmingham, Ala., writes: " If my heart did not go out for the Negro, as a human being, or I cared less for my God and an earnest wish to walk in His ways, I would kill the Negro or die trying. God must intend that TIME shall work out His ways and not the men of my generation, for after a longer life than most, and all of it spent with and among the Negroes, I give it up. . . . Credit the Southern people with preserving the Negro, with teaching him Christ, with good will. . . . Education will do some good—perhaps more than I believe, but I verily believe that we must have the Negro all born again before we can teach him what to do."

(III) Of the more hopeful group of reflective men in the South there are many spokesmen, who suggest various sorts of remedies not always in accord.

Ex-Congressman William H. Fleming, of Georgia, puts it that " We do not know what shifting phases this vexing race problem may assume, but we may rest in the conviction that its ultimate solution must be reached along the lines of honesty and justice. Let us not in cowardice or want of faith needlessly sacrifice our higher ideals of private and public life. Race differences may necessitate social distinction. But race differences cannot repeal the moral law. . . . The foundation of the moral law is justice. Let us solve the negro problem by giving the negro justice and applying to him the recognized principles of the moral law. This does not require social equality. It does not require that we should surrender into his inexperienced and incompetent hands the reins of political government.

But it does require that we recognize his fundamental rights as a man."

Senator John Sharp Williams, of Mississippi, protests against "Indiscriminate cursing of the whole negro race, good and bad alike included. . . . Above all, remember this: it is not the educated negro who commits unspeakable crime; he knows the certain result. It is the brute whose avenues of information are totally cut off."

Leroy Percy, of Greenville, Miss., pleads for protection of the black man: "Daily, in recognition of the weakness of human nature, the prayer goes up from millions to a higher power: 'Deliver me from temptation—temptation which I cannot face and overcome I pray Thee to deliver me from.' There is no greater temptation known to man than the hourly, daily, yearly dealing with ignorant, trusting people. . . . So justice, self-interest, the duty which we owe to ourselves and those who follow us, all demand that we should not permit to go unchallenged, should not acquiesce in the viciously erroneous idea that the negro should be kept in helpless ignorance."

From this summary of general views it is evident that even the most moderate white men pleading for the rights of their black neighbors practically all tacitly accept certain postulates as to any possible remedies, which they believe to be quite beyond discussion and which may be analyzed as follows:

(I) The first is the dominance of the white race, which will not surrender any of the present privileges. As Page puts it: "The absolute and unchangeable superiority of the white race—a superiority, it appears to him, not due to any mere adventitious circumstances, such as superior educational and other advantages during some centuries, but an inherent and essential superiority, based on

343

superior intellect, virtue, and constancy. He does not believe that the Negro is the equal of the White, or ever could be the equal." That means that the low Negro is inferior to the low White, the average Negro to the average White, and the superior Negro, however high his plane, moral and intellectual, is also to be put into a position of permanent inferiority to the higher Whites. Because inferior morally and mentally, he is held also in political inferiority. The South does not intend that even intelligent and educated Negroes shall have a share in making or administering the laws.

(II) Partly from a sense of its own superiority, partly from a disdain of a formerly servile race, chiefly from a well-founded belief that amalgamation would be a great misfortune for the community, the South is determined that there shall be no legalized admixture of the races. That miscegenation is still going on in an unknown degree heightens the determination that it shall at least be put under the ban of law; the very danger makes the South more determined that the races shall be kept separate.

(III) The dominant white Southerners are further absolutely determined that any settlement of the question shall come from their volition; and that means that the Southern Negro is not expected to exercise anything more than a mild academic influence. The character of the Negroes, their thriftlessness or industry, their crime or virtue, their stupidity or their intelligence, may deflect the white mind one way or another; their preferences, outside the iron fence which the South has erected round the question, will receive some attention; but they will have to accept what the white people assign to them.

(IV) The South is as yet little awakened to the idea

344

that the status of the lower Whites is a part of the whole race problem. Inasmuch as the Poor White is emerging from seclusion and poverty, people do not sufficiently realize that he needs education, intellectual and moral; that his passions, his animal instincts, his violence stand in the way of the uplift of both races.

(V) The North is expected by the South not to act by legislation or any other active method in behalf of the Negro. The Southerners in general consider the Fifteenth, or suffrage Amendment, to be an affront, which they avoid by shifty clauses in their constitutions and would repeal if they could. Some Southerners resent even inquiry about the South, and apparently remember how their fathers received visiting abolitionists.

(VI) It would, however, be a great injustice to the immense number of broad-minded people in the South to leave the impression that nobody down there welcomes investigation or reads criticisms. Upon the negro question in general there are two different and opposing Southern points of view. The one-sided and arrogant statements of the Vardamans, the Dixons, the Graveses, and the Tillmans have no right to call themselves the voice of the South, in the face of the appeals to common justice and American principles of fair play that flow from the pens of the Bassetts, the Murphys, the Mitchells, the Flemings, and the Percys. It is a happy omen that the South is divided upon its own question; for it means that the taboo has been taken off discussion; that Southern men may honestly differ on the question of the rights and the character of the Negro.

On the one side is a numerous class of Whites, some coarse and ignorant, others of power and vitality, including many small farmers and managers of plantations, and also a large element in the towns, who are not much interested in the uplift of the Whites and do not wish well to the Negro, but are full of a blind hostility to the negro race and take the ground that this is a white man's government, and accept the Negro only as a tool for their use.

On the other side stand a great part of the high-bred, well-educated and masterful element; the people who count in the church, the club and university, the pulpit and the bench; people who have a material interest and genuine public spirit in providing for the future of their own commonwealth. In general the best people in the South, the most highly trained, most public-spirited, most religious, wealthiest, and most responsible people wish well to the Negro. The plantation owner, the manufacturer, the railroad manager, want efficient laborers; the minister wants God-fearing people; the judge wants law-abiding men; the educator wants good schools; they all want to raise the community, the bottom as well as the top. How far is the superior class in the South to control the action of legislatures and the movement of public sentiment, and the behavior of those of a ruder cast? Which of these two classes speaks for the South?

CHAPTER XXV

THE WRONG WAY OUT

EXCEPT within the postulates stated in the last chapter, there can be no rational expectation of improvement of race relations in the South. Even within those conditions many suggestions are from time to time made which are out of accord with white and negro character, with the physical conditions, or with the general trend of American life. Before coming to practical remedies, it is necessary to examine and set aside these no-thoroughfares.

First of all, can the Southern race question be solved by any action of the North? The Reconstruction amendments with the clause authorizing Congress to enforce them by " appropriate legislation " seem intended to give the federal government power to protect the Negro against either state legislation or individual action; but the Supreme Court in the Civil Rights decision of 1883 held that the action of Congress under those amendments was confined to meeting positive official action by state governments. The Fourteenth Amendment provides for a special penalty in case of deprivation of political rights, by reducing the representation in Congress of the states which limit their suffrage. Any such legislation must be general in terms and would therefore apply to the Northern states in which there are educational or tax qualifications. Beyond that difficulty is the remembered ill effect of Reconstruction laws, and the conviction in the North that the negro problem is not one simply of race hostility and definition of rights—that the Negroes are in many ways a menace. To take the matter a second time out of the hands of the people on the ground, even though they are not solving their own problems, would mean a storm in Congress, a weight on the administration, possibly a contest with the Supreme Court, which no responsible Northern public man likes to contemplate.

Through the control of Congress over federal elections there is another opportunity to interfere in behalf of the Negro, but the federal laws put on the statute book in Reconstruction times were repealed in 1894; and nobody now proposes to renew them. By the recent experience of the nation in the Philippines, Porto Rico, and Cuba, a lesson has been taught of the difficulty of handling non-European races. The nation begins to doubt the elevating power of self-government. For whatever reason, there is no evidence of any intention in the North to make the Negro the ward of the nation. The writer is one of those who believe that any general federal legislation would revive friction between the sections, would sharpen the race feeling in the South, and in the end could accomplish little for the uplift of the Negro; even federal aid to education could hardly be so managed as to keep up the feeling of white responsibility from which alone proper education of the Negro can be expected.

Is there any likelihood of a private propaganda in behalf of the Negro like that of the abolitionists? A considerable class of Northern people have a warm sense of resentment at what they think the injustice and cruelty of the superior race, especially in the withdrawal of the suffrage by state constitutional amendments; and there is a lively interest in the education of Negroes and in work among the Poor Whites. A propaganda, with societies, public meetings, journals, and a literature is, however, no longer possible—the North has too much on its own hands in curing the political diseases of its cities, in absorbing the foreigners; like Congress, it recognizes that the South is sincere, even if somewhat exaggerated, in its nervousness about the Negroes. The most that can be expected of Northern individuals in the way of bettering Southern conditions is attempts like that of this volume to get into the real nature of the problems and to offer good advice.

Notwithstanding the horror felt toward amalgamation, from time to time in unexpected Southern quarters reappears the suggestion that it is impossible for the two races to live alongside each other separate, and that the logical and unavoidable outcome is fusion; that the relentless force of juxtaposition is too much for law or prejudice or race instinct. Over and over again one is told that nowhere in history is there an example of two races living side by side indefinitely without uniting. This is not historically true; Mohammedans and Hindoos (originally of the same race) have lived separate hundreds of years in India; Boers and Kaffirs have been side by side for near a century; the English colonists and the American Indians were little intermixed. Amalgamation could only be accomplished by a change in white sentiment about as probable as the Mormonization of the Northern Whites; and if it were possible, it would lead to a new and worse race question, the rivalry of a mixed race occupying the whole South against a white race in the rest of the country, which would make all present troubles seem a pleasant interlude. Amalgamation as a remedy welcomed by the Southern

349

Whites is unthinkable; as a remedy against their convictions, brought about by time, it is highly unlikely.

At the other extremity is the idea, now more than a century old, that the way to get rid of the race question is to remove one of the races altogether. This notion of curing the patient by sending him to a hospital for incurables goes back to 1775. Jefferson favored it; the Colonization Society organized it in 1816, and in the forty years from 1820 to 1860 succeeded in sending about ten thousand Negroes to Liberia. Abraham Lincoln favored it. It is often suggested nowadays. This plan, if it could be carried out, would so completely relieve the immediate difficulties that it deserves the most careful consideration.

The first objection at the outset is ten million objections—namely, the Negroes themselves, who have never taken kindly to expatriation, for the simple reason that it is flying to evils that they know not of. The second difficulty is to find a place to receive the exiles. Experiments in the West Indies, in Central America, and in Africa have all been failures. No European country or colonies will welcome people sent away on the ground that they are inimical to white civilization; and the settlements of American Negroes in savage Africa have been entire failures. As has been shown above, Liberia, after nearly ninety years of existence, has no influence on the back country; its trade is scanty, its health is depleted, and its conditions are in every way less favorable to physical and moral well-being than those of the United States.

Then follows the financial difficulty; to be sure a correspondent of a Georgia newspaper suggests: " Let the government appropriate $20,000,000 for five successive years each for deportation, judiciously forcing off first the ages from eighteen to forty-five, as far as can be done without too violent a separation of dependent ages, and five years will substantially settle the exodus. All separations can be reunited in a few years and not a negro's heart broken." But a single hundred millions would be only a drop in the bucket. To bring over the ten million foreigners now in the United States, and get them started in a country abounding in work and opportunities, has probably averaged a cost of a hundred dollars a head, or one thousand millions. The thing must be done completely, if at all; for from the point of view of its advocates, to expatriate a part of the race would be like cutting out a portion of a cancer; and where are you going to find, say, a thousand million dollars to carry away ten million people upon the proceeds of whose continued labor in America you must depend for the Southern share of the money?

In the next place, would a world which still has tears for the Acadians deported from Nova Scotia in 1755, which is aroused by the banishment of political suspects to Siberia, be impressed with the high civilization of a nation which would send ten million people to their death in a continent where as yet neither Briton, Frenchman, Portuguese, or German has ever been able to establish any considerable colony of European emigrants? If the superior race, with all its resources, prudence, and medical skill cannot live in Africa, what would become of ten million Negroes deported on the plea that they were not capable of participating in the white man's civilization? Though descended from Africans there is no reason to suppose that they have transmitted immunity from the deadly tropical diseases.

Again, there is not a state, city, or county populous with Negroes in the South which would not resent, and if need be resist, the sudden taking away of its laborers. Whenever the question is brought to an issue, the Southern people admit that, with all the race difficulties, the Negro does raise the cotton and drive the mule; and without him the white man must take the hoe and the reins. As John Sharp Williams puts it: " The white people of the South do not want to hasten the departure of the good negroes; . . . whenever you suggest that he leave the Southern darky replies in Scriptural phrase, ' Ask me not to leave thee.' They are here, and they are going to remain here so long as there is a cotton field in sight." The people who preach expatriation, deportation, elimination, or whatever they choose to call it, are not the people who employ the Negro or wish him well, or would be pleased to see him succeed in any hemisphere.

A milder suggestion is that the essential Negro be slowly and quietly replaced by somebody else. What somebody else? Shall it be Northerners? Senator Williams, of Mississippi, says: " I would like to see established a great land company with a capital of about a million dollars, to buy lands in the cotton States and sell them out to home-seeking immigrants on a ten years' instalment plan." In 1907 the Southern press was convinced that a great flow of immigration had set in from the North, but in reality outside of Florida and Texas nearly all colonies of Northerners have been unsuccessful, though there is a slow stream of people, partly from the Northwest, who take up farms in the South and mix with the Southern white population. These people are prone to be dissatisfied with the schools; they are in despair over the wretched domestic service; the women are filled with terror by the lynchings and by the frequent cause of them; the newcomers dislike the Negroes more than the Southern-born people dislike them, and cannot be depended upon to remain a permanent part of the population. In any case, they do not replace the negro laborer for wages.

The only hope of a substitute population of plantation hands is in the foreign immigrants, who have been described in a previous chapter, and of whom, up to 1909, the South seems to have expected a brisk influx. The federal government even set out to build immigrant stations in Charleston and Savannah. But in 1907 all the Southern ports (excepting Baltimore) together received only 21,000 out of 1,300,000. To-day the whole scheme is a failure and there is no prospect of importing large numbers of foreigners to work for wages. A member of Congress from Mississippi recently declared from his seat in the House that there was a conspiracy of federal and Italian officials to prevent Italians from coming into his state.

The first reason for the failure of the promising plan is the many undoubted cases, and the more rumored and reported instances, of peonage of white men. In the second place the Italians, who have been chiefly relied upon, have no intention of spending their lives and bringing up their children as plantation laborers; they work so well and are so profitable to both the plantation owners and themselves that after a few years they save money enough to do something that they like better, and that is the end of their service on other people's land. The experience of South Carolina in 1906, detailed in the chapter on Immigration, seems conclusively to prove that most foreigners prefer the North because they think they are better treated there.

The fundamental difficulty with the whole plan of immigration is that a great many people in the South believe that the average foreigner is an undesirable member of the community. They have no familiarity with that

grinding-down process by which even unpromising races
are transformed into Americans. They read of the
" Black Hand," which is not very different from some
forms of the old Ku Klux Klan; of the Vendetta, which
can be paralleled in the Southern mountains; and they
show little willingness to receive even the better foreign
elements on equal terms. It is a fair question whether if
the Italians, for example, should come to have a majority
of votes in Louisiana they would ever be permitted to
elect and inaugurate a governor out of their own number;
whether the phrase " White man's government " does not
apply as much against the " Dago " as against the Negro.

If the Negroes cannot be replaced, is it not possible to
segregate them into districts of their own? For forty
years a process has been going on by which the black
counties grow blacker and the white counties become whiter;
Negroes move into the counties where there is most work
and therefore the greatest number of laborers, and the
Whites gradually move out of the districts in which the
Negroes are very numerous. Could not that process be
carried still farther? Some people in despair predict that
the Whites will eventually find their way into the West
and Northwest, leaving the fruitful South to the Negro.
Although there is a steady drift of white people out of the
Southern states, it is of the same kind as the movement
from New England and the Middle states to the West,
and the Whites have not the slightest intention of aban-
doning their section; buildings go up, mills appear, sky-
scrapers intensify the city, and in every Southern state the
Whites grow richer and more powerful.

The desired result might be brought about if the
Negroes would move to other parts of the Union, and much
is made of the present drift into the Northern cities, but the

conditions of life are not favorable to them there, and their number is only kept up by new immigrations. Booker Washington advises the Negro to stay in the South because " The fact that at the North the Negro is confined to almost one line of employment often tends to discourage and demoralize the strongest who go from the South, and to make them an easy prey to temptation." Many of the keenest observers in the South desire that the Negroes should spread through the country, partly to relieve the pressure in the South, and partly in the conviction that it would furnish an object lesson to the Northern people of the disadvantage of the presence of Negroes. Whatever the number of emigrant Negroes out of the South, the number left there goes on steadily increasing from decade to decade; and whenever they show a disposition to leave in large numbers, the Southerners oppose and resist, because they see no hope of supplying their place with any other than more negro laborers.

Could the two races divide the land into districts? Such a separation is favored both by Bishop Turner, a negro leader, and by John Temple Graves, of Atlanta, a negro hater, and there are a few examples of such separate communities. Many white counties and a few white towns will not admit Negroes; and in perhaps half a dozen colored villages no white man lives. Here is perhaps an opportunity for considerably reducing race friction, for there is no reason to suppose that such separate towns go backward in civilization; and they give opportunities for negro business and professional men, which are important for the encouragement of the best members of the race. The most serious practical objection is, however, that such towns take away laborers, actual or potential, from the white plantations; and the industrial cotton system depends on keeping those Negroes on other people's land.

A broader proposition is phrased by Reed in the "Brother's War"—"Let us give the negro his own State in our union. . . . We are rich enough and have land enough to give the negro this State, which is due from us. His especial need is to exercise political and civil privileges, in his own community, all the way up from the town meeting to congress." Possibly this remedy might have been applied forty years ago, but it is now absolutely unworkable. When Reed suggests that the Negro be allowed to take over some state and carry it on as a negro community, the instant question is, which state? Louisiana will not allow her laborers to go *en masse* to Texas; and Texas would drive them back with shotguns from the border if they tried to move. The blackest states have the least disposition to become blacker, the lighter states are just as determined to remain light; and since there is no longer any great area of good land not taken up by anybody, colonization of the Negro within the limits of the United States is impossible.

Could the desired result of keeping Whites and Negroes from too confining a contact be reached by a less drastic method? A favorite suggestion eloquently championed by Grady is "race separation," which he defined to mean: "That the whites and blacks must walk in separate paths in the South. As near as may be, these paths should be made equal—but separate they must be now and always. This means separate schools, separate churches, separate accommodation everywhere—but equal accommodation where the same money is charged, or where the State provides for the citizen." That is, in every city Negroes are to occupy separate quarters, go to separate schools, ride in separate sections of the street cars, use separate sidewalks, buy in separate stores, have separate churches, places of amusement, social organizations, banks, and insurance companies. This system, which in many directions has already been carried out, rests upon a conviction of the Negro's ability to maintain an economic and intellectual life of his own, without danger to the white race. It has the great disadvantage of cutting off the third of the population which most needs uplift from the influences which bear for progress. It still further diminishes that association of the superior with the inferior race, that kindly interest of employer in employee, that infiltration of culture and moral principles which is the mightiest influence among the white people.

Furthermore, where is the black man to acquire the skill to carry on his own enterprises, to build cotton gins and oil mills, to stock stores, to found banks, if he is to be separated from the white man? Where is he to buy his goods? Here the whole system breaks down; the drummer is no respecter of persons, and not only is willing to sell to a solvent Negro, but is likely to insist that the negro merchant shall not give all his orders to a colored wholesaler. Then what is to be done with the hundreds of thousands of landowners, tenants, croppers, and wage hands, who depend on advances from the Whites? There is no such thing as commercial segregation; as in other directions, when any remedy is proposed which means the cutting off of negro labor, or of the profits derived from negro custom, the South invariably draws back.

On the other hand, race separation would give greater opportunities to the Negroes and reduce the contact with the lower class of the Whites, out of which comes most of the race violence in the South. It is substantially the method applied in Northern cities, though nowhere to any such degree as in the South. It is a method which, with all its hardship to Negroes of the higher class, comes nearest being a *modus vivendi* between the races.

As for white communities without Negroes, there are many such in the mountain regions, and an unsuccessful effort was made in the town of Fitzgerald, Ga., by Northern immigrants to keep the Negroes out of it, but in such places who will do the odd jobs and perform the necessary rough labor? How shall houses be built, drays be driven and dirt shoveled, if there are no Negroes?

Try which way you may, there seems no method consonant with the interests of the South and the principles of humanity by which Negroes can be set apart from the white people. It was not the choice of their ancestors to change their horizon; nor were the Africans now in the United States consulted as to their neighbors; but they were born on American soil; they have shared in the toil of conquering the continent; they have their homes, their interests, and their traditions; they have never known any life except in dependence on and close relations with the Whites. However happier the South and the whole country might be were there no race question, there seems no possibility of avoiding it by taking away all race contact.

A method of supposed relief widely applied, frequently invoked, and strenuously defended, is to terrorize the Negro. And the North is not free from that spirit. As Mr. Dooley philosophizes: " He'll ayther have to go to th' north an' be a subjick race, or stay in th' south an' be an objick lesson. 'Tis a har-rd time he'll have, anyhow. . . . I'm not so much throubled about th' naygur whin he lives among his opprissors as I am whin he falls into th' hands iv his liberators. Whin he's in th' South he can make up his mind to be lynched soon or late an' give his attintion to his other pleasures iv composin' rag-time music on a banjo, an' wurrukin' f'r th' man that used to own him an' now on'y owes him his wages. But 'tis the divvle's own hardship . . . to be pursooed by a mob iv abolitionists till he's dhriven to seek police protection." Still the Northern police do give protection against assaults on the Negro which Southern police sometimes refuse. Lawlessness is the plague of the South. Attention has already been called to the negro crime against person and life, the shocking frequency of white crime, the weakness and timidity of the courts, and the resort to lynching as an alleged protest against lawlessness. The number of homicides and mob murders is not so serious as the continual appeals to violence by editors and public men who are accepted as leaders by a large minority and sometimes a majority of the white people. Thus John Temple Graves calls for " a firm, stern, and resolute attitude of organization and readiness on the part of the dominant race. . . . Is this black man from savage Africa to keep on perpetually disturbing the sections of our common country? Is this running sore to be nursed and treated and anodyned and salved and held forever to our breasts?" Southern newspapers abound in fierce and exciting headlines: " The Burly Black Brute Foiled!" " A Ham Colored Nigger in the Hen House!" " The Only Place for You is Behind a Mule," and so on—what somebody has called " The wholesale assassination of negro character." Senator Tillman in a public lecture has said: " On one occasion we killed seven niggers; I don't know how many I killed personally, but I shot to kill and I know I got my share." And in another speech, in November, 1907, in Chicago, the same man, who has repeatedly been elected to the

Senate from a once proud state, said: " No matter what
the people in the North may say or do, the white race in
the South will never be dominated by the Negro, and I
want to tell you now that if some state should ever make
an attempt to ' save South Carolina,' we will show them
in their fanaticism that we will make it red before we
make it black."

Observe that this ferocity is not directed against the
Negro simply because he does ill, but equally if he does
well. Thus a correspondent in Georgia writes: " Let me
tell you one thing,—every time you people of the North
countenance in any way, shape or form any form of social
equality, you lay up trouble, not for yourselves, or
for us so much, but for the negro. *Right or wrong the
Southern people will never tolerate it, and will go through
the horrors of another reconstruction, before they will permit it to be. Before we will submit to it, we will kill
every negro in the Southern states.* This is not idle boast-
ing or fire-eating threats, but the cold, hard facts stated in
all calmness." Could hate, jealousy, and meanness reach a
higher pitch than in the following declaration of Thomas
Dixon, Jr., sent broadcast through the country in the
Saturday Evening Post two years ago? " Does any sane
man believe that when the Negro ceases to work under
the direction of the Southern white man, this ' arrogant,'
' rapacious,' and ' intolerant ' race will allow the Negro to
master his industrial system, take the bread from his
mouth, crowd him to the wall and place a mortgage on
his house? Competition is war—the most fierce and brutal of all its forms. Could fatuity reach a sublimer height
than the idea that the white man will stand idly by and
see this performance? What will he do when put to the
test? He will do exactly what his white neighbor in the

360

North does when the Negro threatens his bread—kill him!" Could blind race hostility go farther than in the Atlanta Riots of 1907, for which not one murderer has ever been subjected to any punishment?

These violent utterances come almost wholly from the Superior Race. The Negroes have their grievances; but any intemperate publication toward the white race would almost certainly lead to a lynching. An instance has actually occurred where a Negro was driven out of a community, and glad to escape with his life, because he had in his newspaper said with regard to a woman of his own race whose character had been assailed, that she was as virtuous as any white woman. Doubtless some of the cruel and incendiary language that has been quoted is intended for home consumption; it is supposed to be a striking way of saying to the Negroes that they ought to behave better; and alongside every one of these vindictive utterances could be placed a message of hope and encouragement from Southern white men to the blacks. These expressions of white ferocity in condemnation of negro ferocity are overbalanced by such strong words as those of Senator Williams: "It cannot be escaped by the extermination of either race by the other. That thought is absolutely horrible to a good man, a believer in the divine philosophy of Jesus Christ, who taught mutual helpfulness, and not mutual hatred to mankind." Nevertheless, it remains true that a large number of Southern people who are in places of influence and authority advise that the race problem be settled by terrorizing the Negro.

The commonest form of terror is lynching, a deliberate attempt to keep the race down by occasionally killing Negroes, sometimes because they are dreadful criminals, frequently because they are bad, or loose-tongued, or influential, or are acquiring property, or otherwise irritate the Whites. A saucy speech by a Negro to a white man may be followed by swift, relentless, and tormenting death. In every case of passionate conflict between two races the higher loses most, because it has most to lose; and lynch law as a remedy for the lawlessness of the blacks has the disadvantage of occasionally exposing innocent white men to the uncontrollable passion of other white men, of filling the mind with scenes of horror and cruelty, of lowering the standard of the whole white race.

This subject is inextricably connected with the crimes by Negroes, for which lynching is held to be an appropriate punishment. The statistics collected by Mr. Cutler, and stated in a previous chapter, show in the twenty-two years from 1882 to 1903 a record of 1,997 lynchings in the South; of the Negroes lynched, 707 were charged with violence to women and 783 with murder. These figures absolutely disprove the habitual statements in the South that lynching is common to all sections of the Union; that it is almost always caused by rape; and that rape is a crime confined to Negroes. The details of some of these cases would show that the mob not infrequently gets an innocent person; that it is liable to be carried away into the most horrible excesses of burning and torture; that a lynching is really a kind of orgy in which not only the criminal class among the Whites, but people who are ordinarily swayed by reason simply let go of themselves and indulge the primeval brutishness of human nature. Said Confucius: "The Master said, 'I hate the manner in which purple takes away the luster of vermilion. I hate the way in which the songs of Ch'ing confound the music of Gna. I hate those who with their sharp mouths overthrow kingdoms and families.'"

THE WRONG WAY OUT

Professor Smith, of Tulane University, is spokesman for thousands of respectable and educated men when he says: "Atrocious as such forms of rudimentary justice undoubtedly are, and severely reprehensible, to be condemned always and without any reserve, it cannot be denied that they have a certain rough and horrible virtue. Great is the insult they wreak on the majesty of the law and brutalizing must be their effect upon human nature, yet they do strike a salutary terror into hearts which the slow and uncertain steps of the courts could hardly daunt. In witness stands the fact that lynch-lightning seldom strikes twice in the same district or community. Such frightful incidents tend to repeat themselves at wide intervals, both of time and place."

They tend to repeat themselves immediately; it is not an accident that Mississippi, in a large part of which the Negroes are renowned for their freedom from the crime so much reprehended, nevertheless, has more lynchings than any other state; it is because Mississippi has the lynching habit. Strange that in a community like the South, so intelligent, so proud of the superiority and the supremacy of the white race, the deeds of fifty abandoned black men each year should throw millions of Whites into a frenzy of excitement; and that for the crime of those fifty, ten million innocent people are held responsible. Lynching is no remedy for race troubles, and never has been; it intensifies the race feeling a hundredfold; it is a standing indictment of the white people who possess all the machinery of government, yet cannot prevent the fury of their own race. "Surely," says President Roosevelt, "no patriot can fail to see the fearful brutalization and debasement which the indulgence of such a spirit and such practices inevitably portend. . . . The nation, like the individual,

363

cannot commit a crime with impunity. If we are guilty of lawlessness and brutal violence, whether our guilt consists in active participation therein or in mere connivance and encouragement, we shall assuredly suffer later on because of what we have done. The corner stone of this republic, as of all free governments, is respect for and obedience to the law." That the South can get on without lynchings is shown by the gradual diminution in the number of instances. In 1901 there were 135, in 1906 only 45, and in this good result the protests of the good people in the South have been aided by the criticism of the North. Murders of Whites by Negroes are probably just as frequent, but they are more likely to go to the courts.

Some things can still be done to reduce the crime of the individual without increasing the crime of the mob. John Temple Graves has suggested for the Negro that: " Upon conviction of his crime he would cross a ' Bridge of Sighs ' and disappear into a prison of darkness and mystery, from which he would never emerge, and in which he would meet a fate known to no man save the Government and the excutioners of the law—that the very darkness and mystery of this punishment would strike more terror to the soul of superstitious criminals than all the vengeance of modern legal retribution."

A kindred suggestion is that a special court of Whites shall be set up to deal with certain aggravated crimes, outside of the technicalities of the ordinary criminal law. If the Negroes would deliver up those of their own number whom they suppose to have committed such crimes, they would relieve themselves of the odium of protecting the worst criminals. The Whites are right in insisting on a stronger feeling of race responsibility, but where is their own sense of race responsibility when the Salisbury lynchers, the Atlanta murderers and the scoundrel Turner, who practically kidnapped and then tortured to death a Negro woman, are protected by public sentiment? Extraordinary remedies are not necessary if the white people will make their own courts and sheriffs do their duty, by speedy trials, followed by swift and orderly punishment; and most of all by disgracing and driving out of society men who take upon themselves the hangman's office without the hangman's plea of maintaining the majesty of law.

Lynching is part of the same spirit as that which inspires peonage, the meanest of all crimes in the calendar; for to steal a poor Negro's labor is to rob a cripple of his crutches; to knock down the child for his penny; it is the fleecing of the most defenseless by the most powerful. One of the remedies for the ills of the South is that the white people shall sternly set themselves against the crime of peonage, which exists in every state of the Lower South, either with or without the color of law; and which secures the most expensive labor that the South can possibly employ, since it alarms and discourages a thousand for every man whose forced labor is thus stolen.

The terrible thing about all the suggestions of violence and hatred as a remedy is that they react upon the white race, which has most to lose in property and in character. "There are certain things," said Governor Vardaman, of Mississippi, in a public proclamation, "that must be done for the control of the negro which need not be done for the government of the white man. In spite of the provisions of the federal constitution the men who are called upon to deal with this great problem must do that which is necessary to be done, even though it may have the appearance at times of going somewhat without the law. . . .

If the people of the respective communities of this state will only come together and resolve to convert every negro into a laborer and self-supporter, even though it be necessary to make him a laborer upon the county's or the state's property, they will serve their communities and their state well." No idea is more futile than that you can drive people with whips into the Kingdom of Heaven; that you can teach an inferior race to observe laws by yourself breaking them; that you can put one half the community outside the law, while claiming American liberty for the other half. Though the negro race has little to urge in public, it feels the degradation and the hurt. Violence solves no problems; it does not even postpone the evil day. The race problem must be solved by applying to Negroes the same kind of law and justice that the experience of the Anglo-Saxon has found necessary for its own protection.

CHAPTER XXVI

MATERIAL AND POLITICAL REMEDIES

THE methods of dealing with the race question discussed in the last chapter all go back to the idea that the Negro can be improved only by some process distasteful to him. Race separation he dislikes, expatriation he shudders at, and violence brings on him more evils than it removes, to say nothing of the effect on the Whites. The world has tried many experiments of civilizing people by the police, and they are all failures, from the Russian Empire to the West Side of New York, especially since both the Cossacks and the metropolitan police have faults of their own. In the South and in Russia alike there is doubtless a feeling that the people at the bottom of the scale are things below the common standard, that force is necessary because they will not listen to reason.

None of the forcible remedies meets the most obvious difficulty in the South—that the present condition of the lower race is not a foundation for great wealth and high prosperity. If the Negro has reached his pitch, if he is to remain at his present average of morals and industry and productivity, the South may well be in despair, for it is far below that of the low Southern White, and farther below that of the Northwestern farmer. The condition of the black is a menace to society—if it must stay at the present level.

In the chapter on " Is the Negro Rising? " some reasons are given for believing that the status of the race has
much improved in the last forty years and is still gaining.
Upon this critical point numbers of both races testify.
Kelly Miller says of the achievements of his people:
" Within forty years of only partial opportunity, while
playing as it were in the backyard of civilization, the
American negro has cut down his illiteracy by over fifty
per cent; has produced a professional class some fifty thousand strong, including ministers, teachers, doctors, lawyers,
editors, authors, architects, engineers and all higher lines
of listed pursuits in which white men are engaged; some
three thousand negroes have taken collegiate degrees, over
three hundred being from the best institutions in the North
and West established for the most favored white youth;
. . . negro inventors have taken out some four hundred
patents as a contribution to the mechanical genius of
America; there are scores of negroes who, for conceded
ability and achievements, take respectable rank in the
company of distinguished Americans."

This opinion is not confined to members of the negro
race; even so cordial an enemy of the Negro as John
Temple Graves admits that " The leaders of no race in
history have ever shown greater wisdom, good temper and
conservative discretion than distinguishes the two or three
men who stand at the head of the negro race in America
to-day "; and elsewhere he declares that there are two good
Negroes for every bad Negro, a proportion which does not
obtain in every race. Thomas Nelson Page is of opinion
that, " Unquestionably, a certain proportion of the Negro
race has risen notably since the era of emancipation," and
John Sharp Williams commits himself to the statement that
" Fully ninety per cent of the negro race is behaving itself

as well as could be expected; it is at work in the fields, on the railroads, and in the sawmills, and does not, for the most part, know that there is a fifteenth amendment." A cloud of witnesses confirm the belief that a fourth to a fifth of all the Negroes in the South are somewhat improving and slowly saving. Some of them have hearkened to the advice of an English writer: "Try to realize two things: first, that you are living in a commercial republic; a country whose standard, in all things, is material; second, that you are the greatest economic power in this country."

The possibility of a general industrial uplift depends upon several factors which are not easy to fix. It is a question whether the lower four fifths of the negro race has anything like the potentiality of the upper fraction, for it is made up mostly of plantation Negroes, who have certainly advanced a long way from slavery times, are better clothed, better fed, better housed, better treated, but are still a long way below most of the Whites in their own section. The most appalling thing about the negro problem is, this mass of people on the land who are doing well in the sense that they work, make cotton, yield profits, help to make the community prosperous, but who are ignorant, stupid, and have no horizon outside the cotton field and the cornfield. In spirit they still hark back to Whittier's plantation song,

> De yam will grow, de cotton blow,
> We'll hab de rice an' corn;
> O nebber you fear if nebber you hear
> De driver blow his horn.

Is there anything stirring in the minds of that great, good-natured, inert and unthinking mass which will bring

369

them up where the reproach now heaped upon them shall fade away? Still more, if they try to arise, will the Whites permit them? That is no idle question, for rising means that some of them will seek other pursuits, and the white people have already given notice that certain avenues of labor are closed to them. Contrary to many assertions confidently made, the Negroes are not as a race crowded out of the skilled trades in the South; but the trades union is bound to appear and the effort will be to shut negro mechanics out of the unions altogether, as has been done in some Northern places. The Negro as he rises to higher possibilities may find those possibilities withdrawn. Listen to the philosophy of Thomas Dixon, Jr., a Christian minister: "If the Negro is made master of the industries of the South he will become the master of the South. Sooner than allow him to take the bread from their mouths, the white men will kill him here, as they do North, when the struggle for bread becomes as tragic. . . . Make the Negro a scientific and successful farmer, and let him plant his feet deep in your soil, and it will mean a race war. . . . The Ethiopian cannot change his skin, or the leopard his spots. Those who think it possible will always tell you that the place to work this miracle is in the South. Exactly. If a man really believes in equality, let him prove it by giving his daughter to a Negro in marriage. That is the test." This is nothing more nor less than the negro preacher's exhortation to his congregation: "My dear hearers, dar is two roads a-lyin' straight before you, and a-branchin' off de one from de odder at the nex' corners; one of 'em leads to perdition, and de odder to everlastin' damnation. Oh, my friends, which will you choose?" If the Negro will not rise, argues Dixon, he gives nothing to the community, away with him! If he does rise, he may take work that otherwise some white man might do, lynch him!

The real argument of competition works just the other way. The inferior Negro is not likely to take the bread out of the mouth of the superior white man; but, when relieved from the abnormal conditions of slavery and of Reconstruction, he may still be able to hold his own in the struggle for existence. Emancipation threw upon the Negro the responsibility for his own keeping. The most that he can ask is a fair field without artificial hindrances or limitations; and in such a field a race on the average inferior may nevertheless find tasks in which it excels, and may maintain its race life unimpaired. Kelly Miller says: " You were born with a silver spoon in your mouth, I was born with an iron hoe in my hand "; and the world needs the hoe hand just as much as the silversmith.

It would appear that for the uplift of the Negro something is needed on the white side: remembrance of the foundations of American liberty, of the workings of Christianity, of the economic truth that you are not made poor because your neighbor gets on in the world. The curse of the South is that its people do not more genuinely realize that the more active, industrious, and thrifty a people become, the more their neighbors receive out of the enlarged contribution to the community. If the Negroes were all as intelligent as Roscoe Conkling Bruce, as forehanded as Benson of Kowaliga, as lyric as Paul Dunbar, the Whites in the South might get rich out of the trade of the Negro, and some of them see it so. For instance, President Winston, of the Agricultural College of North Carolina: " Greater industrial efficiency would prove an everlasting bond between the races in the South. It is the real key to the problem. Let the Negro make himself indispensable

371

as a workman, and he may rely upon the friendship and affection of the whites. . . . Public sentiment in the South still welcomes the Negro to every field of labor that he is capable of performing. The whole field of industry is open to him. The Southern whites are not troubled by his efficiency but by his inefficiency." Meantime the really industrious Negroes, of whom there are a couple of million or more, follow the advice of Paul Dunbar:

> I've a humble little motto
>   That is homely, though it's true,—
> Keep a-pluggin' away.
> It's a thing when I've an object
>   That I always try to do,—
> Keep a-pluggin' away.
> When you've rising storms to quell,
> When opposing waters swell,
> It will never fail to tell,—
>   Keep a-pluggin' away.

The self-interest of the planter in the efficiency of his labor does not necessarily lead him to see the highest interests either of the negro race or of the South, under the present industrial system, which makes a plantation a workshop rather than a farm. The ownership of rich cotton lands only means wealth if you can find negro laborers and keep them at work. One of the most powerful uplifting agencies in all agricultural countries is the desire to own land, and one of the most frequent texts of Booker Washington is that now is the time for the Negro to acquire land, for it will never again be so cheap; but where is the land to be found? Although ownership has almost completely changed since the Civil War, good lands are aggregating more and more into large tracts. The white farmer finds it difficult to hold his own against the capitalist and the syndicate, and even the thrifty black is beset by special difficulties.

In the first place, the rural Negro has, unless by his saving from sawmill and turpentine work, little opportunity to make money with which to buy a farm, except from the farm itself: hence he buys on time, pays a heavy interest charge, and is at every disadvantage. In the second place, few planters are willing to break up their land into small tracts; to do so takes away their livelihood, their only opportunity of making available their knowledge of cotton planting and of dealing with cotton hands. Some of them are absolutely opposed to letting the Negroes have land. Mr. Bell, of Alabama, one of the largest landowners in the South, is credited with saying that he " has no use for a Nigger that pays out." That is to say, he prefer his hands to be unprogressive and in debt. Perhaps the South fails to realize that the wealth of the Western, Middle, and New England states comes from encouraging people to do the best they know how. The more industrious the people are, the more business there is of every kind and for everybody. The South would be happier and more prosperous if it could accept the Western system of moderate-sized detached farms, on each of which there is an intelligent owner or tenant.

The large number of negro landowners (though many of them perhaps are mortgaged) and the evident prosperity of those communities in which the greatest number of them hold their land, seems to show that landowning is a motive that ought to be strongly set before them. The old notion of Reconstruction times that the federal government ought to furnish " forty acres and a mule " was not so far wrong; it would have been perfectly possible for the nation to acquire land in large tracts, to subdivide it, and give or sell it at nominal rates, so as to offer every thrifty Negro the chance of proprietorship; but that opportunity, if it ever existed, has long gone by, and the Negro must depend upon himself if he wishes to buy land.

The present system is not only industrial; it tends to make a peasant out of the Negro, and peasant is a term of reproach in the United States, though in France, Germany, and Italy there are rich peasants as well as poor ones, peasants who employ labor as well as those who have nothing but their hands. The American objection to a peasant system is its fixity; the peasant is an hereditary laborer on the land, usually the land of another; he leaves it to other people to carry on the state, to elevate the community. Nevertheless, it is simply the truth that under the present system of tenancy employment and day wages, nearly half of the negro race in the South is in effect a peasantry. Perhaps that is their fate. Perhaps the Alabama lawyer's doctrine, so comfortable for the white man, is to prevail: " It's a question who will do the dirty work. In this country the white man won't: the Negro must. There's got to be a mudsill somewhere. If you educate the Negroes they won't stay where they belong; and you must consider them as a race, because if you let a few rise it makes the others discontented."

The question of who is to do the crude, disagreeable and dirty work, has solved itself in the North which has had one stratum after another of immigrants who were willing to take it, each shoving his predecessor higher up in the scale of employment; but no foreigners will come into the South in order to relieve the Negro of hewing of wood and drawing of water. It looks as though the majority of the race would be compelled to accept some con-

374

dition on the land, without a share in the government and without much prospect of getting into other kinds of life. The prospect is discouraging in itself, and it readily shades into restraint, subjection, and peonage—the worst of remedies for a race low in origin, which has just emerged from a debasing servitude, and which needs all the stimulus of ambition and opportunity.

The South has proved its capacity for organizing and directing ignorant labor, but a peasant system has more dangers for the upper than the lower class. The gentlemen of eighteenth-century France, with all their high breeding, did not understand the people under them and were hated of their peasants; the Pashas of Egypt were degraded by their mastery over thousands of fellahin; the Russian boyars have so alienated the peasants that they have almost rent the empire in twain. To accept a peasant system would be a confession that the South must remain in the lower stage of economic progress which goes with such a system. The duty and the privilege of the South is still to seek the way of enlightment; to make the Negro a better laborer instead of crystallizing him into a race of dependents.

Material progress is necessary for the Negro and equally for the Poor White, not simply that he may be better clad and have better health, but because it brings with it other influences which go to elevate mankind. You cannot make good citizens and virtuous people out of a dirty, ill-fed family in a one-room house; the remedy of intellectual and moral uplift is as important as the material side. Thrift works both ways: the man who buys good clothes for his children wants to send them to Sunday school; the poor children in Sunday school beg their fathers to give them good clothes. Such intellectual and moral agencies are at work, though here again some white leaders object to them. For instance, John Temple Graves asks: " Will the negro, with his increasing education and his surely and steadily advancing worth and merit, be content to accept, in peace and humility, anything less than his full and equal share in the government of which he is a part?" Here is one of the stumbling blocks in the way of the progress of the race.

For thrift and saving habits the South has always lacked one of the approved aids; it has few savings banks, few ordinary banks which attract the deposits of Negroes, and few steady investments in small denominations. For this reason the proposed Postal Savings Banks would be a boon to the South, and would help toward the purchase of land and other property. The Negroes' own fraternal orders and stock companies furnish some opportunities for savings. Regulation of drinking and gambling places will also make saving likelier among the laborers. That difficulties and conflicts of interest would rise between Whites and Negroes was foreseen at the time of Reconstruction, and it was honestly supposed by the thinking people of the North that the ballot would at the same time protect the black against white aggression, and would educate him into the sense of such responsibility that there would not be negro aggression. Giving the negro suffrage, however, while at the same time through the Reconstruction state constitutions disfranchising his former master, brought about a condition of unstable equilibrium, and the strongest, best organized, and most determined race of course prevailed. For some years after the restoration of white supremacy in the Southern states, colored men were still allowed to vote in districts like the Sea Islands of South Carolina, and the Delta of Mississippi, where they were predominant, but since 1885 there has not been any genuine negro suffrage in any state of the South, in the sense that Negroes were assured that their votes could be cast and would be counted even if they made a difference in the result. The last remnant of a successful combination of negro voters with a minority of the Whites was in the North Carolina election of 1896.

By the series of constitutional amendments begun in 1890, and since spread through the South, a property or intelligence qualification has practically been established for Negroes while not applying to poor or illiterate Whites. In the Northern states race difficulties, so far as they take form in politics, are settled by the usual course of elections; in the South it is the unalterable intention of the Whites that the Negroes shall not participate in choosing officials or in making laws either for white men or for themselves.

Furthermore, the South is bitterly opposed to the holding of offices by Negroes except the small local appointments. Though Negroes are one third in number in the South, and more than one half the population in two states, they have not a single state administrative official, member of legislature, or judge. The opposition to negro office holding extends to federal appointments, although a considerable number of places, some of them important, are still held by Negroes. They obtain appointments as railway mail clerks and letter carriers by competitive examination, and a few of them are selected for collectorships of internal revenue and of customs, on the basis that the Negroes are part of the community and entitled to some recognition. To exclude them altogether from the public service, as they have been almost excluded from the suffrage, may somewhat diminish race friction, but it is a mark of inferiority which the whole negro race resents.

CHAPTER XXVII

MORAL REMEDIES

THE regeneration of a race, as of mankind, is something that must proceed from within and work outward. Hence the most obvious remedy for race troubles is that both races should come up to a higher plane of living. What has been the progress of the Negro in that direction; what is the likelihood of further advance? The chance of the blacks is less than it would be if the white race had a larger part in it. The Negro is insensibly affected by the spirit of the community in which he lives. He knows that though ruffians threaten him with revolvers or with malignant looks that have a longer range, there are also broad-minded and large-hearted white men who bid him rise; but he is almost cut off from the machinery of civilization set in motion by his white neighbor; he cannot use or draw books from the public library; he practically cannot attend any churches, lectures, or concerts, except those provided directly for him. On the plantation he hardly sees a white face, except those of the managers and their families. He has little opportunity to talk with white men; none for that interchange of thought which is so much promoted by sitting round the same table. He can attend no colleges or schools with white students. In the common schools and in many institutions above, he meets only negro teachers. He is far more cut off from the personal touch and influence of white men and women of high quality than he was in slavery times.

Within his own race he experiences the influences of some notable minds, and, with few exceptions, the men recognized by the Negroes as their chief leaders counsel moderation and preach uplift. Many of the lesser leaders are deficient in character, and a large fraction of the ministers of the gospel do not, by their lives or conversation, enforce the lessons which they teach from the pulpit; they also have not the advantage of training by white teachers. In the process of separation of races, the negro mind has gone far toward losing touch with the white mind. The best friends of the race are grieved and humiliated from time to time to find that they had expected something which the Negroes did not recognize as due from them—service, loyalty, gratitude. Thousands of people believe that the Negro makes it the object of his life to cheat a white man. Thousands of Negroes feel that they are not bound by promises or contracts made to their own hurt.

Since the white race is not in such friendly relations with the Negro as to impress upon him the causes of white superiority, some Southern writers would like to see a sort of benevolent state socialism applied to the Negro, such as laws under which the coming and going of the blacks should be regulated, their implements secured, and labor distributed where it was needed. Like many other suggestions, this remedy would cure the Negro's shiftlessness by taking away his self-control, and would apply to the lazy black man a régime which would be abhorrent if employed upon the lazy white man.

Where the Whites appreciate and aid the Negroes, the color line cuts them off from making the distinctions which are the rewards of the energetic and successful in other communities. The negro poet, the essayist, and the educator have no fellowship with those neighbors who could appreciate their genius. So far as the South can prevent it, the most energetic and successful negro business man can hope for no public office. The machinery for uplifting the Negro through white influence is no longer in operation. The inferior race is thrown back upon members of the inferior race for its moral stimulus; and then is reproached because it does not form higher ideals and advance more rapidly. The successful Negro exercising a good influence among his fellows cannot be admitted to the white man's club, cannot be made the intimate of men of kindred aims. As Senator Williams says: " When we find a good negro we must encourage him to stay good and to grow better. We are doing too little of that. The old adage, ' Give a dog a bad name and you have made a bad dog,' is a good one. Indiscriminate cursing of the whole negro race, good and bad alike included, is an exemplification of the adage. I have frequently thought how hard it was for a good negro, especially during campaign times, to stay good or to grow better when he could not come within sound of a white speaker's voice without hearing his whole race indiscriminately reviled without mention of him as an exception, even in the neighborhood where he was known to be one."

One of the strongest civilizing forces both North and South has been the Church, through which has been spread abroad not only the incitements to life on a high plane, but the intellectual stimulus of the preacher's voice, of the association of keen men, of Bible study. The Negro has the outward sign of this influence, the force of which is recognized by all candid people; but his clergy are not, as a class, moral leaders, and here, as in so many other

380

directions, he is deprived of the leadership of the Whites. For similar populations in the North there is an apparatus of missions, and the schools and colleges planted by Northerners in the South are almost all substantially missionary movements; but the South dislikes them and makes almost no effort to rival them. The Christian church, which is the bearer of civilization to Africa, China, the American Indians, leaves the Negroes in great part to christianize themselves if they can.

The white man has another opportunity of helping upward his dark neighbor through his control of legislatures and courts. Garner would solve the problem—" not by denying him the advantages of education, but by curbing his criminal instincts through a more rigid enforcement of the law. The laws against carrying concealed weapons, against gambling, and against vagrancy should, if necessary, be increased in severity and enforced with a vigilance and certainty which will root out gambling, force the idle vagrant to work, and send the pistol carrier to prison. The abolition of the saloon and the extirpation of the ' blind tiger' and the cocaine dive would remove the most potent external causes of negro criminality. . . . Conditions could be materially improved by the establishment of a more adequate police surveillance and control and the introduction of a more effective police protection, for it is a well-known fact that in most Southern communities this protection is notoriously insufficient. It is also well worth considering whether some reasonable and effective measures might not be taken to prevent the movement of the negroes to the towns and cities and their segregation in particular localities." Says an Alabamian lawyer: " A different and milder set of laws ought to be enacted for him than for the white man. . . . His best

friends in the South are among our 'gentlemen.' The low
White has no use for him. He hates the Negro and the
Negro hates him." From the federal government, as has
been shown above, no effective legislation can be expected;
but may not something be done by special state action?

Many observers are alive to the possibility of removing
temptations which are thought to be specially alluring to
the Negro. The ill-disposed country black is a rover, a
night-hawk, and has his own kinds of good times, including
a supply of whisky; the bad town Negro finds his pleasures
right at hand, and is frequently abetted in them by the
white man. To be sure, low drinking houses, gambling
houses and worse places, flourish among all races in New
York, and are no more likely to be exterminated in New
Orleans than in the Northern city for such considerations.
John Sharp Williams would resort to "some sort of
common-sense remedies of the negro question upon the
criminal side, principally in the nature of preventives. In
the first place, they suggest the rigid enforcement of vagrant laws by new laws whenever, in justice and right, they
need strengthening. In the second place, they suggest a
closing of all low dives and brothels where the vagrant,
tramp, and idle negroes consort and where their imagina-
tions—they being peculiarly a race of imagination and
emotion—are inflamed by whisky, cocaine, and lewd pictures. It must be remembered that that which would not
inflame the imagination of a white man will have that
effect upon the tropical, emotional nature of the darky.
. . . We ought, like Canada and Cape Colony, to have
mounted rural police or constabulary, whose duty it would
be to patrol the country districts day and night." The
cry in the Southern newspapers against negro dives generally ignores the fact that many of them are carried on by

white people, and others are partially supported by white custom. At the bottom of humanity race distinctions disappear, and you could find, if you searched for it, in many Southern towns, beneath the lowest negro deep a lower white deep. The difficulty with Southern legislation is that it is more hostile to negro dives than to white dives.

A more promising legislative remedy is an efficient vagrant law, by which the hopelessly idle, the sponges on the industry of their race, should receive the dread punishment of work. Northern states which are unable to find statutes and magistrates strict enough to put an end to the intolerable white tramp nuisance, have little cause to criticise the Southern loafers, of whom the Whites are found in quite as large a proportion as the Negroes. Several states already have vagrant laws, but they are applied chiefly to Negroes, often very inequitably, and play into the iniquitous system by which sheriffs make money in proportion to the number of prisoners that they arrest and keep in jail. The *Birmingham Age Herald* says that to abolish imprisonment for nonpayment of criminal costs is " as much out of our reach as is a flight to Mars. . . . We must build jails to suit the operations of the collectors of fees. There is no help for it."

Suggestions that there be a kind of negro court for the less serious negro crimes, have been made by Thomas Nelson Page and others; and Negroes could probably administer as good local justice as some of their dominant race. In the island of St. Helena, for instance, where seven thousand people for a long time had no local court, a white magistrate was sent over who sat day after day drunk on the bench, finally shot a man (the second homicide on that island in forty years), and was put on his trial, but still held his judicial office. Perhaps a special negro

383

court for petty crimes would increase the sense of responsibility; but it collides with the present system of selling petty criminals to the planters.

Something could be done by an efficient system of rural police such as is needed all over the country, North and South. In Georgia and South Carolina bills have lately been pending for a state mounted police which would be a sort of revival of the volunteer patrols of slavery times. The suggestion is fought hard, however, on the ground that white men might be obliged to give an account of themselves as well as Negroes.

The only thoroughgoing legislative measure which seems likely to help the Negro is prohibition, which is now sweeping through the Lower South. It is a region which suffers from hard drinking, and there has long been a strong sentiment against the traffic; but the tumultuous success of prohibition laws in communities like Alabama and Mississippi is due in great part to the conviction of employers of labor in cotton mills, in ironworks, in the timber industry, and on the land, that they are losing money because their laborers are made irregular by drunkenness. That objection applies as much to the selling of liquor to Whites as to Negroes; but the drinking white men have an influence over prosecuting officers that the Negroes cannot command; and it looks as though the result would be a kind of prohibition which shuts off the stream from the dusky man's throat while leaving it running for the white man. If the South succeeds in keeping liquor away from the Negro in the Southern cities, it will show more determination than exists in any Northern center of population.

In general, legislation is not a remedy for the race question, because breaches of the law come from both sides;

384

and nobody is skillful enough to draft a bill which will, if righteously applied, apply only to criminal and dissolute Negroes. The cutting down of drinking shops, the arrest of the drones, a rural police, enforcement of the liquor laws, will help in the South because it will bring about a feeling of responsibility in both races—but race hostility is not caused by laws, is not curable by laws, and relies upon defying laws.

Perhaps the most striking failure of the Whites to exercise an influence over the Negroes is through the negro schools. They are, to be sure, carried on under laws made by white men, administered by state and county white officials, but there the relation ends. Even from the point of view of an unsympathetic superior race, the schools are badly supervised; and when it comes to the teachers, the lower race is thrown back upon teachers of the lower race. In the North the raw children from the alien families are Americanized by their fellows in the public schools, under the influence of teachers taken from the class of the population which has most opportunity for training. Not so in the South, where the blind are expected to lead the blind, where negro teachers trained by Negroes are expected to inculcate the principles of white civilization.

The refusal of the South to permit white people, and especially white women, to teach the Negroes, is a plant of recent growth. In slavery times the white mistresses and their daughters habitually taught the household servants their duties and set before them a standard of morals. Beyond that, they were often proud of teaching capable slaves to read and write. On every theory of the relation of the races this transmittal of civilization was not only allowable, but a sacred duty. Nowadays the mis-

385

tresses have the smallest control over or influence upon their domestic servants; and, with few exceptions, the South absolutely refuses to improve the low estate of the Negroes by permitting the white young people to teach them.

The arguments against putting white teachers into negro schools are altogether weak. The first is that it is unsafe for white women, but the Northern women who have been for years among Negroes as teachers have no fear nor cause for fear; and the influence of a pure and refined white woman would tend to diminish some of the worst crimes of the black race. It is urged, however, that even men could not teach Negroes, first, because the Negroes would not trust their girls to them; secondly, because it would cut off the field or negro employment; thirdly, because a white man does not wish to teach Negroes; and, finally, because none but inferior men would seek such employment.

Surely the poor little black children are not likely under any circumstances to suppose that they are the equals of the members of the proud families that held their fathers in slavery! The white people sorely need the employment; the Negroes still more need the example and admonition of trained and high-minded people. The relation is not unknown. In the public schools of Charleston, for forty years, the negro children have been taught by white ladies, and as well taught as the white children. In Alabama, and even in Virginia, public schools were for a time taught by Whites, and you hear of sporadic cases elsewhere, as in a district of Louisiana, where the mother of the chairman of the school board was a teacher, and she was so incapable that no white school would have her on any terms, so they compromised by giving her a negro school. With these small exceptions, a relation between the races, through which none of the dreaded evils of race equality could come about, was rejected; and that is the main reason why the negro schools have been poor and continue inferior. The Southern woman is not below the Northern in a sense of duty; the Southern schoolmarm is the equal of her Yankee sister in refinement and in pluck; and the Southern woman was the only class of people in the South who could at the same time have taught the pickaninnies to read, and the older people to recognize that the Whites were their best friends.

Of all the remedies suggested, education is the most direct and the most practical because it has so far been neglected; education is needed for the safety of the race. As Leroy Percy, the successful planter, puts it: "You cannot send these men out to fight the battle of life helplessly ignorant. In slavery, he was the slave of one, and around him was thrown the protecting care of the master. In freedom you cannot, through the helplessness of ignorance, make him the slave of every white man with no master's protection to shield him"; and he adds, "The education of the Negro, to the extent indicated, is necessary for the preservation of the character and moral integrity of the white men of the South." Professor Garner roundly declares that "Governor Vardaman's contention that education increases the criminality of the negro is nothing but bold assertion and has never been supported by adequate proof."

Education is just as much needed to break windows into dark minds, to open up whatever of the spiritual the Negro can take to himself. It is the one remedy in which the North can take direct part, and never was there more need of maintaining the schools in the South, supported

387

chiefly by Northern contributions; for they have the opportunity to teach those lessons of cleanliness of body and mind, of respect for authority, of thrift, personal honesty, of human relations, which the public schools are less fitted to inculcate. Many of these schools have white teachers, all have white friends; they interfere in no way with the education furnished by the South; they teach no lessons harmful to the Negro or the white man; they perform a function which the Whites in the South offer to their own race by endowed schools and colleges, and which they do not attempt to provide for the Negroes. Education is not a cure-all, education is only the bottom step of a long flight of stairs; but neither race nor individual can mount without that step.

Throughout this book it has been steadily kept in mind that there are two races in the South between which the Southern problem is divided; and that there can be no progress without both races taking part. Here is the most difficult part of the whole matter: the two races, so closely associated, are nevertheless drifting away from each other. Time was when men like Wade Hampton, of South Carolina, and Senator Lamar, of Mississippi, expected that Whites and Negroes would coöperate in political parties; time was when former slaveholders joined with former slaves in a confident attempt to bring the Negroes up higher. Those voices of encouragement still are heard, but there is in them a note of weariness. Almost everybody in the South would be pleased if the Negroes (of course without prejudice to the white domination) would rise or rise faster. It would mean also much to the white race if the cook always came in the morning, and the outside man never got drunk, and the cotton hand would raise a bale to the acre, and the school child would

388

learn to read about how to keep his place toward the white man.

Every thinking man in the South knows that he is worse off because the Negro is not better off. That is the reason of the rising dissatisfaction, wrath and resentment in the minds of many Whites. They feel that the Negro has no sense of responsibility to the community; they accuse him of sullenness, of a lack of interest in his employment and his employer. Just what the Negro thinks in return is hard to guess. "Brer Rabbit, 'e ain't sayin' nuffin"; but it is plain that the races are less friendly to each other, understand each other less, are less regardful of each other's interests, than at any time since freedom was fairly completed. We have the unhappy condition that while both races are doing tolerably well, and likely to do better, race relations are not improving.

In other parts of the country where there are such rivalries, efforts are made to come to an understanding. Each side has some knowledge of the arguments of the other; they appeal to the same press; the leaders sooner or later are brought together in legislatures or in a social way, and gradually come to understand each other's difficulties. Some efforts have been made in the South to study this question in association. The Negroes have now several organizations which bring people together for discussion. The Agricultural and Industrial Fairs which they are beginning to carry on are one such influence. The negro schools of the Calhoun and Talladega type do something; the large annual conferences organized by Atlanta, Tuskegee, and Hampton, with their subsequent publications, are a kind of clearing house of opinions on the conditions of the Negro and of sound advice. A few years ago the attempt was made in the so-called Niagara

Movement to organize the Negroes in defense of their political rights.

On the side of the Whites there has been the Ogden Movement, for the improvement of the Southern white education, part of the outcome of which has been the formation of the General Education Board and Southern Education Board. The *South Atlantic Quarterly,* published at Trinity College, North Carolina, encourages a free exchange of views on Southern conditions; and though the *Manufacturers' Record* lays the responsibility for the Atlanta riots upon the Southern white people who have been urging moderation in the South, the Southern educational movement goes on steadily, and seems to be gaining ground.

An effort was made after the riots to bring about a Southern commission of three white men from each state, to discuss plans for keeping up the race integrity of the Whites, including the Negro to stay on the soil, educating both races, and reforming the courts, but it was allowed to fail. Some Southern newspapers bitterly attacked it on the ground that no discussion was necessary; that everybody knew all the facts that were cogent, and that any such discussion of the negro problem would be likely to bring down criticism from "doctrinaires, theorists and self-constituted proprietors of the universe in the North." To the Northern mind this seems one of the most alarming things about the whole matter. The labor question in the Northeast, the land question in the Northwest, are openly discussed man to man, and newspaper to newspaper. Nobody thinks that the conditions in the South are agreeable; everybody would like to see some betterment; and the refusal to discuss it simply makes the crisis worse.

MORAL REMEDIES

This opposition is still stronger against any form of joint discussion between representatives of the white and negro races. The real objection seems to be that it would be a recognition that the Negro had a right to some share in adjusting his own future, and that what he thinks about the question ought to have weight with the white people. This is another of the cruel things about the whole situation. The whole South is acquainted with the negro criminal and the shiftless dweller on the borders of the cities; almost no white people are acquainted by personal observation with the houses, with the work, and still less with the character and aims of the best element of the Negroes. For this reason, Northern investigators have a certain advantage in that they may freely read the statements of both sides, supplement them out of personal experience and conversation, and try to strike a balance. There are plenty of reasonable people in both races, each of whom knows his own side better than anybody else can possibly know it; hence mutual discussion, common understanding, some kind of programme toward which public sentiment might be directed, would seem an obvious remedy, and is upheld by such men as Thomas Nelson Page; yet it is a remedy which is never tried.

All the suggestions that have been discussed above may be roughly classified into remedies of push and remedies of pull, and this classification corresponds to the points of view of the two dominant classes of Southern Whites. In studying the books, the articles and the fugitive utterances on this subject, in talking with men who see the thing at first hand, in noting the complaints of the Negroes and the Whites alike, it is plain that there is in the South a strong negro-hating element, larger than people like to admit, which appeals to drastic statutes, to unequal judicial punishments, to violence outside of the law; in a word, to "keeping the nigger down." Alongside it the thinking class of Southern people (which appears to be gaining ground) seeks the elevation of both races, and especially of that one which needs it most. Meanwhile the Negro sits moodily by, waiting for the superior race to decide whether he shall be sent to the calaboose or to school.

The Southern problem is thus brought down in its last analysis to the simple question whether the two races can permanently live apart and yet together. That depends, in the first place, on the capacity of the Negro to improve far enough to take away the reproach now heaped upon him; and in the second place in the willingness of the Whites to accept the deficiencies of the negro character as a part of the natural conditions of the land, like the sterility of parts of the Southern soil, and to leave him the opportunity to make the most of himself.

The three fundamental duties of the white man, according to Judge Hammond, of Atlanta, are to see " that his own best interest lies in the cultivation of friendly relations with the negro. . . . To treat the negro with absolute fairness and justice . . . advising him and counseling him about the important affairs of his everyday life." These duties lie upon the white man because, as Thomas Nelson Page states it: " Unless the whites lift the Negroes up, the Negroes will drag them down."

Nobody, white or black, North or South, is able to point out any single positive means by which the two races are both to have their full development and yet to live in peace. Every positive and quick-acting remedy when examined is found invalid. Violence of language or of behavior of both sides does nothing whatever to remove the real difficulties. The agencies of uplift are slow and uncertain and nobody can positively predict that they will do the work. The South, with all its magnificent resources, is far behind the other sections of the Union, both in wealth and productive power. It can only take its proper place in the Union by raising the average character and energy of its people—of all its people—for it cannot be done by improving either race while the other remains stationary.

In a word, the remedy is patience. Dark as things look in the South, it is subject to mighty forces. In many ways the strongest influence for peace and concord in the South is simply self-interest. The most intelligent and thoughtful men in the South see clearly that unless the people can be made to improve, the section will always lag behind. Side by side with this force is the spirit of humanity, of practical Christianity, which forbids that milions of people shall be cut off from the agencies of evangelization. The South is behind no other part of the country in a sense of the greatness of moral forces.

From every point of view, the obvious thing for the South is to make the best of its condition and not the worst, to give opportunities of uplift to all those who can appropriate them, to raise the negro race to as high a point as it is capable of occupying. This is a long, hard process, full of disappointment and perhaps of bitterness. The problem is not soluble in the sense that anyone can foresee a wholly peaceful and contented community divided into two camps; but the races can live alongside, and cooperate, though one be superior to the other. That superiority only throws the greater responsibility on the upper race. Nobody has ever given better advice to the South than Senator John Sharp Williams—" In the face of this great problem it would be well that wise men think more, that good men pray more, and that all men talk less and curse less." In that spirit the problem will be solved, because it will be manfully confronted.

MAP AND TABLES

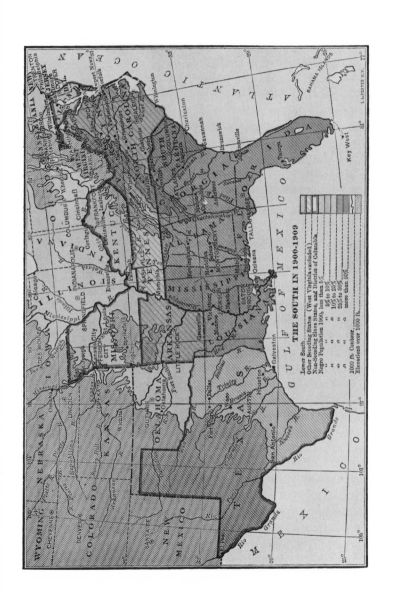

THE SOUTH IN 1900-1909

Lower South.
Other Seceding States. (West Virginia excluded.)
Non-Seceding Slave States, and District of Columbia.

Negro Population 1900 less than 5%.

       "   "   5% to 10%.

       "   "   10% to 25%.

       "   "   25% to 50%.

       "   "   more than 50%.

1000 ft. Contour.
Elevations over 1000 ft.

COMPARATIVE POPULATION (1900)

White Elements Contrasted

(*In Thousands*)

Northern Groups (1900).	Whites	Colored	Total	Equivalent Southern Groups (1900).	Whites	Colored	Total
1 Colorado......	529	9	540	1 Alabama.........	1,001	827	1,829
2 Indiana........	2,459	58	2,516	2 Arkansas........	945	367	1,312
3 Indian Ter.....	303	37	392	3 Florida..........	297	231	529
4 Iowa..........	2,219	13	2,232	4 Georgia..........	1,181	1,035	2,216
5 Kansas........	1,416	52	1,470	5 Louisiana........	730	651	1,382
6 Michigan.......	2,399	16	2,421	6 Mississippi.......	641	908	1,551
7 Minnesota......	1,737	5	1,751	7 North Carolina...	1,264	624	1,894
8 Nebraska......	1,059	6	1,066	8 South Carolina...	558	782	1,340
				9 Tennessee........	1,540	480	2,021
				10 Virginia.........	1,193	661	1,854
				Total 10 States....	9,350	6,566	15,928
				11 Texas...........	2,427	621	3,049
Total........	12,121	196	12,388	Total 11 Seceding States....	11,777	7,187	18,977
9 North Dakota..	312	...	319	12 Delaware........	154	31	185
10 Oklahoma......	368	19	398	13 Dist. of Columbia.	192	87	279
11 South Dakota..	381	...	402	14 Kentucky........	1,862	285	2,147
12 Utah..........	272	1	277	15 Maryland........	952	235	1,188
13 Wisconsin......	2,058	3	2,069	16 Missouri.........	2,945	161	3,107
14 California......	1,403	11	1,485				
15 Idaho.........	154	...	162				
16 Montana.......	226	2	243				
17 Oregon........	395	1	414				
18 Vermont.......	343	1	344				
Double Total	18,033	234	18,501	Total South....	17,882	7,986	25,883

COMPARATIVE POPULATION (1900)—SOUTHERN GROUPS
(In Thousands)

	Races			Distribution			Foreign Whites			Estimates	
	White	Negro	Total	Total	Urban	Rural	Foreign Born	Native [foreign parents]	Total	1905	1906
1 Alabama	1,001	827	1,829		134	1,695	14	30	44	1,986	2,018
2 Arkansas	945	367	1,312		71	1,241	14	33	47	1,403	1,422
3 Florida	297	231	529		79	450	19	24	43	613	629
4 Georgia	1,181	1,035	2,216		244	1,972	12	25	37	2,406	2,444
5 Louisiana	730	651	1,382		314	1,068	52	108	160	1,513	1,539
6 Mississippi	641	908	1,551		41	1,510	8	20	28	1,682	1,708
7 North Carolina	1,264	624	1,894		97	1,797	4	8	12	2,032	2,059
8 South Carolina	558	782	1,340		100	1,240	5	12	17	1,435	1,454
9 Tennessee	1,540	480	2,021		270	1,751	18	41	59	2,147	2,172
10 Virginia	1,193	661	1,854		272	1,582	19	33	52	1,953	1,973
Total 10 States	9,350	6,566	15,928		1,622	14,306	165	334	499	17,170	17,418
11 Texas	2,427	621	3,049		344	2,705	178	289	467	3,455	3,537
Total Seceding States	11,777	7,187	18,977		1,966	17,011	343	623	966	20,625	20,955
12 Delaware	154	31	185		77	108	14	22	36	193	194
13 District of Columbia	192	87	279		279	. . .	20	38	58	303	308
14 Kentucky	1,862	285	2,147		363	1,784	50	139	189	2,291	2,320
15 Maryland	952	235	1,188		557	631	93	179	272	1,261	1,275
16 Missouri	2,945	161	3,107		956	2,151	216	524	740	3,320	3,363
Total Border States	6,105	799	6,906		2,232	4,674	393	902	1,295	7,368	7,460
Total South	17,882	7,986	25,883		4,198	21,685	736	1,525	2,261	27,993	28,415

COMPARATIVE POPULATION (1900)—EQUIVALENT NORTHERN GROUPS
(In Thousands)

	RACES			DISTRIBUTION			FOREIGN WHITES			ESTIMATES	
	White	Negro	Total	Total	Urban	Rural	Foreign Born	Native [foreign par. ents]	Total	1905	1906
1 Colorado	529	9	540	540	206	334	90	127	217	603	616
2 Indiana	2,459	58	2,516	2,516	608	1,908	142	364	506	2,678	2,711
3 Indian Territory	303	37	392	392		392	5	10	15	498	519
4 Iowa	2,219	13	2,232	2,232	375	1,857	306	652	958	2,210	2,206
5 Kansas	1,416	52	1,470	1,470	205	1,265	127	276	403	1,546	1,612
6 Michigan	2,399	16	2,421	2,421	747	1,674	540	832	1,372	2,557	2,585
7 Minnesota	1,737	5	1,751	1,751	470	1,281	505	806	1,311	1,980	2,026
8 Nebraska	1,059	6	1,066	1,066	169	897	177	326	503	1,068	1,068
9 North Dakota	312	..	319	319	10	309	113	133	246	440	464
10 Oklahoma	368	19	398	398	20	378	16	38	54	558	590
11 South Dakota	381	..	402	402	10	392	88	156	244	455	466
12 Utah	272	1	277	277	70	207	53	116	169	310	316
13 Wisconsin	2,058	3	2,069	2,069	634	1,435	516	956	1,472	2,229	2,261
Total	15,512	219	15,853	15,853	3,524	12,329	2,678	4,792	7,470	17,132	17,440
14 California	1,403	11	1,485	1,485	650	835	317	442	759	1,621	1,648
15 Idaho	154	..	162	162		162	22	43	65	198	206
16 Montana	226	2	243	243	66	177	62	71	133	294	304
17 Oregon	395	1	414	414	99	315	54	85	139	465	475
18 Vermont	343	1	344	344	39	305	45	73	118	349	350
19 Washington	496	3	518	518	165	353	102	129	231	599	615
Total	3,017	18	3,166	3,166	1,019	2,147	602	843	1,445	3,526	3,598
Double Total	18,529	237	19,019	19,019	4,543	14,476	3,280	5,635	8,915	20,658	21,038
20 Arizona	93	2	123	123		123	22	26	48	140	144
21 Illinois	4,735	85	4,822	4,822	2,272	2,550	965	1,498	2,463	5,319	5,419
22 Nevada	35	..	42	42		42	9	12	21	42	42
23 New Mexico	180	2	195	195		195	13	18	31	213	216
24 New Hampshire	411	1	412	412	159	253	88	80	168	429	433
25 Wyoming	89	1	93	93	22	71	17	24	41	102	104
26 West Virginia	915	43	959	959	74	885	22	49	71	1,057	1,076
Total	6,458	134	6,646	6,646	2,527	4,119	1,136	1,707	2,843	7,302	7,434
Grand Total	24,987	371	25,665	25,665	7,070	18,595	4,416	7,342	11,758	27,960	28,472

COMPARATIVE VALUATION OF PROPERTY (1860-1909)—SOUTHERN GROUPS
(In Millions)

	1860 Population (thousands)	1860 Asses'd Valuation	1890 Population (thousands)	1890 Real Valuation	1890 Asses'd Valuation	1904 Population (thousands)	1904 Real Valuation	1904 Assessed Valuation	1906 Population (thousands)	1906 Assessed Valuation	1907 Assessed Valuation	1908 Assessed Valuation	1909 Asses'd Valuation
1 Alabama	964	432	1,513	623	259	1,955	965	323	2,018	344	451	451	484
2 Arkansas	435	179	1,128	455	175	1,385	804	250	1,422	250	302	302	327
3 Florida	140	69	391	389	92	596	431	100	629	131	142	142	131
4 Georgia	1,057	618	1,837	852	416	2,368	1,167	505	2,444	578	700	700	705
5 Louisiana	708	436	1,119	495	234	1,487	1,032	301	1,539	459	459	459	524
6 Mississippi	791	410	1,289	454	167	1,656	688	223	1,708	223	223	223	393
7 North Carolina	993	292	1,618	584	235	2,004	842	433	2,059	489	575	575	565
8 South Carolina	705	490	1,151	401	168	1,416	586	210	1,454	250	267	267	271
9 Tennessee	1,111	382	1,768	888	383	2,122	1,104	352	2,172	475	475	475	444
10 Virginia	1,596	657	1,656	862	415	1,933	1,288	424	1,973	424	424	424	580
Total	8,500	3,965	13,470	6,003	2,544	16,922	8,907	3,121	17,418	3,623	4,018	4,018	4,424
11 Texas	604	267	2,235	2,106	781	3,374	2,836	1,082	3,537	1,139	1,139	1,139	2,174
Total Seceding States	9,104	4,232	15,705	8,109	3,325	20,296	11,743	4,203	20,955	4,762	5,157	5,157	6,598
12 Delaware	112	40	168	176	66	191	230	76	194	76	76	76	76
13 Dist. Columbia	75	40	230	344	153	298	1,040	198	308	198	279	279	312
14 Kentucky	1,155	528	1,859	1,172	548	2,263	1,527	668	2,320	644	644	644	753
15 Maryland	687	296	1,043	1,085	529	1,246	1,511	644	1,275	644	765	765	765
16 Missouri	1,182	267	2,679	2,398	888	3,278	3,760	1,243	3,363	1,489	1,553	1,622	1,547
Total	3,211	1,171	5,979	5,175	2,184	7,276	8,068	2,829	7,460	3,051	3,317	3,386	3,453
Total South	12,315	5,403	21,684	13,284	5,509	27,572	19,811	7,032	28,415	7,813	8,474	8,543	10,051

400

COMPARATIVE VALUATIONS OF PROPERTY (1860-1909)—EQUIVALENT NORTHERN GROUPS

(In Millions)

	1860 Population [thousands]	1860 Assess'd Valuation	1890 Population [thousands]	1890 Real Valuation	1890 Assess'd Valuation	1904 Population [thousands]	1904 Real Valuation	1904 Assessed Valuation	1906 Population [thousands]	1906 Assessed Valuation	1907 Assessed Valuation	1908 Assessed Valuation	1909 Assess'd Valuation
1 Colorado	34		412	1,146	221	590	1,208	465	616	465	465	465	465
2 Indiana	1,350	411	2,192	2,095	857	2,646	3,106	1,360	2,711	1,598	1,598	1,768	1,776
3 Indian Terr.			180			477	459		519				
4 Iowa	675	205	1,912	2,287	519	2,214	4,049	642	2,206	635	590	599	613
5 Kansas	107	23	1,427	1,799	348	1,534	2,253	378	1,612	378	425	2,454	2,511
6 Michigan	749	164	2,094	2,095	898	2,530	3,282	1,578	2,585	1,596	1,654	1,654	1,649
7 Minnesota	172	32	1,302	1,692	589	1,934	3,344	871	2,026	871	1,037	1,037	1,091
8 Nebraska	29	7	1,059	1,276	185	1,068	2,010	295	1,068	313	329	392	392
9 North Dakota			183	337	88	416	736	117	464	196	196	227	280
10 Oklahoma			62			526	636		590	97	97	97	860
11 South Dakota			329	425	140	444	680	173	466	173	173	284	321
12 Utah	40	4	208	349	106	303	488	50	316	146	146	146	146
13 Wisconsin	776	186	1,687	1,833	577	2,197	2,839	1,358	2,261	1,385	1,385	1,385	2,479
Total	3,932	1,032	13,047	15,334	4,528	16,870	25,090	7,287	17,440	7,853	8,095	10,508	12,583
14 California	380	140	1,208	2,534	1,101	1,594	4,115	1,551	1,648	1,595	1,879	1,995	2,337
15 Idaho			84	208	26	191	343	67	206	81	81	116	121
16 Montana			132	453	113	283	746	153	304	234	251	252	280
17 Oregon	52	19	314	590	166	454	852	174	475	188	188	188	598
18 Vermont	315	85	332	266	162	348	360	168	350	188	184	184	186
19 Washington	12	4	349	761	218	582	1,052	298	615	329	573	573	790
Total	759	248	2,419	4,812	1,786	3,452	7,468	2,411	3,598	2,615	3,156	3,308	4,312
Double Total	4,691	1,280	15,466	20,146	6,314	20,331	32,558	9,698	21,038	10,468	11,251	13,816	16,895
20 Arizona			60	189	28	137	306	45	144	45	76	81	84
21 Illinois	1,712	389	3,826	5,067	810	5,220	8,817	1,083	5,419	1,083	1,127	1,127	1,264
22 Nevada	7	21	46	180	25	42	221	28	42	44	44	44	74
23 New Mexico	94	124	154	231	-43	209	332	42	216	43	43	43	64
24 New Hampshire	326		377	325	263	426	517	221	433	232	238	245	249
25 Wyoming			61	170	33	100	330	47	104	51	64	68	186
26 W. Virginia			763	439	187	1,037	840	242	1,076	875	850	850	1,068
Total	2,139	534	5,287	6,601	1,389	7,171	11,363	1,708	7,434	2,373	2,442	2,458	2,989
Grand Total	6,830	1,814	20,753	26,747	7,703	27,502	43,921	11,406	28,472	12,841	13,693	16,274	19,884

COMPARATIVE BANKING STATISTICS (1865–1906)—SOUTHERN GROUPS

(In Thousands of Dollars)

	NATIONAL BANKS, 1865.				All Banks, 1896. Deposits.	NATIONAL BANKS, 1905.				ALL BANKS, 1906.	
	No.	Capital.	Deposits.	Assets.		No.	Capital.	Deposits.	Assets.	Deposits.	Clearings.
1 Alabama	2	…	…	…	6,856	67	5,993	21,235	37,809	52,004	238,514
2 Arkansas	0	…	…	…	3,555	28	2,650	8,803	15,323	19,533	62,608
3 Florida	0	…	…	…	5,531	34	2,840	14,085	22,837	31,878	…
4 Georgia	1	100	350	466	10,952	63	6,371	22,527	43,333	68,131	594,700
5 Louisiana	1	500	5,089	6,572	25,307	35	5,905	30,091	55,678	83,634	984,264
6 Mississippi	1	50	86	163	8,909	25	2,970	8,578	16,139	44,727	…
7 North Carolina	2	68	52	141	9,722	48	3,850	14,057	26,499	47,377	19,484
8 South Carolina	0	…	…	…	9,891	24	2,986	9,059	18,819	41,095	68,415
9 Tennessee	7	340	939	1,850	21,723	68	8,425	36,417	66,079	86,706	594,979
10 Virginia	10	1,089	3,910	7,246	28,244	85	8,344	42,277	76,381	95,132	411,353
Total 10 States	24	2,147	10,426	16,438	130,690	477	50,334	207,129	378,897	570,217	2,974,317
11 Texas	0	…	…	…	31,747	440	32,295	101,285	189,484	130,364	946,197
Total 11 Seceding States	24	2,147	10,426	16,438	162,437	917	82,629	308,414	568,381	700,581	3,920,514
12 Delaware	11	1,328	1,555	4,479	7,020	24	2,274	8,164	14,220	24,552	65,309
13 Dist. Columbia	6	1,550	5,483	18,396	18,677	12	4,827	21,868	41,391	47,861	284,214
14 Kentucky	11	2,272	2,129	6,841	41,502	124	14,686	40,208	89,523	105,252	674,079
15 Maryland	27	11,910	15,212	38,923	87,354	89	17,294	61,986	130,422	171,313	1,442,156
16 Missouri	11	3,574	5,622	14,144	117,150	101	23,580	117,079	309,821	347,613	4,373,738
Total Border States	66	20,634	30,001	82,783	271,703	350	62,661	249,305	585,377	696,591	6,839,496
Whole South	90	22,781	40,427	99,221	434,140	1,267	145,290	557,719	1,153,758	1,397,172	10,760,010

402

COMPARATIVE BANKING STATISTICS (1865-1906)—EQUIVALENT NORTHERN GROUPS
(In Thousands of Dollars)

		National Banks, 1865.				All Banks, 1896.	National Banks, 1905.				All Banks, 1906.	
		No.	Capital.	Deposits.	Assets.	Deposits.	No.	Capital.	Deposits.	Assets.	Deposits.	Clearings.
1	Colorado	1	200	162	427	29,967	74	7,093	66,618	102,970	93,243	399,242
2	Indiana	70	12,260	10,526	33,259	52,386	197	20,551	91,727	160,193	203,333	511,813
3	Indian Terr.	0				704	133	5,629	11,657	24,059	15,529	308,990
4	Iowa	36	3,196	5,110	11,128	78,440	281	17,665	69,709	134,197	262,176	99,533
5	Kansas	2	200	2,479	2,910	30,529	171	10,313	50,236	84,155	118,269	830,735
6	Michigan	35	4,148	4,307	11,665	103,671	88	12,720	74,719	115,736	278,579	1,374,158
7	Minnesota	11	1,345	1,894	4,582	68,494	229	18,606	83,491	145,250	179,699	524,947
8	Nebraska	2	115	337	525	30,866	159	10,885	56,822	106,743	114,645	27,935
9	North Dakota	0				7,032	97	3,498	14,519	22,396	35,416	
10	Oklahoma	0				756	98	3,780	12,822	21,881	26,985	
11	South Dakota	0				7,217	72	2,790	13,752	20,510	41,982	18,554
12	Utah	0	200	262	463	6,366	17	1,948	10,758	18,392	38,331	267,961
13	Wisconsin	34				68,864	115	13,585	85,736	124,241	189,181	476,709
	Total	191	21,664	25,077	64,959	485,292	1,731	129,063	642,566	1,080,723	1,597,368	4,840,677
14	California	0				202,874	95	23,065	92,111	181,699	593,979	2,506,729
15	Idaho	0				1,969	27	1,275	8,282	11,392	19,194	
16	Montana	0				16,801	29	2,895	18,855	27,005	37,663	42,113
17	Oregon	0				9,262	43	3,160	24,285	38,193	34,535	259,704
18	Vermont	27	4,863	1,019	10,384	40,572	50	5,935	12,796	27,362	65,240	843,145
19	Washington	0				9,229	36	4,013	36,100	51,225	91,309	
	Total	27	4,863	1,019	10,384	280,707	280	40,343	192,429	336,876	841,920	3,651,691
	Double Total	218	26,527	26,096	75,343	765,999	2,011	169,406	834,995	1,417,599	2,439,288	8,492,268
20	Arizona	0				1,548	13	705	4,319	6,247	13,708	
21	Illinois	76	10,715	15,783	39,812	213,799	346	48,709	276,382	572,972	714,421	11,174,325
22	Nevada	0				580	4	407	1,333	2,136	5,813	
23	New Mexico	0				2,311	23	1,342	7,194	11,012	10,782	
24	New Hampshire	38	4,635	1,390	10,814	71,922	55	5,330	15,307	31,044	93,083	
25	Wyoming	0				2,651	19	1,085	6,630	9,498	11,620	
26	West Virginia	12	1,652	2,325	4,807	17,746	79	6,604	24,848	43,079	76,465	50,918
	Total	126	17,002	19,498	55,433	310,557	539	64,182	336,013	675,988	925,892	11,225,243
	Grand Total	344	43,529	45,594	130,776	1,076,556	2,550	233,588	1,171,008	2,093,587	3,365,180	19,717,511

COMPARATIVE MANUFACTURES (1905)

SOUTHERN GROUPS

(Money Values in Thousands of Dollars)

	No. of Establishments.	Wage Earners.	Capital.	Annual Wages.	Cost of Material.	Value of Products.
1 Alabama........	1,882	62,173	105,383	21,878	60,458	109,170
2 Arkansas.......	1,907	33,089	46,306	14,544	21,799	53,864
3 Florida..........	1,413	42,091	32,972	15,767	16,532	50,298
4 Georgia..........	3,219	92,749	135,212	27,392	83,625	151,040
5 Louisiana........	2,091	55,859	150,811	25,316	117,035	186,380
6 Mississippi......	1,520	38,690	50,256	14,819	25,801	57,451
7 North Carolina...	3,272	85,339	141,001	21,375	79,268	142,521
8 South Carolina...	1,399	59,441	113,422	13,869	49,969	79,376
9 Tennessee........	3,175	60,572	102,439	22,806	79,352	137,960
10 Virginia.........	3,187	80,285	147,989	27,943	83,649	148,856
Total 10 States..	23,065	610,288	1,025,791	205,709	617,488	1,116,916
11 Texas...........	3,158	49,066	115,665	24,469	91,604	150,528
Total, 11 Seceding States....	26,223	659,354	1,141,456	230,178	709,092	1,267,444
12 Delaware........	631	18,475	50,926	8,158	24,884	41,160
13 Dist. of Columbia.	482	6,299	20,200	3,658	7,732	18,359
14 Kentucky........	3,734	59,794	147,282	24,439	86,545	159,754
15 Maryland........	3,852	94,174	201,878	36,144	150,024	243,376
16 Missouri.........	6,464	133,167	379,369	66,644	252,258	439,549
Total Border States.......	15,163	311,909	799,655	139,043	521,443	902,198
Whole South.....	41,386	971,263	1,941,111	369,221	1,230,535	2,169,642

COMPARATIVE MANUFACTURES (1905)

EQUIVALENT NORTHERN GROUPS

(Money Values in Thousands of Dollars)

	No. of Establish-ments.	Wage Earners.	Annual Wages.	Capital.	Cost of Material.	Value of Products.
1 Colorado........	1,606	21,813	107,664	15,100	63,114	100,144
2 Indiana..........	7,044	154,174	312,071	72,056	220,507	393,954
3 Indian Terr......	466	2,257	5,016	1,114	4,849	7,909
4 Iowa............	4,785	49,451	111,427	22,997	102,844	160,572
5 Kansas..........	2,475	35,570	88,680	18,883	156,510	198,245
6 Michigan........	7,446	175,229	337,894	81,279	230,081	429,120
7 Minnesota.......	4,756	69,636	184,903	35,843	210,554	307,858
8 Nebraska.......	1,819	20,260	80,235	11,022	124,052	154,918
9 North Dakota....	507	1,755	5,704	1,031	7,096	10,218
10 Oklahoma........	657	3,199	11,108	1,655	11,545	16,550
11 South Dakota....	686	2,492	7,585	1,422	8,697	13,085
12 Utah............	606	8,052	26,004	5,157	24,940	38,926
13 Wisconsin.......	8,558	151,391	412,647	71,472	227,255	411,140
Total..........	41,411	695,279	1,690,938	339,023	1,392,044	2,242,639
14 California.......	6,839	100,355	282,647	64,657	215,726	367,218
15 Idaho..........	364	3,061	9,689	2,059	4,069	8,769
16 Montana........	382	8,957	52,590	8,652	40,930	66,415
17 Oregon..........	1,602	18,523	44,024	11,444	30,597	55,525
18 Vermont........	1,699	33,106	62,659	15,221	32,430	63,084
19 Washington......	2,751	45,199	96,953	30,087	66,166	128,822
Total..........	13,637	209,201	548,562	132,120	389,918	689,833
Double Total...	55,048	904,480	2,239,500	471,143	1,781,962	2,932,472
20 Arizona.........	169	4,793	14,396	3,969	14,595	28,083
21 Illinois..........	14,921	379,436	975,845	208,405	840,057	1,410,342
22 Nevada.........	115	802	2,892	693	1,628	3,096
23 New Mexico......	199	3,478	4,638	2,153	2,236	5,706
24 New Hampshire..	1,618	65,366	109,495	27,693	73,216	123,611
25 Wyoming.......	169	1,834	2,696	1,261	1,301	3,523
26 West Virginia....	2,109	43,758	86,821	21,153	54,419	99,041
Total..........	19,300	499,467	1,196,783	265,327	987,452	1,673,402
Grand Total....	74,348	1,403,947	3,436,283	736,470	2,769,414	4,605,874

COMPARATIVE CHARITIES AND COLLECTIONS (1904-1905)—SOUTHERN GROUPS

	Juvenile Delinquents, June 30, 1904.	Prisoners (June 30, 1904).			Insane in Hospitals (Jan. 1, 1905).			Paupers (Jan. 1, 1905).		
		White.	Negro.	Total.	White.	Negro.	Total.	White.	Negro.	Total.
1 Alabama	37	270	1,798	2,068	1,222	490	1,712	414	357	771
2 Arkansas		251	632	884	562	107	669	476	167	643
3 Florida	31	140	1,094	1,234	457	283	740	80	70	150
4 Georgia	99	544	2,029	2,579	2,049	915	2,964	602	407	1,009
5 Louisiana	36	325	1,355	1,680	1,122	467	1,589	149	14	163
6 Mississippi		114	1,122	1,238	981	598	1,579	223	280	503
7 North Carolina		269	912	1,185	1,532	545	2,077	981	578	1,559
8 South Carolina		142	903	1,045	709	498	1,207	415	289	704
9 Tennessee	246	600	1,397	1,997	1,457	336	1,793	1,343	641	1,984
10 Virginia	279	401	1,494	1,895	2,239	1,200	3,439	1,112	883	1,995
Total 10 States	728	3,056	12,736	15,805	12,330	5,439	17,769	5,795	3,686	9,481
11 Texas		1,835	2,667	4,504	3,081	401	3,482	742	221	963
Total Seceding States	728	4,891	15,403	20,309	15,411	5,840	21,251	6,537	3,907	10,444
12 Delaware	98	66	94	160	288	78	366	229	63	292
13 District of Columbia	405	12	34	46	2,074	517	2,591	90	160	250
14 Kentucky	301	923	1,298	2,221	2,632	508	3,140	1,396	306	1,702
15 Maryland	1,070	750	1,117	1,867	2,189	325	2,514	1,325	405	1,730
16 Missouri	670	1,752	1,040	2,793	4,923	273	5,196	2,257	244	2,501
Total Border States	2,544	3,503	3,583	7,087	12,106	1,701	13,807	5,297	1,178	6,475
Total South	3,272	8,394	18,986	27,396	27,517	7,541	35,058	11,834	5,085	16,919

406

COMPARATIVE CHARITIES AND CORRECTIONS (1904-1905)—EQUIVALENT NORTHERN GROUPS

	Juvenile Delinquents, June 30, 1904.	Prisoners (June 30, 1904).			Insane in Hospitals (Jan. 1, 1905).			Paupers (Jan. 1, 1905).		
		White.	Black.	Total.	White.	Black.*	Total.	White.	Black.*	Total.
1 Colorado	288	901	120	1,022	880	31	911	452	10	462
2 Indiana	872	1,719	419	2,138	4,324	125	4,449	3,206	129	3,335
3 Indian Territory	714	1,131	122	1,255	4,603	60	4,663	2,055	41	2,096
4 Iowa	372	1,918	801	2,876	2,539	121	2,660	693	93	786
5 Kansas	1,114	1,857	124	1,995	5,483	81	5,564	2,796	57	2,853
6 Michigan	360	995	59	1,067	4,263	14	4,277	557	8	565
7 Minnesota	164	430	85	519	1,592	16	1,608	477	10	487
8 Nebraska	39	198	5	203	473	4	477	233	3	236
9 North Dakota		21	..	22	394	19	413	58	4	62
10 Oklahoma		217	9	245	591	31	622	161	3	164
11 South Dakota	65	212	11	223	373	3	376	184	3	187
12 Utah	79									
13 Wisconsin	543	1,311	32	1,366	5,024	25	5,049	1,707	6	1,713
Total	4,610	10,910	1,787	12,931	30,539	530	31,069	12,579	367	12,946
14 California	474	3,036	165	3,355	5,705	305	6,010	4,156	136	4,292
15 Idaho		183	8	196	277	3	280	111	1	112
16 Montana	78	519	38	571	563	16	579	420	9	429
17 Oregon	93	360	21	399	1,276	47	1,323	378	11	389
18 Vermont	137	262	12	274	883	2	885	414	11	425
19 Washington	158	841	37	911	1,420	27	1,447	311	7	318
Total	940	5,201	281	5,706	10,124	400	10,524	5,790	175	5,965
Double Total	5,550	16,111	2,068	18,637	40,663	930	41,593	18,369	542	18,911
20 Arizona	31	289	13	318	258	12	270	180	11	191
21 Illinois	1,386	2,550	629	3,180	10,184	264	10,448	5,238	149	5,387
22 Nevada		99	5	129	175	11	186	162	4	166
23 New Mexico		236	15	265	112	1	113			
24 Wyoming		195	26	230	104	3	107			
25 New Hampshire	181	411	5	416	608	2	610	1,064	12	1,076
26 West Virginia	314	535	604	1,139	1,417	86	1,503	846	115	961
Total	1,912	4,315	1,297	5,677	12,858	379	13,237	7,490	291	7,781
Grand Total	7,462	20,426	3,365	24,314	53,521	1,309	54,830	25,859	833	26,692

* Not possible for figures of Jan. 1, 1905, to distinguish between blacks and other colored insane and paupers; not important except in California where on Dec. 31, 1903, there were 218 Mongolian insane.

COMPARATIVE COMMON SCHOOL EDUCATION (1905)—SOUTHERN GROUPS

	Estimated Population [thousands]	Estimated School Population [thousands]	ENROLLMENT AND ATTENDANCE: Number Pupils Enrolled [thousands]	ENROLLMENT AND ATTENDANCE: Average Number Pupils Attending [thousands]	Average Days of School	TEACHERS: Number	TEACHERS: Average Monthly Salary	Value of School Property [thousands]	REVENUE: Annual Revenue [thousands]	REVENUE: Revenue per Person of School Age	EXPENDITURE: Annual Outgo [thousands]	EXPENDITURE: Outgo per Average Attendance	EXPENDITURE: Outgo per $10,000 Actual Property
1 Alabama	1,986	663	400	210	103	5,400	28	2,200	1,589	2.39	1,475	7.03	13.0
2 Arkansas	1,403	474	336	207	88	7,826	40	3,171	2,042	4.31	1,955	9.43	21.5
3 Florida	613	185	123	84	108	2,925	38	1,290	946	5.20	945	11.30	21.9
4 Georgia	2,406	803	499	311	118	10,360	34	4,010	2,397	3.03	2,328	7.47	19.2
5 Louisiana	1,513	493	210	146	130	4,680	40	3,660	2,219	4.51	2,169	14.83	15.0
6 Mississippi	1,682	572	404	233	123	8,922	31	2,190	1,881	3.35	1,869	8.01	27.1
7 North Carolina	2,032	676	474	280	95	9,687	31	3,183	1,859	2.78	1,936	6.90	24.6
8 South Carolina	1,435	497	303	200	106	6,059	30	2,000	1,310	2.64	1,305	6.51	20.3
9 Tennessee	2,147	687	508	349	113	9,784	36	5,172	3,102	4.52	2,933	8.41	23.6
10 Virginia	1,953	618	362	215	128	9,072	29	4,298	2,432	3.94	2,378	11.05	16.6
Total 10 States	17,170	5,668	3,619	2,235	...	74,715	...	31,174	19,777	...	19,293	...	...
11 Texas	3,455	1,156	756	502	112	17,116	53	11,897	6,406	5.54	6,400	12.76	21.9
Total Seeding States	20,625	6,824	4,375	2,737	...	91,831	...	43,071	26,183	...	25,693	...	...
12 Delaware	193	51	37	25	170	897	40	1,627	499	9.75	540	17.93	21.4
13 Dist. of Columbia	303	66	51	41	181	1,478	64	5,816	1,680	25.54	1,676	41.28	15.1
14 Kentucky	2,291	709	501	310	90	10,449	44	6,118	2,723	3.94	2,663	8.59	17.4
15 Maryland	1,261	352	227	140	192	5,150	47	4,790	3,163	8.99	2,961	21.32	18.2
16 Missouri	3,320	978	729	471	152	17,385	47	22,593	10,330	10.56	10,102	21.46	26.3
Total Border States	7,368	2,156	1,545	987	...	35,359	...	40,944	18,395	...	17,942	...	...
Total South	27,993	8,980	5,920	3,724	...	127,190	...	84,015	44,578	...	43,635	...	...

			ENROLLMENT AND ATTENDANCE			TEACHERS			REVENUE		EXPENDITURE		
	Estimated Population [thousands]	Estimated School Population [thousands]	Number Pupils Enrolled [thousands]	Average Number Attending per Pupils [thousands]	Average Days of School	Number	Average Monthly Salary	Value of School Property [thousands]	Annual Revenue [thousands]	Revenue per Person of School Age	Annual Outgo [thousands]	Outgo per Average Attendance	Outgo per $10,000 Actual Property
1 Colorado	603	149	138	92	158	4,454	47	10,265	4,172	28.62	3,985	41.89	33.0
2 Indiana	2,678	741	550	416	160	16,495	54	29,059	11,927	16.09	11,501	27.67	30.1
3 Indian Territory	498	170	48	28	115	1,325	44	750	643	3.78	715	25.10	14.0
4 Iowa	2,210	681	540	376	160	29,619	38	23,305	11,195	16.43	10,316	27.47	26.4
5 Kansas	1,546	470	382	264	145	12,036	42	10,525	5,506	11.72	5,830	22.08	25.2
6 Michigan	2,557	692	521	408	168	16,823	45	25,963	9,760	14.11	9,630	23.60	27.9
7 Minnesota	1,980	579	430	281	161	13,320	44	22,018	9,163	15.82	8,470	30.19	24.1
8 Nebraska	1,068	322	279	185	170	9,680	44	11,309	5,218	16.29	5,304	28.64	23.8
9 North Dakota	440	115	107	68	141	5,714	44	4,334	2,435	21.21	2,530	37.27	31.5
10 Oklahoma	558	175	158	90	104	3,687	37	2,123	1,429	8.17	1,488	16.49	21.4
11 South Dakota	455	132	109	75	140	5,150	38	4,550	2,341	17.67	2,380	31.61	32.9
12 Utah	310	101	76	56	153	1,718	62	3,538	1,655	16.76	1,657	29.50	34.0
13 Wisconsin	2,229	670	465	291	169	14,004	38	16,575	8,531	12.74	8,240	28.34	27.8
Total	17,132	4,997	3,803	2,630		134,025		164,314	73,975		72,046		
14 California	1,621	370	315	239	170	9,026	67	27,551	9,271	25.05	9,771	40.80	22.8
15 Idaho	198	57	57	41	136	1,547	58	1,892	914	16.09	912	22.39	29.1
16 Montana	294	65	45	31	107	1,268	56	4,832	1,278	20.68	1,236	39.28	16.6
17 Oregon	465	122	108	78	158	4,022	45	4,671	2,013	16.57	2,052	26.27	21.2
18 Vermont	349	82	67	48	157	3,417	32	2,964	1,290	15.80	1,324	27.39	32.6
19 Washington	599	151	170	119	167	5,179	55	9,808	3,648	24.10	3,220	27.09	38.6
Total	3,526	847	762	556		24,459		51,718	18,414		18,515		
Double Total	20,658	5,844	4,565	3,186		158,484		216,032	92,389		90,561		
20 Arizona	140	36	22	14	135	538	76	900	438	12.08	457	32.67	14.3
21 Illinois	5,319	1,456	985	812	169	27,860	60	64,555	22,670	15.59	22,823	28.11	24.7
22 Nevada	42	9	7	5	159	357	68	270	271	30.04	258	49.69	11.7
23 New Mexico	213	65	38	26	114	828	54	801	368	5.64	362	14.09	10.6
24 New Hampshire	429	93	78	50	152	2,416	36	4,493	1,360	14.69	1,557	31.22	26.6
25 Wyoming	102	26	18	12	140	728	51	454	366	14.27	388	31.78	9.0
26 West Virginia	1,057	326	248	163	123	7,636	35	5,811	2,744	8.42	2,767	16.97	30.1
Total	7,302	2,011	1,396	1,082		40,363		77,284	28,217		28,612		
Grand Total	27,960	7,855	5,961	4,268		198,847		293,316	120,606		119,173		

COMPARATIVE COMMON SCHOOL EDUCATION (1907)

SOUTHERN GROUPS

	Teachers.	Pupils Average Attendance [thousands].	FINANCES.		
			Value of School Property [thousands].	Annual Revenue [thousands].	Annual Expenditure [thousands].
1 Alabama.........	7,757	249	4,569	2,287	2,620
2 Arkansas.........	8,113	221	4,039	2,428	2,414
3 Florida...........	3,362	91	2,001	1,384	1,352
4 Georgia..........	10,379	317	5,822	2,831	2,850
5 Louisiana........	5,615	160	4,098	2,952	2,169
6 Mississippi.......	9,499	285	2,190	1,511	2,641
7 North Carolina....	10,146	297	4,250	2,519	2,378
8 South Carolina....	6,228	222	2,200	1,531	1,416
9 Tennessee........	9,829	353	6,332	3,314	2,705
10 Virginia..........	9,468	220	5,718	3,323	3,357
Total 10 States..	80,396	2,415	41,219	24,080	23,902
11 Texas............	17,867	499	15,178	7,443	7,402
Total, 11 Seceding States....	98,263	2,914	56,397	31,523	31,304
12 Delaware....... .	897	25	1,627	499	540
13 Dist. of Columbia..	1,575	43	7,005	2,164	2,012
14 Kentucky........	9,245	310	6,368	4,263	4,051
15 Maryland.........	5,290	135	4,790	3,424	3,307
16 Missouri..........	17,847	493	27,847	10,853	8,482
Total South......	133,117	3,920	104,034	52,726	49,696

COMPARATIVE COMMON SCHOOL EDUCATION (1907)

EQUIVALENT NORTHERN GROUPS

	Teachers.	Pupils Average Attendance [thousands].	FINANCES.		
			Value of School Property [thousands].	Annual Revenue [thousands].	Annual Expenditure [thousands].
1 Colorado........	4,944	106	10,207	5,836	4,476
2 Indiana..........	16,841	420	31,499	13,816	12,012
3 Indian Terr......	2,740	61	2,175	790	920
4 Iowa.............	28,508	366	24,950	11,619	10,681
5 Kansas...........	12,743	277	11,000	6,294	6,874
6 Michigan........	17,286	423	30,944	15,260	12,086
7 Minnesota.......	13,928	322	26,000	11,085	10,803
8 Nebraska........	10,059	186	12,755	5,809	5,561
9 North Dakota....	6,109	72	4,900	3,000	2,900
10 Oklahoma.......	4,386	103	3,624	2,053	1,629
11 South Dakota....	5,358	65	5,138	2,702	2,730
12 Utah...........	2,010	61	3,577	1,996	2,056
13 Wisconsin.......	14,491	328	23,243	10,223	8,946
Total.........	139,403	2,790	190,012	90,483	81,674
14 California.......	9,714	248	36,680	10,914	12,219
15 Idaho...........	1,897	48	3,162	1,240	1,370
16 Montana........	1,741	35	3,489	1,597	1,716
17 Oregon..........	4,228	77	5,732	2,671	2,474
18 Vermont........	3,984	49	3,416	1,255	1,271
19 Washington......	6,209	131	12,448	5,397	5,504
Double Total...	167,176	3,378	254,939	113,557	106,228
20 Arizona.........	626	15	1,158	610	620
21 Illinois..........	28,083	770	69,142	30,958	30,106
22 Nevada.........	322	7	523	345	490
23 New Mexico......	923	25	1,000	524	484
24 New Hampshire...	2,916	50	5,240	1,379	1,453
25 Wyoming........	787	14	914	609	436
26 West Virginia.....	8,061	165	7,113	3,490	3,361
Grand Total....	208,894	4,424	340,029	151,472	143,178

411

COMPARATIVE SECONDARY SCHOOLS (1905)—SOUTHERN GROUPS

	Students					Teachers			Value of Plant		
	Public		Private								
	White	Negro	White	Negro	Total	Public	Private	Total	Public [thousands]	Private [thousands]	Total [thousands]
1 Alabama	4,646	231	1,485	116	6,478	223	112	335	831	516	1,347
2 Arkansas	3,215	295	1,562	159	5,231	144	77	221	620	419	1,039
3 Florida	1,493	102	242	95	2,382	114	21	135	501	134	635
4 Georgia	7,015	139	2,499	585	10,238	320	207	527	1,339	1,111	2,450
5 Louisiana	2,927	80	1,320	35	4,362	155	102	257	909	457	1,366
6 Mississippi	3,998	286	1,375	160	5,819	225	89	314	1,027	509	1,536
7 North Carolina	2,958	14	4,185	383	7,540	123	270	393	553	896	1,449
8 South Carolina	4,380	278	748	344	5,750	214	83	297	689	612	1,301
9 Tennessee	5,459	605	3,528	90	9,682	242	215	257	1,145	865	2,010
10 Virginia	4,095	545	4,302	338	8,264	193	273	466	596	1,424	2,020
Total 10 States	40,636	2,575	20,230	2,305	65,746	1,953	1,449	3,402	8,210	6,943	15,153
11 Texas	19,427	1,134	3,710	221	24,492	842	264	1,106	4,323	1,988	6,311
Total Seceding States	60,063	3,709	23,940	2,526	90,238	2,795	1,713	4,508	12,533	8,931	21,464
12 Delaware	1,340	53	238	...	1,631	63	30	93	487	200	687
13 Dist. of Columbia	2,968	891	1,117	...	4,976	196	203	399	536	1,007	1,543
14 Kentucky	6,155	651	3,261	51	10,118	297	289	586	1,597	850	2,447
15 Maryland	6,362	350	2,094	...	8,806	261	248	509	1,149	3,125	4,274
16 Missouri	26,278	1,080	3,365	89	30,812	1,140	311	1,451	6,532	2,072	8,604
Total Border States	43,103	3,025	10,075	140	56,343	1,957	1,081	3,035	10,301	7,254	17,555
Grand Total	103,166	6,734	34,015	2,666	146,581	4,752	2,794	7,546	22,834	16,185	39,019

413

	STUDENTS.					TEACHERS.			VALUE OF PLANT.		
	Public.		Private.								
	White.	Negro.	White.	Negro.	Total.	Public.	Private.	Total.	Public. [thousands].	Private. [thousands].	Total. [thousands].
1 Colorado	8,079	56	323		8,458	347	49	396	2,634	200	2,834
2 Indiana	34,848	658	1,831	2	37,339	1,596	185	1,781	9,540	836	10,376
3 Indian Territory	340	26	423		789	20	19	39	352	239	591
4 Iowa	32,210	134	2,577		34,921	1,367	147	1,514	8,452	643	9,095
5 Kansas	19,715	310	832		20,857	756	67	823	4,636	604	5,240
6 Michigan	33,077	110	1,523		34,710	1,412	148	1,560	8,905	639	9,544
7 Minnesota	18,073	62	2,381		20,516	767	205	972	5,244	1,731	6,975
8 Nebraska	17,425	49	1,461	1	18,836	749	126	875	4,309	505	4,814
9 North Dakota	2,218	1	48		2,267	119	3	122	725		725
10 Oklahoma	1,917	78	286		2,281	87	14	101	551	145	696
11 South Dakota	4,543	7	340		4,890	229	34	263	1,566	255	1,821
12 Utah	1,785	2	2,731		4,578	84	144	228	268	1,049	1,317
13 Wisconsin	23,956	17	1,476		25,449	1,051	166	1,217	6,457	1,539	7,996
Total	198,186	1,510	16,232	3	215,931	8,584	1,307	9,891	53,639	8,385	62,024
14 California	23,125	64	2,749		25,938	930	349	1,279	4,616	2,722	7,338
15 Idaho	930	1	366		1,297	48	22	70	441	179	620
16 Montana	2,641	4	200		2,845	133	26	159	980	139	1,119
17 Oregon	4,125	12	811	1	4,949	165	74	239	1,157	309	1,466
18 Vermont	4,378	3	1,523	1	5,805	196	98	294	1,234	775	2,009
19 Washington	8,168	40	524		8,732	346	62	408	2,050	496	2,546
Double Total	43,367	124	6,173	2	49,666	1,818	631	2,449	10,478	4,620	15,098
Double Total	241,553	1,634	22,405	5	265,597	10,402	1,938	12,340	64,117	13,005	77,122
20 Arizona	285	1	55		341	13	4	17	128	80	208
21 Illinois	48,212	461	3,434	6	52,113	1,945	314	2,259	11,757	2,985	14,742
22 Nevada	171				171	10		10	69		69
23 New Mexico	638	3	33		674	34	3	37	381		381
24 New Hampshire	4,766	3	2,281	14	7,064	227	185	412	1,478	1,108	2,556
25 Wyoming	560	3	35		598	29	5	34	372	75	447
26 West Virginia	2,408	63	1,019		3,480	121	83	204	1,052	367	1,419
Total	57,040	534	6,857	20	64,451	2,379	594	2,973	15,237	4,615	19,852
Total	298,593	2,168	29,262	25	330,048	12,781	2,532	15,313	79,354	17,620	96,974

COMPARATIVE HIGHER EDUCATION (1905)—SOUTHERN GROUPS

	Teachers.	STUDENTS.				FINANCES.			
		Under-graduates.	Graduates.	Pro-fessional.	Total.	Value of Plant.	Productive Funds.	Benefac-tions.	Total Income.
						Thousands.	Thousands.	Thousands.	Thousands
1 Alabama	258	1,895	47	241	2,183	1,845	1,306	17	393
2 Arkansas	154	894	7	272	1,173	913	208	15	247
3 Florida	109	311	1	37	349	722	614	22	176
4 Georgia	430	3,719	19	311	4,049	3,972	1,161	153	701
5 Louisiana	266	1,172	101	716	1,989	2,877	3,560	13	404
6 Mississippi	315	2,021	72	87	2,180	2,229	1,510	21	589
7 North Carolina	465	3,255	49	588	3,892	3,699	1,441	186	645
8 South Carolina	295	2,878	37	66	2,981	2,740	783	159	542
9 Tennessee	681	2,770	80	1,870	4,720	4,659	3,050	310	718
10 Virginia	450	3,741	81	472	4,294	5,475	2,747	850	857
Total 10 States	3,393	22,656	494	4,660	27,810	29,131	16,380	1,746	5,272
11 Texas	513	2,954	46	862	3,862	3,975	1,059	2	776
Total Seceding States	3,906	25,610	540	5,522	31,672	33,106	17,439	1,748	6,048
12 Delaware	29	173	1		174	270	83		68
13 Dist. of Columbia	501	875	146	1,790	2,811	9,416	1,510	355	517
14 Kentucky	448	2,281	42	1,080	3,403	2,934	2,287	257	420
15 Maryland	540	2,433	206	405	3,044	16,218	5,388	110	1,131
16 Missouri	929	3,736	203	1,417	5,356	8,063	8,005	253	1,164
Total Border States	2,447	9,498	598	4,692	14,788	36,901	17,273	975	3,300
Total South	6,353	35,108	1,138	10,214	46,460	70,007	34,712	2,723	9,348

414

		STUDENTS.				FINANCES.			
	Teachers.	Under-graduates.	Graduates.	Pro-fessional.	Total.	Value of Plant.	Productive Funds.	Benefac-tions.	Total Income.
						Thousands.	Thousands.	Thousands.	Thousands.
1 Colorado	425	1,826	140	333	2,299	2,713	812	75	525
2 Indiana	462	5,004	136	295	5,435	6,312	2,964	80	1,022
3 Indian Territory	21	25	...	...	25	171	...	12	16
4 Iowa	775	4,165	238	1,102	5,505	5,959	3,251	342	1,426
5 Kansas	609	3,396	120	487	4,003	4,287	1,232	130	710
6 Michigan	560	4,198	144	1,538	5,880	6,076	2,863	106	1,324
7 Minnesota	595	2,770	140	1,138	4,048	3,506	2,118	50	883
8 Nebraska	502	2,283	153	650	3,086	2,588	1,254	193	599
9 North Dakota	88	267	11	49	327	1,096	1,151	50	368
10 Oklahoma	62	323	3	50	376	546	...	...	145
11 South Dakota	138	516	19	48	583	1,299	199	73	275
12 Utah	146	580	2	...	582	1,044	326	1	282
13 Wisconsin	452	3,741	157	198	4,096	4,548	2,464	311	1,106
Total	4,835	29,094	1,263	5,888	36,245	40,145	18,634	1,423	8,681
14 California	882	5,285	380	617	6,282	10,755	35,270	470	1,999
15 Idaho	22	173	1	...	174	288	213	...	93
16 Montana	52	322	12	...	334	695	523	...	177
17 Oregon	201	1,078	20	193	1,291	907	680	17	191
18 Vermont	89	574	1	193	768	1,430	1,073	101	149
19 Washington	170	1,315	85	104	1,504	2,015	295	33	607
Total	1,416	8,747	499	1,107	10,353	16,090	38,054	621	3,216
Double Total	6,251	37,841	1,762	6,995	46,598	56,235	56,688	2,044	11,897
20 Arizona	26	33	6	...	39	234	...	...	55
21 Illinois	1,634	8,889	1,368	3,809	14,066	20,112	17,052	1,133	3,072
22 Nevada	33	178	3	...	181	282	147	2	98
23 New Mexico	54	105	9	...	114	292	...	...	91
24 New Hampshire	119	1,038	36	60	1,130	1,996	2,750	110	279
25 Wyoming	18	62	3	...	65	358	26	...	59
26 West Virginia	106	889	2	220	1,111	1,122	276	115	217
Total	1,990	11,194	1,427	4,089	16,710	24,396	20,251	1,360	3,871
Grand Total	8,241	49,035	3,189	11,084	63,308	80,631	76,939	3,404	15,768

COMPARATIVE NORMAL AND INDUSTRIAL SCHOOLS (1905)—SOUTHERN GROUPS

	Normal Schools (Public and Private).				Reform and Industrial Schools (Public).		Finances.	
	Teachers for Normal Students.	Number of Normal Students.	Value of Plant.	Total Income.	Teachers.	Number of Students.	Value of Plant.	Total Expenditures.
1 Alabama	89	1,866	988,000	310,000	2	78	37,000	8,000
2 Arkansas	15	292	112,000	17,000				
3 Florida	34	350	55,000	30,000	1	52	25,000	3,000
4 Georgia	77	831	370,000	82,000	1	49	30,000	3,000
5 Louisiana	35	638	130,000	31,000				
6 Mississippi	23	269	7,000	6,900				
7 North Carolina	114	1,872	707,000	166,000				
8 South Carolina	48	502	370,000	74,000				
9 Tennessee	84	1,652	600,000	109,000	28	1,279	170,000	87,000
10 Virginia	62	1,146	1,274,000	267,000	6	351	59,000	24,000
Total 10 States	581	9,418	4,613,000	1,092,000	38	1,809	321,000	125,000
11 Texas	51	1,510	372,000	120,000	2	180	50,000	35,000
Total Seceding States	632	10,928	4,985,000	1,212,000	40	1,989	371,000	160,000
12 Delaware					6	229	165,000	20,000
13 Dist. of Columbia	21	181			15	436	460,000	71,000
14 Kentucky	26	434	114,000	29,000	9	744	200,000	57,000
15 Maryland	22	475	227,000	33,000	31	1,486	1,122,000	147,000
16 Missouri	106	3,324	1,188,000	186,000	18	1,247	771,000	124,000
Total	175	4,414	1,529,000	248,000	79	4,142	2,718,000	419,000
Grand Total	807	15,342	6,514,000	1,460,000	119	6,131	3,089,000	579,000

COMPARATIVE NORMAL AND INDUSTRIAL SCHOOLS (1905)—EQUIVALENT NORTHERN GROUPS

	Normal Schools (Public and Private).				Reform and Industrial Schools (Public).		Finances.	
	Teachers for Normal Students.	Number of Normal Students.	Value of Plant.	Total Income.	Teachers.	Number of Students.	Value of Plant.	Total Expenditures.
1 Colorado	35	490	250,000	71,000	12	549	180,000	67,000
2 Indiana	140	3,877	905,000	268,000	8	1,186	280,000	103,000
3 Indian Territory	...	...	...	...	...	...	...	...
4 Iowa	129	2,757	518,000	203,000	29	986	420,000	99,000
5 Kansas	54	1,040	396,000	79,000	6	575	299,000	75,000
6 Michigan	122	2,416	795,000	216,000	56	2,149	850,000	198,000
7 Minnesota	96	1,968	983,000	202,000	16	250	381,000	81,000
8 Nebraska	64	1,533	415,000	73,000	11	310	340,000	61,000
9 North Dakota	15	397	108,000	26,000	...	...	...	...
10 Oklahoma	72	1,471	405,000	118,000	...	...	...	...
11 South Dakota	44	702	390,000	46,000	2	89	86,000	26,000
12 Utah	8	182	100,000	19,000	...	...	...	...
13 Wisconsin	173	2,723	1,075,000	313,000	30	900	671,000	136,000
Total	952	19,546	6,340,000	1,634,000	170	6,994	3,507,000	846,000
14 California	101	1,614	1,179,000	198,000	9	676	529,000	156,000
15 Idaho	21	239	145,000	33,000	1	20	50,000	5,000
16 Montana	14	126	100,000	30,000	2	127	45,000	24,000
17 Oregon	46	466	163,000	65,000	2	110	50,000	46,000
18 Vermont	19	256	20,000	21,000	4	240	60,000	25,000
19 Washington	47	753	350,000	101,000	6	48	...	...
Total	248	3,444	1,957,000	448,000	24	1,221	734,000	256,000
Double Total	1,200	22,990	8,297,000	2,082,000	194	8,215	4,241,000	1,106,000
20 Arizona	18	288	183,000	46,000	1	55	35,000	16,000
21 Illinois	146	2,997	3,011,000	337,000	47	3,765	2,200,000	636,000
22 Nevada	...	...	...	...	...	...	...	...
23 New Mexico	15	206	135,000	36,000	...	177	...	...
24 New Hampshire	9	119	125,000	27,000	4	...	100,000	30,000
25 Wyoming	...	...	...	...	...	...	...	...
26 West Virginia	75	1,339	642,000	139,000	10	505	170,000	67,000
Total	263	4,949	4,096,000	585,000	62	4,502	2,505,000	749,000
Grand Total	1,463	27,939	12,393,000	2,667,000	256	12,717	6,746,000	1,855,000

417

INDEX

INDEX

A

Abbott, E. H., articles by, on Southern question, 18.

Advance system on cotton plantations, 268; lien loans, 268; impositions, 269-270, 272; specimen accounts, 271; Christmas money, 272.

Africa, negroes in, 94-97. *See also* Colonization.

Afro-American as name for Negro, 92.

Agriculture. Southern crops, 24, 220; poor white farmers and tenants, 41, 45; foreign laborers, 57; white small farmers, 60; negro life, 115-116; Negroes as laborers, 127; farms owned by Negroes, 144-145; amount of negro products, 145; actual wealth of Southern states, 220-221; population 221; reclamation of swamps, 221; comparative wealth of seceding states, 237-238; of whole South, 241; comparative value of cotton and other Southern crops, 251. *See also* Cotton.

Alabama. Mining, 24; Republican party, 173; negro voters, 176; leasing of convicts, 201; contract law and peonage, 283; illiteracy, 293; per-capita school tax, 295; comparative statistics, 395-415.

Albany, Ga., negro school near, 312.

Alderman, E. A., and negro progress, 179.

Alexander's Magazine, 18.

Alexandria, La., Italians at, 56.

Amalgamation of races. Evil of, 157; determination against, 344, 349. *See also* Miscegenation, Mulattoes.

American Colonization Society and Liberia, 96, 97. *See also* Colonization.

American Magazine, articles in, on race question, 18.

Americus, Ga., as trade center, 26.

Amusements, negro, 116.

Andersonville, Ga., statue to Wirz in, 88.

Andrew, J. A., protest of, against class prejudice, 165.

Appalachian Forest Reserve, proposed, 223.

Architecture, Southern standard of, 26, 304.

Arizona, comparative statistics of, 395-415.

Arkansas. Illiteracy, 293; comparative statistics, 395-415.

Armstrong, S. C., and Hampton Institute, 334. *See also* Hampton.

Art galleries in South, 304.

Assessment. *See* Taxation.

Association of Colleges, 300.

Atlanta. Size, 28; progress, 29, 242; foreign population, 51; negro population, 107; race riot, 206, 390.

Atlanta, University of. Conferences, 131, 389; founding, 309. *See also* Colleges.

Atlanta Evening News and race riot, 206.

Atlanta Georgian, on lynching, 213.

Augusta, Ga., water power of, 26.

Austin. Capitol, 27; progress, 29.

Avary, Myrta L., on educational value of slavery, 84.

B

Baker, R. S., articles by, on race question, 18.

Baldwin Co., Ala., Northerners in, 48.

Bale, cotton. Making, 259; round, 259; careless construction, 274.

Baltimore. Foreign population, 51; as port, 229, 233; schools, 296, 315.

Banishment of Negroes, 195, 205, 206.

Banking, Southern, 225; comparative statistics of, 236, 238, 402-403; and cotton culture, 263; need of savings banks, 376.

Baptist Church, negro, 117.

"Basket-name," 138.

Bassett, J. S., and race problem, 72, 345.

Beaufort County, S. C., negro suffrage in, 176. *See also* Sea Islands.

"Before Day Clubs," 190.

Bell, of Alabama. Plantation, 254; and negro uplift, 373.

Benevolent institutions, comparative statistics of, North and South, 237, 406-407.

Benson settlement, 141, 371.

Berea College and negro education, 317.

Bernhard of Saxe-Weimar, Duke, on cotton seed, 260.

Bibliography of Southern problem, 7-19; bibliographies, 7; anti-negro works, 8-12; conservative Southern books, 12-14; works by Negroes, 14-17; monographic studies, 17; magazine articles, 18; necessity of first-hand investigation, 19.

Birmingham, Ala. Iron trade, 25; progress, 29, 242.

Birmingham Age Herald on punishment of vagrancy, 383.

Black-and-tan Republicans, 173.

Black Belt. Extent, 21; manufactures, 25; trade centers, 26; richness of soil, 220.

Blount College and coeducation, 290.

Blowing Rock, N. C., view from, 31.

"Bohunks," 54.

"Boomer" described, 34.

Boyd, J. E., and peonage, 285.

Brawley, W. H., and peonage, 285.

Brookhaven, Miss., violence in, 199, 211, 212, 214.

Brown, W. G., "Lower South," 14.

Brownsville incident, 129, 194.

Bruce, P. A., on Virginians of seventeenth century, 82.

Bruce, R. C., as leader, 371.

Brunswick, Ga., as port, 22, 229.

Business. Leadership in South, 62; Negroes in, 130.

C

Cairo, Ill., mob in, 207.

Calhoun, J. C., Northern education of, 290.

Calhoun, Ala. Negro community, 141; school, 318, 389.

California. School expenditures, 295; comparative statistics, 397-417.

Cann, Judge, on concealment of negro criminals, 193.

Capital, in South, 225; comparative statistics of banking, 402-403; of manufacturing, 404-405.

Carnegie Educational Fund and Southern colleges, 300.

Catholic Church and Negroes, 117.

Cavaliers, myth of Southern descent from, 81.

Census Bureau, data from, 235. *See also* Population.

Ceylon, advance system in, 272.

Chain gangs in South, 200.

Chamberlain, D. H., on lynching, 213.

Charleston. As port, 22, 229; character, 28; negro morality, 108; Crum incident, 171.

Charleston News and Courier, character of, 70.

Chattanooga, lynching at, 212.

Chesnutt, C. W., as writer, 15, 325.

Child labor in South, 264.

Chinese and South, 54.

"Christmas money," 272.

Churchill, W. S., on Negroes in Africa, 95.

Cities. Chief Southern, 22; growth of smaller Southern, 26; effect on Whites and Negroes, 27; urban population of South, 28; progress of Southern, 28; negro life, 114, 167; schools, 291, 296, 314, 315.

Civil War. Poor Whites and, 40; present Southern attitude toward secession, 84; towards Northern leaders, 85; belief in impoverishment through emancipation, 86; Andersonville and statue of Wirz, 88; negro soldiers, 129.

Clay Eaters, name for Poor Whites, 38.

Clearings, bank, comparative statistics of, North and South, 402-403.

Climate of South, 24, 25.

Coal in South, 224, 225.

Cole, peonage case, 282.

Colleges, Southern. Antebellum, 290; present development, 292, 302; comparative statistics, 296, 300, 414-415; for women, 301, 302; ranking institutions, 302; state university funds, 302; and politics, 302; Northern instructors, 303; endowments, 307; postbellum negro, 309; character of negro, 315, 317; need of negro, 317, 336; number of negro graduates, 318; objections to negro, 331-332; academic versus industrial training for Negroes, 332-336.

Collier's Weekly on Southern progress, 247.

Colonization of Negroes. Attempts, 96-97; not a solution of race problem, 350-352.

Colorado, comparative statistics of, 397-417.

Colored person as name for Negro, 92.

Columbia, S. C. Water power, 26; progress, 29; manufacturing output, 276.

Columbus, Ga., water power in, 26.

Commerce. Southern ports, 22, 228-229; South and Panama

Canal, 22; Southern inland centers, 26; of Liberia, 96; Southern inland transportation, 226-230; through Southern ports, 233; and race separation, 357.

Concealed weapons, carrying of, in South, 37, 64, 196, 216.

Conferences, negro, 131, 389.

Congress, no interference by, in race problem, 347-348.

Consumption, negro mortality, 108.

Convicts. Number, North and South, 197; Southern treatment, 200-202, 286.

Coöperative Educational Association of Virginia, 306.

Corbin, Austin, Sunny Side plantation, 57, 256, 281.

Cordova, S. C., and negro education, 327.

Corn, comparative value of crops of, 237, 241, 242, 248, 251.

Cotton. Extent of belt, 21, 252; Southern manufactures, 25, 274, 276; Poor Whites and manufacture, 45, 275; foreign and negro cultivators, 58; value of crop, 237, 241, 248; making of, 250-260; Southern claim of importance, 250; monopolizes Southern interest, 250; compared with other Southern crops, 251-252; and race problem, 252, 261, 267; history, prices, 252; staples, 252; fertilizing, 253; application of term plantation, 253-255; types of plantations, 255-256; white laborers, 255, 262, 264, 267; labor system, 257, 261; cultivation, 257-258; yield per acre, 258; ginning and baling, 258, 274; round bale, 259; seed as product, 260; hands, 261-277; independent negro raisers, 262; relation of negro hands to plantation, 262, 266; character of labor, 263; management of plantation, 263-264; working division of plantations, 264; renters, croppers, and wage hands, 265-266; extra work, 266; instability of negro laborers, 266; negro monopoly of labor, 267, 277; necessity of training of laborers, 267, 273, 274; complaints of negro hands, 267; advance system and its effect, 268-273; wastefulness of culture and distribution, 273; selection of seed, 274; culture and practical peonage, 279.

Cotton seed. Seed trust of Sea Island staple, 252; value as product, 260; selection, 274.

"Cotton-weed," 256.

Courts. Conduct of criminal trials in South, 198-199; suggestion of negro, 383. *See also* Crime.

Crackers, name for Poor Whites, 38.

Crime in South. Mountaineer, 37; concealed weapons, 37, 64, 196, 216; mulattoes and, 112; and its penalties, 181-204; in North, 183; Northern ideas of Southern, 184; proportion of homicides, 184, 197; character of white homicides, 185; criminality of Negroes, 186-189; negro education and, 188, 189, 192, 328, 334, 343, 387; Negroes and organized, 189; conditions promoting negro, 190; Before Day Clubs, 190; negro assault on white women, 191-193, 208; concealment of negro criminals, 193; criminal example of Whites, 194, 207; whipping of Negroes, 194, 205; banishment of Negroes, 195, 205, 206; homicide of Negroes by Whites, 195-196; treatment of Negroes by police, 196; relative convictions, North and South, 197; conduct of murder trials, 198; negro trials and protection, 199; chain gangs, 200; prisons, 201; leasing of convicts, 201, 286; prison reform, 202; pardons, 203; white responsibility for inefficient criminal justice, 203; race riots, 205-208; lynching, 208-217, 361-365; prevalence, 216; influences working against, 216; and race animosity, 339; preventative measures for negro, 381-384; comparative statistics of prisoners, North and South, 406-407. *See also* Peonage.

Croppers on cotton plantations, 266.

Crum, W. D., opposition to appointment of, 171.

INDEX

Cuba, Negroes in, 98.

Cullman, Ala., excludes Negroes, 167.

Cutler, J. E., on lynching, 191, 208, 362.

D

Dallas, progress, 29.

Davis, Jeff, as political leader, 63.

Davis, Jefferson, on Southland, 2.

Dayton plantation, 255.

Death-rate, negro, 107-110.

Debts, comparative public, of South, 246.

Delaware, comparative statistics of, 397-417.

Democratic party, effect of control of, in South, 72, 173, 174.

Deposits, bank, comparative, statistics of, North and South, 402-403.

District of Columbia, comparative statistics of, 397-417.

Divorce, negro, 135.

Dixon, Thomas, Jr. As writer on race question, 9; on Southern temperament, 68; on Reconstruction, 86; on miscegenation, 155; and suppression of negro development, 180, 345, 370; on Booker Washington and Tuskegee, 319, 332; on cost of negro education, 328; on terrorizing Negroes, 360.

Domestic servants, negro, 124-127.

Domination, negro, as live question, 160.

"Dooley, Mr." on terrorizing Negroes, 358.

Dothan, Ala., abortive lynching in, 211.

Douglass, Margaret, negro school held by, 309.

Drink. Negroes and, 109, 117; Southern manufacture of liquor, 225; Southern prohibition, 384.

Drug habit, negro, 109.

Du Bois, W. E. B. Bibliographies of negro question, 8; as writer and investigator of negro question, 16-17, 114; literary style, 16, 325; on race problem, 69; on gospel of work, 120; on suffrage and leadership, 131; on race prejudice, 161; "Litany of Atlanta," 207; on race separation and progress, 318; on right to education, 325, 333, 336.

Dunbar, P. L. And negro question, 16; on unaccountability, 187; on industry, 372.

Dunleith plantation, 265.

Durham, N. C., tobacco manufacture in, 225.

E

Edmonds, R. H., on Southern potential wealth, 231.

Education, negro. Illiteracy, 98, 293, 294, 320; in North, 99; negro teachers, 130, 314; and

426

INDEX

crime, 188, 189, 192, 328, 334, 343, 387; race separation, 168, 313; of cotton hands, 267, 273; problem, 308; antebellum, 308; during and after Civil War, 309; beginning of public schools, 310; present status of public schools, 310; white opposition, 311, 323-337; typical rural schools, 311-313; refusal of authorities to provide schools, 313; interaction of poor schools and attendance, 313, 320; character of urban schools, 314; secondary and higher, 314; private schools, white opposition, 315-317, 319, 332; colleges, 315, 317-318; boycotting of white teachers, 316; influence of private schools, 318; Hampton and Tuskegee and industrial, 319; question of federal aid, 321, 348; private funds, 322; as help in race problem, 320, 385-388; needs, 320-321, 385-387; questions of negro capability, 323-327; question of harmful, 327; cost to South, 328; as unreasonable burden on Whites, 328-331; opposition to academic, 331; public industrial training, 332; academic versus industrial, 332-334; contradictory objections, 333, 337; professional, 335; opposition to secondary, 335; necessity of academic, 336; fundamental race objection, 336; negro complaints, 336; comparative statistics, secondary, North and South, 412-413.

Education, white, in South. Of Mountaineers, 36, 37; of Poor Whites, 44; comparative statistics of seceding states, 237, 248, 294, 408-417; of whole South, 241, 248, 295, 408-417; on basis of white population, 295; divergent views of need, 288; tradition of culture, 289; antebellum, 289-290; postbellum, 290; development of public schools, 291; of secondary and higher systems, 292; normal, 292; comparative illiteracy, 292-294; urban schools, 296; rural schools, 296-299; rural superintendence, 299; secondary, 299; of women, 299, 301; colleges, 300-303; professional, 303; influence of travel, 304; hopeful conditions, 304, 306; museums and art galleries, 304; libraries, 305; literature, 305; historical societies, 305; taxes, 306; promotive associations, 306; Northern aid, 306; federal aid, 307; standard, 339.

Electric railroads in South, 227.

Eliot, C. W. On South and Union, 5; on education in South, 288.

Emancipation, Southern belief in impoverishing effect of, 86, 219.

Eyre, J. E., and negro insurrection, 98.

427

F

Family life, negro, 116, 324.

Farming. *See* Agriculture, Cotton.

Fenwick's Island, inhabitants of, 107.

Fernandina as port, 229.

Fertilizing in cotton culture, 253.

Fifteenth Amendment. Reason for, 175, 376; present South and, 345. *See also* Suffrage.

Fisheries, Southern, 225.

Fisk University, founding of, 309.

Fitzgerald, Ga. Northern community, 49; Negroes excluded, 167, 358.

Flaxseed, Southern crop, 251.

Fleming, W. H., on remedy of race problem, 342, 345.

Florida. And immigration, 52; leasing of convicts, 201; comparative statistics, 397-417.

Forests, Southern wealth, 22; 221-223; lumbering and advancement of Mountaineers, 36; lumbering and Poor Whites, 45; efforts for forest reserve, 223; naval stores, 223.

Fourteenth Amendemnt, enforcement of, and race problem, 347.

Freedmen's Bureau and negro education, 309.

Frontier life of Southern Mountaineers, 23, 33, 37.

G

Gadsden, on South and immigration, 53.

Gallagher peonage case, 280.

Galveston. As port, 22, 233; rivalry with New Orleans, 228; lecture courses, 305.

Gambling, negro, 189.

Garner, J. W. On agitation of race question, 341; on legislative remedy of problem, 381; on negro education and crime, 387.

General Education Board, and Southern education, 300, 306, 307, 390; and negro schools, 322.

Georgia. Loss of natives, 47; valuations, 238; rural police, 384; comparative statistics, 397-417.

Georgia, University of, standing of, 302.

Ginning of cotton, 259, 274.

Glenn, G. R., on negro capability, 326.

Goldsboro, Fla., negro community at, 142.

Gonzales, N. G., murder of, 185.

Grady, H. W. On race problem, 69, 151; on Lincoln, 85; on faithfulness of slaves in war time, 139; on race separation, 356.

Graham, Jeffrey, case of descendants of, 156.

Graves, J. T. On negro advancement, 140, 345, 368, 376; on negro segregation, 355; on terrorizing Negroes, 359; on legal terror, 364.

Greenville, Miss., as trade center, 26.

Griffin, A. P. C., bibliographies of, on negro question, 8.

H

Hammond, Judge, on white duties in race problem, 392.

Hampton, Wade, on coöperation with Negroes, 388.

Hampton Institute. Opposition, 317; influence, 319; justification, 333; basis of success, 334; conferences, 389.

Hardy, J. C., on training of cotton laborers, 274.

Harris, J. C., as writer, 305.

Hay, comparative value of Southern crop of, 241, 251.

Hayti, Negroes in, 98.

Health. Southern, 25; negro death-rate, 107-110; mulatto, 111.

Helms, Glenny, peonage case, 284.

Hermitage plantation, 254.

Hill, W. B., and negro development, 179.

Hill Billies, name for Poor Whites, 38.

Historical societies, Southern, 305.

History. Southern attitude, 80-90; separate, of antebellum South, 80; Southern adherence to traditional views, 81; Cavalier myth, 81; belief in an-

tebellum prosperity, 82; and in advantages of slavery to Negroes, 83; present attitude towards Civil War, 84-85, 88; towards Reconstruction, 85-88; towards post-Reconstruction times, 89, 218.

Hoffman, F. L. "Race traits," 10; on negro death-rate, 107-108; on negro physical inferiority, 132

Home life. See Family life.

Horseback riding in South, 23.

Hotels. Race separation in South, 170; improvement of Southern, 227.

Houses. Of Mountaineers, 34, 36; of Poor Whites, 43; negro farm, 115, 254-256.

Houston, progress, 29.

Howell, Clark. Gubernational campaign, 173; on progress of South, 247, 248.

I

Idaho, comparative statistics of, 397-417.

Illinois, comparative statistics of, 399-417.

Illiteracy. Comparative Southern, 237, 292; negro, 293, 320; decreasing, 293-294. See also Education.

Immigration, foreign. And South, 50-58; foreign population of South, 50; and antebellum South, 51; Southern encouragement, 51; South Carolina's experiment, 52, 56;

foreign groups in South, 53, 56-57; obstacles, 54-56; and negro question, 57; and cotton laborers, 264, 267; not remedy of race problem, 353; and peonage, 353; and crude labor, 374; comparative statistics of foreign population, North and South, 398-399.

Indian question, 76.

Indian Territory, comparative statistics of, 399-417.

Indiana. Colonization of Negroes in, 112; comparative statistics, 397-417.

Indianapolis. Negro question, 112; negro schools, 313.

Indianola, Miss., incident of negro postmistress in, 171.

Industrial education of Negro. Hampton and Tuskegee, 319; public, 332; versus academic, 332-334; dangers, 334.

Industry. See Agriculture, Business, Commerce, Forests, Labor, Manufactures, Mining, Wealth.

Insane, comparative statistics of, North and South, 406-407.

Iowa, comparative, statistics of, 397-417.

Iron, Southern mining and manufacture of, 25, 224.

Italians in South, 53, 56-57, 272, 281.

J

Jackson, Miss., capitol at, 27.

Jacksonville as port, 22.

Jamaica, Negroes in, 98.

Jefferson, Thomas, and colonization of Negroes, 350.

Jim Crow cars, 168-171.

Johnson, E. A., on race antagonism, 160.

Jones, T. G., and peonage, 282, 286.

Jones, Tom, Negro, lynched, 213.

Jonesville, La., Dayton plantation near, 255.

Jury duty, Negroes and, 203.

Juvenile criminals in South, 202; comparative statistics of delinquents, 406-407; of reform schools, 416-417.

K

Kansas. Negro migration, 112; comparative statistics, 395-415.

Kelsey, Carl. "Negro Farmer," 17; on negro immorality, 134, 135.

Kentucky. Liquor manufacture, 225; problem of negro education, 307; taxation for negro schools, 329; comparative statistics, 397-417.

Kowaliga, Ala., negro community at, 141.

Ku-Klux Klan, evil of, 87.

L

Labor. Of Poor Whites, 45; in cotton mills, 45, 275; foreign and negro, 55, 57; white, on cotton plantations, 57, 255, 262,

264, 267; negro, in North, 100;
negro, in South, 120-131; Negroes and gospel of work, 120;
Negroes and unskilled, 120;
white control of negro, 121;
willingness of blacks, 121-124;
negro managers, 123; negro
domestic servants, 124-127;
blacks as farm laborers, 127;
skilled negro, 127, 225, 370;
unions and negro, 128, 370;
whipping on plantations, 194;
manufacture of iron, 224; influence of Southern, on comparative wealth, 232, 235, 246,
247, 277; system on cotton plantation, 254, 257, 261; cotton
hands, 261-277; character, on
cotton plantation, 263; child,
in South, 264; cotton renters,
croppers, and wage hands,
265-266; instability of negro,
266; negro monopoly of cotton
culture, 267, 277; necessity of
training of cotton hands, 267,
273, 274; negro complaints,
267; advance system and its
effect, 268-273; peonage in
South, 278-287; postbellum
vagrant laws, 279; Negroes as
peasants, 374-376; immigration and crude, 374; comparative statistics of manufacturing wages, North and South,
404-405. See also Immigration.

Lake Charles, La., Northerners
at, 48.

Lake City, S. C., attack on negro postmaster at, 171.

Lamar, L. Q. C., on coöperation
with Negroes, 388.

Land, negro ownership of, and
uplift, 144, 372-374.

Lanier, Sidney, as writer, 305.

Lawyers, negro, 130, 335.

Lead in South, 224.

Leadership in South. Antebellum, 59; postwar changes, 60-
62; social, 62; business, 62; political, 63; homogeneity, 63;
tone, 64; Negroes and negro
leaders, 130, 379.

Leasing of convicts in South,
201, 286.

Lee, S. D., on negro labor, 121.

Legislation as remedy of race
problem, 381-385.

Leland University, founding of,
309.

Leonard, John, negro settlement
started by, 141.

Liberia, failure of, 96-97, 350.

Libraries in South, 305.

Lien loans on cotton plantations,
268.

Lilywhite Republicans, 173.

Lincoln, Abraham. Minor's
"Real Lincoln," 85; Grady on,
85; and colonization of Negroes, 350.

Liquor. See Drink.

Literature. Southern, 305; negro, 325.

Little River, plantations on, 255.

Lockhart, Texas, peonage case,
280.

London, murders in, 184.

Louisiana. Immigration, 52, 56,
57; school system, 292; illiter-

acy, 293; negro illiteracy, 294; rural schools, 299; comparative statistics, 397-417.

Louisville, tobacco manufacture in, 225; schools, 296.

Louisville *Courier-Journal*. On South and immigration, 48.

Lower South, extent, 20. *See also* South.

Lumber. *See* Forests.

Lynching. Cutler's researches, 208; origin and early practice, 208; proportion, North and South, 209, 210; not confined to cases of rape, 209, 362; methods of lynchers, 210; mistakes, 211; conduct of officials, 211; and of militia, 212; justified, 212; reasons for practice, race hostility, 213-215; suggestion of legalization, 215; as remedy for race problem, 361-364; reduction, 364.

M

McDonogh, John, educational bequest by, 289.

McKinley, William, price of wheat and election of, 261.

Macon Telegraph on Northern criticism, 243.

Madison, Ga., popular hysteria in, on negro question, 164.

Magic, negro belief in, 137.

Malaria in South, 25.

Manufacturers' Record. On immigration, 54; on Southern wealth, 242, 243; on wealth in cotton, 250; opposition to

Northern educational aid, 307; on Atlanta riots, 390.

Manufactures of South, 24, 224-225; cheap power, 26, 225; cotton, 45, 274-276; importation of aliens, 52; comparative statistics, North and South, 237, 238, 276, 404-405.

Marriage. *See* Miscegenation.

Maryland. And South, 20; problem of negro education, 307, 329; comparative statistics, 397-417.

Massachusetts and school tax, 329.

Mean Whites, name for Poor Whites, 38.

Medicine. Negro physicians, 129, 335; schools in South, 303.

Memphis, progress, 242.

Methodist Church. Negro, 117; educational commission of Southern, 300.

Michigan, comparative statistics of, 397-417.

Military service, negro, 129.

Militia and lynchings, 212.

Miller, Kelly. On Dixon, 10; as writer, 15, 325; on race antagonism, 160; on negro advancement, 368, 371.

Mining in South, 24, 224.

Minnesota, comparative statistics of, 397-417.

Minor, C. L. C. On Negroes under slavery, 83; "Real Lincoln," 85.

Miscegenation, 151-154; and principle of social inequality, 154, 156; prohibition of marriage, 155; white exclusion of mulattoes, 156; remedy, 157; and calamity of amalgamation, 157.

Mississippi. Postbellum vagrant laws, 168; negro voters, 176; valuations, 238; illiteracy, 294, school statistics, 295; lynchings, 363; comparative statistics, 395-415.

Missouri. And South, 20; illiteracy, 292; comparative statistics, 397-417.

Mitchell, S. C., and negro development, 179, 345.

Mitchell Co., N. C., Negroes excluded from, 166.

Mobile. As port, 22, 229; progress, 28.

Monroe, La., as trade center, 26.

Montana, comparative statistics of, 397-417.

Montgomery, founder of negro community, 141.

Montgomery, Ala., progress, 29.

Morals. Mountaineer, 35; poor white, 43; negro, 108-109, 134-137; mulatto, 112; miscegenation, 151-157. *See also* Crime.

Morristown, Tenn., treatment of Negroes in, 167.

Mound Bayou, Miss., negro community at, 141.

Mt. Moriah, Ala., school at, 297.

Mountaineers, Southern, as frontiersmen, 23, 33, 37; conditions, 30-38; uniqueness, 30; region, 31; descent, 31-33; self-sustenance, 32; lowest type, "boomer," 33-35; higher type, 35; advancement, 35-38; crime, 37; and negro question, 38; as laborers in cotton mills, 275; Northern aid for education, 306.

Mulattoes. And negro "race traits," 102; proportion, 110-111; physique, 111; character, 112; social position, 112, 156, 339; and private negro schools, 316; literature, 325.

Murders. Proportion in South, 184; varieties, 185; of Negroes by Whites, 195-196; conduct of trials, 198; lynchings for, 209, 362.

Murphy, E. G. "Present South," 13; on democratic development, 65; on race problem, 69, 79, 345; on South and Northern criticism, 73; on survival of Negroes, 109; on race association, 150; and negro development, 179; on Poor Whites, 293; on Negro academic training, 331.

Museums, Southern, 304.

N

Nashua, N. H., manufacturing output of, 276.

National banks, comparative statistics of, North and South, 402-403. *See also* Banking.

Naval stores, Southern, 223.

Nebraska. Illiteracy, 292; comparative statistics, 397-417.

"Negro a Beast," 11.

INDEX

Negroes. Writers, 14-17, 325; periodicals, 18; of Sea Islands, 22, 107, 110, 137, 142; effect of urban life, 27, 114; and Mountaineers, 38; and foreign immigration, 55, 57; temperament of Northern and Southern, 74; present attitude of North on question, 75; Northern responsbility and interest in question, 75-79; persistence of question, 77; necessity of solution, 78; Southern belief in benefits of slavery, 83, 341; character, 91-105; population, 91, 106, 397-399; names for, 91; white generalizations on, 92; character and capability in Africa, 94-96; failure of Liberia, 96-97, 350; conditions in West Indies, 97-99; in North, 99-101; question of inferiority, 101-105, 339; "race traits," 101, 110; lack of opportunity, 103; and white standards, 103; arrested development, 104, 326; irresponsibility, 104; life, 106-119; diffusion, 106; ruralness, 107; survival and death-rate, 107-110; divergent types, 110; proportion and character of mulattoes, 110-112; Northward drift, 112, 354; white ignorance of negro life, 114, 124, 340, 391; investigations of life, 114; rural houses, 115; family life, 116, 324; amusements, 116; religious life, 117, 380; secret societies, 118; as managers, 123; and military service, 129; as business and professional men, 129-130, 335; attitude towards leaders, 130, 379; conferences, 131, 389; question of advancement, 132-148; physical structure and inferiority, 132-134; morality, 134-137; not retrograding, 137, 143; morals under slavery, 138; faithfulness during Civil War, 139; evidences of advancement, 139-142; communities, 141; proportion of uplift, 143, 146, 339, 368-369; accumulation of property, 143-148; savings, 143, 376; real estate, 144-145, 372-374; and tax-paying, 147; race association, 149-165; problem of association, 149-151; miscegenation, 151-157; remedy for it, 157; position of mulattoes, 156, 339; evil of amalgamation, 157, 349; growth of race antagonism, 158-161, 216, 340, 389; white fear of negro domination, 160, 172; Negroes on race antagonism, 160; basis of antagonism, 161; question of social equality, 162-165, 340; race separation, 166-180, 356-358; exclusion from settlements, 166; increasing segregation, 167; quarters in cities, 167; church separation, 167; postbellum vagrant laws, 168, 279; discrimination in travel, 168-171; and public positions, 171-174, 377;

disfranchisement, 1 7 4 - 1 7 8 , 347-348, 376-377; white suppression of development, 178-180, 370-371; illustrations of white antagonism, 181-183; rough language by Whites, 194; and present vagrant laws, 200; and jury duty, 203; testimony, 203; race riots, 205-207; thriftlessness, 271; and newspapers, 324; summary of race problem, 338-341; race separation and principle of equality, 339, 344; perpetual inferiority and subjection, 339, 340, 343, 344; agitation against, 341; postulates as to possible remedies of race problem, 343-346; wrong remedies, 347-366; no help from Congress, 347-348; nor from Northern propaganda, 348; nor from colonization 350-352; nor from substitution of white laborers, 352-354; nor from segregation, 354-358; terrorizing as remedy 358-366; material and political remedies, 367-377; advantage to Whites in negro uplift, 371, 373; as peasant class, 374-376; moral remedies, 378-394; influence of race separation on uplift, 378-381, 388-391; suggestion of socialistic control over, 379; need of equitable vagrant laws, 383; special courts, 383; and prohibition, 384; necessity of discussion of race problem, 389; essentials of remedy, 392-394;

comparative statistics of insane and paupers, North and South, 406-407. *See also* Cotton, Crime, Education, Labor, Lynching, Peonage, Whites.

Nevada, comparative statistics of, 399-417.

New Hampshire, comparative statistics of, 399-417.

New Mexico, comparative statistics of, 399-417.

New Orleans. As port, 22, 233; population and trade, 28; foreign population, 51; negro population, 107; negro morality, 108; rivalry with Galveston, 228; belt line, 228; progress, 242; McDonogh bequest, 289; discontinuance of negro high school, 315.

New York City, murders in, 184.

Newport News as port, 229, 233.

Newspapers. *See* Press.

Niagara Movement, 389.

Nixburg, Ala., negro community near, 141.

No 'Count, name for Poor Whites, 38.

Norfolk, Va. As port, 22, 229, 233; Mrs. Douglass' negro school, 309.

Normal schools in South. Development, 292; comparative statistics, 296, 416-417. *See also* Teachers.

North. Extent, 1; Northerners in South, 48-50; position of Southerners in, 49; Southern suspicion, 71, 73, 89; Southern belief in hostility, 74; present attitude on race problem, 75; responsibility and interest in problem, 75-79; condition of Negroes in, 99-101; negro drift, 112, 354; crime, 183; idea of crime in South, 184; criminal spirit in, and in South, 197-199; lynching in, 209, 210; comparative wealth (*see* Wealth); aid for Southern white education, 306; for negro education, 315-317, 322; and solution of Southern race problem, 345, 347-349, 391; comparative statistics, 397-417.

North Carolina. And immigration, 52; and Mecklenburg Declaration, 81; early negro suffrage, 175; comparative statistics, 397-417.

North Carolina, University of. Founding, 290; standing, 302.

North Dakota. School statistics, 295; comparative statistics, 397-417.

Norwood, T. M., generalization by, on Negroes, 93.

O

Oak Grove, Ala., negro school at, 312.

Oats, comparative value of crops of, 241.

Odum, H. W., negro researches by, 114.

Ogden, R. C., and Southern Education Board, 306, 390.

Oklahoma. And South, 20; comparative statistics of, 397-417.

Onancock, Va., banishment of Negroes from, 206.

Opelika, Ala., public buildings in, 27.

Open-air life in South, 23, 25.

Oregon, comparative statistics of, 397-417.

Outlook, articles in, on Southern question, 18.

P

Pace, J. W., peonage case, 282.

Page, T. N. "Negro," 12; on educational value of slavery, 83; on failure of Negro, 101; on negro immorality, 134; on race antagonism, 150; on negro capability, 326, 368; on evils of negro education, 327; on white dominance, 343; on negro court, 383; on mutual discussion of race problem, 391; on need of negro uplift, 392.

Panama Canal and Southern commerce, 22.

Pardon of criminals in South, 203.

Paupers, comparative statistics of, North and South, 406-407.

Peabody fund, 322.

Peasant class, Negroes as, 374-376.

Penn School in Sea Islands, 316.

Pensacola as port, 22, 229.

Pensions, Southern income, 234.

Peonage. And immigration, 56, 353; in South, 278-287; rise, 278; federal law against, 278; principle, 279; development in cotton culture, 279; of Whites, 280-281; restraint of movements of Negroes, 281-282; of Negroes under cover of laws, 282-283, 365; illustrations, 283-285; federal prosecutions, 285; Southern approval, 286; federal investigation, 286; and leasing of convicts, 286; and negro shiftlessness, 287.

Percy, Leroy. On remedy of race problem, 343, 345; on negro education, 387.

Pests, Southern, 25.

Petroleum in South, 225.

Philadelphia, negro mortality in, 107.

Phosphates in South, 225.

Physical conditions of South, 20-29; swamps, 221.

Physicians, negro, 129, 335.

Physique, negro, and inferiority, 132-134.

Plantation. Application of term, 253-255; present types, 255-256. *See also* Agriculture, Cotton.

"Plow" division of farms, 264.

Poe, E. A., as Southern writer, 305.

Police. Treatment of Negroes, 196; need of rural, 211, 382, 384.

Politics. Southern leadership, 63; cause and effect of Solid South, 72, 173, 174; colonization of Negroes in Indiana, 112; Negroes and public positions, 171-174, 377; Negroes and Republican party in South, 173; negro suffrage, 174-178, 347-348, 376-377.

Poor Whites. Traditional home, 21; conditions, 38-47; names for, 38; diffusion, 38; antebellum isolation, 38-41; and Civil War, 40; as farmers, 41, 45, 46; advancement, 41-47; morals, 43; education, 44, 293; as wage earners, 44-45; in cotton mills, 45, 275; northward and westward drift, 46; term a misnomer, 47; turbulence, 64; and Southern problem, 344; need of uplift, 375.

Population. Southern urban, 28; of South, 30; Southern, of Northern birth, 48; foreign, in South, 50; negro, 91, 106; negro death-rate, 107-110; Southern agricultural, 221; comparative statistics, North and South, 397-399.

Ports of the South, 22, 28, 228-229, 233.

Portsmouth, Va., as port, 229, 233.

Post-office. Negro employees, 171, 172; need of Postal Savings Banks in South, 376.

Potatoes, comparative value of crop of, 241.

Press, Southern. Character, 70; negro journalists, 130, 324; Negroes and newspapers, 324.

Price. Of farm lands, 220; of cotton, 252.

Prisons in South, 201; reform, 202; comparative statistics of prisoners, 406-407

Professions. Negroes in, 129, 335; schools in South, 292, 303.

Prohibition as remedy of race problem, 384.

Property. *See* Land, Taxation, Wealth.

Protestant Episcopal Church and race separation, 167.

Pulaski Co., Ga., increasing negro population of, 167.

Pullman Car Co. and Jim Crow cars, 169.

R

Race. *See* Negroes, Remedies, Whites.

Railroads of South. Race separation, 168-171; development, 226-227; New Orleans belt road, 228; control, 229; comparative mileage of seceding states, 237; of whole South, 248.

Rape, negro, of white women, 191-193; early examples, 208; lynching not confined to, 209, 362; not on increase, 209; and justification of lynching, 213, 214.

Real estate, negro, 144-145.

Reclamation of Southern swamps, 221.

Reconstruction. Present Southern attitude, 85-88; Ku-Klux, 87; and race antagonism, 159; negro suffrage, 175, 376; educational measures, 292, 310.

Red Necks, name for Poor Whites, 38.

Reed, J. C. On Dixon, 9; on Negroes under slavery, 83; on Ku-Klux, 87; on negro segregation, 355.

Religion. Of Mountaineers, 35; of Negroes in Africa, 94; negro, in South, 117, 129; question of negro paganism, 137; race separation, 167; training of Southern ministers, 303; Church and race problem, 380.

Remedies of race problem. Summary of problem, 338-340; essential conditions, 340; types of altitude of Southern Whites, 340-343; postulates, 343-345; division of Whites, 345-346, 391; wrong, 347-366; no Congressional interference, 347-348; no Northern private propaganda, 348; no amalgamation, 349; no colonization, 350-352; no substitutes for negro laborers, 352-354; no segregation, 354-356; possibility of race separation, 356-358; terrorizing, 358-366; legalized terror, 364; material, 367-376; possibility and permission of general negro uplift, 367-372; land-buying by Negroes, 372-374; Negroes as peasants, 374-376; aids for thrift, 376; political, 376-377; moral, 378-394; influence of race separation,

378-381; character of negro leaders, 379; benevolent state socialism, 379; influence of Church, 380; legislative and judicial, 381-385; negro education, 385-388; need of race coöperation and discussion, 388-391; last analysis of problem, 392-394; white duties, 392; patience, 392-394.

Renters on cotton plantations, 256, 266.

Restaurants, race separation in, in South, 170.

Rhett, Barnwell, Northern education of, 290.

Rice as Southern crop, 251.

Richmond. Race separation, 167; tobacco manufacture, 225; progress, 242.

Richmond Times Despatch on immigration, 54.

"Riders" on cotton plantations, 258, 263.

Riots, race, 205-208, 390.

Roads, Southern, 227.

Roosevelt, Theodore. Booker Washington incident, 162; and appointment of Negroes, 171, 174; rewards faithful state official, 211 ; on lynchings, 363.

Rural life. Open-air life, 23, 25; preponderance in South, 27-29; negro propensity, 107; police, 221, 382, 384; schools, 296-299, 311-313; relative lack of progress, 242. *See also* Agriculture.

Russell, C. W., on peonage, 286.

S

St. Louis, schools in, 296.

Salisbury, N. C., lynching in, 210.

Sand Hillers, name for Poor Whites, 38.

Santo Domingo, Negroes in, 99.

Savannah as port, 22, 28, 229.

Savings banks, need of, in South, 376.

Saxons, Taine on, 102.

Sea Islands, 22; Negroes of, 107, 110, 137, 142; trucking, 220; cotton, seed trust, 252; ginning and bagging of cotton, 259; war-time negro schools, 309; present education, 316.

Secession, present Southern attitude toward, 84.

Secondary education. Development of Southern, 292, 299; comparative statistics, North and South, 296, 412-413; negro, 314; hostility to negro, 319, 335.

Secret societies, negro, 118.

Shannon, A. H. "Racial Integrity," 12; on mulattoes, 111.

Shipp, J. F., and lynching, 212.

Shreveport. Public buildings, 27; Italians at, 57.

Shufeldt, R. W., "Negro a Menace," 8.

Sinclair, W. A. "Aftermath of Slavery," 15; as writer, 325.

Slater fund, 322.

Slavery. Effect on South, 2; and Southern attitude towards history, 80; traditional belief in prosperity under, 82, 218; and in benefit to Negro, 83, 341; domestic servants, 126; negro morals under, 138; personal race association under, 158; chattel, and leasing of convicts, 201; in Philippines, 279; and education of Negroes, 308. *See also* Peonage.

Smith, Hoke. Gubernatorial campaign, 173; on negro education, 329; on white control over Negroes, 341.

Smith, W. B. "Color Line," 13; on South and outside public opinion, 77; on negro inferiority, 133; apology for lynching, 363.

Social life in South. Open-air, 23; of Northerners, 49; leadership, 59-62; character, 62; crudeness of behavior, 64; democratic uplift, 65; of Negroes in North, 100; miscegenation and social inequality of Negroes, 154, 156; exclusion of mulattoes, 156; question of negro equality, 162-165, 340; race equality and negro officials, 171; negro homes, 324.

Socialism and race problem, 379.

Solid South, cause and effect of, 72.

South. As part of Union, 1-3; individuality, 2, 30; author's preparation for judging, 3-6; materials on, 7-19; physical conditions, 20-29; extent, 20; physical divisions, 20-22; Black Belt, 21; forests, 22;

climate, 24; mining, 24; pests, 25; health, 25; architecture, 26, 304; rural preponderance, 27-29; comparative statistics, 397-417. *See also* Agriculture, Cities, Civil War, Commerce, Cotton, Crime, Education, History, Immigration, Labor, Leadership, Manufactures, Negroes, Peonage, Politics, Population, Reconstruction, Remedies, Slavery, Social life, Wealth, Whites.

South Atlantic Monthly and discussion of race problem, 390.

South Carolina. Loss of natives, 47; immigration experiment, 52, 56; postbellum vagrant laws, 168; murders in, 184; valuations, 238; cotton manufactures, 275, 276; peonage in, 284; illiteracy, 293; school statistics, 295; rural police, 384; comparative statistics, 397-417.

South Dakota, comparative statistics of, 397-417.

Southern Education Association and negro education, 327.

Southern Education Board, 300, 306, 390.

"Southern South," meaning of term, 6.

Spartanburg, water-power in, 26.

Spencer, Samuel, and immigration, 52.

Springfield, Ill., race riot in, 207.

Springfield, Ohio, race riot in, 207.

INDEX

Statistical Abstract, data from, 235, 243.

Steamboat, race separation on Southern, 169.

Stock, Southern, 251.

Stone, A. H. Studies of negro question, 17; on foreign and negro cotton hands, 58; on negro accumulation of property, 146; on lien loans, 268.

Stone and Webster, and electric power and transportation, 227.

Straight University, founding of, 309.

Street railways. Race separation on Southern, 170; interurban trolleys, 227.

Suffrage. Northern distrust of negro, 100; effect of disfranchisement on negro leadership, 131; negro, 174-175; negro disfranchisement, 175-177, 345; reason for disfranchisement, 178; enforcement of Fourteenth Amendment, 347; federal control of elections, 348.

Sugar, Southern crop of, 251.

Sugar beets, Southern crop of, 251.

Sulphur in South, 225.

Sulu Archipelago, slavery in, 279.

Sunny Side. Italian labor at, 57; plantation, 256; alleged peonage case, 281.

Superstitions, negro, 138.

Swamps, Southern, 25; reclamation of, 221.

Syracuse, Ohio, Negroes excluded from, 166.

T

Taine, H. A., on Saxons, 102.

Talassee, school at, 297.

Talladega, school at, 389.

Tar Heels, name for Poor Whites, 38.

Taxation. Negroes and, 147, 330; assessment valuations as comparison of Southern wealth, 235; comparative valuations of seceding states, 236; of whole South, 239-241, 244, 248, 400-401; on basis of white population, 246; ante- and post-bellum valuation in South, 237; school, in South, 295, 306; burden of, for negro schools, 328-331.

Teachers, Southern. Of rural white schools, 298; of negro schools, 310, 314, 320; boycott of Northern, of negro schools, 316; need of white, for colored schools, 385-387; comparative statistics, North and South, 408-417.

Temperament of Southern Whites, 66-79; difficulty in determining, 66; emotionalism, 66, 164; influence of race problem, 67-69, 74; diversity on problem, 69-70; impatience of dissent, 70, 72, 390; suspicion of Northerners, 71, 73, 74, 89; attitude towards criticism, 71-73, 243; exaggeration, 73; of Negroes, 74; Whites, and outside interest in race problem, 75-79; attitude towards history, 80-90, 218; veneration for ancestors, 81.

Tennessee. School statistics, 295; comparative statistics, 397-417.

Tensas River, plantations on, 255.

Testimony, negro, 203.

Texas. Urban population, 29; immigration from other states, 47; foreign settlement, 53; value of farms, 238; school statistics, 248, 295, 306; comparative statistics, 397-417.

Texas, University of, standing of, 302.

Theft, Negroes and, 186.

Thomas, William Hannibal. "American Negro," 15; on negro morals, 134.

Thomas, William Holcombe. On race association, 150; on homicides, 197.

Thorsby, Ala., Northern community at, 49.

Tillman, B. R. As political leader, 63; anti-negro generalizations, 93; on newly imported slaves, 110; attitude on negro disfranchisement, 177; on lynching, 213; and race problem, 345, 359.

Tillman, J. H., killing of Gonzales by, 185.

Tobacco. Southern manufacture, 224; comparative value of crop, 241.

Toombs, Robert, on South under slavery, 82.

Trade. See Commerce.

Transportation. Race separation in South, 168-171; Southern conditions, 226-230.

Trucking in South, 24, 220, 251.

Trudics peonage case, 280.

Tulane University, standing of, 300, 307.

Turner, H. M., on negro segregation, 355.

Turner peonage case, 284, 365.

Turpentine, Southern industry, 223.

Tuskegee Institute. Conferences, 131, 389; influence, 319; number of students, 332; opposition, 332; basis of success, 334.

U

Union, South and, 1, 5.

Urban life. See Cities.

Utah, comparative statistics of, 397-417.

V

Vagrant laws, Southern. Postbellum, 168, 279; present, 200; need of equitable, 383.

Valdese, N. C., Italians at, 57.

Valdosta, Ga., negro teachers in, 314.

Vardaman, J. K. As political leader, 63; abuse of Negro, 72, 93; on negro inferiority, 101; on leasing convicts, 202; pardons, 202; opposition to negro education, 327, 371; and race problem, 345; on illegal control of Negroes, 365.

Venereal disease, Negroes and, 108.

Vermont. School statistics, 295; comparative statistics, 397-417.

Vice. *See* Morals.

Virginia. And Hampton Institute, 317; comparative statistics, 397-417.

Virginia Coöperative Education Association, 306.

Virginia, University of. Founding, 290; standing of, 203.

W

Wage hands on cotton plantations, 265.

Wages. *See* Labor, Teachers.

Wanderer, Negroes imported in, 110.

Washington, B. T. Works on negro problem, 15; negro hostility to, 130; on acquiring land, 144, 372; incident of lunch with Roosevelt, 162; Dixon on, 180, 319, 332; on South as home of Negro, 262, 355; on treatment of cotton hands, 267; influence of Tuskegee, 319; as writer, 325; as leader, 333, 334.

Washington, George, and fertilizing, 253.

Washington, State of, comparative statistics of, 399-417.

Watauga Co., N. C., Negroes excluded from, 166.

Water-power in South, 26, 225.

Waterways, Southern, 226.

Watson, T. E., on cry of negro domination, 160.

Watterson, Henry, on Southern wealth, 231.

Wealth, Southern. Private, 62; enlarged views, 89, 231, 247; negro accumulation, 143-148; actual, 218-230; under slavery, 218; postbellum poverty, 219; recent great increase, 219; agricultural, 220-221; forests, 221-224; mineral, 224; in manufactures, 224-225 : capital and banking, 225; commercial, 226-229, 233; comparative, North and South, 231-249; Southern claims considered, 232, 247, 249, 276, 338; influence of labor conditions, 232, 235, 246, 247, 277; pensions, 234; proper basis for comparison, 234; comparative tables, 234, 400-417; materials for comparison, 235; comparative, of seceding states, 236-239, 248; of whole South, 239-245, 248; on basis of white population, 246-247; uneven advance of Southern, 242; actual and comparative rate of Southern accumulation, 243-245.

West Indies, capacity of Negroes in, 97-99.

West Virginia. And South, 20; comparative statistics, 399-417.

Wheat. As an export, 233; Southern crop, 251; price and election of McKinley, 261.

Whipping on plantations, 194.

White Trash, name for Poor Whites, 38.

Whitecapping, 195.

Whites, Southern. Effect of city life, 27; position of Northerners in South, 48-50; small farmers, 60; division on, and discussion of race problem, 67-72, 345-346, 391; generalizations on Negroes, 92; Southern exaltation, 102; ignorance of negro life, 114, 124, 340, 391; race association, 149-165; problem of association, 149-151; miscegenation, 151-157; remedy for it, 157; exclusion of mulattoes, 156 ; evil of amalgamation, 157, 344, 349; growth of race antagonism, 158-161, 216, 340, 389; fear of negro domination, 160, 172; Negroes on race antagonism, 160; basis of prejudice, 161; race separation, 160-180; fear of negro social equality, 162-165, 340; suppression of negro development by, 178-180; illustration of race antagonism, 181-183; responsibility for inefficient criminal justice, 203; comparative wealth of South on basis of white inhabitants, 235, 246; laborers on cotton plantations, 255, 262, 264, 267; peonage of, 280-281; advancement, 339; domination, 339, 343; perpetual superiority, 340; violent agitation of race problem, 341; despair over problem, 342; to control settlement of problem, 344; terrorizing of Negroes, 358-366; advantages to, of negro uplift, 371, 373; necessity of coöperation with Negroes, 388-391; duties in problem, 392; comparative statistics of population, 397-399. *See also* Crime, Education, History, Immigration, Leadership, Mountaineers, Negroes, Poor Whites, Remedies, Social life, Temperament.

Whittaker, assault by, 186.

Williams, G. W., "Negro Race in America," 14.

Williams, J. S. On immigration, 51, 352; senatorial campaign, 72; on increasing race antagonism, 159, 361; on basis of race prejudice, 161; on remedy of race problem, 343, 394; on negro emigration, 352; on good conduct of negroes, 368; on recognizing negro worth, 380; on prevention of negro crimes, 382.

Wilmington, Del., lynching in, 210.

Wilmington, N. C. As port, 22, 229; banishment of Negroes, 206.

Winston, G. T. On South, 5; on negro criminality, 188; on negro uplift, 371.

Wirz, Henry, statue to, 89.

Wisconsin. School statistics, 295; comparative statistics, 397-417.

INDEX

Women. Labor on cotton plantations, 265; school education in South, 299; college education, 301, 302.

Wool, Southern crop of, 251.

World Almanac, statistics from, 235, 248.

World's Work, articles in, on Southern question, 18.

"Worth, Nicholas." "Autobiography," 18; on Southerners and criticism, 72; on Southern exaggeration, 73; on historical ignorance, 83; on race antagonism, 159; on training cotton hands, 267.

Wyoming, comparative statistics of, 399-417.

Z

Zinc in South, 224.

(1)

THE END